T0320020

EU Policymaking at a Crossroads

NEW HORIZONS IN EUROPEAN POLITICS

Series Editor: José M. Magone, *Berlin School of Economics and Law, Germany*
Founding Series Editor: Julie Smith, *Robinson College, Cambridge, UK*

The New Horizons in European Politics series is an invaluable forum for original research across the spectrum of European politics, promoting innovative cross-disciplinary analysis of contemporary issues and debates. Covering a diverse range of topics, the series examines issues such as: the impacts of the severe challenges brought about by the financial crisis; economic issues, including integration and monetary union; the politics of the EU and other governmental and nongovernmental institutions; environmental politics and the ongoing struggle to mitigate climate change; and the politics of trade, energy and security in Europe. Both international and comparative in its approach, this exciting series encompasses theoretical and empirical work from both well-established researchers and the next generation of scholars.

Titles in the series include:

Constraining Democratic Governance in Southern Europe
From 'Superficial' to 'Coercive' Europeanization
José M. Magone

The Politics of Regional Cooperation and the Impact on the European Union
A Study of Nordic Cooperation and the Visegrad Group
Mats Braun

Revisiting EU-Africa Relations in a Changing World
Edited by Valeria Fargion and Mamoudou Gazibo

Awaking Europe in the Triple Global Crisis
The Birth Pangs of the Emerging Europe
Attila Ágh

The Politicisation of Social Europe
Conflict Dynamics and Welfare Integration
Francesco Corti

The Everyday Making of EU Foreign and Security Policy
Practices, Socialization and the Management of Dissent
Anna Michalski, Niklas Bremberg, August Danielson and Elsa Hedling

Party Realignment in Western Europe
Electoral Drivers and Global Constraints
Magnus Hagevi, Sofie Blombäck, Marie Demker, Jonas Hinnfors and Karl Loxbo

EU Policymaking at a Crossroads
Negotiating the 2021–2027 Budget
Edited by Sybille Münch and Hubert Heinelt

EU Policymaking at a Crossroads

a Crossroads

Negotiating the 2021–2027 Budget

Edited by

Sybille Münch

Professor of Political Science, Stiftung Universität Hildesheim and Visiting Professor, Center for the Study of Democracy, Leuphana University, Lüneburg, Germany

Hubert Heinelt

Professor for Public Administration, Public Policy and Urban Research at the Institute for Political Science, Technische Universität Darmstadt, Germany

NEW HORIZONS IN EUROPEAN POLITICS

Edward Elgar
PUBLISHING

Cheltenham, UK • Northampton, MA, USA

Published by
Edward Elgar Publishing Limited
The Lypiatts
15 Lansdown Road
Cheltenham
Glos GL50 2JA
UK

Edward Elgar Publishing, Inc.
William Pratt House
9 Dewey Court
Northampton
Massachusetts 01060
USA

A catalogue record for this book
is available from the British Library

Library of Congress Control Number: 2022946174

This book is available electronically in the **Elgar**online
Political Science and Public Policy subject collection
http://dx.doi.org/10.4337/9781788977654

ISBN 978 1 78897 764 7 (cased)
ISBN 978 1 78897 765 4 (eBook)

Printed and bound by CPI Group (UK) Ltd, Croydon, CR0 4YY

Contents

v

Figures

Tables

Contributors

Marlon Barbehön, Research Assistant (Postdoc), Institute of Political Science, Heidelberg University, Germany.

Peter Becker, Senior Associate, Research division EU/Europe at the Stiftung Wissenschaft und Politik (SWP), German Institute for International and Security Affairs, Berlin, Germany.

Peter Biegelbauer, Senior Scientist, Center for Innovation Systems and Policy, AIT Austrian Institute of Technology, Austria.

Basil Bornemann, Senior Researcher and Lecturer, Department of Social Sciences, University of Basel, Switzerland.

Antoine de Cabanes, PhD student in Political Science, ISPOLE, UCLouvain, Belgium.

Michael Dinges, Senior Expert Advisor and Thematic Coordinator, Center for Innovation Systems and Policy, AIT Austrian Institute of Technology, Austria.

Peter H. Feindt, Professor of Agricultural and Food Policy, Humboldt-Universität zu Berlin, Germany.

Clément Fontan, Professor in European Economic Policies, Ispole, IEE, UCLouvain, Université Saint-Louis Bruxelles, Belgium.

Pascal Grohmann, PhD researcher at the Agricultural and Food Policy Group at Humboldt-Universität zu Berlin, Germany.

Astrid Häger, Senior Researcher and Lecturer at the Agricultural and Food Policy Group at Humboldt-Universität zu Berlin, Germany.

Hubert Heinelt, Professor for Public Administration, Public Policy and Urban Research at the Institute for Political Science, Technische Universität Darmstadt, Germany.

Katja Lamprecht, Expert Advisor, Center for Innovation Systems and Policy, Austrian Institute of Technology, Vienna, Austria.

Sybille Münch, Professor of Political Science, Stiftung Universität Hildesheim.

Wolfgang Petzold, former EU official, who worked for the European Commission's Regional and Urban Policy Directorate-General and the Committee of the Regions.

Uwe Puetter, Professor for Empirical Research on Europe, Europa-Universität Flensburg, Germany.

Sabine Saurugger, Professor of Political Science, Sciences Po Grenoble-UGA, Grenoble, France.

Matthias Weber, Head of the Center for Innovation Systems and Policy, Austrian Institute of Technology, Austria & Visiting Professor, Laboratoire Interdisciplinaire Sciences, Innovations, Technologies (LISIS), Université Gustave Eiffel, France.

PART I

The negotiations about the Multiannual
Financial Framework 2021–2027 and their
context

1. The EU at a crossroads. Negotiations about the Multiannual Financial Framework 2021–2027: introduction to the book

Hubert Heinelt and Sybille Münch

THE GENERAL BACKGROUND

The adoption of the EU's Multiannual Financial Framework (MFF), the long-term budget for the period 2021–2027, marked an end to prolonged and difficult negotiations. The first long-term budget without the United Kingdom, with the final steps taken while most member states were facing yet another shutdown to tackle a second wave of Covid-19 infections, and revealing differences of opinion that go to the core values of the European Union, this was 'a historic budget for a historic moment', as then European Parliament President David Sassoli put it (Bayer, 2020). 'The financial framework sets the maximum amount of commitment appropriations in the EU budget each year for broad policy areas ("headings") and fixes an overall annual ceiling on payment and commitment appropriations' (European Commission, 2016) and hence shapes EU policies for years to come. The fact that the negotiations for 2021–2027 took place in a very specific context, characterised by many controversies, is reflected in the fact that the discussion on the former Multiannual Financial Framework (for 2014–2020) took 20 months, as opposed to the current one, which had already taken 29 months by the time of the extraordinary meeting of the European Council in July 2020 (European Parliamentary Research Service, 2020, p. 1).

Even before the outbreak of the coronavirus pandemic in March 2020, it had been clear that the EU was at a crossroads – as already emphasised, for example, by the European Commission (2017) three years earlier. Many observers asserted that Europe had been reeling for some years: the financial crisis of 2008, the subsequent sovereign debt crisis in some member states of the Eurozone and the following austerity measures, the rise of Eurosceptic parties in member states' parliaments and the European Parliament (EP), growing right-wing populism, the Brexit referendum[1] and the exit of the UK from the EU, as well as the unsolved burden-sharing in the face of the arrival of refugees. The heated debates around these developments are an expression of the fact that *the EU and its further development are 'politicized' as never ever before* (Hutter et al., 2016).[2] This politicisation refers – as convincingly argued by Grande and Hutter (2016, pp. 8–12; with reference to Schattschneider, 1957) – to (issue) salience, actor expansion and actor polarisation, that is, the visibility, the range as well as the intensity and direction of politicisation. One can easily agree with Grande and Hutter (2016, pp. 12–16) that this unknown degree of politicisation was initially triggered by the euro crisis and caused by conflicts over solidarity, identity and sovereignty and thus the scope of cooperation and membership, as well as institutional design and authority, of the European Union. The same could be argued regarding the subsequent refugee crisis and the impact of the coronavirus pandemic (see below in this introductory chapter and in Chapter 8 in this volume).

One expression of this unprecedented politicisation is the rise of populism in Europe.[3] Generally, populism may appear in different forms and this diversity holds true for the European Union in particular (for an overview see Kriesi & Pappas, 2015). Populism may currently arise from a 'new conflict between globalization "winners" and "losers"' (Kriesi, 2014, p. 369; Kriesi & Pappas, 2015, p. 3) and a resulting new cleavage between 'integration' (in the globalised world) and 'demarcation' (of territorially defined communities; Kriesi et al., 2008)[4] as well as growing disappointment about the promises of representative democracy and distrust in the role of political parties as mediators between the 'people' and decision-making authorities (Kriesi, 2014, p. 364ff. with reference to Mair, 2009). 'According to populist narrative, a political elite has developed who does not understand the "people" – a political one (the people as sovereign), a cultural one (the people as a nation) and an economic one (the people as a class)' (Kriesi, 2014, p. 362).[5] In the case of the European Union, however, there is not just an abstract conflict between 'winners' and 'losers' of globalisation but conflicts about concrete measures of Europeanisation that are enforced by political decisions resulting in obvious benefits for some and burdens for others. Furthermore, the unfulfilled promise that everyone will gain from Europeanisation in general and the 'common market' in particular – a promise which had led to an 'increasing public support [of European integration particularly] from 1985 until 1991' (Grande & Hutter, 2016, p. 21, with reference to Çiftçi, 2005) has given way to disappointment and resentment. For members of the Eurozone these conflicts and redistributive effects are even more apparent.

Moreover, the growing disappointment about the unfulfilled promises of representative democracy and distrust in the role of political parties that can be observed in most member states are amplified by the particularities of the EU decision-making processes. In the multilevel system of the EU, "'non-majoritarian" forms of representation [are important] in a range of arenas that are not directly electorally accountable, little visible, and operating "back-stage"' (Kriesi, 2014, p. 365). Therefore, the perception prevails that EU policymaking is dominated by 'Eurocrats' who are supported by political elites in the member states and an overall permissive consensus that European integration is without alternative. And the impression that decisions are made and power is exercised by unaccountable rulers acting 'back-stage' is again even more widespread in those member states of the Eurozone where bodies like the Troika play a crucial role, but where also a battle over different ideas took place over how to address the debt problem (Schmidt, 2015; Brunnermeier et al., 2016; Kriesi & Grande, 2016).

THE MULTIANNUAL FINANCIAL FRAMEWORK NEGOTIATIONS AS STRUGGLE OVER IDEAS

This edited volume foregrounds the 'struggle over ideas' (Stone, 2002) that unfolded during the negotiations of the MFF and the recovery package against the backdrop of the aforementioned conflicts over solidarity, identity and sovereignty and thus the scope of cooperation and membership, as well as institutional design and authority. These aspects, which formed the background for the negotiations on the Multiannual Financial Framework for the years 2021 to 2027, are dealt with in the contributions which form the first part of this book. These chapters are set against the observation that 'Europe's challenges show no sign of abating', as the European Commission (2017, p. 7) declared in its White Paper on the 'Future of Europe'. The chapters in the second part of the book try to *anticipate, describe and discursively explain changes* in selected policy areas.

In regarding 'Europe as a discursive battleground' (Diez, 2001), the authors tackle the negotiations about the Multiannual Financial Framework 2021–2027 and the recovery package as well as their consequences for different policy areas from an interpretive perspective. We use 'interpretivism' rather than 'constructivism', a term that might admittedly be more common among authors writing from an international relations background, in order to create a synthesis of advances in critical policy studies and European integration research.[6] Our notion embraces those post-positivist approaches that have gathered under the label 'argumentative' (Fischer & Forester, 1993)[7] or 'interpretive policy analysis' (Yanow, 1995; Münch, 2016) or that more recently go by the name of 'critical policy studies' (Fischer et al., 2015). Here, political processes are no longer explained solely either on the basis of actors maximising interests or policymaking as rational problem solving nor by historical path-dependency or the determining impact of institutional structures. Instead, policymaking is understood as language-mediated and shaped interpretation processes and interpretive struggles. One of the fundamental goals of policy-making, we maintain following Fischer (1998, p. 12), is not only to change an existing reality but to construct a common understanding of a problem. These are generally clearly differentiated from positivist approaches, which are based on naturalistic assumptions in ontological terms and objectivist assumptions in epistemological terms (Barbehön et al., 2019, p. 144).

As demonstrated in our *Handbook of European Policies* (Heinelt & Münch, 2018a), the 'struggle over ideas' (Stone, 2002, p. 11) and processes of collectively giving meaning to (i.e. interpreting) constraints and opportunities are the essence of policymaking in this perspective (Hajer & Wagenaar, 2003; Heinelt, 2019). Therefore, we focus 'on meanings that shape action and institutions, and the way in which they do so' (Bevir & Rhodes, 2004, p. 130), and agree with Wagenaar (2011, p. 4): 'Meaning influences people's behavior.' This implies 'an actor-centered approach to interpretive explanation', as outlined by Nullmeier (2018, p. 72). As the contributions to our previous handbook on EU policies have clearly demonstrated, interpretive or 'argumentative' approaches have proven to be particularly fruitful in circumstances where policy change is not clearly determined by institutions and where rational choice's neglect of ideas in processes of preference formation and transformation becomes particularly apparent. In a similar vein, Roederer-Rynning and Greenwood have successfully applied interpretivism to highlight how a significant part of EU law-making in practice takes place in secluded arenas, stressing its 'relevance for the study of informal processes and governance (Finlayson 2004)' (Roederer-Rynning & Greenwood, 2020, p. 2). While Joerges and Neyer (1997) also claim that the debates behind closed doors in many fields of EU policymaking could be spaces where the logic of argumentation prevails, since member states in these forums do not compete with each other openly, we have wondered elsewhere whether the traditionally intergovernmental and secretive mode in some policy areas, like migration, has slowed down interpretive accounts and discourse analyses in particular (Münch, 2018, p. 306). Drawing from Vivien Schmidt (2018, p. 36), one could claim that in the case of the negotiations for the MFF, both the '"coordinative" discourse of elite policy construction at the EU level and a "communicative" discourse between elites and the public involving national level policy discussion, contestation, and legitimization' become particularly apparent.

In essence, the aim in this volume is not to explain the course and results of negotiations from the interests of member state governments, which are simply given (as a null hypothesis). The focus of interpretive policy analysis on meaning-making implies that 'it seeks knowledge about how human beings, scholars included, make individual and collective sense of their particular worlds' (Schwartz-Shea & Yanow, 2012, p. 46). Since we cannot always just ask actors what they think because they might not be aware of what they are doing or – particularly in politics – be unwilling to tell us what they are thinking, critical interpretive policy analysis turns to arguments in policy discourse as a unit of analysis. It examines the normative assumptions upon which problematisations and policy solutions are based (Fischer, 2016, p. 96). It therefore takes the statements (in written or oral form) of actors seriously and infers from them the reasons for their actions (cf. Wiesner et al., 2017, p. 4). Or to quote Bevir and Rhodes (2004):

> Understanding needs an ethnographic form of inquiry: we have to read practices, actions, texts, interviews and speeches to recover other people's stories. Explanation needs a historical form of inquiry: we have to locate their stories within their wider webs of belief, and these webs of belief against the background of traditions they modify in response to specific dilemmas. (p. 135)

For readers interested in an overview of what lead to the adoption of the MFF, in what follows we trace the discursive dynamics and milestones of the negotiations around the MFF and the new recovery instrument, aimed at alleviating the economic crisis caused by the coronavirus pandemic (in the next section), irrespective of specific policy areas that are going to be analysed in the second part of the book. Following this chronological reconstruction, in the section after that we outline the different discourse coalitions among the member states' governments that formed around different storylines and conclude with some tentative expectations about the development of specific policy areas following the new long-term budget.

ON THE WAY TO THE MULTIANNUAL FINANCIAL FRAMEWORK 2021–2027 AND THE NEW RECOVERY INSTRUMENT, 'NEXT GENERATION EU'

The negotiations over the MFF started in 2016 and initially took a typical course (see Becker, Chapter 2 in this volume). The process, however, took a different course and gained particular momentum with the outbreak of the pandemic. As highlighted by the European Commission (2020):

> The economic impact of the crisis will differ greatly across Member States. Some had the misfortune of being hit harder by CoVid-19 than others. But the impact also depends on Member States' economic structures and capacity to absorb and respond to the resulting economic shock, including through *financial* buffers in the public and private sector. ... Furthermore, the economic impact of the crisis also differs substantially across regions within countries, showing a pronounced impact of the crisis in all corners of the EU. (p. 3)

These different degrees of being affected by the pandemic did not only lead to a call for the assurance of an old idea of European integration – namely cohesion; emphasising the 'human tragedy' of the pandemic, the European Parliament, among others, called for standing 'together in solidarity' (European Parliament, 2020a, p. 3). The emerging awareness that a common recovery package was needed to address the massive economic, financial and social impact of the pandemic in April 2020 led to a Joint Statement of the European Council (2020a) on 'A Roadmap for Recovery'. This roadmap was meant to pave the way 'Towards a more resilient, sustainable and fair Europe' (the subtitle of this statement) by a 'coordinated exit strategy, a comprehensive recovery plan and unprecedented investment' to 'relaunch and transform' the EU economy.

After the French and German governments proposed a 'Recovery Fund'[8] of €500 billion beyond the MFF, financed by borrowing on behalf of the EU and made available to member states either by loans or grants, the European Commission presented (on 28 May 2020) proposals for a European recovery package.[9] It consisted of three elements (for details see Bachtler et al., 2020, as well as Becker, Chapter 2 in this volume):

- A revised proposal for the Multiannual Financial Framework 2021–2027.
- A 'recovery instrument' titled 'Next Generation EU' consisting of €750 billion to be financed and distributed based on the proposal of the French and the German governments. Most of the €750 billion should be distributed through a new instrument called the 'New Recovery and Resilience Facility' and the rest through already existing channels like the cohesion policy.
- The third element of the European recovery package proposed by the Commission consists of resources already available outside the EU budget – namely through the European Stability Mechanism, the European Investment Bank and the SURE programme (for 'temporary Support to mitigate Unemployment Risks in an Emergency').

After (critical) reactions among the member states and from the European Parliament as well as videoconference discussions of the President of the European Council, Charles Michel, with every member of the European Council, on 10 July 2020 Michel presented a 'negotiating box' which formed the basis for negotiations at an extraordinary five-day meeting of the European Council (from 17 to 21 July 2020). The main results of this meeting were the following (for more details see European Council, 2020b, as well as Chapter 2 in this volume):

- The size of the Multiannual Financial Framework for 2021–2027 is lower than that for 2014–2020 – namely just €1.074 trillion (in contrast to

  €1.324 trillion proposed by the European Parliament (2020a) and €1.1 trillion suggested by the European Commission in its last proposal from May
  2020).
- The size of the recovery fund titled 'Next Generation EU' (NGEU)
  remained at a total of €750 billion, as proposed by the European
  Commission. However, the amount of grants was reduced from €500 billion
  to €390 billion and the amount of loans increased from €250 billion to
  €360 billion.
- Existing rebates (or 'budget correction mechanisms') were not only
  retained for Austria, Germany, Denmark, the Netherlands and Sweden, but
  even increased for them.
- Finally, even though a rule of law conditionality for funding was unanimously accepted, after long and hard negotiations only a vague formulation
  was included in the Council's final conclusions, which was interpreted
  differently by government representatives of individual member states
  immediately after the Council meeting.

Despite the reduction in the budget for the Multiannual Financial Framework
and the share of grants within the recovery fund, and the maintenance and even
increase of rebates for some member states, the fact that the EU is now allowed
to issue common debt should not be underestimated. This is interpreted as
'a historic step in European integration and a clear expression of solidarity
following the coronavirus crisis' (European Parliamentary Research Service,
2020, p. 3).

  Only two days after the end of the Council meeting the European Parliament
adopted by broad majority a resolution on the conclusions of the extraordinary
European Council meeting. In this resolution the European Parliament (2020b)
emphasised that

- the 'Parliament is the guarantor of a transparent and democratic recovery',
  and that
- 'under such unprecedented and exceptional circumstances [of the pan-
  demic], people in the EU have a collective duty of solidarity'.

Although the European Parliament welcomed in its resolution

- 'the EU Heads of State and Governments' acceptance of a recovery fund
  to kick-start the economy [and] acknowledges the creation of the recovery
  instrument, which represents a historic move for the EU', it
- 'deplores ... the reduction of the grant component in the final agreement'
  and does
- 'not accept ... the political agreement on the 2021–2027 MFF as it stands'
  and

–   'warns that the cuts to the MFF go against the EU's objectives'.

This applies particularly to cuts in programmes related to health, education, research and the digital transformation. Furthermore, cuts in programmes supporting the transition of carbon-dependent regions, which run counter to the EU's Green Deal agenda, were criticised. In addition, it was stated that the European Parliament 'believes that the proposed cuts to asylum, migration and border management imperil the EU's position in an increasingly volatile and uncertain world' (European Parliament, 2020b). Against the background of these statements, it was not surprising that the European Parliament stressed that it 'will not rubber-stamp a *fait accompli* and is prepared to withhold its consent for the MFF until a satisfactory agreement is reached in the upcoming negotiations between Parliament and the Council' (ibid.). Moreover, the European Parliament 'regrets the fact that the European Council significantly weakened the efforts of the Commission and Parliament to uphold the rule of law, fundamental rights and democracy in the framework of the MFF and the Next Generation EU (NGEU) instrument' (ibid.). Finally, it was emphasised in this resolution that the European Parliament (EP) 'regrets the fact that once again some Member States negotiated in the spirit of operating budgetary balances while completely disregarding the overall benefits of membership of the single market and the EU as a whole' (ibid.).

On 10 November 2020, the EP's budget negotiators and the Council Presidency approved the outline of an agreement on the next Multiannual Financial Framework and the recovery instrument (Next Generation EU), after ten weeks of negotiations. This agreement, which needs to be endorsed by the EP and unanimously adopted by the Council, includes in particular the following (for details see Becker, Chapter 2 in this volume):

–   An increase of EU programmes, particularly for research (Horizon), health and Erasmus+ (exchange of students and academic staff) by €15 billion through additional means (€12.5 bn) and reallocations (€2.5 bn) for the next financial period.
–   A greater involvement of the EP in the oversight of revenue under Next Generation EU.
–   Funding targets for ensuring the achievement of biodiversity and climate objectives.

In the light of the comments made by the EP and their representatives after the Council meeting in July 2020, the not-yet-clearly defined involvement of the EP in the control of the spending of revenue under Next Generation EU, the marginal financial strengthening of individual instruments and the emphasis placed on certain policy objectives, which are well in line with a large number of member state governments, must, from an EP perspective, represent a modest outcome of the negotiations (even though the EP's budget negotiators claimed the opposite in their statements; see European Parliament 2020c).

A few days earlier (on 5 November 2020), the German presidency of the Council and the European Parliament's negotiators had already agreed on a provisional agreement concerning a new regime of a rule of law conditionality. This provisional agreement builds on the political compromise reached at the European Council's meeting in July 2020.

Against the background of these agreements reached by the EP's budget negotiators and the Council Presidency, Michael Clauß, Permanent Representative of Germany to the EU, emphasised, on 10 November 2020:

> Negotiations with the Parliament took time, but we have finally made it ... This is a well-balanced deal, which addresses the issues raised by the Parliament while respecting the guidance received from the European Council in July. We are now in a position to take the next crucial steps in the process – submitting the different parts of the package to the member states and the Parliament for endorsement. Europe has been hit severely by the second wave of the coronavirus pandemic. We urgently need the recovery fund up and running in order to cushion the dire economic consequences of the pandemic. I hope that everyone understands the urgency of the situation and will now help to clear the way for the swift implementation of the EU budget and recovery package – no one needs new hurdles and further delays. (European Council, 2020c)

However, both the Hungarian and Polish governments immediately signalled a veto of the Multiannual Financial Framework and the recovery instrument in view of the rule of law conditionality. This led Michael Roth, the then Minister of State for Europe at the German Federal Foreign Office, to make the following statement in an interview with the newspaper *Die Welt* on 12 November 2020:

> With the agreement on a new multi-annual budget and the recovery package, we have made a real breakthrough after long negotiations. The EU is sending a clear signal of capacity to act and solidarity. We are setting an important course for our common future. I cannot imagine that anyone could now have any serious interest in stopping this train by stepping on the brakes. That would be extremely dangerous. After all, it is in all our interests and our joint responsibility to ensure that the urgently needed recovery funding flows quickly and mitigates the social and economic consequences of the pandemic. Anyone who blocks the road here is shooting himself in the foot.[10]

This was a clear hint towards Hungary and Poland, who would shoot themselves in the foot when they refused to agree to the next Multiannual Financial Framework and the recovery instrument.

Nevertheless, to underline their position, the heads of government of Hungary and Poland, Viktor Orbán and Mateusz Morawiecki, emphasised after a meeting on 26 November 2020 that neither Poland nor Hungary would accept a proposal that appears unacceptable to the other (Gnauck & Löwenstein, 2020).

The Polish Foreign Minister, Zbigniew Rau, defended the Polish government's position in a guest op-ed for the *Frankfurter Allgemeine Zeitung* (on 27 November) as follows:

> The EU Treaty states that the Union acts on the basis of competences conferred on it by the states. 'The exercise of these competences is subject to the principles of subsidiarity and proportionality. … All competences not conferred on the Union by the Treaties shall remain with the Member States' (Article 5 TEU). … We cannot allow the EU and its institutions to expand their competences through the assumption of rights. That is forbidden by the principle of legalism! … The 27 countries have concluded an agreement – in the form of the EU Treaty – that violations of the fundamental principles of our Union are to be investigated in a particular procedure. This procedure is objective because it must take into account the opinions of all: The rule of unanimity in Article 7 of the EU Treaty is based on this. … However, without amending the Treaties, we will not accept instruments other than those defined in Article 7 TEU. (Rau, 2020; translation by the authors)

He concluded by highlighting not only the legitimacy but also the legality of political decisions made at home and by stylising the Polish government as the defender of the rule of law, as it were:

> Yes, the dispute between Poland and the institutions is about the rule of law. But it is not about reforming the Polish judiciary, as this is not within the remit of European integration – the EU institutions merely arrogate to themselves competences in this area. No member state ever had the right to interfere in the German or Polish judiciary, it could therefore not hand over such a power to the European institutions. (Ibid.)

In an interview with the *Frankfurter Allgemeine Zeitung* (of 3 December 2020), the Polish Prime Minister Mateusz Morawiecki comments on the concerns that have led the Polish government to threaten the veto:[11]

> Our main concern is that this mechanism [fixing the rule of law conditionality] can be used very arbitrarily and for political motives. Today someone does not like the Polish government, then we put them on the pillory. Tomorrow it can be the government of Italy or Portugal, then we take away their funds. This is paradoxical: this mechanism circumvents the treaties. It is supposed to safeguard the rule of law and is itself a fundamental violation of it.

And he added in the same interview (see note 11), which may be characteristic of his interpretation of the situation:

> … we in Poland also know what an order imposed by some centre means. This is what the Soviet system looked like: A distant central committee, a fictitious independence and equality of the "partner countries" with actual dependence, exploitation and neo-colonialism. … This is only a memento from fortunately bygone times. But one should learn from it.

Finally, on 9 December 2020, the Polish and Hungarian governments agreed with the German EU Presidency on a solution to the budgetary blockade, which was approved by the heads of state and government of all member states one day later.[12] The Polish and Hungarian governments withdrew their threat to block the decisions on the budget and the recovery fund, and the heads of state and government of the other member states agreed that the new rule of law mechanism would only be applied after a possible decision by the European Court of Justice. The Hungarian and Polish governments argued that the controversial rule of law mechanism contradicts Article 7 of the EU Treaty. According to this article, sanctions can only be imposed if the member states (with the exception of the state concerned) decide unanimously. In contrast, the new controversial instrument provides for a qualified majority. Yet, on 16 February 2022 the European Court of Justice ruled to dismiss the requests by the Polish and Hungarian governments (European Parliament, 2022).

In addition, an 'interpretative declaration' was provided on the application of the rule of law mechanism. If a state objects to sanctions, the heads of state and government may to seek to 'formulate a common position' at an EU summit. This is a slightly strengthened form of the regulation already agreed in July 2020. However, it does not give Hungary and Poland a veto.

Against this background the European Council stated on its website on 11 December 2020:

> For the first time, a commitment to the rule of law and a mechanism to protect the budget have been anchored in the new Multiannual Financial Framework. In the event of violations, the European Commission would be able to submit concrete proposals for action, which the Council could then confirm by qualified majority.[13]

The reactions to this compromise were different in Hungary and Poland. The compromise was seen by Hungarian government officials and the press close to Viktor Orbán from a different perspective, as expressed by the Hungarian Foreign Minister Péter Szijjártó: 'We won because we fought for the national interests.' Had that not been the case, 'Brussels would have decided that we must either accept illegal migrants or be deprived of EU money'.[14] In contrast, it was said from the circle around the EU-critical Polish Justice Minister

Zbigniew Ziobro that the 'interpretative declaration' is only a political resolution and not binding law. The EU Commission has often disregarded such resolutions. There is a threat of 'economic and political colonization of Poland by the left-wing ideologues in Brussels and Berlin'. One does not want a 'centralist Euro-kolkhoz, but a Europe of fatherlands'.[15]

DISCOURSE COALITIONS AMONG THE MEMBER STATES' GOVERNMENTS IN THE STRUGGLE OVER IDEAS ABOUT THE MFF AND THE RECOVERY FUND

The degree of politicisation of the negotiations about the MFF and the Next Generation EU (NGEU) instrument is also expressed in different positions of distinct groups of member states' governments. This may have something to do with the interests of certain governments who have either tried to limit the budget of the MFF and the nature of financial support under the Next Generation EU instrument or to limit, retain or even increase funding for individual EU policies such as agricultural or cohesion policy. These groups of member state governments, however, did not simply insist on their objective (i.e. a certain level of budgetary resources for cohesion policy) according to easily understandable or presumable financial interests, but interpreted the given situation in a certain way and justified how, according to this interpretation, the MFF and the Next Generation EU instrument should necessarily be financially equipped and targeted in terms of policy contents.

In the spirit of the interpretive premises that underpin this volume, we follow Maarten Hajer (1995, p. 58f.) and focus on the duality of structures around the constitutive role of discourses in policymaking as well as equally around the 'discoursing subjects', that is, creative, intelligent individuals who nevertheless have to move within a context that both enables and limits their actions. Social constructions or interpretations are thus not a function of the interests of (individual or collective) actors and interests are not given, but are constituted through discourse. In the struggle for discursive hegemony, actors join together to form discourse coalitions. 'A discourse coalition is thus the ensemble of a set of storylines, all organized around a discourse. The discourse coalition approach suggests that politics is a process in which different actors from various backgrounds form specific coalitions around specific storylines' (Hajer, 1993, p. 47). In contrast to Sabatier (1998), who employs his advocacy coalition framework as the basis for 'a rigorous causal theory of policy change' (Fischer, 2003, p. 112), Hajer's (1995) discourse coalitions are united by narrative storylines that interpret events and courses of action in concrete social context, not by relatively stable beliefs. In contrast to Hajer's approach, where the discourse coalitions are mostly identified by the discourse analyst, some of the coalitions we encounter in the MFF negotiations self-identify as belonging to certain groups.

Seen in this way, member state governments formed certain discourse coalitions in a struggle over ideas (Stone, 2002) about the next MFF and the recovery instruments (see Figure 1.1). Drawing from argumentative policy analysis we follow Fischer (2003, p. 60), for whom every policy-related idea represents an argument or set of arguments that favours different world views.[16]

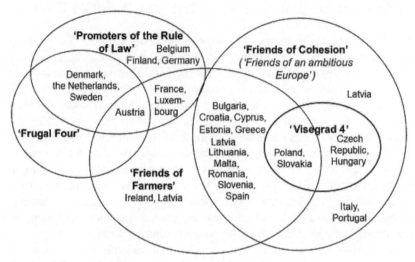

Source: Authors' own presentation based on https://de.slideshare.net/petzowg/simulating-the-eu -budget-20212027?qid=8c561b66-fa92-4369-bc71-1e5df7fe4205&v=&b=&from_search=12 (last accessed 21 February 2022).

Figure 1.1   *Discourse communities of member state governments in the struggle over ideas about the MFF and the recovery fund*

We reconstruct five such discourse coalitions based on statements before and during the negotiations not only by individual governments but – more interestingly – also in joint (non-)papers.[17]

The 'Friends of Cohesion'

The focus on cohesion policy gives the name 'friends of cohesion' to a group of net recipient member states consisting of Bulgaria, Croatia, Cyprus, Czech Republic, Estonia, Greece, Hungary, Latvia, Lithuania, Malta, Poland, Portugal, Romania, Slovakia, Slovenia and Spain. This group of member states – to which Italy could be added – defined cohesion policy as a crucial instrument 'in the context of important challenges such as climate change, demographic trends, innovation, job creation and sustainable growth' in a Joint Declaration on the MFF from February 2020.[18] For most of them the common agricultural policy plays a similarly important role to the cohesion policy. Therefore, the Joint Declaration stated that the cohesion policy and the common agricultural policy 'are crucial to confront the economic and social disparities that might arise from the Digital and Climate transitions'. Finally, it was emphasised in this Joint Declaration that the 'Cohesion Policy and the Common Agricultural Policy have a positive impact on the daily life of European citizens and represent a highly valuable asset that enhances their trust and connection to the European project and therefore require a sufficient level of financing'.

Even before the outbreak of the coronavirus pandemic, when the size of the MFF was still the main topic of the debate, the 'friends of cohesion' had renamed themselves the 'friends of an ambitious Europe'. Hungarian Prime Minister Viktor Orbán, on 22 February 2020, explained the reasoning to media representatives:

> ... the Friends of Cohesion group of countries has decided to rename itself the 'Budget for an Ambitious Europe Group', [because] its members have accepted the proposition that 'if we want an ambitious Europe, we need an ambitious budget'. The group's member countries have suggested that the financial calculations should be compared to a European Parliament proposal for each of the 27 Member States to contribute a standard rate of 1.3 per cent of GNI to the budget.[19]

In a similar vein, the Spanish government asked for an 'ambitious MFF' in a non-paper on a European recovery strategy from 19 April 2020.[20] Nevertheless, it underlined:

> Allocations for Cohesion Policy and Common Agriculture Policy should be maintained. There is also a need to make room for new programs, to improve the Union's resilience in areas like health, R&D, migration or external action. European agriculture has proven to be a key element of stability, self-sufficiency and geopolitical autonomy in times of crisis. It is therefore key to ensure that the Common Agricultural Policy provides appropriate support to ensure the ability of farmers to adjust to the increasing needs and reinforce the contribution of this sector to the ecological transition. Likewise, cohesion policy can play an important role in avoiding divergence of countries and regions in the aftermath of the health crisis.

Furthermore, the Spanish government demanded 'appropriate flexibility', implying that the use of the financial resources allocated to member states from the MFF should not focus on EU priorities.

With respect to a new economic recovery fund, the non-paper of the Spanish government argued that it 'should be established based on grants to Member

States, thus not raising national public debt levels'. These grants should be made available 'to member states through the EU budget based on a national allocation key related to the impact of the COVID 19 crisis on the basis of clear and transparent indicators, such as percentage of population affected, drop of GDP, increase in unemployment levels, etc.' Although the 'Fund should support the financing of post-crisis economic reconstruction in a coherent way at European level. Priority should be given to national programs that jumpstart the ecological and digital transition of the economy, and that boost its industrial and technological autonomy.' Furthermore, it emphasised that '[special] attention should be given to those sectors most affected by the global lock-down and virus contention measures, such as tourism and transport' – and not those sectors given priority at the EU level, for instance by the Green Deal (as demanded particularly by the 'frugal four'; see below).

The 'Friends of the Farmers'

Some members of the 'friends of cohesion' or the 'friends of an ambitious Europe', for whom not only the cohesion policy but also the common agricultural policy are key, form a group that could be called 'friends of the farmers'. Their core arguments for a common agricultural policy are those outlined in the Joint Declaration of the 'friends of cohesion' mentioned earlier. Members of the 'friends of cohesion' who are also members of the 'friends of the farmers' are Bulgaria, Croatia, Cyprus, Estonia, Greece, Lithuania, Malta, Romania, Slovenia and Spain. They are joined by Ireland and Latvia, who are not members of the 'friends of cohesion'. Furthermore, Austria, France and Luxembourg belong to the 'friends of the farmers' because the common agricultural policy is also a core issue for the governments of these three member states. However, the governments of these three member states are also part of two other discourse coalitions, which are dealt with further below.

The 'Visegrad 4'

A particular subgroup of the 'friends of cohesion' (or, the 'friends of an ambitious Europe') is the Visegrad Group consisting of the governments of the Czech Republic, Hungary, Poland and Slovakia.[21] 'The Visegrad Group (also known as the "Visegrad Four" or simply "V4") reflects the efforts of the countries of the Central European region to work together in a number of fields of common interest within the all-European integration' (Visegrad Group, n.d. a). However, these common interests are explicitly not limited to financial matters or security concerns. Instead, it is stressed: 'Czechia, Hungary, Poland and Slovakia have always been part of a single civilization sharing cultural and intellectual values and common roots in diverse religious traditions, which they wish to preserve and further strengthen' (ibid.).

Behind this and similar statements there is a common identity construction which developed in these states after the end of the East–West confrontation (see Balazs & Griesler, 2020; Braun, 2020 and therein especially the introduction by Balazs, 2020). It is based on the one hand on the delineation from their eastern neighbours, which are seen as characterised by the Orthodox Church. On the other hand, it is rooted in a historically founded aversion to dominance by an 'imperial' centre. According to this frame, Brussels took the place of Moscow and Vienna, and Berlin has remained a place from which – if at all – at best rarely anything good can be expected.

It is emphasised that this group, officially formed on 15 February 1991 (Visegrad Group, n.d. b), 'is not institutionalized in any manner. It is based solely on the principle of periodical meetings of its representatives at various levels (from the high-level meetings of prime ministers and heads of states to expert consultations).' However, it is admitted: 'Official summits of V4 prime ministers take place on an annual basis. Between these summits, one of the V4 countries holds presidency, part of which is the responsibility for drafting a one-year plan of action' (Visegrad Group, n.d. c).

That the one-year plan of each presidency is not merely symbolic is made clear by the programme of the Polish Presidency (1 July 2020 to 30 June 2021), which states: 'The task of the Polish Presidency will be to present [a] common position toward the details of architecture of the European Recovery Instrument (ERI)/Next Generation EU), in the final stage of the negotiation of the package MFF-ERI.'[22] Furthermore, the programme of the Polish Presidency of the 'Visegrad 4' highlights: 'The V4 is at the heart of building a wider coalition which can include up to 17 member states and may act as a counterbalance to the so-called net payers.'[23]

However, the main concern of this group – and especially of Hungary and Poland – in the negotiations about the MFF and the recovery instrument was challenging the rule of law conditionality for EU funding.

The 'Promoters of the Rule of Law'

The main opponents of the 'Visegrad 4' in the struggle over ideas about the MFF and the recovery fund are not just the 'net payers' (as argued in the quoted programme of the Polish Presidency) but the 'promoters of the rule of law'. This group consists of the governments of Austria, Belgium, Denmark, Germany, Finland, France, Luxembourg, the Netherlands and Sweden. The core ideas of this group are expressed in the following quote from an opinion editorial by the Belgian Foreign Minister at that time, Didier Reynders, the then German State Secretary of European Affairs, Michael Roth, and the

Dutch Foreign Minister at that time, Stef Blok, published in the *Frankfurter Allgemeine Zeitung* on 20 March 2019:

> What makes the European Union unique ... is our community of values. ... At the heart of our fundamental European values are respect for human dignity, freedom, democracy, equality, the rule of law and respect for human rights. In the European Treaties, these fundamental values are not hidden somewhere in an annex behind a long list of legal provisions. No, they are enshrined in Article 2 of the Treaty on European Union ... It shows that fundamental values are rooted in our European identity and are part of our common narrative. ... Among the fundamental values, the rule of law occupies a special place. Some have called it the 'guarantee of guarantees': It acts as a safeguard that allows democracies to function properly. It ensures that citizens and businesses can invoke their rights before independent courts. Indeed, the rule of law is the foundation of our societies. (Reynders et al., 2019)

The 'Frugal Four'

Parts of the 'promoters of the rule of law' – namely the governments of Austria, Denmark, the Netherlands and Sweden – form the 'frugal four', who have strongly influenced the negotiations in a well-concerted way. In a 'non-paper' the 'frugal four'[24] agreed that the 'COVID-19 crisis is affecting all EU Member States hard. Socially and financially. It is in the interest of all to restore growth to Member States' economies as soon as possible. This calls for European solidarity and a common recovery strategy.' They 'therefore suggest setting up a temporary, one-off Emergency Fund to support the economic recovery and the resilience of our health sectors to possible future waves. ... What we cannot agree to, however, are any instruments or measures leading to debt mutualisation nor significant increases in the EU-budget.'

Particularly the latter was justified by the argument that 'all Member States will suffer from an unprecedented economic contraction in 2020, with only a partial recovery in 2021. This means that ... national public finances are already under severe pressure. Additional funds for the EU ... will strain national budgets even further' (ibid.).

The basic idea was 'to provide temporary, dedicated funding through the MFF and to offer favourable loans to those who have been most severely affected by the crisis'. The loans should be provided by

> an Emergency Recovery Fund based on a 'loans for loans' approach ... and designed along the following lines:
>
> – A thorough *needs assessment* that targets sectors and segments that are most hit.
> – Recovery support should ensure that all Member States are better prepared for the next crisis. A *strong commitment to reforms and the fiscal framework* is essential to promote potential growth.

- Directed towards activities that contribute most to the recovery such as *research and innovation, enhanced resilience in the health sector* and ensuring a green transition that underpins the EU's ambitious *climate, growth and digital agendas*. …
- Adherence to *Rule of Law and Fundamental Rights* and *protect spending from fraud* …
- As part of the recovery effort, we need to *restore and deepen the Single Market* by having a common innovation and industrial policy, setting a joint action agenda before 2021 and by completing the Capital Markets Union. (Ibid.; emphasis in the original)

These statements make it clear that the 'frugal four' did agree to the establishment of a recovery fund even before the extraordinary meeting of the European Council. However, they did not just insist that this fund should only be used for issuing loans. They also stress that the fund is to be used to promote reforms and improve the budgetary situation (the 'fiscal framework') in the recipient countries in order to secure or increase their economic competitiveness. Furthermore, the fund should be used to 'restore and deepen the Single Market' as well as to complete the Capital Markets Union and contribute to the achievement of other goals that have already been on the EU agenda – namely 'a green transition' and 'the EU's ambitious climate, growth and digital agendas'. This, together with the emphasis that the granting of financial aid from the fund is *conditional* on respect for the rule of law and fundamental rights, means that the 'frugal four' want to use the money from a recovery fund to achieve ('ambitious') objectives that have already been formally defined at EU level – and in no case to stabilise structures in the member states according to the interests of their respective governments.

This strategy – agreeing to a recovery fund to respond to the COVID-19 crisis but using its financial means to 'prepare for the sustainable resurrection of our economies, by stimulating public and private investments, looking for new business opportunities and innovations, and creating employment' – was already made clear in a non-paper of the Dutch government presented on 21 April 2020. This non-paper, titled 'Outline for an EU Green Recovery. The Netherlands' priorities for a green recovery',[25] stressed that the 'recovery strategy … should include the green transition … and should be integrated with the mid- and long-term sustainability goals and actions of the Green Deal'. This should mean in concrete terms, for example with regard to the Common Agricultural Policy (CAP) – as emphasised in this non-paper – the provision of:

the right incentives for all farmers to contribute to common objectives, including through a shift from income support to targeted payments, in particular for innovation, circular agriculture, climate, sustainability and more nature-inclusive production that enhances biodiversity. The next CAP should include an objective and clear assessment-regime for National Strategic Plans.

A clear assessment regime for national recovery and resilience plans for 2021–2023, that is, the plans for using funding from the recovery fund, Next Generation EU, was also particularly demanded by Mark Rutte, Prime Minister of the Netherlands, at the extraordinary meeting of the European Council in July 2020. Moreover, this request was successful because, as a result of the negotiations at this meeting (see European Parliamentary Research Service, 2020, p. 4),

> Member States will be required [based on the Commission's country-specific recommendations], to prepare national recovery and resilience plans for 2021–23, in line with the European Semester. The plans will be reviewed in 2022. The assessment of these plans will be approved by the Council by qualified majority vote (QMV), on a proposal by the Commission – and not by unanimity as was suggested in the course of the negotiations and heavily debated.

The Finnish government, who joined the 'frugal four' at the extraordinary meeting of the European Council in July 2020, had already emphasised in a document (Finnish Government Communications Department, 2020) published on 4 June 2020 that the 'Commission's proposal for the recovery instrument is not acceptable to Finland as such' and asked, for example, for the 'following key changes':

– '[T]he support to be provided from the recovery instrument should, in principle, be in the form of loans.'
– 'The size of the recovery instrument must be smaller, and it must be proportionate to the subsequent burden of payment incurred by the Member States and its duration.'
– 'The long-term restriction of the budgetary sovereignty of the Member States must be kept to a minimum.'

Furthermore, the Finnish government welcomed 'the linking of the recovery instrument with the Green Deal'. Finally, it is remarkable that the Finnish government not only highlighted that the 'planned package of measures [of the MFF and the recovery instrument] is of major economic and political significance', but also 'stresses the importance of sufficient public debate in the context of the preparation [of the planned package of measures], both in Finland, in Europe and in the national Parliament. For the decisions to be legitimate, broad acceptance by citizens is necessary.'

Interim Résumé: Five Partly Overlapping Discourse Coalitions and Two Unlinked Camps

In summary, it can be said that although there are overlaps between some of the five discourse coalitions, in the end two interconnected discourse coalitions are facing each other: on the one hand the 'friends of cohesion' and the 'Visegrad 4', and on the other hand the 'frugal four' and the 'promoters of the rule of law'. There is no overlap between these two camps. The only overlaps are made by the 'friends of the farmers'. On one side, Austria belongs to the 'frugal four' and together with France and Luxembourg to the 'promoters of the rule of law', and on the other side, Bulgaria, Croatia, Cyprus, Czech Republic, Estonia, Greece, Hungary, Latvia, Lithuania, Malta, Poland, Romania, Slovenia and Spain are members of the 'friends of cohesion' and Poland and Slovakia are also members of the 'Visegrad 4'.

If one contrasts the central concerns of the 'friends of cohesion' and the 'Visegrad 4' with those of the 'frugal four' and the 'promoters of the rule of law' then the main points in the struggle over ideas about the next MFF and the recovery instruments become clear:

- *More funding with as little conditionality as possible* versus *less funding with conditionality*.
- In terms of recovery measures, the controversy boils down to *grants* or *loans* – or as much or as little of either one or the other.
- And the 'promoters of the rule of law' are not only concerned with conditionality in general, but above all with *rule of law conditionality* which the 'Visegrad 4' wanted to prevent in any case.

STRUCTURE AND CONTENT OF THIS BOOK

To capture the 'struggle over ideas' during the MFF negotiations, its discursive context, its consequences for core policy areas and its implications for how to theorise European integration, this edited volume proceeds in three steps.

The first part of the book introduces the readers to the chronology of events and their context. Peter Becker starts with a detailed account of the procedures leading to the adoption of the MFF, the peculiarities leading up to the MFF covered in this volume and the main results of the negotiations. Marlon Barbehön takes the continuing crisis mode of EU governance as his starting point. In his theoretically informed contribution, he scrutinises the triad of crisis, time and budgetary policy. By treating time as both a technique and a product of communicative operations, he reconstructs how different rationales 'temporalise' complexity in specific ways, hence making the crisis governable.

Zooming in on the euro crisis, Clément Fontan and Antoine de Cabanes trace the historical roots of the battle over ideas that shape the euro area asymmetry and its crisis. Furthermore, they draw conclusions on what the political responses back then can teach us about the controversies around the MFF negotiations ten years later.

The second part in this volume dissects different policy areas and how they were interpreted and shaped during the negotiations about the Multiannual Financial Framework 2021–2027.

In the areas of EU agricultural policy (CAP), addressed by Peter H. Feindt, Pascal Grohmann and Astrid Häger, and EU cohesion policy, scrutinised by Wolfgang Petzold, an awareness gradually emerged that a common recovery package to address the massive economic, financial and social impact of the pandemic could facilitate the negotiations on the MFF. By early 2020, the financial size of the MFF, its distribution between traditional policies (agricultural and cohesion policy) and innovative ones were the core controversies in the negotiations – in addition to the rebates for some member states and the rule of law conditionality. The debate on the financial size of the Multiannual Financial Framework 2021–2027 faded into the background and the controversy focused on whether the European Recovery Plan or the new recovery instrument ('Next Generation EU') should provide grants or loans to member states (and in what proportions) and how and under which conditions the newly mobilised financial resources should be used. The debate about the use of the newly mobilised financial resources concerns not only the rule of law conditionality. As argued by Wolfgang Petzold, the 2021 reform of EU cohesion policy may open avenues for a radical policy change because pressure on this traditional EU policy may stem from the delivery mechanism of the new Recovery and Resilience Facility to which EU cohesion policy is strongly interwoven. In contrast, as Peter H. Feindt, Pascal Grohmann and Astrid Häger show, the CAP's policy pathway, budget structure or budget share were not changed because discourse coalitions and political opportunity structures resulting from the context of the negotiations favoured the continuation of this established policy.

In his chapter, Basil Bornemann sheds light on the European Green Deal (EGD), which was envisioned as the European Union's new long-term growth strategy. He highlights how, in spite of the pandemic, the EGD's underlying ideas remained important reference points during the budget negotiations, arguing that this is an expression of a 'sustainabilisation' of European policymaking.

Asylum and migration are policy areas that had proven to be particularly polarised in the run-up to the MFF negotiations. In her chapter on the migration and border management heading of the MFF, Sybille Münch detects a high degree of continuity when it comes to notions of migration management, border protection and motives drawing migration into the realm of security.

In the field of EU research, technological development and innovation policy, Matthias Weber, Peter Biegelbauer, Michael Dinges and Katja Lamprecht trace the process and the discourses that have led to the proposal of the European Framework Programme for Research and Innovation's 'Horizon Europe'.

Both the challenges to decision-making in the negotiations about the Multiannual Financial Framework 2021–2027 and the resulting changes in the EU policy areas discussed in detail in the second part of this book will complement and update existing handbooks and edited volumes on EU policies.[26]

In the third part in this volume authors ask what the negotiations about the Multiannual Financial Framework 2021–2027 mean for theories of European integration.

Drawing from new intergovernmentalism, Uwe Puetter documents the commitment of the German government to consensus politics in the European Council and the Council and explains why Chancellor Merkel actively sought to accommodate challenger governments in Budapest and Warsaw during the MFF negotiations.

Sabine Saurugger asserts that the processes covered in this volume show signs of both path-dependency and innovation, as well as the influence of cognitive frames, which question a purely cost–benefit reading of the process.

As the contributions to this edited volume demonstrate, EU budget negotiations work like a burning glass through which Lasswell's (1936) definition of politics – 'who gets what, when and how' becomes visible. Rather than treating the process leading up to the final MFF as an expression of given cost–benefit analyses on behalf of member states and other institutional stakeholders, the chapters zoom into the 'struggle over ideas' (Stone, 2002) as the essence of policymaking as understood by interpretivism. Distributions among the headings in the Multiannual Financial Framework reflect specific readings of problem representations that can change throughout the long process of negotiations or show high degrees of continuity and ideational embeddedness. Different discourse coalitions can draw from different narratives and frames to persuade and justify their positions. In line with Bevir and Philipps (2019), who aim at 'decentering European governance', we highlight the significance of narratives, rationalities and resistance in European governance and uncover both contingency and conflict.

NOTES

1. For an account of British Eurosceptic discourses and their affective power see Hawkins (2015, p. 141):

    First, despite clear similarities with anti-EU discourses elsewhere, the radical separation constructed between Britain and the EU, is indicative of a particularly British strand of opposition to the EU. Second, British Euroskepticism in its current form predates the populist reemergence of the 1990s and is traceable at least to the negotiations of the British budgetary contribution which emerged in the late 1970s … Third, British Euroskepticism is a mainstream political phenomenon, not associated with extremist parties as in many EU member-states, where the mainstream consensus is pro-European.

2. For a multidimensional concept of (de)politicisation, comprising strategy, process and outcome, cf. Feindt et al. (2020).

3. Even though populism remains a highly contested concept, discursive style and performance often feature in media reporting on populism and have been considered by discourse analysis more recently as well. By deploying certain styles,

    populist politicians come forward as candid and authentic – albeit disruptive. Conversely, the discursive 'bad manners' and abrupt style shifting that disrupt expectations of 'appropriate' political communication are precisely at least in part what invests these discursive performances with overtones of candidness and authenticity. Moreover, populist politicians appeal to 'the people' by claiming the moral high ground, subverting and undermining the establishment, and producing identity performances that signify closeness to 'the people', as opposed to the perceived remoteness of mainstream political elites. (Ekström et al., 2018, p. 10)

4. Or a new cleavage between 'cosmopolitanism' and 'communitarianism' (as argued, for example, by Zürn & de Wilde, 2016).

5. For a critical discourse analysis account of populism see Wodak et al. (2013). Writing in the tradition of the Essex School of discourse analysis, which has been featured among critical policy scholars as well, Stavrakakis et al. (2017, p. 421) put forward the 'hypothesis that many parties are better categorized as nationalist, xenophobic, maybe even elitist, and only secondarily – if at all – as "populist"'.

6. Barbehön (2015, pp. 132–134) traces the specific genesis of constructivism in EU studies and its epistemological consequences. See Kurowska and Bliesemann de Guevara (2020) for an interpretive methodology in international relations.

7. Hajer (2002, p. 63) claims that the term argumentative turn is more appropriate than interpretivism, since it is not only about the words or images in the speakers' heads, but also about the confrontation with counter-positions in the sense of a debate. We concede that interpretivism as umbrella term is associated with a number of inconsistencies and has recently been increasingly replaced by the self-designation critical policy studies. On the one hand, the generic term interpretive policy analysis brought together both researchers who can be classified as belonging to an interpretative-hermeneutic current – that is, who focus on the interpretative performance of acting and interacting actors – as well as poststructuralist authors who, following Foucault, shed light on how subjects are constituted through discourse in the first place. On the other hand, the interpretive approach was seen as a necessary, but not sufficient condition for critique. Interpretive approaches did not destroy the dogmatic core of traditional interpretation, as Habermas accused, they only clarified it. A hermeneutic understanding must be supplemented by critical reflection if it is to open up perspectives for an emancipatory practice (Saretzki, 2015).

8. A French–German Initiative for the European Recovery from the Coronavirus Crisis, Pressemitteilung der Bundesregierung 173/20, 18 May 2020.
9. Amended proposal for Common Provisions Regulation, COM(2020) 450 final, Brussels.
10. www.auswaertiges-amt.de/de/newsroom/roth-welt-rechtsstaatsmechanismus/ 2415882 (last accessed 14 March 2022; translation by authors).
11. www.faz-biblionet.de/faz-portal/faz-archiv?q=Die+EU+reagiert+sich+ gern+an+Polen+und+Ungarn+ab&source=&max=10&sort=&offset=0&& _ts=1608117479603&DT_from=03.12.2020&timeFilterType=0#hitlist (last accessed 15 March 2022; translation by the authors).
12. In view of the blocking attitude of the Hungarian and Polish governments, there were plans to establish the recovery fund without Hungary and Poland, that is, only by the remaining 25 member states, which would have meant that Hungary and Poland would not have been able to benefit from this jointly loan-financed support instrument.
13. www.eu2020.de/eu2020-en/news/article/european-council-climate-protection -mff-terror/2425588 (last accessed 16 December 2020).
14. See *Frankfurter Allgemeine Zeitung*, 11 December 2020, No. 289, p. 2 (translation by the authors).
15. See *Frankfurter Allgemeine Zeitung*, 11 December 2020, No. 289, p. 2 (translation by the authors).
16. For a discussion on differences between ideas in variable-based research and in post-positivist accounts see Münch (2016, p. 27).
17. In addition to the positions of the different discourse coalition briefly described below, see the more detailed presentations in Bachtler et al. (2020, pp. 18–31) and also in European Parliamentary Research Service (2020, pp. 4–6).
18. www.portugal.gov.pt/download-ficheiros/ficheiro.aspx?v=c6825828-42dc -4090-8378-929c760c58a3 (last accessed 21 January 2021).
19. www.kormany.hu/en/the-prime-minister/news/an-ambitious-europe-needs-an -ambitious-budget (last accessed 21 January 2021).
20. See https://g8fip1kplyr33r3krz5b97d1-wpengine.netdna-ssl.com/wp-content/ uploads/2020/04/Spain-.pdf (last accessed 21 January 2021).
21. Sometimes (like at the extraordinary meeting of the European Council in July 2020) the 'Visegrad 4' are joined by the Slovenian government.
22. www.gov.pl/attachment/6fbcecec-34a3-4e70-a58b-d0ce194458a9, p. 4 (last accessed 15 March 2022).
23. www.gov.pl/attachment/6fbcecec-34a3-4e70-a58b-d0ce194458a9, p. 8 (last accessed 15 March 2022).
24. See www.rijksoverheid.nl/documenten/publicaties/2020/05/26/non-paper -eu-support-for-efficient-and-sustainable-covid-19-recovery (last accessed 15 March 2022).
25. www.euractiv.com/wp-content/uploads/sites/2/2020/04/Netherlands-non-paper -on-Green-Recovery-21-April-2020.pdf (last accessed 15 March 2022).
26. See for an overview of these publications Heinelt and Münch (2018b, p. 1). Subsequent publications are, for example, the volumes edited by Heinelt and Münch (2018a) and Zahariadis and Buonanno (2017).

REFERENCES

Bachtler J., Mendez, C. & Wishlade, F. (2020). 'The Recovery Plan for Europe and Cohesion Policy: An Initial Assessment'. European Regional Policy Research Consortium Paper 20/1, European Policies Research Centre.

Balazs, A. B. (2020). 'Introduction – All happy regions are alike'. In A. B. Balazs & C. Griessler (eds), *The Visegrad Four and the Western Balkans: Framing Regional Identities*, Nomos, 9–24.

Balazs, A. B. & Griessler, C. (eds) (2020). *The Visegrad Four and the Western Balkans: Framing Regional Identities*, Nomos.

Barbehön, M. (2015). *Die Europäisierung von Städten als diskursiver Prozess: Urbane Konstruktionen des Mehrebenensystems und die lokale Umsetzung europäischer Politik*, Nomos.

Barbehön, M., Münch, S., & Schlag, G. (2019). 'Interpretationen in der Politikwissenschaft'. *Zeitschrift für Politikwissenschaft*, 29(2), 141–151.

Bayer, L. (2020). 'European Parliament approves 2021–2027 EU budget'. Politico (16 December 2020). www.politico.eu/article/parliament-approves-2021-2027-eu-budget (last accessed 17 January 2021).

Bevir, M., & Philipps, R. (2019). *Decentring European Governance*, Routledge.

Bevir, M., & Rhodes, R. A. W. (2004). 'Interpreting British governance'. *The British Journal of Politics and International Relations*, 6(2), 130–136.

Braun, M. (2020). 'Postfunctionalism, identity and the Visegrad group'. *Journal of Common Market Studies*, 58(4), 925–940.

Brunnermeier, M. K., James, H., & Landau, J.-P. (2016). *The Euro and the Battle of Ideas*, Princeton University Press.

Çiftçi, S. (2005). 'Treaties, collective responses and the determinants of aggregate support for European integration'. *European Union Politics*, 6(4), 469–492.

Diez, T. (2001). 'Europe as a discursive battleground: discourse analysis and European integration studies'. *Cooperation and Conflict*, 36(1), 5–38.

Ekström, M., Patrona, M., & Thornborrow, J. (2018). 'Right-wing populism and the dynamics of style: a discourse-analytic perspective on mediated political performances'. *Palgrave Communications*, 4(1). https://doi.org/10.1057/s41599-018-0132-6.

European Commission (2016). 'Financial Framework 2014–2020'. https://ec.europa.eu/budget/biblio/documents/fin_fwk1420/fin_fwk1420_en.cfm (last accessed 18 January 2021).

European Commission (2017). 'White Paper: The Future of Europe', COM(2017)2025.

European Commission (2020). 'Repair and Prepare for the Next Generation', Commission Staff Working Document, SWD 2020/98 final.

European Council (2020a). 'A Roadmap for Recovery: Towards a more resilient, sustainable and fair Europe', Joint Statement by Members of the European Council.

European Council (2020b). 'Special Meeting of the European Council (17, 18, 19, 20 and 21 July 2020) – Conclusions'. www.consilium.europa.eu/media/45109/210720-euco-final-conclusions-en.pdf (last accessed 14 March 2022).

European Council (2020c). 'Next Multiannual Financial Framework and recovery package: Council presidency reaches political agreement with the European Parliament', Press release.

European Parliament (2020a). 'Resolution on EU action to combat the COVID-19 pandemic and its consequences', 2020/2616 (RSP).

European Parliament (2020b). 'Resolution on the conclusions of the extraordinary European Council meeting of 17–21 July 2020', 2020/2732 (RSP).

European Parliament (2020c). 'Long-term EU Budget and Own Resources: Statements by Parliament's negotiators', Press release, 10 November 2020.

European Parliament (2022). 'Rule of Law: ECJ has removed last obstacle to application of the Conditionality mechanism', Press release, 16 February 2022.

European Parliamentary Research Service (2020). 'Outcome of the special European Council meeting of 17–21 July 2020'. www.europarl.europa.eu/RegData/etudes/BRIE/2020/654169/EPRS_BRI(2020)654169_EN.pdf (last accessed 15 March 2022).

Feindt, P. H., Schwindenhammer, S., & Tosun, J. (2020). 'Politicization, depoliticization and policy change: a comparative theoretical perspective on agri-food policy'. *Journal of Comparative Policy Analysis: Research and Practice*, 1–17. https://doi.org/10.1080/13876988.2020.1785875.

Finlayson, A. (2004). 'The interpretive approach in political science: a symposium'. *The British Journal of Politics and International Relations*, 6(2), 129–164.

Finnish Government Communications Department (2020). 'Ministerial Committee on EU Affairs outlined Finland's positions on the financial framework package and the recovery instrument', Press release 392/2020, 4 June 2020. https://vnk.fi/en/-/eu-minva-linjasi-suomen-kantoja-rahoituskehyskokonaisuuteen-ja-elpymisvalineeseen (last accessed 15 March 2020).

Fischer, F. (1998). 'Beyond empiricism: policy inquiry in postpositivist perspective'. *Policy Studies Journal*, 26(1), 129–146.

Fischer, F. (2003). *Reframing Public Policy. Discursive Politics and Deliberative Practices*, Oxford University Press.

Fischer, F. (2016). 'What is critical? Connecting the policy analysis to political critique'. *Critical Policy Studies*, 10(1), 95–98.

Fischer, F., & Forester, J. (eds) (1993). *The Argumentative Turn in Policy Analysis and Planning*, Duke University Press.

Fischer, F., Torgerson, D., Durnová, A., & Orsini, M. (eds) (2015). *Handbook of Critical Policy Studies*, Edward Elgar Publishing.

Gnauck, G., & Löwenstein, S. (2020). 'Kein Weichling sein: Warum Ungarn und Polen bei ihrem Veto gegen die Corona-Hilfen und den EU-Haushalt hart bleiben'. *Frankfurter Allgemeine Zeitung*, 277, 6. www.faz-biblionet.de/faz-portal/faz-archiv?q=Keine+Weichling+sein&source=&max=10&sort=&offset=0&&_ts=1608118155177&DT_from=27.11.2020&timeFilterType=0#hitlist (last accessed 15 March 2022).

Grande, E., & Hutter, S. (2016). 'Introduction: European integration and the challenge of politicisation'. In S. Hutter, E. Grande, & H. Kriesi (eds), *Politicising Europe: Integration and Mass Politics*, Cambridge University Press, 3–31.

Hajer, M. (1993). 'Discourse coalitions and the institutionalization of practice: the case of acid rain in Britain'. In F. Fischer & J. Forester (eds), *The Argumentative Turn in Policy-Analysis and Planning*, Duke University Press, 43–76.

Hajer, M. (1995). *The Politics of Environmental Discourse. Ecological Modernization and the Policy Process*, Oxford University Press.

Hajer, M. (2002). 'Discourse analysis and the study of policy making'. *European Political Science*, 2(1), 61–65.

Hajer, M., & Wagenaar, H. (eds) (2003). *Deliberative Policy Analysis. Understanding Governance in the Network Society*, Cambridge University Press.

Hawkins, B. (2015). 'Fantasies of subjugation: a discourse theoretical account of British policy on the European Union'. *Critical Policy Studies*, 9(2), 139–157.

Heinelt, H. (2019). *Challenges to Political Decision-Making: Dealing with Information Overload, Ignorance and Contested Knowledge*, Routledge.

Heinelt, H., & Münch, S. (2018a). *Handbook of European Policies: Interpretive Approaches to the EU*, Edward Elgar Publishing.

Heinelt, H., & Münch, S. (2018b). 'Introduction'. In H. Heinelt & S. Münch (eds), *Handbook of European Policies*, Edward Elgar Publishing, 1–16.

Hutter, S., Grande, E., & Kriesi, H. (2016). *Politicising Europe*, Cambridge University Press.

Joerges, C. & Neyer, J. (1997). 'From intergovernmental bargaining to deliberative political processes: the constitutionalisation of comitology'. *European Law Journal*, 3(3), 273–299.

Kriesi, H. (2014). 'The populist challenge'. *West European Politics*, 37(2), 361–378.

Kriesi, H., & Grande, E. (2016). 'The euro crisis: a boost to the politicisation of European integration?' In S. Hutter, E. Grande, & H. Kriesi (eds), *Politicising Europe: Integration and Mass Politics*, Cambridge University Press, 240–276.

Kriesi, H., & Pappas, T. S. (2015). *European Populism in the Shadow of the Great Recession*, ECPR Press.

Kriesi, H., Grande, E., Lachat, R., Dolezal, M., Bornschier, S., & Frey, T. (2008). *West European Politics in the Age of Globalization*, Cambridge University Press.

Kurowska, X., & Bliesemann de Guevara, B. (2020). 'Interpretive approaches in political science and international relations'. In L. Curini & R. Franzese (eds), *The SAGE Handbook of Research Methods in Political Science & IR* (Vol. 2), Sage, 1221–1240.

Lasswell, H. (1936). *Politics: Who Gets What, When, How*, Whittlesey House.

Mair, P. (2009). 'Representative versus Responsible Government', MPIfG Working Paper 09/8. www.mpifg.de/pu/workpap/wp09-8.pdf.

Münch, S. (2016). *Interpretative Policy-Analyse. Eine Einführung*, Springer VS.

Münch, S. (2018). 'EU migration and asylum policies'. In H. Heinelt & S. Münch (eds), *Handbook of European Policies: Interpretive Approaches to the EU*, Edward Elgar Publishing, 306–330.

Nullmeier, F. (2018). 'How to explain discursive change: an actor-centered approach to interpretive explanation'. In H. Heinelt & S. Münch (eds), *Handbook of European Policies: Interpretive Approaches to the EU*, Edward Elgar Publishing, 72–90.

Rau, Z. (2020). 'Die EU-Verträge sind heilig'. *Frankfurter Allgemeine Zeitung*, 277, 10. www.faz-biblionet.de/faz-portal/faz-archiv?q=Die+EU-Vertr%C3%A4ge+sind+heilig&source=&max=10&sort=&offset=0&&_ts=1608115168766&DT_from=27.11.2020&timeFilterType=0#hitlist (last accessed 15 March 2022).

Reynders, D., Roth, M., & Blok, S. (2019). 'Die Rechtsstaatlichkeit aller EU-Mitglieder prüfen'. *Frankfurter Allgemeine Zeitung*, 67, 8. www.faz-biblionet.de/faz-portal/document?uid=FAZ__FD1201903205665135&token=2e61c83f-2ab3-4497-b1e6-e3c1fce6ef0c&p._scr=faz-archiv&p.q=%28%22Europ%C3%A4ische+Union%22.1F.%29&p.source=&p.max=10&p.sort=&p.offset=0&p._ts=1647345531241&p.DT_from=20.03.2019&p.DT_to=20.03.2019&p.timeFilterType=0 (last accessed 15 March 2022).

Roederer-Rynning, C., & Greenwood, J. (2020). 'Black boxes and open secrets: trilogues as "politicised diplomacy"'. *West European Politics*, 44(3), 485–509. https://doi.org/10.1080/01402382.2020.1716526.

Sabatier, P. A. (1998). 'The advocacy coalition framework: revisions and relevance for Europe'. *Journal of European Public Policy*, 5(1), 98–130.

Saretzki, T. (2015). 'Habermas, critical theory and public policy'. In F. Fischer, D. Torgerson, A. Durnová, & M. Orsini (eds), *Handbook of Critical Policy Studies*, Edward Elgar, 67–91.

Schattschneider, E. (1957). 'Intensity, visibility, direction and scope'. *The American Political Science Review*, 51(4), 933–942. doi:10.2307/1952444.

Schmidt, V. A. (2015). 'The forgotten problem of democratic legitimacy. Governing by the rules and ruling by the numbers'. In M. Matthijs & M. M. Blyth (eds), *The Future of the Euro*, Oxford University Press, 90–114.

Schmidt, V. A. (2018). 'The role of ideas and discourse in European integration'. In H. Heinelt & S. Münch (eds), *Handbook of European Policies*, Edward Elgar Publishing, 35–54.

Schwartz-Shea, P., & Yanow, D. (2012). *Interpretive Research Design: Concepts and Processes*, Routledge.

Stavrakakis, Y., Katsambekis, G., Nikisianis, N., Kioupkiolis, A., & Siomos, T. (2017). 'Extreme right-wing populism in Europe: revisiting a reified association'. *Critical Discourse Studies*, 14(4), 420–439.

Stone, D. A. (2002). *Policy Paradox: The Art of Political Decision Making* (rev. edn), Norton.

Visegrad Group (n.d. a). 'About the Visegrad Group'. www.visegradgroup.eu/about (last accessed 10 November 2020).

Visegrad Group (n.d. b). 'History of the Visegrad Group'. www.visegradgroup.eu/about/history (last accessed 10 November 2020).

Visegrad Group (n.d. c). 'Aims and Structure'. www.visegradgroup.eu/about/aims-and-structure (last accessed 10 November 2020).

Wagenaar, H. (2011). *Meaning in Action: Interpretation and Dialogue in Policy Analysis*, M.E. Sharpe.

Wiesner, C., Haapala, T., & Palonen, K. (2017). *Debates, Rhetoric and Political Action*, Palgrave Macmillan.

Wodak, R., Khosravinik, M., & Mral, B. (2013). *Right-wing Populism in Europe: Politics and Discourse*, A&C Black.

Yanow, D. (1995). 'Practices of policy interpretation'. *Policy Sciences*, 28(2), 111–126.

Zahariadis, N., & Buonanno, L. (2017). *The Routledge Handbook of European Public Policy*, Routledge.

Zürn, M., & de Wilde, P. (2016). 'Debating globalization: cosmopolitanism and communitarianism as political ideologies'. *Journal of Political Ideologies*, 21(3), 280–301.

2. The negotiations about the Multiannual Financial Framework 2021–2027: what happened when with what result?

Peter Becker

INTRODUCTION

The European budgetary system, as we know it today, has grown slowly in a more than 25-year-long process with strong signs of path dependency (Laffan, 1997; Ackrill and Kay, 2006; Lindner, 2006).[1] In the six negotiation processes since 1988 – always fierce struggles – the EU has created this well-established procedure, including an unspoken dramaturgy – a special 'budgetary acquis' (Laffan, 2000). Most conflicts and issues are largely predictable, the roles of the actors are known, and national negotiating positions accepted. The process can be roughly divided into three phases, each dominated by different actors and following very different rules. In the beginning, it is always the Commission drafting the new Multiannual Financial Framework (MFF), which sets the framework for further negotiations. Then, in the second phase, the member states determine the talks, initially in the Council and finally at the level of the heads of state and government in the European Council, seeking a political compromise on the overall financial package. Only then, in negotiations between the Council and the European Parliament, is this political agreement translated into European legislation. The lengthy process – negotiations usually take more than two years after the Commission has presented its proposals – is characterised by the antagonism between net payers and net receivers and the national net balances remain the decisive points for assessing the outcome.

The negotiations on the MFF for 2021–2027 broke with this traditional and largely predictable procedure, that is, the negotiation process deviated from the path mapped out, the negotiations addressed new issues, and the outcome is far from the status quo. Until the first, as usual unsuccessful, attempt to reach an agreement by the heads of state and government at an extraordinary summit on 20–21 February 2020, the European budget negotiations followed this familiar path. Yet, with the outbreak of the Covid-19 pandemic in the EU immediately after this first summit, the framework for the negotiations changed fundamentally.

Only in the Treaty of Lisbon were this process and the MFF as the central component of European budgetary policy incorporated into European treaty law. The Multiannual Financial Framework has to be adopted as a European regulation by unanimous agreement of all member states in the Council. However, this consensus of all member states can only be reached through a political agreement of the heads of state and government in the European Council. According to Art. 312 of the Treaty on the Functioning of the European Union (TFEU), the European Parliament must be kept properly informed of the progress of negotiations and at the end of the process, the Parliament can approve or reject by majority vote the draft regulation negotiated by the member states. Hence, the Lisbon Treaty implies the search for and willingness to compromise of all institutions and all member states, and sets limits on excessive or rigid negotiating positions.

THE NEGOTIATIONS – THIS TIME IT WAS DIFFERENT

The Negotiations until the Outbreak of the Pandemic – Talks along Traditional Paths

The Commission started the process, as usual, by submitting its proposal for the MFF 2021–2027, after having prepared it well in advance. Already in 2016, the Commission used the mid-term review of the MFF 2014–2020 to launch its first ideas, putting particular emphasis on new and better-equipped flexibility instruments (Becker, 2016). Moreover, the Commission combined its initiative to discuss the future of Europe with the issue of reforming the European budget. In an innovative reflection paper on the future of EU finances in June 2017, the Commission discussed key budgetary challenges for the coming years. It developed five scenarios for the future ranging from a sharp reduction of the budget, through a continuation of the current system, to a system to create a truly federal EU budget (European Commission, 2017). After a high-level conference on the future of the European budget in January 2018, a paper prepared for the meeting of the European Council in February 2018 (European Commission, 2018a) and extensive hearings of all commissioners and departments inside the Commission in April 2018, on 2 May 2018, Commission President Jean-Claude Juncker and Budget Commissioner Günther Oettinger presented 'a new, modern long-term budget' (European Commission, 2018b) to the European Parliament. The Commission proposed a total amount of commitments of €1,134 billion in constant 2018 prices and an additional €26 billion outside the financial framework for flexibility instruments, specific facilities and reserves, such as the European Solidarity Fund, the Globalisation Fund or the European Peace Facility (Lehner, 2018; Becker, 2018). The European Development Fund (EDF), previously managed and financed outside the MFF, should be incorporated into the financial framework. Funding for the Common Agricultural Policy (CAP) should be cut by about 5 per cent and structural funds by 7 per cent according to the calculations of the European Commission,[2] justified by the Brexit gap and the new political priorities laid down in the European Council's strategic agenda (European Council, 2019). The funding for border management, migration and asylum policies was to be almost tripled to €34.9 billion (in current prices), funds for the Erasmus programme nearly doubled, and significantly more money should be made available for digitisation. To stabilise the Eurozone, the Commission proposed a new reform assistance programme to support member states in implementing structural reforms with a total amount of €25 billion (in current prices). The proposal also included a new 'political conditionality', that is, the linking of disbursement of European funds to the respect of the rule of law. On the revenue side, the Commission proposed a basket of new own resources to improve the EU's financial resources, including new revenues stemming from the emissions trading scheme and contributions based on a new levy on non-recyclable plastic waste. Contributions based on a consolidated corporate tax base were also part of the proposal. The Commission intended to phase out the current rebates and special schemes in the own resources system by the end of the MFF in 2027 (Becker, 2019).

Initially, the member states reacted cautiously and insisted on their most extreme positions and objectives. The 'Friends of Cohesion'[3] pleaded for a continuation of agricultural and cohesion policy spending at the same levels and a bigger budget in general. The like-minded group of net contributors was not able to agree on a joint position paper, in contrast to previous MFF negotiations.

The second phase of the process started when the Bulgarian presidency, in the first half of 2018, quickly established the necessary working structures for the MFF negotiations in the Council and began to examine the Commission's proposals, without, however, entering into concrete negotiations. The subsequent Austrian presidency in the second half of 2018 intensified this work and tabled early on the envisaged structure of the so-called 'negotiating box' (Council of the European Union, 2018a) and then, on 31 October 2018, the first draft of this essential instrument of MFF negotiations (Council of the European Union, 2018b). This non-paper of the presidency had the task of fixing interim agreements and political compromises of the member states in the form of European Council conclusions. However, the key financial elements were still missing, both for the overall amount of the MFF and for the distribution across expenditure headings as well as compromises to adapt the system of own resources.[4] The succeeding Romanian presidency, in the first half of 2019, attempted to hammer out a revised negotiating box for the Council, bringing the negotiations closer to an overall compromise. However, the Romanian draft was strongly criticised in May 2019 and, despite revision, this negotiating box was rejected by the Council as a basis for further negotiations. The positions between the net contributor and net beneficiary member states were still too far apart. Only the Finnish presidency in the second half of 2019 was able to bring new momentum to the negotiations and tabled a new negotiating box in early December 2019, including concrete figures for the first time (Council of the European Union, 2019a). This Finnish proposal foresaw a total amount of €1,087 billion or 1.07 per cent of the gross national income (GNI) of the EU-27 and less drastic cuts in traditional spending policies than demanded by the net payers, that is, the European Structural Funds and the CAP.

Nevertheless, and as usual, all member states complained about this Finnish negotiation box. Central and Eastern European member states argued for full alignment of direct payments for their farmers, and together with net beneficiaries of Southern Europe in the group 'Friends of Cohesion' (Friends of Cohesion, 2019), they criticised the total amount of the Finnish proposal as being insufficient. The French government rejected any cuts in the CAP's first pillar as absurd and unacceptable for France. Since the group of net contributors had not yet been able to agree on common position papers, Sweden, Denmark, the Netherlands and Austria had formed a new group of strict net contributors, the so-called 'Frugal Four'. They vehemently argued that after Brexit the MFF for a smaller EU-27 should be smaller too and limited to 1 per cent of the reduced GNI; the proposed total amount for the new MFF of 1.07 per cent of the EU GNI in the Finnish negotiating box, therefore, was far too high for them. Given their high net payments, they stuck to their rebate schemes and argued in a joint position paper with Germany that they 'continue to need corrections that keep pace with the increasing size of the MFF'. According to their calculation, these five member states feared that they would have to 'finance around half of the net payments to the EU budget in 2020, and the contributions would rise to three quarters of net payments by the end of the period in 2027' (Council of the European Union, 2019b). France, together with 16 other member states, called for all rebates to be completely abolished from the first day of the new MFF (Council of the European Union, 2019c). The proposal for a new rule-of-law mechanism added another point of dispute to the traditional conflict lines. While the Nordic and some West European member states argued strongly in favour of this political conditionality, Poland and Hungary, at that time supported by the Italian government, remained negative.

At the end of 2019, the negotiations in the Council thus had reached an impasse – this was also in line with the normal process of MFF negotiations. Despite the strong criticism and limited agreement on the new negotiating box, the Finnish presidency presented its proposal to the European Council on 12 December 2019. The Finns thus handed over the MFF dossier from the Council to the European Council and the new President of the European Council, Charles Michel, accepted the dossier (Ludlow, 2020a). In January 2020, the cabinet of the new President of the European Council held bilateral talks with the 'sherpas' (the personal advisers for European policy of all heads of state and government) and tested options for a first attempt to hammer out a compromise in the European Council on 20–21 February 2020. As the Finnish proposal could not serve as the starting point for the negotiations in the European Council, Charles Michel presented a new negotiating box for this summit on 14 February (Council of the European Union, 2020a). In this new proposal, he slightly increased the total amount of the MFF to €1087.3 billion or 1.074 per cent of GNI of the EU-27, but also included an additional €7.5 billion for the new Just Transition Fund (JTF) proposed by the European Commission (European Commission, 2020a). In a concession to the 'Frugal Four' and Germany, Michel reintroduced the rebates, albeit decreasing, and expiring at the end of the MFF period (D'Alfonso et al., 2020).

However, the presentation of the negotiating box just a few days before the summit did not trigger any easing of entrenched positions. On 17 February 2020, the 'Frugal Four' published a joint article in the *Financial Times* in which they reaffirmed their well-known negotiating positions and docu-mented their unity (Kurz, 2020). Earlier, on 1 February 2020, the 'Friends of Cohesion' had reiterated their demands for the continuation of the Structural Funds at the same levels and an immediate abolition of all rebates (Friends of Cohesion, 2020).

As expected, and as usual,[5] the extraordinary meeting of the European Council on 20–21 February 2020 was unable to reach a political consensus on a new financial framework. President Michel, together with Commission President von der Leyen, had tried in bilateral and multilateral talks during the two days to bring the heads of state and government closer to a comprehensive compromise. But even a final Commission compromise non-paper presented on the second day of the summit did not lead to success or a rapprochement. According to this paper, the total amount should be further reduced to 1.069 per cent of the EU GNI while traditional spending priorities of the EU budget (Structural Funds and CAP direct payments) should receive top-ups and the rebates for the 'Frugal Four' and Germany should remain.

The Negotiations after the Lockdown

At the beginning of March 2020, the outbreak of the Covid-19 pandemic in the EU put an end to all considerations on how and when a consensus could be reached by the European Council in its second attempt. Negotiations both at working level in Council working groups (with the exception of the Permanent Representatives Committee) and at political level had to be switched to telephone or videoconferences. The heads of state and government were no longer able to meet and negotiate in person and had to use videoconferencing as well. Additionally, the immediate economic and social consequences of the pandemic and the lockdown of European economies and societies quickly became apparent, raising expectations and hopes for European solidarity and financial support in countries most affected by the pandemic, namely Italy and Spain.

After an initial crisis reaction and efforts in April 2020, the MFF came to the fore as a key crisis management tool. In mid April, European Council President Michel and Commission President von der Leyen stated in their joint roadmap for a European economic recovery plan, that in order to minimise the medium- to long-term consequences of the pandemic, 'The future MFF will be a key instrument to support a lasting recovery' (President of the European Commission and President of the European Council, 2020a). The European Council finally endorsed the proposal for 'a Marshall Plan-type investment effort' in a videoconference on 23 April 2020 and instructed the Commission to prepare elements for a European reconstruction fund without delay (President of the European Council, 2020). The recovery fund should be linked to the new MFF, be of a sufficiently high amount and be specifically dedicated to dealing with the consequences of the crisis. At the same time, the Commission should revise its proposal for the 2021–2027 MFF, taking into account the current crisis and its consequences.

Finally, after a few postponements, the Commission presented its comprehensive package, with a new proposal for the next MFF and additional recovery funds, dubbed 'Next Generation EU' (NGEU) on 27 May 2020 (European Commission, 2020b; European Commission, 2020c). The revised MFF 2021–2027 should increase to €1.1 trillion and be complemented by an additional but temporary €750 billion recovery fund, from which €500 billion should be disbursed as grants and €250 billion as loans. To finance this massive European economic stimulus package, the Commission proposed that the EU should take on common debt, for which the own resources ceiling should be increased to 2 per cent of the EU GNI.

Previously some member states had tabled position papers hinting to the Commission at a corridor for a possible compromise and indicating the red lines of their national interests (Becker, 2020; De la Porte and Jensen, 2021). Undoubtedly, a Franco-German initiative, which was presented on 18 May

2020 at a joint press conference by Chancellor Merkel and French President Macron (Press and Information Office of the Federal Government, 2020) had been of particular importance. The Franco-German coalition argued for a limited in time and scope, but ambitious, recovery fund as a stimulus to the European economy in the framework of the EU budget. This additional fund of €500 billion should be made available for the European Green Deal[6] and digitisation of the internal market, and to finance this package, the EU should take on temporary common debt (Howarth and Schild, 2021). As an answer to this Franco-German proposal, the 'Frugal Four' published a short position paper very quickly, on 23 May 2020 (Frugal Four, 2020; see also Fleming, 2020). They also advocated a temporary recovery fund to boost the European economy and to strengthen national health systems. Under no circumstances, however, they said, should the European Union be allowed to take on common debts.

Although the Commission did not present a completely new MFF package, the Commission proposed significant shifts and redeployments from its original proposal of May 2018. With this proposal, the Commission took a great political risk, because it was clear that this was the only and decisive attempt to broadly anticipate the consensus in the European Council and the subsequent approval of the European Parliament. While the previous negotiations in the Council were not rendered completely obsolete and some key elements of the first attempt to reach an agreement in February 2020 remained in place, the new proposal changed the content of the negotiations. The traditional distribution conflict between net contributors and net beneficiaries no longer dominated the negotiations, but the link between the MFF and the very much needed stimulus for European economies did.

Charles Michel invited the heads of state and government to Brussels for the second attempt to agree on the MFF 2021–2027 on 17 July 2020. Once again, he and his cabinet held a large number of informal meetings with members of the European Council in preparation for the special summit. Additionally, there were many bilateral discussions and much travelling by individual heads of state and government (Drachenberg, 2020). As in February, Michel presented his own new negotiating box (Council of the European Union, 2020b) to sketch out the compromise. He proposed a total amount for the new MFF of €1,074.3 billion and an additional €750 billion for the recovery budget NGEU, as proposed by the Commission. This huge recovery package should be financed by raising common debt of the EU. In addition, Charles Michel proposed to create a new reserve for the consequences of Brexit, amounting to €5 billion and to stick to the rule of law conditionality. In addition to the no-longer-disputed levy on non-recyclable plastic waste, he also recommended a timetable to introduce additional resources, such as a European digital levy, a CO_2 border adjustment mechanism and an extension of the emissions trading system. Thus, Charles Michel tried to provide some gains for each side and for the European Parliament – and thus to satisfy all.

The summit, originally scheduled to last two days, lasted epically long and, according to Charles Michel, was on the brink of failure at least twice. The European Council President, often together with the President of the European Commission and the Franco-German coalition, sought compromises in various bilateral and multilateral formats; he and his team used interruptions in these tough negotiations to draft various new proposals. Finally, after nearly five hard and somewhat painful days and nights of negotiations, the heads of state and government reached an agreement on all points of conflict (European Council, 2020; see also Table 2.1). The fiercest quarrel in the European Council was over four points (Ludlow, 2020b):

(1) The key point in the negotiations was, as usual, the total amount of the overall package and the respective financial envelopes of the MFF and the recovery budget NGEU. Already in the run-up to the summit, this issue had been dominated by debates on the division of the funds for NGEU into loans and non-repayable grants and debates about the distribution criteria. The negotiations were based on the European Commission's proposal to allocate €500 billion in grants from the new NGEU. The final compromise provides for €390 billion in grants and €360 billion in loans.[7] Although the Commission's distribution key had been strongly criticised, the heads of state and government, without diving too deeply into technical distribution issues, agreed to endorse in principle the controversial allocation method for the first two years. The criteria will only be applied to the allocation of 70 per cent of the money in 2021 and 2022, while the allocation key will be changed for the remaining 30 per cent to be allocated up to 2023 and paid out until 2026. Then, the controversial criterion of average unemployment before the outbreak of the pandemic will be replaced by the indicator of the real decline in economic development in 2020 and 2021.

(2) The second point of hard negotiations circled around the conditions under which NGEU funds should be distributed and paid out as well as on monitoring the implementation of member states' reform commitments as a condition for receiving European funding. Especially on this issue of conditionality, a difficult marathon of negotiations developed between the 'Frugal Four/Five', led by Dutch Prime Minister Marc Rutte on the one hand, and the southern European member states most affected by the pandemic, Italy, Spain and Portugal, on the other. Finally, a suspension clause on the disbursement of these funds was agreed: if one or more member states have doubts about the Commission's assessment of

the implementation of the national recovery and resilience plans, they may refer the matter to the European Council.

(3)   Another point of hard negotiations had been the reform of the European system of own resources and the maintenance of rebates. Since the Franco-German coalition had already proposed to finance the additional recovery fund by mandating the Commission to borrow through common European debt, a solution on this point was already mapped out. Moreover, the rebates as an instrument of burden-sharing were no longer questioned in principle and rebates in favour of the 'Frugal Four' and Germany remained at the same or even higher levels.

(4)   The link between respect for the rule of law and the disbursement of European funds had been the final point of negotiations, with bitter disputes between the heads of state and government. This controversial political conditionality was directed in particular against Hungary and Poland, both of whom already had proceedings pending under Article 7 of the Treaty on European Union (TEU) to be suspended from EU membership for serious violations of the fundamental values. The Hungarian Prime Minister, Viktor Orbán, called for unanimous decision-making to start the process of political conditionality and thus the possibility of a veto for member states threatened with sanctions. The European Council finally reached a compromise containing three rather vague and ambiguous paragraphs on a conditionality regime to protect the MFF and the NGEU (European Council, 2020, paragraphs 22 to 24). Although the disputed rule of law conditionality was included in the European Council conclusions and Hungary was unable to obtain a unanimous agreement, the substantive solution for this quarrel had only been postponed.

The first comments following this historically long and conflict-ridden European Council on the new MFF and a temporary recovery budget ranged from relief that a compromise could be reached at all to criticism that the reform budget was insufficient. The French President, Emmanuel Macron, and the Presidents of the Commission spoke about a 'historic moment' (President of the European Commission and President of the European Council, 2020b; Belz, 2020) and the President of the European Council Charles Michel even saw a 'Copernican turning point' (Mussler, 2020).

The Final Phase – The Negotiations between Council and European Parliament

The compromise of the European Council on 21 July 2020 was the culmination, but not yet the end of the process. This political compromise still had to be transferred into European legislation in difficult trilogue negotiations

Table 2.1   *The Multiannual Financial Framework 2021–2027*

Commitment appropriations	MFF 2021–2027 (€ billion – prices 2018)								NGEU 2021–2023 (€ billion – prices 2018)	
	2021	2022	2023	2024	2025	2026	2027	Total		
1. Single Market, Innovation & Digital	19,712	19,666	19,133	18,633	18,518	18,646	18,473	132,781	Invest EU	5.6
2. Cohesion, Resilience & Values	49,741	51,101	52,194	53,954	55,182	56,787	58,809	377,768	Horizon Europe	5.0
2. Economic, Social, Territorial Cohesion	45,411	45,951	46,493	47,130	47,770	48,414	49,066	330,235	REACT-EU	47.5
2. Resilience & Values	4,330	5,150	5,701	6,824	7,412	8,373	9,743	47,533		
3. Natural Resources & Environment	55,242	52,214	51,489	50,617	49,719	48,932	48,161	356,374	Rural Development	7.5
3. Market Related & Direct Payments	38,564	38,115	37,604	36,983	36,373	35,772	35,183	258,594		
4. Migration & Border Management	2,324	2,811	3,164	3,282	3,672	3,682	3,736	22,671	rescEU	1.9
5. Security & Defence	1,700	1,725	1,737	1,754	1,928	2,078	2,263	13,185	Just Transition Funds	10.0
6. Neighbourhood & World	15,309	15,522	14,789	14,056	13,323	12,592	12,828	98,419	Recovery & resilience facility	672.5
7. European Public Administration	10,021	10,215	10,342	10,454	10,554	10,673	10,843	73,102	Total	750.0
7. Administrative Expenditure	7,742	7,878	7,945	7,997	8,025	8,077	8,188	55,852		

	MFF 2021–2027 (€ billion – prices 2018)								NGEU 2021–2023 (€ billion – prices 2018)
Commitment appropriations	**2021**	**2022**	**2023**	**2024**	**2025**	**2026**	**2027**	**Total**	
Commitment appropriations total	**154,049**	**153,254**	**152,848**	**152,750**	**152,896**	**153,390**	**155,113**	**1,074,300**	
Payment appropriations total	156,557	154,822	149,936	149,936	149,936	149,936	149,936	1,061,058	**Total MFF & NGEU** (€ billion – prices 2018) **1,824.3** (commitments)
Outside the MFF									
Solidarity and Emergency Aid Reserve	1,200	1,200	1,200	1,200	1,200	1,200	1,200	**8,400**	
European Globalisation Adjustment	186	186	186	186	186	186	186	1,302	
Brexit Adjustment Reserve	p.m.	p.m.	p.m.	p.m.	p.m.	p.m.	p.m.	5,000	
Flexibility Instrument	772	772	772	772	772	772	772	5,404	
Outside the MFF – Total	**2,158**	**2,158**	**2,158**	**2,158**	**2,158**	**2,158**	**2,158**	**20,106**	
MFF + outside the MFF – Total (commitments)								1,094,406	

Source: European Council (2020).

between the German Council presidency, the Commission and the European Parliament's negotiators. As usual, the Parliament put together a huge package, comprising all elements of the MFF and NGEU and the new legislative acts, required as basic acts for European spending programmes. Here the Parliament enjoys political power as an equal legislator in co-decision procedures, and all actors involved are aware that although these acts are negotiated in differentiated forums, the components are closely interrelated and form an overall negotiation package and no separate solutions are possible. The intention of the German presidency was to finalise the trilogue negotiations by the end of September. However, these negotiations did not develop as smoothly and quickly as planned.

The European Parliament had already presented its demands very early and repeatedly (European Parliament, 2018c), and had already named a negotiating team of six parliamentarians for the negotiations with the Council on the MFF, NGEU and the reform of the system of own resources. Just before the summit on June 18, 2020, the heads of the five biggest parliamentary groups in the European Parliament had emphasised their demands and the Parliament had immediately after the summit substantiated its objectives for the trilogue negotiations with its resolution from July 23, 2020 (European Parliament, 2020). In this resolution, the Parliament criticised in principle the cuts in European health, research and education programmes, reiterated its demands for an obligatory MFF mid-term review and for being involved in the implementation and monitoring of the new reconstruction and resilience facility. In particular, however, the ambivalent formulation of the rule of law conditionality was not acceptable to MEPs. The Parliament stuck to its initial demands already adopted by a broad majority in a resolution on March 14, 2018, even before the European Commission had presented its first MFF-proposal (European Parliament, 2018a; European Parliament, 2018b). In its resolution from November 2018, then the Parliament demanded a total amount for the next MFF of €1,324 billion, top-ups for modern research and innovation policies, and argued that too little funding in the budget would lead to unacceptable cuts in agricultural, structural and cohesion policy (European Parliament, 2018c). In the trilogue negotiations, the Parliament demanded additional funding for 15 so-called flagship programmes, such as Horizon Europe, InvestEU, Erasmus+ or the Just Transition Fund, and the Parliament's chief negotiator, Johan van Overtveldt, substantiated this demand in October 2020 in a letter to the German presidency requesting an additional €39 billion 'fresh' top-up funding. According to calculations from the Council, however, the Parliament's total demands could amount to an additional €90 billion.[8]

As expected, the German presidency gave in only on some minor points, for example, the mid-term review, and remained resolute on the question of changing the figures of the next MFF as agreed by the European Council and increasing specific headings of the MFF. The member states were only willing to top up some flagship programmes by some €15 billion and to increase the flexibility of the budget. These additional funds should be financed with reallocations and additional means such as, for example, the use of competition fines which are currently offset against member states' contributions. The German presidency also admitted a greater involvement of the European Parliament in the implementation and monitoring of NGEU by setting up a 'constructive dialogue' between Parliament and Council. Moreover, an indicative timetable was conceded to establish new own resources over the next seven years, as long as this agreement does not change the political compromise of the European Council on this issue. The final agreement between the Council and the European Parliament did not change the figures and headings laid down in the European Council's compromise of 21 July 2020.

The political agreement in the trilogue negotiations reached on 10 November 2020 after ten weeks of intensive negotiations, however, did not win the approval of all member states in the Council. The Hungarian and the Polish governments vetoed the agreement on the MFF and NGEU after the Permanent Representatives Committee had adopted, with a qualified majority, the compromise with the European Parliament on the legislative act for the rule of law mechanism. Since the Parliament rejected any change of the rule-of-law agreement, the German presidency had to negotiate with the two vetoing member states to resolve the impasse. Only in informal and confidential negotiations was the German presidency, supported by the Council Secretariat, able to hammer out a final deal on the political conditionality, which was approved in the European Council in December 2020 (Ludlow, 2020c). The heads of state and government agreed on some political clarifications and to focus the application of the rule of law regulation on the protection of the financial interests of the Union, without changing the wording of the regulation.

This recurring ambivalent solution in the European Council opened the way for the adoption of the overall MFF/NGEU legislation package, first in the European Parliament on 16 December 2020 and then in the Council on 18 December 2020. The final step then was the publication of the new legislation in the EU official journal on 22 December 2020.[9]

THE RESULT – THE NEW FINANCIAL FRAMEWORK AND THE RECOVERY BUDGET

The new MFF comprises around €1,074 billion (for commitments in 2018 prices);[10] this corresponds to 1.12 per cent of the GNI of the EU-27. The total amount of the MFF is roughly divided into thirds as the Commission had originally requested in 2018, with one third for the cohesion policy, the second third for the CAP and the last third for the remaining policies. Compared with the European Commission's proposal of 27 May 2020, this compromise represents a significant reduction of around €26 billion or 2.3 per cent and compared with the former MFF 2014–2020, a reduction of about €9 billion or 0.1 per cent of EU-27 GNI (see also Table 2.2). However, the reduction of the MFF total amount was compensated by the additional economic stimulus budget, NGEU. Taking both budgets together, the total amount of funds available to the EU significantly increased; in total, the EU thus has €1,824 billion or 1.9 per cent of the EU GNI at its disposal.

For NGEU, a maximum total budget of €750 billion has been agreed, but limited to the three years up to 31 December 2023, with final payments possible until 31 December 2026. At the heart of NGEU stands the new recovery and resilience facility (RRF) with a total budget of €672.5 billion, of which €312.5 billion will be disbursed as non-repayable grants (Regulation 2021/241). The remaining €77.5 billion of NGEU will be used to temporarily increase and complement existing programmes in the EU budget; for example, €5 billion will be added to the EU's Horizon Europe research programme, €5.6 billion to the InvestEU financial instruments to promote investments, an additional €10 billion to the Just Transition Fund (JTF) to help regions and sectors exit from fossil fuels and €47.5 billion for the new ReactEU programme to top up payments from European structural funds at the beginning of the new programming period. However, member states rejected the Commission's proposals for both an entirely new €26 billion programme of direct support and recapitalisation of European companies and €7.7 billion for a new European health programme.

According to the Commission's breakdown, Poland will remain the biggest recipient of European structural funds with about €66.4 billion (in 2018 prices), followed by Italy with €37.3 billion. Looking at the CAP, the Commission calculated that France, with €51 billion (in current prices), is the biggest recipient of European funds for market-related expenditure and direct payments followed by Germany with €34.4 billion and Spain with €34.1 billion; for the second pillar of the CAP, that is, European funds for rural development, France will receive €10.5 billion, followed by Italy with €9.7 billion, Germany with €7.9 billion and Spain with €7.8 billion. When looking at the new instruments, the ReactEU allocations as top-ups for European structural funds, the Just Transition Fund and the grants allocation of the recovery and resilience facility, the Commission calculated that Italy and Spain, the member states most affected by the pandemic crisis, will receive by far the biggest share from the recovery and resilience facility allocated for the first two years, with €44.7 billion for Italy and €43.5 billion for Spain (in 2018 prices). France will become the third-largest recipient of payments from this facility with €22.7 billion. Poland, however, will receive the biggest share from the Just Transition Funds, with €3.5 billion, followed by Germany with €2.2 billion.[11]

Table 2.2   *The development of the proposals*

€ billion (2018 prices)	MFF 2014–2020 (EU-27)	1. Proposal of COM May 2018	Negotiation Box FIN-Pres. Dec. 2019	1. Negotiation Box Michel Feb. 2020	2. Proposal of COM May 2020	additional NGEU	2. Negotiation Box Michel July 2020	additional NGEU	MFF & NGEU	additional NGEU
Total Commitments	**1,094.4**	**1,134.6**	**1,087.3**	**1,094.8**	**1,100**	**750**	**1,074.3**	**750.0**	**1,074.3**	**750.0**
in % GNI	1.0%	1.08%	1.07%	1.074%	1.079%	–	1.054%	–	1.054%	–
Single Market, Innovation, Digital	121.6	166.3	151.8	149.5	140.7	69.8	131.3	70.0	132.8	12.5
Cohesion, Resilience & Values	391.7	392.0	374.0	380.0	374.5	–	380.5	–	377.8	–
Cohesion Policy	273.3	330.6	323.2	323.2	323.2	50.0	323.6	50.0	330.2	47.5
Natural Resources & Environment	399.6	336.6	346.6	354.1	357.0	–	355.6	–	356.4	–
Market-Related Expenditure and Direct payments	291.5	254.2	254.2	256.7	258.3	15.0	258.2	15.0	258.6	15.0
Just Transition Funds	–	–	–	7.5	10.0	30.0	7.5	30.0	7.5	10.0
Migration and Border Management	8.9	30.8	23.4	21.9	31.1	–	21.9	–	22.7	–
Security and Defence	4.6	24.3	14.7	14.3	19.4	9.7	13.6	–	13.2	–
Neighbourhood and World	97.1	108.9	103.2	101.9	102.7	15.5	98.4	15.5	98.4	–

Source: Author's own composition.

However, the payments of NGEU to member states will not be unconditional, and the use of the money should not take place without European monitoring and surveillance. The member states were required to develop so-called national recovery and resilience plans by April 2021 (Sapała, 2021; European Commission, 2022) in which the member states must present a coherent reform and investment agenda to strengthen national growth, safeguard and create jobs and improve their national economic and social resilience. In principle, the measures shall serve the EU's economic policy objectives and 'support … the Union's green and digital priorities' (European Council, 2020, paragraph A2).

The central reform of European budgetary policy, apart from the agreement on the temporary economic budget, NGEU, however, was the innovation on the revenue side of the EU budget. For the first time, the Commission 'will be authorised to borrow funds on behalf of the Union on the capital markets' (European Council, 2020, paragraph A3) of up to €750 billion; repayment of this common debt is to be made with the additional new own resources and is to be completed by 31 December 2058 at the latest. In addition, and for the first time since 1988, a new own resource was introduced with the levy on non-recyclable plastic packaging waste. Moreover, at the demand of the European Parliament, additional new own resources are to follow by 2027. The Commission has been instructed to present proposals in 2021 for a digital levy and a carbon border adjustment mechanism. On 22 December 2021 the European Commission presented a proposal to create three new own resources and to introduce these additional resources by 1 January 2023 at the latest – a carbon border adjustment mechanism, contributions to the European budget stemming from the emissions trading system (ETS) and, from the OECD, a framework on base erosion, profit shifting and a global minimum taxation (European Commission, 2021).

As usual, the agreement was achieved by including some special arrangements and payments in favour of individual member states. In total €7.2 billion was distributed to 17 member states, ranging from €200 million for rural development in the Slovak Republic to €1.6 billion for rural development in France (CPMR, 2020, Annex 1). Moreover, one traditional topic of MFF negotiations remained: the demand from some member states to get some kind of rebate. The 'Frugal Four', together with Germany, were able to push through the continuation of rebate regulations on their contributions and in some cases, even increase them significantly (European Council, 2020, paragraph 152; Council of the European Union, 2020c).[12] However, unlike the previous UK rebate, these rebates were not granted for an unlimited period of time; they only apply to the new MFF 2021–2027 and therefore have to be renegotiated in the negotiations on the next MFF from 2028 onwards.[13]

THE LONG-TERM CONSEQUENCES OF THE 'HISTORIC' COMPROMISE

The European Council's five days of negotiations led to significant changes in the well-established procedure for European budget negotiations. However, the agreement on many points also confirmed elements of the special path dependency and the orientation towards the status quo (Ladi and Tsarouhas, 2020; Schmidt, 2020; Salvati, 2021; Becker and Gehring, 2022). The difficult but ultimately successful negotiations showed that a joint effort of the Presidents of the European Council and of the European Commission together with the Franco-German coalition was needed to push through fundamental changes in European budgetary policy (Crespy and Schramm, 2021). The European Commission took advantage of the coincidence of the pandemic crisis and the European budget negotiations to link its proposal for a new MFF 2021–2027 to its major economic policy reform project – the transition of European economies to climate-neutral, sustainable and digital growth models – and to underpin these policy priorities with the necessary funding. However, the original proposal of May 2018 presented by the previous Commission under President Jean-Claude Juncker did not take the political priorities of the new von der Leyen Commission sufficiently into account – neither the European Green Deal and the mechanism for a fair transition nor the promotion of digitisation were sufficiently funded in the original proposal of the Juncker Commission. Moreover, the Commission tried to use the pandemic crisis and the urgency of European responses to expand its policy options. The new instruments, such as the business support programme or the European health programme, would have been tantamount to extending the Commission's competencies. The member states' response to this attempt – also traditionally – was status quo oriented and restrictive.

Also, the cuts made by the European Council to the Commission's proposal confirmed the well-known lines of MFF negotiations. The European Council's compromise of 21 July 2020 required cuts to be made in particular in 'modern' policies, such as European research and education programmes, or the funding for the common European external border guard. On the other hand, funding for 'traditional' policies increased, that is, the CAP and the Structural Funds – when taking both elements (i.e. MFF and NGEU) of the comprehensive budget compromise together (see also Table 2.3).

The European Council also made use of familiar instruments to facilitate compromise finding, such as additional side payments or derogations and the use of technocratic levers. The new Just Transition Fund seems to be such an instrument of financial compensation for hesitant states like Poland, as are the increase in the member states' collection costs of European customs duties,

Table 2.3   *The changes: MFF 2014–2020 compared to MFF 2021–2027*

€ billion (prices 2018)	MFF 2014–2020 (EU-27)	MFF 2021–2027	additional NGEU	Changes compared to MFF 2014–2020	additional NGEU
Single Market, Innovation, Digital	121.6	132.8	12.5	+ 11.2 bn **+ 9.2%**	+ 23.5 bn **+ 19.3%**
Cohesion & Values	391.7	377.8	–	– 13.9 bn – 3.5 %	–
Cohesion Policy	273.3	330.2	47.5	+ 56.9 bn **+ 20.8%**	+ 104.4 bn **+ 38.2%**
Natural Resources & Environment	399.6	356.4	–	– 43.2 bn – 10.8%	–
Market Related & Direct Payments	291.5	258.6	15.0	– 32.9 bn **– 11.3%**	– 17.9 bn **– 6.1%**
Just Transition Funds	–	7.5	10.0		
Migration & Border Management	8.9	22.7	–	+ 13.8 bn **+ 155%**	
Security & Defence	4.6	13.2	–	+ 8.6 bn **+ 187%**	
Neighbourhood & World	97.1	98.4	–	+ 1.3 bn **+ 1.3%**	
Total Commitments	**1094.4**	**1074.3**	750.0	**– 20.1 bn – 1.8%**	**1,824.3 bn + 66.6%**

Source: Author's own composition; figures taken from European Council (2013). 'Conclusion of the European Council (7–8 February 2013)'. EUCO 37/13, Brussels; and European Council (2020). 'Extraordinary European Council (July 17, 18, 19, 20 and 21, 2020) – Conclusions'. EUCO 10/20, Brussels.

benefitting mainly the Netherlands, or the special payments from the structural funds in favour of eastern German states. Moreover, the rebate schemes continue to be an instrument for balancing the lack of will or at least insufficient capacity for reform on the expenditure side of the budget on the one hand and the favouring by individual member states of 'traditional' policies, in particular agricultural policy, on the other.

Nevertheless, triggered by the necessary strong European response to the pandemic crisis, the EU created, in the stimulus budget NGEU, a completely new element of European budgetary policy. NGEU, as the EU's 'exceptional response' to the pandemic, will remain in the European policy toolbox, although it is an instrument limited in time and amount and hence will always be an exceptional measure or crisis response. The new funds, however, will not be spent without conditions. In order to be able to supervise the expansion of the EU's financial possibilities and the additional economic policy options available to the EU, the 'Frugal Four' group, at least, insisted on additional conditions. The linking of NGEU with the European Semester for the coordination of economic policies will create a new form of conditionality and thus enable the Commission and the member states to monitor the use of the European funds. The compromise on the suspension clause can increase the transparency of the evaluation procedure and thus at least initiate a public debate on the sense, efficiency and effectiveness of using European funds. Thus, the process of evaluating national recovery and resilience plans can be politicised. The higher the sum of non-repayable grants will be, the stricter the criteria for the efficient and sustainable use of the funds will become, and the more other European member states will claim to monitor the implementation in national policies of other member states. This principle of conditionality might become a new guideline for European spending policies.

The main changes have been made on the revenue side of the MFF. In the future, the Commission will borrow to finance the budget itself and use the new own resources for the repayments. The EU is thus expanding its budgetary policy instruments and possibilities. It will also have new own resources which will not only finance the EU budget but also provide political guidance for its climate and digital policy objectives. The huge integration step towards the introduction of a real European tax has become smaller – even though the introduction of a European tax will require a treaty change.

Brexit did not play a direct role in the decisive negotiations in July 2020: the already very fierce distribution conflicts were only aggravated by Brexit, but far less so than by the pandemic crisis. However, the consequences of Brexit became apparent for the political dynamics and tactical considerations of the negotiations. The Dutch attempt to fill the gap with the new group, the 'Frugal Four', has only been partially successful. It is true that the 'frugal' countries were able to create a counterweight to the net recipients from southern and eastern Europe and their sometimes-exaggerated expectations. However, the group lacked the political weight of the UK and the credible radicalism to enforce its demands. The negotiations showed, however, that the more traditional interest groups of member states were declining. The fact that the net contributors were not able to present joint position papers, neither at the beginning nor later during the negotiations, underlined this weakening of the internal cohesion of this group. With the 'Frugal Four', a new group of net paying member states emerged, not only arguing with net recipient countries but also with the Franco-German coalition. The Franco-German coalition obviously stayed together during the long summit negotiations, and President Michel was able to rely on its help in his difficult search for a compromise (De la Porte and Jensen, 2021; Krotz and Schramm, 2022).[14] With the joint initiative of 18 May 2020, the duo paved the way for the European Commission in preparing the second MFF proposal, including the recovery funds. At the same time, however, it became clear that a Franco-German understanding could perhaps point the way to an agreement between the EU-27, but that this alone would not be sufficient to achieve a compromise.

The role and the influence of the European Parliament on MFF negotiations remains limited. The Parliament does not sit at the negotiating table during the crucial negotiations between member states in the European Council. Modifications or adjustments to the compromise are thus hardly possible, and the more difficult the negotiations in the European Council are, the more limited the influence of the Parliament becomes.

NOTES

1. I am grateful to the two anonymous reviewers for their constructive criticism and valuable comments. Any remaining errors are of course the responsibility of the author.
2. These figures had been presented by Commissioner Oettinger on 14 May 2018 in the Council. However, the member states and the European Parliament questioned these figures. See Agence Europe, Bulletin Quotidien Europe, 'BUDGET; Several member states oppose reduction in agriculture and cohesion budgets after 2020'. 15 May 2018 and 'EU-Parlament wirft Kommission Haushaltstricks vor; Haushaltskommissar Oettinger korrigiert Zahlen für den Finanzrahmen 2021 bis 2027', *Frankfurter Allgemeine Zeitung*, 24 May 2018, p. 5.
3. On the discourse coalitions of member states see Heinelt and Münch, Chapter 1 in this volume.
4. The different and sometimes contradictory positions of the member states on specific points and issues were reflected in over 100 bracketed formulations in this negotiating box.
5. The Dutch Prime Minister Marc Rutte arrived at the European Council building in Brussels looking demonstrably unenthusiastic, with a biography of the Polish composer Frederic Chopin. He emphasised that he intended to read the book because he did not expect the negotiations to produce results.

6. On the European Green Deal, see Bornemann, Chapter 7 in this volume.
7. For the 'Frugal Four' – who were supported by Finland in the course of the nego-tiations and changed therefore into the 'Frugal Five' – the reduction of grants below the €400 billion limit was of high symbolic importance.
8. https://twitter.com/sfischer_eu/status/1316341227319693317 (last accessed 4 April 2021).
9. The legislation package included two regulations, the new decision on own resources and the new Interinstitutional Agreement:
   - Regulation (EU, Euratom) 2020/2092 of the European Parliament and of the Council of 16 December 2020 on a general regime of conditionality for the protection of the Union budget, *Journal of the European Union*, L 433 I, 22.12.2020, pp. 1–10.
   - Council Regulation (EU, Euratom) 2020/2093 of 17 December 2020 laying down the multiannual financial framework for the years 2021 to 2027, *Journal of the European Union*, L 433 I, 22.12.2020, pp. 11–22.
   - Interinstitutional Agreement between the European Parliament, the Council of the European Union and the European Commission on budgetary dis-cipline, on cooperation in budgetary matters and on sound financial man-agement, as well as on new own resources, including a roadmap towards the introduction of new own resources Interinstitutional Agreement of 16 December 2020 between the European Parliament, the Council of the European Union and the European Commission on budgetary discipline, on cooperation in budgetary matters and on sound financial management, as well as on new own resources, including a roadmap towards the intro-duction of new own resources, *Journal of the European Union*, L 433I, 22.12.2020, pp. 28–46.
   - Council Decision (EU, Euratom) 2020/2053 of 14 December 2020 on the system of own resources of the European Union and repealing Decision 2014/335/EU, Euratom, *Journal of the European Union*, L 424, 15.12.2020, pp. 1–10.
10. To this amount an additional €21.1 billion outside the MFF for various reserve and flexibility instruments must be added.
11. The European Commission's calculations on the pre-allocations per member state can be found here: https://ec.europa.eu/info/strategy/eu-budget/long-term -eu-budget/2021-2027/spending/budget-pre-allocations (last accessed 5 April 2021).
12. According the conclusions of the European Council, the GNI-based contribu-tions of Denmark will be reduced by €377 million per year, Austria by €565 million per year, Sweden by €1,069 million per year and the Netherlands by €1,921 million per year. The rebate in favour of Germany would be €3,671 million per year.
13. A separate arrangement is the increase of collection costs for customs duties, which is equivalent to an indirect rebate scheme in favour of the Netherlands due to the high level of imports of goods via the port of Rotterdam. Under this scheme, member states are allowed to retain 25 per cent of the customs duties they levy on goods imported on behalf of the EU and paid to the EU budget as collection costs.
14. The Franco-German cooperation was so close that after the five-day summit Angela Merkel and Emmanuel Macron even presented their assessment of the results in a joint press conference.

REFERENCES

Ackrill, R., and Kay, A. (2006). 'Historical-institutionalist perspectives on the development of the EU budget system'. *Journal of European Public Policy*, 13(1), 113–133.

Becker, M., and Gehring, T. (2022). 'Explaining EU integration dynamics in the wake of COVID-19: a domain of application approach'. *Journal of European Public Policy*, DOI: 10.1080/13501763.2022.2027000.

Becker, P. (2016). 'The EU budget's mid-term review. With its promising reform proposals, the Commission lays the groundwork for the next, post-2020 budget'. SWP Comment, 2016/C 48.

Becker, P. (2018). 'Pragmatismus und Flexibilität: der Fokus der EU-Kommission bei ihrem Vorschlag für den neuen Finanzrahmen'. *Wirtschaftsdienst*, 98(6), 387–391.

Becker, P. (2019). 'A new budget for the EU. Negotiations on the Multiannual Financial Framework 2021–2027'. SWP Research Paper, 11, Berlin.

Becker, P. (2020). 'The EU budget as an opportunity in the crisis. The EU Commission's Proposal for a New Financial Framework and a Reconstruction Fund'. SWP Comment, 2020/A 56.

Belz, N. (2020). 'Ein Moment des Triumphs für Macron; Der französische Präsident möchte in der Einigung eine historische Wende der EU sehen, aber dafür ist es zu früh. *Neue Zürcher Zeitung*, 23 July.

CPMR (Conference of Peripheral Maritime Regions) (2020). 'Analysis of the European Council agreement: the EU Recovery Instrument and the MFF 2021–2027'. Policy Analysis July 2020.

Council of the European Union (2018a). 'Multiannual Financial Framework 2021–2027 – Structure of the Negotiation Box'. Doc. 12175/18, Brussels.

Council of the European Union (2018b). 'Multiannual Financial Framework (2021–2027), possible elements of the future draft Negotiation Box in relation to horizontal issues, Headings I, II, III, IV, V, VI and VII'. Doc. 13471/18, Brussels.

Council of the European Union (2019a). 'Multiannual Financial Framework (MFF) 2021–2027: Negotiating Box with figures'. Doc. 14518/1/19 REV 1, Brussels.

Council of the European Union (2019b). 'Non-paper on the continued need of corrections in the next multiannual financial framework (2021–2027) from 5 delegations (AT, DE, DK, NL, SE)'. Working Paper 13320/2019 INIT, Brussels.

Council of the European Union (2019c). 'Compensations on the revenue side of the EU budget: Non-paper from 18 delegations (BG, CY, CZ, EE, EL, ES, FR, HU, IT, LU, LT, LV, MT, PL, PT, RO, SI, SK)'. Working Paper WK 12341/2019 INIT, Brussels, 4 November.

Council of the European Union (2020a). 'Special Meeting of the European Council – Draft conclusions'. Doc. 5846/20, Brussels.

Council of the European Union (2020b). 'Special meeting of the European Council – Draft Conclusions'. Doc. 9515/20, Brussels.

Council of the European Union (2020c). 'Council Decision (EU, Euratom) 2020/2053 of 14 December 2020 on the system of own resources of the European Union and repealing Decision 2014/335/EU'. *Journal of the European Union*, L 424, 1–10.

Crespy, A., and Schramm, L. (2021). 'Breaking the budgetary taboo: German preference formation in the EU's response to the Covid-19 crisis'. *German Politics*, DOI: 10.1080/09644008.2021.2020253.

D'Alfonso, A., Pari, M., and Sapała, A. (2020). 'Negotiations on the next MFF and the EU recovery instrument. Key issues ahead of the July European Council'. EPRS (European Parliamentary Research Service), Briefing. Brussels, July.

De la Porte, C., and Jensen, M.D. (2021). 'The next generation EU: an analysis of the dimensions of conflict behind the deal'. *Social Policy Administration*, 55(2), 249–402.

Drachenberg, R. (2020). 'Outcome of the special European Council meeting of 17–21 July 2020'. EPRS (European Parliamentary Research Service), Post-European Council Briefing, Brussels.

European Commission (2017). 'Reflection Paper on the Future of EU Finances'. COM(2017)358, 28, Brussels.

European Commission (2018a). 'A new, modern Multiannual Financial Framework for a European Union that delivers efficiently on its priorities post-2020. The European Commission's contribution to the Informal Leaders' meeting on 23 February 2018'. COM(2018) 98 final, Brussels.

European Commission (2018b). 'A modern budget for a Union that protects, strengthens and defends. Multiannual Financial Framework 2021–2027'. COM(2018) 321 final, Brussels.

European Commission (2020a). 'Proposal for a Regulation of the European Parliament and of the Council establishing the Just Transition Fund'. COM(2020) 22 final, Brussels.

European Commission (2020b). 'The EU budget powering the recovery plan for Europe'. COM(2020) 442 final, Brussels.

European Commission (2020c). 'Europe's moment: Repair and Prepare for the Next Generation'. COM(2020) 456 final, Brussels.

European Commission (2021). 'The next generation of own resources for the EU Budget'. COM(2021) 566 final, Brussels.

European Commission (2022). 'Report on the implementation of the Recovery and Resilience Facility'. COM(2022) 75 final, Brussels.

European Council (2013). 'Conclusion of the European Council (7–8 February 2013)'. EUCO 37/13, Brussels.

European Council (2019). 'A new strategic agenda 2019–2024'. Brussels.

European Council (2020). 'Extraordinary European Council (July 17, 18, 19, 20 and 21, 2020) – Conclusions'. EUCO 10/20, Brussels.

European Parliament (2018a). 'The next MFF: preparation of Parliament's position on the post-2020 MFF'. European Parliament resolution P8_TA (2018) 0075.

European Parliament (2018b). 'Multiannual financial framework 2021–2027 and own resources'. European Parliament resolution P8_TA (2018) 0226.

European Parliament (2018c). 'Interim report on the Multiannual Financial Framework 2021–2027 – Parliament's position with a view to an agreement'. European Parliament resolution P8_TA (2018) 0449.

European Parliament (2020). 'Resolution on the Conclusions of the Extraordinary European Council of 17–21 July 2020'. P9_TA (2020) 0206, Brussels.

Fleming, S. (2020). '"Frugal four" present rival Covid recovery fund plan. Austria, Denmark, the Netherlands and Sweden want loans from a time-limited fund rather than grants'. *Financial Times*, 23 May.

Friends of Cohesion (2019). 'Joint Declaration on the Multiannual Financial Framework 2021–2027'. Prague.

Friends of Cohesion (2020). 'Joint Declaration on the Multiannual Financial Framework 2021–2027'. Beja.

Frugal Four (23 May 2020). 'Non-paper EU support for efficient and sustainable COVID-19 recovery EU'. www.politico.eu/wp-content/uploads/2020/05/Frugal -Four-Non-Paper.pdf (last accessed 18 March 2022).

Howarth, D., and Schild, J. (2021). 'Nein to "Transfer Union": the German brake on the construction of a European Union fiscal capacity'. *Journal of European Integration*, 43(2), 207–224.

Krotz, U., and Schramm, L. (2022). 'Embedded bilateralism, integration theory, and European crisis politics: France, Germany, and the birth of the EU Corona Recovery Fund'. *Journal of Common Market Studies*, 60(3), 526–544.

Kurz, S. (2020). 'The "Frugal Four" advocate a responsible EU budget'. *Financial Times*, 17 February.

Ladi, S., and Tsarouhas, D. (2020). 'EU economic governance and Covid-19: policy learning and windows of opportunity'. *Journal of European Integration*, 42(8), 1041–1056.

Laffan, B. (1997). *The Finances of the European Union*. St. Martin's Press.

Laffan, B. (2000). 'The big budgetary bargains: from negotiation to authority'. *Journal of European Public Policy*, 7(5), 725–743.

Lehner, S. (2018). 'Ein Haushalt für die Zukunft der Europäischen Union: Die Vorschläge der Europäischen Kommission für den Mehrjährigen Finanzrahmen 2021–2027'. *ifo-Schnelldienst*, 71(12), 10–13.

Lindner, J. (2006). *Conflict and Change in EU Budgetary Politics*. Routledge.

Ludlow, P. (2020a). 'Coming to terms with failure'. *European Council Studies*, 1, 7–35. DOI: https://doi.org/10.11116/ECS.2020.1.2.

Ludlow, P. (2020b). 'European Council Notes 2020/04–05. May to July: The MFF and the Recovery Funds'. *European Council Studies*, 4–5, 1–55, 10. DOI: https://doi.org/10.11116/ECS.2020.4-5.2.

Ludlow, P. (2020c). 'Covid-19, rule of law conditionality, climate change, the EU and the Eastern Mediterranean, security and a Euro summit'. *European Council Studies*, 9, 1–39. DOI: https://doi.org/10.11116/ECS.2020.09.2.

Mussler, W. (2020). 'Charles Michel: "Erheblich mehr Geld für Zukunftsinvestitionen als früher"'. *Frankfurter Allgemeine Zeitung*, 25 July.

President of the European Commission and President of the European Council (2020a). 'A roadmap for recovery. Towards a more resilient, sustainable and fair Europe'. Brussels.

President of the European Commission and President of the European Council (2020b). 'Opening remarks by President von der Leyen at the joint press conference with President Michel following the Special European Council meeting of 17–21 July 2020'. Brussels.

President of the European Council (2020). 'Conclusions of the President of the European Council following the video conference with the members of the European Council'. Brussels.

Press and Information Office of the Federal Government (May 18, 2020). 'Franco-German Initiative for Europe's Economic Recovery after the Corona Crisis'. Press Release 173.

Regulation (EU) 2021/241 of the European Parliament and of the Council of 12 February 2021 establishing the Recovery and Resilience Facility, Official *Journal of the European Union*, L 57, 18.2.2021, pp. 17–74.

Salvati, E. (2021). 'Crisis and intergovernmental retrenchment in the European Union? Framing the EU's answer to the Covid-19 pandemic'. *Chinese Political Science Review*, 6, 1–19.

Sapała, M. (2021). 'Recovery plan for Europe: State of play'. EPRS Briefing, European
    Parliamentary Research Service, Brussels, June.
Schmidt, V.A. (2020). 'Theorizing institutional change and governance in European
    responses to the Covid-19 pandemic'. *Journal of European Integration*, 42(8),
    1177–1193.

3. A decisive moment of governing: budgeting (in) the time of crisis

Marlon Barbehön

INTRODUCTION

There is hardly a term as prevalent in modern practices of governing as the notion of *crisis*. In recent years, the European continent faced the financial and economic crisis in 2007/2008, the Brexit crisis triggered by the UK referendum about EU membership in 2016, the refugee crisis from 2015 onwards and, most recently, the coronavirus crisis (Riddervold et al., 2021). All of these events appear as major disruptions which interfere with a normal mode of governing and establish a state of radical uncertainty as to what will follow after each crisis. The EU is 'at a crossroads', as the title of this volume puts it. At the same time, the idea that politics is confronted with crises, and thus in an exceptional state, looks back on a long history, with a much-noticed peak in the 1970s when the governability of modern society was at issue (Crozier et al., 1975; Offe, 1979). The fact that in modernity, there seems to be a *constant* concern with a state of affairs which is by definition *exceptional* even leads to the formula of a 'normality of crisis', indicating the paradox that crises are perceived as both extraordinary and ever-present (on this paradoxical tendency in modern society see Holton, 1987; Koselleck, 2006).

This chapter reflects on the meaning of crisis in the context of the EU's Multiannual Financial Framework (MFF) for 2021–2027. It will do so on the basis of a constructivist and time-theoretical perspective which assumes, firstly, that a 'crisis' comes into existence through practices of *meaning-making*, and, secondly, that in the case of 'crisis', these meaning-making practices are characterised by a specific *temporality*. As already indicated in the paragraph above, the notion of crisis is essentially temporal: by way of remembering a past (stability, normality) and projecting a future (contingency, uncertainty, radical change), the notion of crisis constitutes a present in which (extraordinary) political decisions seem necessary. In modern society, the moment of crisis is thus a pivotal moment of governing, both for legislation in general and spending in particular. Yet while research in political science is typically concerned with 'governing after crisis' (Boin et al., 2008) and with 'the European Union budget in times of crises' (Kaiser & Prange-Gstöhl, 2019), implying that politics occurs in response to and within exogenously given crises, this chapter reads 'crisis' as a social artefact resulting from the meaning-making practices of governing themselves (cf. Mergel, 2012b; de Rycker & Mohd Don, 2013; Wengeler & Ziem, 2013; Barbehön & Münch, 2017). Crises are not simply out there and befalling politics and society, but they are socially constructed entities that emerge in the moment worldly phenomena are being observed, classified and rendered governable according to a specific temporal logic.

To interrogate the relationship between crisis, (budgetary) governing and time, this chapter will build on arguments from systems theory (cf. Luhmann, 1996, 2012, 2013) which allows the theorising of time as both a technique and a product of meaning-making. In the modern and functionally differentiated society, time is constituted, as will be argued in detail below, through the differentiation between past and future, and depending on the way this distinction is drawn in communicative operations, specific presents with specific temporal characteristics emerge. In this sense, practices of meaning-making constitute time by resorting to time (and vice versa), with 'crisis' as a particularly productive semantics in modern practices of societal self-observation. What is more, crisis-ridden presents call for (immediate) political action, yet it is not self-evident what and how decisions should be taken in light of severe destabilisation and radical uncertainty. Practices of governing thus have to find ways to render themselves plausible in this temporal paradox that is constituted by crisis communication. As will be shown in this chapter, the EU's MFF addresses this general temporal challenge in a historically specific way, namely by applying three (interrelated) governing rationales: *recovery*, *resilience* and *prevention*. The aim of this chapter is to interrogate how these rationales specifically inscribe into the 'flow of time' in order to take effect on the difference between past and future, and how they, as a consequence, produce new temporal tensions and contradictions which constitute the basis for governing the next crisis.

TIME AND CRISIS

At the most basic level, a 'crisis' is a sudden departure from the 'normal' and thus a disruption of the (allegedly) continuous flow of time which calls for (immediate) political action. It is therefore instructive to focus on the temporal characteristics of crisis in order to understand how it comes into existence and how it relates to governing. Much of the research dealing with the relationship between crisis and governing starts with the premise that crises *are there*. It is assumed that crises occasionally emerge and become manifest *in* time, and thus time is treated in the Newtonian sense as a given and uniformly flowing stream in which socio-political phenomena materialise. This notion of time, which is rarely made explicit, resembles the container model of space which has repeatedly been problematised within spatial sociology and critical geography for disregarding the mutual constitution between space and the social (cf. Richardson & Jensen, 2003; Löw, 2016). An analogous critique can be made with regard to the status of Newtonian time in the social realm. In Newtonian physics, time is seen as 'invariant, infinitely divisible into space-like units, measurable in length and expressible as number' (Adam, 1990, p. 50). This naturalist idea of time, which by the way does not even apply to the natural world entirely (relativity of time), could not be directly transferred to the social world. This becomes apparent most obviously in the case of the perception of durations, which is not congruent with the temporal extension as it is 'measurable'[1] but contingent upon practices of perception and interpretation. In this sense, 'time is fundamentally a social construction' (Adam, 1990, p. 42).

According to *systems theory*, as one variant for theorising the constructivist nature of temporality (Luhmann, 1976, 1979, 2005; see also Barbehön, 2018, 2022), time is one of three dimensions effective in meaning-making operations (Luhmann, 1996, pp. 74–82). While the factual dimension involves a distinction between this and everything else and the social dimension articulates a difference between alter and ego, the temporal dimension refers to the *difference between past and future*. This latter difference is a specific form of temporalisation (Luhmann, 2013, pp. 251–263) which emerged within the modern, functionally differentiated society. While premodern societies distinguished between eternity and transience, modern societies differentiate between what has happened and what will happen. Thus, time is no longer observed as a feature attached to objects themselves (eternal vs. transient objects), but as a twofold projection surface which enables the location of objects temporally. By distinguishing between what has happened and what will happen, meaning-making operations reduce complexity and construe a present in which certain items of information become manifest while others are kept latent. As soon as these successive presents are observed as a temporal extension, an enduring present emerges in which it becomes possible to locate beginnings and ends, to identify processes, to attribute causes and effects or to accelerate and decelerate (Luhmann, 2005, p. 151). The present is thus not simply 'there', but contingent upon how meaning-making operations distinguish between past and future and how these distinctions are synthesised into an enduring time.

The way in which past and future are constructed and related to one another is guided by *semantics*. In systems theory, semantics are understood as 'historico-cultural materials' (Luhmann, 1993a, p. 7; translation by the author), as typified meaning that co-emerges with the communicative operations in society. Semantics are stored and held available in a collective repertoire of meaning-making, and thus they provide predictability as to how complexity is processed and how communication will assumedly unfold over time. This is where the notion of *crisis* comes into play: From the point of view of systems theory, 'crisis' can be seen as a semantics that establishes a disruptive present by specifically remembering pasts and projecting futures. Communicative operations organised around the semantics of crisis construe *the past* as a phase of stability and functionality which is suddenly being interrupted in a way that could not have been expected prior to the crisis. As an event, crises 'exceed or defeat the expectations of "structure"' (Knight & Stewart, 2016, p. 4), that is, they destabilise the taken-for-granted predictability of the 'flow of time'. There might have been crises of similar kind in the past which allow us to draw analogies (cf. Brändström et al., 2004), but in one way or another this particular crisis is always unique and thus a fundamental challenge to current stocks of knowledge and routines. Accordingly, *the future* that is imagined by the semantics of crisis is essentially uncertain, as we cannot know for sure how long the crisis will last, where and to what extent it will cause enduring damage or whether a return to the former state of stability and functionality is possible at all.

As a result of this specific temporalisation of complexity, the semantics of crisis construes an *enduring present* in the sense of 'a specific placement at the historical past-to-future axis' (Krzyżanowski, 2019, p. 467). Crisis communication establishes a (lasting) moment in which the continuation of established practices is brought to a halt, while at the same time it is unclear what will happen next and how to take effect on the emergent, which is by definition unknown.[2] Moreover, it is this 'liminal phase' (Mergel, 2012a, p. 15) which rearticulates the past as a phase of stability, although this remembered past was probably not experienced in such a way when it was a former present, as it could be assumed that this former present had its own crisis construed against the background of its own remembered past (and so on and so forth). This indicates that not only is the future contingent (Gumbrecht, 2001) but also the past, as communicative operations rather re-construct than re-present what has happened from the viewpoint of an essentially unique present. In this sense, the basic difference between past and future, as the form in which time appears in modern society, is the prerequisite for a crisis to emerge: if the future were determined by the past, the modern notion of crisis as an unforeseen disruption of expectations would be unthinkable and (in the literal sense) meaningless.

What is more, the enduring present of the crisis is a moment in which *action* is needed. The etymological origin of crisis is the Greek word *krísis*, which not only means 'uncertainty' and 'aggravation', but also 'turning point' and 'decision' (Koselleck, 2006, pp. 358–359). In this sense, crisis communication not only ascertains severe defects but also calls for measures to address these. This leads us to the relationship between crisis, time and governing.

GOVERNING (IN) THE TIME OF CRISIS

In his conceptual history of the term 'crisis', Koselleck (2006, p. 358) has pointed out that in ancient Greece 'crisis' was central to the sphere of politics: 'It meant not only "divorce" and "quarrel," but also "decision" in the sense of reaching a crucial point that would tip the scales.' 'Crisis' was, Koselleck (ibid., p. 359) continues, 'a central concept by which justice and the political order (*Herrschaftsordnung*) could be harmonized through appropriate legal decisions'. At the same time, the ancient notion of time grounded on the onto-logical dualism between eternity and transience. Beyond the evanescence of worldly phenomena, there was an 'unmoved mover' (Aristotle), a divine force which moved time but itself was not temporal (Nassehi, 2008, p. 48). This implies that beyond a specific crisis situation there was a stable force which confined the contingency of the crisis and which was to reveal its truth sooner or later. In contrast, in modernity the distinction between eternity and transi-ence has vanished in favour of the radically presentist distinction between past and future (see above), which further enhances the role of the political within a crisis: since there is nothing eternal left, anything might disappear (into the past) or arise (in the future), and thus in a crisis situation everything is up for decision, including phenomena that have traditionally been located in the realm of nature or God (cf. Barbehön & Folberth, 2019).

In its modern form, the political character of the semantics of crisis is thus to be found in the fact that ascertaining a crisis refers to the contingency of social order and the indeterminacy of time (cf. Mergel, 2012a, p. 10). If the status quo were given by nature, God or destiny and thus in a state of eternal validity, its disruption would not be a 'crisis' but rather a 'collapse' in the sense of a definite end time. In this case, the future would not be contingent, as what follows after the collapse would already be determined. We can find this temporality in premodernity, which built on eschatological time and the idea of the Last Judgment as the foreseeable endpoint in the future (Koselleck, 1989, p. 32).[3] In contrast, the notion of crisis only makes sense if it is assumed that what will happen after the crisis is contingent upon what is done now. Although a crisis destabilises routines and taken-for-granted assumptions as to what is to be done in the face of uncertainty, inactivity or apathy do not appear as appropriate options. This is why, in modern society, the notion of crisis is intrinsically linked to notions of response, management or resolution.

In this sense, crisis communication transforms exogeneous dangers which befall a system from outside into endogenous risks that relate to action (cf. Luhmann, 2013, pp. 310–314).[4] The defects that challenge a system's functionality do not simply appear and vanish by chance, but their scale, reach and impact are perceived as a matter of decisions. This could be called the productive side of crisis as it enables the meaningful practice of governing in the first place. What is more, meaning-making operations organised around the semantics of crisis make decisions necessary, as the semantics of crisis 'transfers the problem of time from the realm of experience to the realm of action. ... Time urges to be active' (Luhmann, 1993a, p. 278; translation by the author). Due to the difference between past and future that becomes manifest in the moment of crisis, the world 'loses aspects of reliable presence and acquires aspects of mutability' (Luhmann, 1996, p. 310), and this contingency is the prerequisite to taking a decision which claims to take effect on how time will proceed. Therefore, the time of crisis and political decision-making do not concur somewhat coincidentally, but it is the former which enables and calls for the latter, and as soon as decisions have been taken, the course of time changes, producing the potential sources for a new crisis in a future present. At the same time, governing in the time of crisis – or more precisely: governing the time of crisis – is enmeshed in an ambivalent constellation: it is necessary to decide, yet the past does not carry enough information as to which and how decisions have to be taken in order to bring into existence a time after crisis. There is thus a double contingency as it is neither self-evident what is to be done today nor what the 'new normality' in the aftermath of the crisis will or should look like.

Against the background of this temporal configuration, the logics and rationales of *budgetary policy* as a technique of 'governing through spending' (Egner, 2012; translation by the author) can be elaborated on. Budgetary policy is a peculiar type of political decision as it features a specific temporal architecture. As compared to the regulations in many other policy fields, decisions on public budgets are limited in time (Gosling, 2009, p. 1). From the very beginning of the decision-making process, it is clear that a decision is taken for a limited time span; in national political systems typically for one year, in the case of the EU's MFF, for seven years. This results in a circular temporality in which the end of one budget is the start of the next budget; and if it is not, the entire system runs into a 'shutdown' which brings time to a halt. Budgetary policy is thus an essential component of the 'rhythms of democracy' (Goodin, 1998) which establish predictability and accountability with regard to the system's processing in time, both for the system itself and for its environment. Moreover, budgetary policy is particularly relevant for the (self-)observation of the political system and its operative reproduction: once every (seven) year(s), the political system claims to set the future direction of society by allocating money, the central medium of communication through which the political system is structurally coupled with other social systems (cf. Luhmann, 2002, pp. 382–388). Budgetary policy is thus a specific moment of governing in the sense of a recurring peak of political communication.

In times of crisis, this general significance of budgetary policy is further intensified. As compared to ad hoc emergency decisions that address immediately pressing effects of the crisis, budgetary policy is expected to give a large-scale and long-term answer as to how to overcome the crisis and to build a better future. At the same time, the crisis establishes a situation of radical uncertainty in which the flow of time is interrupted and beliefs from the past are shattered (see above). There is thus a temporal tension inscribed into the relationship between budgetary policy and crisis: while the former claims to be able to plan the future at least up to the start of the next budgetary cycle, the latter destabilises expectations for the future and makes visible that modern society is essentially unplannable (cf. Little, 2012; Mueller, 2020). Against the background of this constellation, budgeting in times of crises has to find ways to plausibilise itself; it has to navigate between the apparent indeterminacy of time and the expectation that this indeterminacy can be tamed through political decisions. Budgetary policy in the context of crises is thus a decisive moment of governing in which the task of communicating that planning for an unknown future is both necessary and possible becomes particularly challenging. In what follows, how the MFF addresses this communicative challenge will be reconstructed by investigating the historically specific semantics that relate a past and future that have fallen into a crisis.

THE TEMPORALITY OF THE EU'S MULTIANNUAL FINANCIAL FRAMEWORK

From the systems-theoretical perspective developed above, the temporalities of crisis and governing are mutually constitutive. Crisis communication establishes a crisis-ridden present by specifically distinguishing between past and future, while a political decision claims to take effect on the difference between what has been, currently is and assumedly will be, what in turn reproduces the premise of temporal contingency and thus lays the ground for the next critical distinction between past and future (and so on and so forth). In the following two subsections, this temporal relationship will be reconstructed for the MFF 2021–2027. It will be shown, firstly, how the communication surrounding the MFF establishes a crisis-ridden present in which decisive action is needed, and how, secondly, the multiannual budget is structured by specific temporal logics of governing which try to plausibilise a 'rational' way of political decision-making in light of disruption, uncertainty and contingency. The aim of the following analysis is thus neither to present detailed case studies on certain crises nor to assess the architecture of the EU's revenues and spending in different policy fields (see the other chapters in this volume on that), but rather to reflect on the temporal linkage between crisis and budgetary policy.

The following analysis takes an *interpretive perspective* (cf. Schwartz-Shea & Yanow, 2012; Bevir & Rhodes, 2016) that aims to reconstruct the social practices through which worldly phenomena are attributed with specific meanings. It is not the aim to assess whether there 'truly' is a crisis or to what extent the budget is an 'effective' answer to the EU's challenges. Rather, the guiding question is how the communicative operations related to the MFF reduce complexity so as to bring order into an ambiguous world and to render it governable. This methodological rationale corresponds with the ontological premises of systems theory which, as a radical constructivist perspective, assumes that meaning is constituted in communication which in turn is structured by contingent socio-historical repertoires. To uncover the communicative repertoire that is effective in the MFF, central documents issued by the European Commission, the European Parliament and the European Council have been analysed regarding *recurring* temporal semantics that relate the budget to current crises. This search for communicative patterns is inspired by Foucauldian discourse analysis which builds on similar theoretical and methodological premises as a systems-theoretical analysis of semantics (cf. Leanza, 2010).

The following analysis is to be understood as an attempt to illustrate the insights that are rendered possible by the theoretical perspective developed above, and not as encompassing empirical research. This also entails that the illustration below only produces a snapshot of the current and historically specific semantic techniques that are prevalent in the MFF 2021–2027. It must be kept in mind that the way the time of crisis is approached and rendered governable is itself temporal, and thus the following analysis does not claim to draw a general picture of the relationship between time, crisis and (budgetary) policy.

The Time Is Now

As argued above, from a time-theoretical point of view budgetary policy is a peculiar type of political decision. It is apparent for everyone that at a certain point in time, namely when the budgetary cycle that is currently operative comes to an end, a decision on the new budget for the upcoming period will be necessary. While every meaningful operation of deciding constitutes such a point in time, that is, an event prior to and after which things were and will be different (cf. Luhmann, 1979, pp. 74–75), in case of a budgetary decision this moment in time is particularly sharply demarcated as it can not only be remembered as a decisive event in retrospect but also anticipated in every single present of the budgetary cycle. At the same time, and since it is a *cycle*, the moment of decision-making will recur over and over again in the future, at least as long as there is no decision taken as regards the cycle itself. This results in an ambivalent temporal configuration in which a decision with an institutionalised recurrence appears as a unique and decisive point in time:

> Once every seven years, the European Union decides on its future long-term budget – the Multiannual Financial Framework. The next such budget, starting on 1 January 2021, will be the first for the European Union of 27. This is a pivotal moment for our Union. It is an opportunity for Member States and the European institutions to unite around a clear vision for the future of Europe. A time to show unequivocally that the Union is ready to back up its words with the actions needed to deliver on our common vision. (European Commission, 2018, p. 1)

The enduring present of the budgetary *process* with all its chronologically organised steps and deadlines, its complex and long-lasting negotiations, its diachronic choreography of proposals and counter-proposals, i.e. something that evolves over time and takes time, is thus compressed to a *decisive moment*; or as the White Paper on the Future of Europe puts it: 'Europe must now choose. ... This can be Europe's hour' (European Commission, 2017, p. 26). From the viewpoint of systems theory, this is a particularly severe reduction of complexity in the temporal dimension of meaning, which also takes effect on the factual and social dimension of following communicative operations, for instance by increasing the possibility of objections against certain budgetary proposals: no political institution or actor can afford to miss 'Europe's hour' and to not make their voices heard in this moment of historical significance. In this sense, it comes as no surprise that budget negotiations are loaded with publicly visible political conflicts, in the case of the MFF 2021–2027, for instance, on the status of the rule of law within the budget's architecture (see Heinelt and Münch, Chapter 1 in this volume).

In the light of crises, this rift in time that is constituted by the decision is even more pronounced. Inasmuch as crisis communication establishes a turning point that abruptly crops the continuation of the past and introduces an uncertain future, there is even more need to act decisively here and now: 'Europe's moment: Repair and Prepare for the Next Generation', reads the title of a proposal of the European Commission (2020a) to address the economic and social consequences of the coronavirus pandemic. On the one hand, it is said that the somewhat sudden openness of the future makes 'Predictions or definitive conclusions ... inevitably fraught with uncertainty', while on the other hand it seems clear that 'the recession in Europe could be deep, damaging and prolonged if we do not take decisive action now' (ibid., p. 2). As the economic outlook is 'full of risk' (ibid.), the EU 'needs more than ever to show that it is ready and willing to act decisively' (ibid., p. 16). What is more, the upcoming decisions on revenue and spending are perceived not only as formative for the next budgetary cycle but also for future generations: 'Choices taken in the coming months will shape the Union for decades to come' (European

Commission, 2018, p. 1), and 'the choices we make today will define tomorrow's future for the next generation' (European Commission, 2020a, p. 2).

These apodictic statements, which combine a sense of severe uncertainty with a strong conviction of agency, only make sense inasmuch as time is perceived as being contingent upon present decisions. This temporal principle, which is historically and culturally not without alternatives (see the classic contributions by Rammstedt, 1975, or Koselleck, 1989), is so deeply rooted in our collective knowledge that these statements appear as plausible without explicit explanations as to why we should assume that the future is unforeseeable but still up for decision. The confidence that deciding upon the unknown is both necessary and possible is also taken from the past, which is pictured as an alternation of crises and successful crisis management:

> The Union has often been built on the back of crises and false starts. From the European Defence Community that never got off the ground in the 1950s, to the exchange rate shocks of the 1970s, through to aborted accessions and rejections in referenda in recent decades, Europe has always been at a crossroads and has always adapted and evolved. (European Commission, 2017, p. 6)

While the history of European integration 'has not always been an easy journey', the EU has always managed to show 'its capacity to reform itself and has proven its value over time' (ibid., p. 26). According to these practices of remembrance, history tells us that crises are not only disruptions but also moments of deciding about the way ahead, which resembles the 'progressive story' that is regularly told about the process of European integration (cf. Schünemann & Barbehön, 2019).

The EU's multiannual budget thus finds itself confronted with the conviction that the time to decide is now. However, in light of the multiple crises which interrupt the continuation of what is known from the past, and which establish uncertainty as regards the future, the question is how exactly decisions shall be taken. As will be shown, the communicative operations surrounding the MFF draw on *three overarching semantics* to engage with this challenge: *recovery*, *resilience* and *prevention*, all of which could be read as specific and historically contingent temporal rationales (cf. Barbehön, 2020, 2022) geared towards governing (in) the time of crisis.

Recovering, Preventing and Fostering Resilience

The notion of *recovery* or *repair* is particularly prevalent in documents related to the coronavirus pandemic, as in a communication of the European Commission (2020a) entitled 'Europe's moment: Repair and Prepare [see below] for the Next Generation' or in the statement 'A Roadmap for Recovery' jointly issued by the presidents of the European Commission and the European Council (European Commission & European Council, 2020). Against the background of severe economic and social disruptions, it is said that political interventions are needed that are able to restore what is currently under pressure. The European Parliament (2020, p. 5), for instance, calls for a 'massive recovery and reconstruction package for investment to support the European economy after the crisis'. In this sense, recovery is conservative in nature as it refers to the past as a state of stability which is supposed to be re-established (at any cost?) under new circumstances, and thus in order to 'understand what Europe needs to do to recover, we must first have a clear picture of what we are facing' (European Commission, 2020a, p. 2). The notion of recovery, and probably even more so the notion of repair, is based on the premise that *before* the crisis occurred, the respective system was running properly, implying a clear and unidirectional relationship between cause and effect in which the crisis 'out there' constitutes an exogenous shock to the established system (and not the other way around or as a reciprocal relationship). The Solvency Support Instrument, for instance, is presented as 'a new and temporary instrument created as part of the European Fund for Strategic Investments to avoid massive capital short-falls and possible defaults of otherwise viable companies due to the COVID-19 crisis' (European Commission, 2020c, p. 7).

From the perspective taken in this chapter, this conservative tendency of recovery could be read as a structural consequence of the time of crisis in the sense that crisis communication squeezes the present into a decisive moment in which action is urgently needed, and thus in a crisis there is 'simply no time' to pose fundamental systemic questions. As the semantic counterpart of crisis is normality, and as the normal is by definition that which is known from the past, the temporality of crisis is intrinsically linked to the idea of recovery. At the same time, the rationale of recovery is regularly complemented by semantics which add another facet to its temporality. For instance, we encounter the idea of 'sustainable recovery' (European Commission, 2018, p. 1, 2020a, p. 5) which adds to the idea of repair a notion of adaptation and change. Instead of simply restoring what has been lost or fallen into a critical state, sustainability implies that something different is (also) needed in order to establish a future present which promises a new stability (on the temporality of sustainability see Bornemann & Strassheim, 2019). More specifically, the European Commission (2020a, p. 1) calls for a 'collective and cohesive recovery that accelerates [since time is scarce] the twin green and digital transitions'. By that, the EU member states shall be supported to 'recover, repair and emerge stronger from the crisis' (European Commission, 2020b, p. 4). Thus, the principle of recovery can be entangled with other temporalities, not least to pursue a political agenda already in place prior to the crisis.[5] In the context of crisis communication, these supplements appear as particularly plausible or even necessary, as a simple repair without adaptations would raise the question whether this would not establish the breeding ground for the next crisis to come.

Even more prominent than recovery and repair is the semantics of *resilience*, which over the last two decades has become an overarching governing rationale in a variety of policy fields (cf. Bröckling, 2012; Folkers, 2018) and which is almost omnipresent in the documents surrounding the MFF: 'Towards a more resilient, sustainable and fair Europe', the subtitle of a statement by the European Council (2020) reads. The semantics of resilience is intrinsically linked to the idea of the future as a reservoir of risks which may materialise into existential threats in future presents. As it is assumed that these risks cannot be anticipated entirely, let alone prevented from occurring, resilience aims at establishing an (adaptive) status that enables a system to withstand external threats as soon as they arise. Resilience is thus not simply about returning to a past status quo but about adapting to changing situations, that is, about 'resilient recovery' (European Council, 2020, p. 2). The aim of the Recovery and Resilience Facility, for instance, is to support 'investments and reforms essential to a lasting recovery, to improve the economic and social resilience of Member States' (European Commission, 2020b, p. 5), and to 'draw the lessons of the crisis and make the single market stronger and more resilient' (ibid., p. 4). A sudden disruption of the status quo is thus communicated as a learning opportunity, in the sense that the crisis 'revealed a number of areas where Europe needs to be more resilient to prevent, protect and withstand future shocks' (European Commission, 2020a, p. 12).

Due to the (paradoxical) maxim that one should prepare for what could not be known entirely, resilience takes a comprehensive meaning. For instance, the European Parliament (2020, p. 3) calls 'for the creation of a European Health Response Mechanism to better prepare and respond in a common and coordinated way to *any type* of health or sanitary crisis' and claims that 'the EU must become more resilient against crises *in general*' (ibid., p. 12); in a similar vein, the European Commission (2020a, p. 3) argues that there is 'a need to build more resilient infrastructure to deal with *unforeseen* events' (all emphases added). These quotes indicate that the semantics of resilience is particularly demanding, as in the light of an unforeseeable future, the risks against which protection is needed are essentially infinite. As Bargués-Pedreny (2020) has put it, resilience 'is "always more" than our practices', a premise which leads to a sense of deficit in which a desired future is basically unachievable. 'There is never an end-state called resilience', Bargués-Pedreny (ibid., p. 265) argues in the context of international security policy, 'where peace and harmony could settle: no mission, initiative, gesture or symbol seems to get them close enough to finally achieve resilience'. Therefore, the semantics of resilience also evokes a notion of urgency and time pressure (cf. Barbehön, 2022) in which measures to build resilient systems are never fast enough: 'The crisis has both underlined the value of European cooperation and demonstrated vividly that the Union must urgently build up its capacity to respond to crises and build resilience to future shocks' (European Commission, 2020b, p. 9).

Finally, there is a third semantics that prevails in the documents in the context of the MFF: *prevention*. Again, the future of prevention is full of risks, yet as compared to the logic of resilience, prevention claims that current decisions are able to avoid the potential risks from materialising at all. The European Parliament (2020, p. 13) argues that 'corporate human rights and environmental due diligence are necessary conditions in order to prevent and mitigate future crises'. Similarly, the European Commission (2020b, p. 10) suggests establishing the EU4Health Programme, which will support 'investments in critical health infrastructure, tools, structures, processes, and laboratory capacity, including tools for surveillance, modelling, forecast, prevention and management of outbreaks'. The programme is supposed to 'help prevent … diseases' by promoting 'evidence-based best practices in prevention and management of diseases' (European Commission, 2020c, p. 10). By way of 'science-driven solutions' (European Commission, 2020b, p. 11), today's decisions will systematically impede what is anticipated for the future.

In a way, prevention is thus a complement to the notion of planning as both construe the future as something that can be deliberately shaped (cf. Leanza et al., 2011). As compared to resilience, the future of prevention is less unforeseeable, as prevention needs a latent object it can work on, and thus prevention builds on the principle of forecast rather than foresight (cf. van der Steen, 2017). In times of crisis, however, this positivist logic of prediction on the basis of a systematic application of knowledge stumbles into a paradox, as in a crisis the past, by definition, does not carry enough information in order to entirely know how the future will look, as otherwise there would not be a crisis in the sense of a critical turning point. Yet despite the radical contingency that crisis communication establishes, (budgetary) governing obviously cannot quite let go of the idea that we are in control of the emergent, if only enough 'evidence' is being gathered and applied (for a critical account of this enduring premise, see Colebatch, 2018).

CONCLUSION

Governing needs time. At first sight, this is a self-evident statement since any activity takes place in and unfolds over time. In this view, time appears (in the Newtonian sense) as a uniform and linear extension, the 'timeline', on which social phenomena are located. This perspective on time and governing enables the interrogation of the successions, sequences, durations and cycles involved in authoritative decision-making, regularly leading observers to problematise the fact that democratic governing 'needs too much time' as against the speed of the societal environment (cf. Scheuerman, 2004; Rosa, 2013). On a more fundamental level, however, governing needs time in the constitutive sense of the term: it needs to establish a time which is not (entirely) determined by nature, God or fate, but contingent upon *decisions*. Governing only makes sense when there is indeterminacy, when there is something that can be decided upon either in this or in that way, and when the decision that is taken actually makes a difference as regards the course of time. This idea of the relationship between time and (political) action is so deeply rooted in how we see the world that it is seldom reflected upon, obscuring the fact that time is not only a neutral container in which governing takes place but also a cultural artefact that emerges in conjunction with the meaning-making practices of governing.

The notion of *crisis* is a particular productive instance of this temporality. Although the term dates back to ancient Greece (Koselleck, 2006), in modern society it features a specific link to the political due to the modern dissociation between the 'space of experience' and the 'horizon of expectation' (Koselleck, 1989, pp. 359–375) which makes essentially everything a matter of decisions. To identify a crisis means inserting a rupture in time which not only establishes an alarming state of instability and uncertainty, but also a present in which it is possible and necessary to take decisions. A crisis calls for immediate and decisive action, for concerted responses and for effective solutions, and, in the long run, for reflexive learning, for structural adaptations and for profound reforms. A crisis is not a tragedy that befalls society in a fateful manner and that inevitably leads to a catastrophe. Despite all the harm a crisis does, it is also politically productive since it poses the task of overcoming and emerging stronger from the crisis. A crisis is thus a *decisive moment of governing* in two ways: it is the moment in which decisions can and have to be taken, and it is (thus) a moment which is crucial to how the future will look. It comes as no surprise then that modern society sees itself in a constant state of crisis, given the fact that there is hardly any phenomenon which is not perceived as being up for decision.

This chapter has utilised these time-theoretical considerations in order to reflect on how crises are rendered governable in and through the MFF 2021–2027. The analysis has shown that the manifold crises of the European continent are construed as a moment for decision-making, that is, not as a state of paralysis but as an opportunity to decide how the common future should look. What is more, this moment is located within a historical continuity of decisive moments: the EU, the story goes, has always found itself being confronted with crises and has always managed to emerge stronger than before. To do so again, the MFF builds on *three semantics* which aim at governing the time of crisis by specifically construing pasts and futures. Firstly, the notion of *recovery* calls for restoring an allegedly stable past and for adapting to new circumstances, for instance by committing to the principle of 'sustainability' which is supposed to establish a state of equilibrium in a future present whose shape, due to the crisis, cannot be known. Secondly, the notion of *resilience* imagines a future full of risks and calls for building robust structures in order to be prepared for what will eventually come, thus demanding to anticipate what is not yet known. Thirdly, the notion of *prevention* even goes a step further by calling for measures which will prohibit latent threats from materialising at all, leading to the essentially unanswerable question of what risks can be taken and what risks deserve preventive efforts (which themselves are the source of new risks). These three semantics are not to be understood as ahistorical techniques to politically deal with time; rather, they are historically specific ways of temporalising complexity which relate to both general trends of modern governing (cf. Barbehön, 2022) and the temporal specificities of EU governance (cf. Goetz, 2009).

The message to be taken from these critical observations is *not* that the EU's responses to the crises are ineffective or inadequate and that the MFF should have taken another route. Assessing the effectiveness of decisions (taken under the heading of recovery, prevention and resilience) is essentially impossible as we can never be sure how a decision will take effect in the future. What is more, the effectiveness cannot even be assessed retrospectively as there will always be different memories as to what has happened and how phenomena influenced each other. Decisions in the sense of communicative operations within a social system necessarily take place in a present 'because the system can neither forge ahead into the future of the environment nor lag behind in its past' (Luhmann, 2012, p. 43). Nevertheless, governing *has to claim* that it is able to deliberately manipulate the emergent, as this is its *raison d'être* in the modern functionally differentiated society. The systems-theoretical perspective applied in this chapter, which of course is only one way of analysing budgetary policy, has allowed the reconstruction of how the MFF tries to come to terms with this task in its communicative operations. A focus on the semantic interrelationship between time, crisis and governing enables the understanding of how ambiguous constellations are reduced in complexity and thus rendered governable, and how this contingent communicative process (de)legitimises certain political arguments as to what is '(un)necessary', '(im)possible' or '(ir)rational'. Therefore, and since they draw a line between what is observed and what remains unobserved (Luhmann, 1993a, p. 35), semantics are inevitably related to structures of power (Barbehön, 2022). The specifically modern idea of time as indefinite and open offers different possibilities to relate political decision-making to past and future, yet this does not only make the world governable, it also entails that the future remains unknowable. Therefore, the goal of repairing the damage in a way that prepares for future threats, or better still, that prevents these threats from materialising at all, is never entirely attainable; or to put it more productively: it constitutes the necessity to take the next political decision over and over again, thus establishing a need for governing into infinity (cf. Foucault, 2007, p. 260).

NOTES

1. What is more, the central cultural artefact for time measurement, the clock, is actually also constructing time. Rather than 'measuring' time as some kind of substance located in the clock's environment, what a clock actually does is produce a constant movement which is then defined as constituting temporal units.
2. It should be mentioned that it is actually *never* obvious what will happen next as meaning-making operations 'can neither forge ahead into the future of the environment nor lag behind in its past' (Luhmann, 2012, p. 43), and thus it is always uncertain how meaning-making practices will unfold in the future. However, in 'normal times' society *assumes* that it knows what will happen – until the next crisis comes to the fore and shatters what has been taken for granted.
3. As Foucault (2007, pp. 255–310) has shown in his lectures on *Governmentality*, the emancipation from eschatological and salvation-historical time, in favour of the idea of an endless time with an open future, was constitutive for the development of a modern rationality of governing, as otherwise there would not be anything to decide upon (see also Hamilton, 2018; Portschy, 2020).
4. According to Luhmann (2013, pp. 310–314), 'risks' and 'dangers' are different ways of observing potential damage: while the sources of a danger are located in a system's environment (for instance, the natural danger of a flood), a risk is contingent upon decisions within the system itself (for instance, the decision whether to construct a dam or not). Risk communication construes a complex future in which potential threats are related to action, evoking considerations as to the probability of threats and the need for preventive measures (Luhmann, 1993b, pp. 33–49). As a constructivist theory, systems theory does not itself distinguish between calculable risks and fundamental uncertainties or known and unknown threats (on that see Knight, 1921), but asks how this distinction is drawn in communicative operations in society.
5. On the European Green Deal, see Bornemann, Chapter 7 in this volume.

REFERENCES

Adam, B. (1990). *Time and Social Theory*, Polity Press.
Barbehön, M. (2018). 'Ever more complex, uncertain and urging? "Wicked problems" from the perspective of anti-naturalist conceptualizations of time'. *Diskurs – Zeitschrift für innovative Analysen politischer Praxis*, 3, 1–20.
Barbehön, M. (2020). 'Die überholte Demokratie? Eine konstruktivistische Perspektive auf das Verhältnis von Beschleunigung und demokratischer Politik'. *Leviathan*, 48(3), 501–524.
Barbehön, M. (2022). 'From time to time: a systems-theoretical perspective on the twofold temporality of governing'. *Critical Policy Studies*, 16(3), 297–314.

Barbehön, M., & Folberth, A. (2019). 'Die Temporalität der Biopolitik – Eine systemtheoretische Perspektive auf die Regierung "symptomfreier Kranker"'. In H. Gerhards & K. Braun (eds), *Biopolitiken – Regierungen des Lebens heute*, Springer VS, 97–120.

Barbehön, M., & Münch, S. (2017). 'Interrogating the city: comparing locally distinct crisis discourses'. *Urban Studies*, 54(9), 2072–2086.

Bargués-Pedreny, P. (2020). 'Resilience is "always more" than our practices: limits, critiques, and skepticism about international intervention'. *Contemporary Security Policy*, 41(2), 263–286.

Bevir, M., & Rhodes, R. A. W. (2016). 'Interpretive political science: mapping the field'. In M. Bevir & R. A. W. Rhodes (eds), *Routledge Handbook of Interpretive Political Science*, Routledge, 3–27.

Boin, A., McConnell, A., & 't Hart, P. (eds) (2008). *Governing after Crisis: The Politics of Investigation, Accountability and Learning*, Cambridge University Press.

Bornemann, B., & Strassheim, H. (2019). 'Governing time for sustainability: analyzing the temporal implications of sustainability governance'. *Sustainability Science*, 14(4), 1001–1013.

Brändström, A., Bynander, F., & 't Hart, P. (2004). 'Governing by looking back: historical analogies and crisis management'. *Public Administration*, 82(1), 191–210.

Bröckling, U. (2012). 'Dispositive der Vorbeugung: Gefahrenabwehr, Resilienz, Precaution'. In C. Daase, P. Offermann, & V. Rauer (eds), *Sicherheitskultur: Soziale und politische Praktiken der Gefahrenabwehr*, Campus, 93–108.

Colebatch, H. K. (2018). 'The idea of policy design: intention, process, outcome, meaning and validity'. *Public Policy and Administration*, 33(4), 365–383.

Crozier, M., Huntington, S. P., & Watanuki, J. (1975). *The Crisis of Democracy: Report on the Governability of Democracies to the Trilateral Commission*, New York University Press.

de Rycker, A., & Mohd Don, Z. (eds) (2013). *Discourse and Crisis: Critical Perspectives*, John Benjamins.

Egner, B. (2012). 'Regieren als Geldausgeben? Zum Einfluss der Koalitionsbildung in den deutschen Landtagen auf die Staatsquote der Bundesländer'. In B. Egner, M. Haus, & G. Terizakis (eds), *Regieren: Festschrift für Hubert Heinelt*, Springer VS, 265–279.

European Commission (2017). 'White paper on the future of Europe. Reflections and scenarios for the EU27 by 2025', COM(2017) 2025.

European Commission (2018). 'A modern budget for a Union that protects, empowers and defends. The Multiannual Financial Framework for 2021–2027', COM(2018) 321 final.

European Commission (2020a). 'Europe's moment: Repair and Prepare for the Next Generation', COM(2020) 456 final.

European Commission (2020b). 'The EU budget powering the recovery plan for Europe', COM(2020) 442 final.

European Commission (2020c). 'The EU budget powering the recovery plan for Europe. Annex', COM(2020) 442 final.

European Commission & European Council (2020). 'A Roadmap for Recovery. Towards a more resilient, sustainable and fair Europe'.

European Council (2020). 'Conclusions to the special meeting of the European Council 17–21 July 2020', EUCO 10/20.

European Parliament (2020). 'EU coordinated action to combat the COVID-19 pandemic and its consequences', P9_TA (2020)0054.

Folkers, A. (2018). *Das Sicherheitsdispositiv der Resilienz: Katastrophische Risiken und die Biopolitik vitaler Systeme*, Campus.

Foucault, M. (2007). *Security, Territory, Population: Lectures at the Collège de France, 1977–78*, Palgrave Macmillan.

Goetz, K. H. (2009). 'How does the EU tick? Five propositions on political time'. *Journal of European Public Policy*, 16(2), 202–220.

Goodin, R. E. (1998). 'Keeping political time: the rhythms of democracy'. *International Political Science Review*, 19(1), 39–54.

Gosling, J. J. (2009). *Budgetary Politics in American Governments* (5th edn), Routledge.

Gumbrecht, H. U. (2001). 'How is our future contingent? Reading Luhmann against Luhmann'. *Theory, Culture & Society*, 18(1), 49–58.

Hamilton, S. (2018). 'Foucault's end of history: the temporality of governmentality and its end in the Anthropocene'. *Millennium: Journal of International Studies*, 46(3), 371–395.

Holton, R. J. (1987). 'The idea of crisis in modern society'. *The British Journal of Sociology*, 38(4), 502–520.

Kaiser, R., & Prange-Gstöhl, H. (eds) (2019). *The European Union Budget in Times of Crises*, Nomos.

Knight, D. M., & Stewart, C. (2016). 'Ethnographies of austerity: temporality, crisis and affect in Southern Europe'. *History and Anthropology*, 27(1), 1–18.

Knight, F. H. (1921). *Risk, Uncertainty and Profit*, Houghton Mifflin Company.

Koselleck, R. (1989). *Vergangene Zukunft: Zur Semantik geschichtlicher Zeiten*, Suhrkamp.

Koselleck, R. (2006). 'Crisis'. *Journal of the History of Ideas*, 67(2), 357–400.

Krzyżanowski, M. (2019). 'Brexit and the imaginary of "crisis": a discourse-conceptual analysis of European news media'. *Critical Discourse Studies*, 16(4), 465–490.

Leanza, M. (2010). 'Semantik und Diskurs: Die Wissenskonzeptionen Niklas Luhmanns und Michel Foucaults im Vergleich'. In R. Feustel & M. Schochow (eds), *Zwischen Sprachspiel und Methode: Perspektiven der Diskursanalyse*, transcript Verlag, 119–146.

Leanza, M., Terpe, S., & Karakayali, S. (2011). 'Politics of the future: between prevention and planning. Editorial'. *Behemoth – A Journal on Civilisation*, 4(2), 1–9.

Little, A. (2012). 'Political action, error and failure: the epistemological limits of complexity'. *Political Studies*, 60(1), 3–19.

Löw, M. (2016). *The Sociology of Space: Materiality, Social Structures, and Action*, Palgrave Macmillan.

Luhmann, N. (1976). 'The future cannot begin: temporal structures in modern society'. *Social Research*, 43(1), 130–152.

Luhmann, N. (1979). 'Zeit und Handlung – Eine vergessene Theorie'. *Zeitschrift für Soziologie*, 8(1), 63–81.

Luhmann, N. (1993a). *Gesellschaftsstruktur und Semantik: Studien zur Wissenssoziologie der modernen Gesellschaft*, Suhrkamp.

Luhmann, N. (1993b). *Risk: A Sociological Theory*, Walter de Gruyter.

Luhmann, N. (1996). *Social Systems*, Stanford University Press.

Luhmann, N. (2002). *Die Politik der Gesellschaft*, Suhrkamp.

Luhmann, N. (2005). 'Weltzeit und Systemgeschichte: Über Beziehungen zwischen Zeithorizonten und sozialen Strukturen gesellschaftlicher Systeme'. In *Soziologische Aufklärung 2: Aufsätze zur Theorie der Gesellschaft* (5th edn), VS Verlag für Sozialwissenschaften, 128–166.

Luhmann, N. (2012). *Theory of Society: Volume 1*, Stanford University Press.

Luhmann, N. (2013). *Theory of Society: Volume 2*, Stanford University Press.

Mergel, T. (2012a). 'Einleitung: Krisen als Wahrnehmungsphänomene'. In T. Mergel (ed.), *Krisen verstehen: Historische und kulturwissenschaftliche Annäherungen*, Campus, 9–22.

Mergel, T. (ed.) (2012b). *Krisen verstehen: Historische und kulturwissenschaftliche Annäherungen*, Campus.

Mueller, B. (2020). 'Why public policies fail: policymaking under complexity'. *Economia*, 21(2), 311–323.

Nassehi, A. (2008). *Die Zeit der Gesellschaft: Auf dem Weg zu einer soziologischen Theorie der Zeit. Neuauflage mit einem Beitrag 'Gegenwarten'*, VS Verlag für Sozialwissenschaften.

Offe, C. (1979). '"Unregierbarkeit". Zur Renaissance konservativer Krisentheorien'. In J. Habermas (ed.), *Stichworte zur 'Geistigen Situation der Zeit': 1. Band: Nation und Politik*, Suhrkamp, 294–318.

Portschy, J. (2020). 'Times of power, knowledge and critique in the work of Foucault'. *Time & Society*, 29(2), 392–419.

Rammstedt, O. (1975). 'Alltagsbewußtsein von Zeit'. *Kölner Zeitschrift für Soziologie und Sozialpsychologie*, 27(1), 47–63.

Richardson, T., & Jensen, O. B. (2003). 'Linking discourse and space: towards a cultural sociology of space in analysing spatial policy discourses'. *Urban Studies*, 40(1), 7–22.

Riddervold, M., Trondal, J., & Newsome, A. (eds) (2021). *The Palgrave Handbook of EU Crises*, Palgrave Macmillan.

Rosa, H. (2013). *Social Acceleration: A New Theory of Modernity*, Columbia University Press.

Scheuerman, W. E. (2004). *Liberal Democracy and the Social Acceleration of Time*, Johns Hopkins University Press.

Schünemann, W. J., & Barbehön, M. (2019). 'EU critique beyond Euroscepticism and progressive stories: introduction to the special issue'. *Culture, Practice & Europeanization*, 4(2), 1–12.

Schwartz-Shea, P., & Yanow, D. (2012). *Interpretive Research Design: Concepts and Processes*, Routledge.

van der Steen, M. (2017). 'Anticipation tools in policy formulation: forecasting, foresight and implications for policy planning'. In M. Howlett & I. Mukherjee (eds), *Handbook of Policy Formulation*, Edward Elgar Publishing, 182–197.

Wengeler, M., & Ziem, A. (eds) (2013). *Sprachliche Konstruktion von Krisen: Interdisziplinäre Perspektiven auf ein fortwährend aktuelles Phänomen*, Hempen Verlag.

4. The Euro crisis: the battle of ideas how to address it – and its effects on European integration

Clément Fontan and Antoine de Cabanes

INTRODUCTION

From the failure of the Werner Plan in the 1970s (see following section) to the current debates on the Recovery and Resilience Facility (RRF), European Union (EU) member states have disagreed on the adequate degree of fiscal and budgetary mutualisation in the Economic and Monetary Union (EMU). These persistent conflicts are in strong contrast to the successful negotiations on the creation of the euro area in the early 1990s, and the deepening of financial integration since then (McNamara, 1998). In fact, since its creation in 1999, the euro area has been shaped by a deep asymmetry between the integration of monetary policy, which is formulated at the supranational level by the European Central Bank (ECB), and budgetary and fiscal policies, which mainly follow an intergovernmental logic (Howarth & Loedel, 2005). With the benefit of retrospect, we know that this asymmetry was one of the main drivers of the economic imbalances of the euro area, which started to unfold from 2007 onwards and were conducive to the euro crisis.

What are the historical roots of the battle of ideas that shape the euro area asymmetry and why was it conducive to the crisis? What does the response of political authorities to the euro crisis teach us about the battle of ideas that underlies the 2021–2027 Multiannual Financial Framework (MFF) negotiations and the present state of distributional conflicts between EU countries?

This chapter aims to answer these questions by shedding light on the ideational struggles about the EMU economic governance before, during and, to a lesser extent, after the euro crisis. In the first section, we underline that the institutional design of the euro area is the outcome of ideational struggles, which have been unfolding and evolving since the 1960s. The second section analyses the battle of ideas between the different policy players who were fighting to frame the causes of the euro area crisis and the subsequent policy solutions. In our conclusion, we draw links between the battle of ideas that took place during the euro area crisis and the negotiations on the Recovery and Resilience Facility (RFF) and the MFF.

In this chapter, we do not take a position on theoretical debates about the nature of ideas. More precisely, we follow the assumption that ideas have a 'Janus-faced nature' (Parsons, 2002). On the one hand, ideas influence power structures to the extent that they shape actors' worldviews, beliefs and their realms of possibility (Diez, 2001). On the other hand, ideas can be mobilised by strategic players in the pursuit of their interests to build unlikely alliances or legitimise controversial decisions (Jabko, 2006).

THE HISTORY OF THE BATTLE OF IDEAS AND THE ORIGINS OF EMU IMBALANCES

The Historical Roots of the Battle of Ideas

Two competing economic visions shaped the early phases of economic integration in the European Economic Community (EEC) in the 1960s (Warlouzet, 2019). On the one hand, the *dirigiste* paradigm encouraged states to play a developmental role in their economy by steering credit in strategic sectors and fostering industrial development. This policy paradigm was influential in the majority of EEC states, including France, Italy, Belgium and the Netherlands. On the other hand, the ordoliberal paradigm promoted markets as the most efficient allocation mechanism but recognised that public authorities must create a proper legal environment to ensure fair competition. However, these interventions should not distort market prices and mechanisms. For example, states should oversee mergers and acquisitions but refrain from engaging in fiscal and monetary expansionary policies since they allegedly destabilise markets and spur inflation. This paradigm has been associated with the *Wirtschaftswunder* and the build-up of a social-market economy in post-war Germany[1] (Bonefeld, 2012). While these two economic paradigms strongly influenced EEC sectoral policies, they failed to set up a macroeconomic framework to coordinate European economies at the supranational level.[2] This failure was caused by political and technical factors (Canihac, 2021). First, under De Gaulle's leadership, France refused to delegate macro-economic competencies to the European Commission, which led to the empty chair crisis.[3] Second, economists had technical difficulties in developing a supranational macroeconomic framework because there was a lack of harmonisation of national statistics and methodological disagreements among them.

This battle of ideas shifted in 1969 with the elaboration of the Werner report, which laid down a plan for economic and monetary unification (Maes, 2004). The report oscillated between two policy options: the 'economist' and the 'monetarist' approaches of integration (Dyson & Featherstone, 1999, pp. 29–30). On the one hand, French officials promoted a 'monetarist' approach whereby monetary integration comes with endogenous effects that would foster economic convergence in the currency area. In their perspective, establishing a common currency should precede economic integration. On the other hand, a German-led 'economist' approach argued that EEC economies must reach a certain level of economic homogeneity before merging into a currency zone, or else monetary policy would not be optimal for participant countries. German policy circles considered common fiscal rules as a prerequisite step for diffusing a culture of economic stability within EEC countries before introducing a common currency. In line with this view, the Bundesbank introduced the 'coronation theory', whereby monetary integration should only come after a significant degree of economic convergence. The Werner report released in 1970 embraced arguments of both approaches as it advised parallel monetary and economic integration and proposed a roadmap for implementing monetary union within a decade.

However, the ambitious strategy of parallel integration of the Werner plan was quickly abandoned in the wake of the collapse of the Bretton Woods system in the early 1970s. EEC governments faced new dilemmas in a world of floating exchange rates where states compete to retain and attract capital, which started to circulate freely (Helleiner, 1994). On the one hand, the growing interconnection of their economies called for a common response to this crisis. EEC policies such as the Common Agricultural Policy (CAP) required a stable exchange rate regime among member states (McNamara, 1998). On the other hand, the crisis triggered national economic retrenchment as EEC states were facing stagflation and the collapse of the post-war growth model. The combination of mass unemployment and high inflation also undermined some core tenets of the Keynesian paradigm, which formed the theoretical basis of the *dirigiste* approach. The first European monetary cooperation project, the European 'currency snake', is an outcome of this dilemma. While the snake aimed at limiting the fluctuations of exchange rates, it only amounted to losing monetary coordination because EEC states were strongly attached to their monetary sovereignty and the pursuit of their national economic objectives. In other words, during the 1970s crisis, the lack of ideational convergence and cooperation between national leaders led to a pause in the supranational economic integration. However, the growing interdependencies between European economies and the build-up of international networks between technocrats and civil servants from different EEC countries paved the way for the relaunch of monetary integration, albeit in the very different economic context of the 1980s (Mourlon-Druol, 2012).

A shift in the battle of ideas occurred at the beginning of the 1980s, as EEC governments gradually converged towards anti-inflationary, pro-market policies. In fact, in 1979, they created the European Monetary System (EMS), which imposed tighter coordination of exchange rates by using the Deutschmark, the strongest European currency, as a de facto peg. Under the EMS, governments soon realised that they were facing a strong trade-off between the pursuit of national economic policies and the respect of the EMS rules.[4] This is well exemplified by the 1983 austerity turn in France. François Mitterrand, the first French socialist president, started to implement an expansionary economic policy following his election in 1981. However, this policy made it difficult to keep stable exchange rates towards the Deutschmark because of increasing outwards capital flows towards Germany and a deteriorating trade balance. In March 1983, the French presidency faced two exclusive policy options: either they pursued their strategy of economic expansion but had to leave the EMS, or France remained in the EMS but had to reverse its policy stance. Following the advice of Jacques Delors, who was the finance minister at the time, the French government did a policy U-turn as it implemented fiscal consolidation measures and raised interest rates to keep the franc at parity with the Deutschmark (Lemoine, 2016). This episode revealed the Deutschmark hegemony in the EMS and the ensuing lack of room for economic manoeuvre for other participating countries (Marsh, 1992). In turn, European social-democratic parties gradually abandoned the Keynesian policy framework to the benefit of pro-market solutions (de Waele et al., 2013).

In sum, the post-war European economic integration has been influenced by two competing economic paradigms, which evolved through various crises. The French promoted a *dirigiste* economic model and believed that monetary integration would strengthen the convergence of European economies. Conversely, German ordo-liberals believed that a shared culture of price stability and a stronger economic convergence between EEC countries was necessary before a further delegation of competencies to the supranational level. While these two paradigms were equally influential in the early stages of the EEC, the 1970s crises, the prioritisation of inflation control policies and the convergence of EMS currencies towards the Deutschmark led to a stronger influence of the German policy model in the 1980s (McNamara, 1998).

The Outcome of the Battle of Ideas: An Asymmetrical Euro Area

In the late 1980s, the Delors Commission pursued an integration strategy that paved the way for the creation of the Economic and Monetary Union (EMU) in 1992. On the one hand, the European Commission promoted the 'market revolution' to form new alliances between EEC states. On the other hand, Jacques Delors strategically narrowed the focus of EMU negotiations on monetary integration to bypass past resistances against budgetary and fiscal integration.

First, the Delors Commission mobilised market rationales to build unlikely political alliances and foster support for further economic integration (Jabko, 2006). For example, the 1983 austerity turn convinced French policymakers that, in a world where capital roams freely, market confidence was necessary to spur economic reforms. From this perspective, the delegation of monetary policy to a supranational central bank would strengthen French sovereignty, as it would benefit from the German 'imported' market credibility in the new currency. Moreover, Italian policymakers saw the European monetary integration process as a window of opportunity to 'modernise' their economy by implementing unpopular economic reforms without taking the electoral blame for it *(vincolo estorno)* (Dyson & Featherstone, 1996). Conversely, German elites saw the creation of a common currency as a way to increase trade, and thus German exports, in the EEC. In sum, the Commission used the market as a 'talisman' to bridge the different economic preferences and perceived interests of governments and enlist them into EMU negotiations (Jabko, 2006).

Second, the Delors Commission strategically narrowed down the EMU negotiations on monetary integration. More precisely, the Commission created the 'Delors Committee', which included the governors of the central banks of the 12 EEC states, three expert personalities and Delors himself. This committee was tasked to elaborate a blueprint for the creation of the economic and monetary union. Central bankers formed an 'epistemic community' since they had a high level of ideational agreement on central banking and monetary issues stemming from their continuous policy coordination since the 1970s (Verdun, 1999). Indeed, they believed that the European monetary integration process should follow the successful template of the Bundesbank, which combined a high level of independence from political authorities and the prioritisation of price stability over other monetary objectives (James, 2012).

The enlisting of central bankers was crucial for the success of the EMU negotiations since they played a decisive role in convincing their governments to delegate their monetary competences to a supranational central bank. More generally, the narrow monetary focus helped to downplay the fiscal and budgetary dimension of economic integration and restrict the EMU negotiation to a small and intimate set of actors in the 'core executive territory' (Dyson & Featherstone, 1999, p. 14). In fact, EMU negotiators were isolated from external pressures and sectoral interests because of the historical 'mystique' surrounding monetary policies and the difficulties that interest groups had in calculating the impact of a common monetary policy on their activities (Grossman, 2004). Finally, the creation of the euro was eased by the fall of the Berlin Wall and the collapse of the USSR. In addition to strengthening market ideas, it also gave EEC countries some negotiating advantage over Germany. In fact, EEC leaders made it clear that they would accept the reunification between West and East Germany only if German leaders gave up the

Deutschmark and agreed to the creation of the euro, in order to compensate for Germany's increased power (Dyson, 1994).

In sum, the Delors Commission managed to build unlikely alliances in favour of the creation of the EMU by strategically manipulating a variety of market ideas according to the pre-existing set of interests and dominant economic paradigms in different European countries. In addition, the Delors Committee enrolled central bankers for the creation of a supranational central bank on the condition that it would follow the template of the Bundesbank. In turn, the narrow focus on monetary integration defused the traditional political resistances against budgetary and fiscal integration, which derailed previous integration projects. In other words, the creation of the EMU is an outcome of the historical battle of ideas (Jabko, 2010). On the one hand, monetary integration preceded a significant degree of economic convergence in line with the 'economist' position defended by French policymakers. On the other hand, the institutional architecture of the EMU is strongly influenced by the Bundesbank template and the ordo-liberal principles.

The Persistence of Asymmetries: Fiscal Rules and Financial Integration rather than Economic Government and Social Harmonisation

Following the signing of the Maastricht Treaty, the focus of the battle of ideas shifted to the kind of economic integration that was required for the smooth functioning of the euro area. In fact, the delegation of monetary competencies to the ECB meant that participating states could not adjust their interest or exchange rates to their domestic economic situation any more. According to the optimal currency area theory, wage flexibility, labour mobility or supranational fiscal transfers can compensate for this rigidity (Mundell, 1961). Since the euro area was faring poorly on these criteria while showing a high level of economic heterogeneity, the majority of American macroeconomists believed that the single currency was doomed. More precisely, they underlined that the lack of a significant federal budget would prevent countries regaining economic competitiveness if they were hit by a crisis (Jonung & Drea, 2010). The Delors Commission relied on these arguments during the EMU negotiations to push forward the creation of a *gouvernement économique*, which would pool budgetary resources and promote some degree of social harmonisation. In 1993, the Commission published a White Paper, proposing the coordination of EU unemployment policies and a crisis resolution mechanism financed by joint borrowing (Verdun, 2003).

However, these proposals met with strong resistance in the European Council in general, and from Germany in particular. German leaders worried that a *gouvernement économique* could lead to a 'transfer union', whereby the fiscal resources of core countries would be transferred to the periphery and create risks of moral hazard (Heipertz & Verdun, 2010). Moreover, they feared that the importing of German credibility at the EMU level would lower national interest rates and allow fiscal profligacy in the euro area periphery (Schoeller & Karlsson, 2021). Fiscal profligacy relates to German elites' historical concerns about inflation, which are often wrongly associated with the rise in power of the Nazi regime (Haffert et al., 2021). Furthermore, in a judgment on the Maastricht Treaty, the German Federal Constitutional Court underlined that the transfer of macroeconomic competencies at the supranational level creates a democratic risk because a European demos is lacking (Weiler, 1995). This ruling did not threaten the creation of the euro but it set legal limits for further integration, in particular the creation of a supranational fiscal authority, which constrained the room for manoeuvre of German policymakers during the euro crisis (see below, 'The euro crisis and the battle of ideas'). Finally, the diversity of welfare states in the EMU prevented a significant degree of social policy integration at the supranational level (Scharpf, 1997).

This opposition shifted the debate about European economic governance, which moved from the *gouvernement économique* proposal to a regime of fiscal rules, enshrined within the Stability Pact in 1997. The Pact imposed debt and deficits limits for euro area member states and granted limited sanction powers to the European Commission. Then, the newly elected French Prime Minister, Lionel Jospin, asked to reopen the negotiations for integrating growth-fostering measures and the *gouvernement économique* in the agreement. Despite Jospin's attempts, he only obtained the addition of the word 'growth' to the title of the pact, which became known as the Stability and Growth Pact (Blyth, 2013). More generally, the pre-eminence of concerns over fiscal rectitude and budgetary sustainability rather than the lack of counter-cyclical macroeconomic capacities were in line with the policy recommendations of dominant economic circles in Europe and North America (Helgadóttir, 2016). In the same vein, the compatibility between a uniform set of rules at the European level and the different growth models in the European economy was overlooked (Johnston & Regan, 2018). In particular, EMU fiscal rules were more suited to (northern) countries relying on price competitiveness and strong exports to generate growth than (southern) growth models that rely on debt accumulation and domestic consumption. In sum, the battle of ideas in the 1990s led to an asymmetric EMU whereby monetary policy is delegated to an autonomous supranational central bank while economic coordination is limited to an intergovernmental regime of fiscal discipline.

Against this background, the European institutions promoted less controversial instruments to break the deadlock on fiscal integration and achieve economic convergence. More precisely, the Commission and the ECB believed that the deepening of financial integration would help to correct imbalances between the core and the periphery of the currency area, and thus foster macroeconomic convergence (Dietsch et al., 2018). The underlying idea was that capital would flow from the centre to the periphery of the euro area and, in turn, boost growth and align business cycles between euro area states. In fact, the lack of alignment of business cycles made it impossible for the ECB to set an appropriate interest rate for the various economic situations of member states: think, for example, about booming Ireland and stagnant Germany in the early 2000s. As with many other areas of European economic integration (Scharpf, 1997), financial integration meant that different market regulations were liberalised similarly. In addition, the cross-border activities of the large universal banks from core euro countries were encouraged (Gabor & Ban, 2016). At first sight, this strategy of financial integration was a success: lending from the core to the periphery rose by 350% between 1999 and 2009 and the sovereign interest rates of peripheral euro states converged on that of Germany (Baldwin & Giavazzi, 2015). However, this strategy had two important side effects. On the one hand, capital inflows were not always directed towards productive investments, but, rather, fuelled speculative bubbles in the euro periphery. On the other hand, the risky but lucrative investment strategies of the core euro area financial institutions in the euro periphery and the US subprime market doubled the size of the balance sheets of the banking system between 1999 and 2008, up to the point that many banks became 'too big to fail' (Gabor & Ban, 2016).

In sum, the battle of ideas between different economic paradigms shaped the long process of European economic integration, from the first stages of the common market to the creation of the single currency. The creation of the euro area showed that a compromise was found between different policy options. On the one hand, the prioritisation of monetary integration was in line with the historical preferences of French negotiators, who were also trying to regain economic sovereignty after the 1983 policy turn. On the other hand, the fact that the ECB was modelled on the Bundesbank template and the implementation of a regime of fiscal rules rather than a *gouvernement économique* clearly shows the pre-eminence of the German economic model in Europe since the 1980s. In other words, the battle of ideas resulted in an asymmetrical EMU, which was conducive to the build-up of macroeconomic imbalances that unravelled from 2007 onwards.

THE EURO CRISIS AND THE BATTLE OF IDEAS

Framing the Crisis: The Ordo-Liberal Victory

The first signs of the global financial crisis (GFC) started to materialise in August 2007, when the ECB injected €95 billion of liquidity into the markets after the closure of three BNP Paribas subsidiaries, which were heavily exposed to the US subprime market. This event reflected the nodal role played by the European universal banking model, which came to function as a 'global hedge fund' in interconnected financial markets (Tooze, 2018, p. 90). The lucrative business strategies of EU banks during the formation of the speculative bubbles brought them to the edge of the abyss when confidence among financial market participants evaporated after Lehman Brothers' bankruptcy in September 2008 (Hardie & Howarth, 2013). To avoid the meltdown of their fragile, interconnected, oversized and over-leveraged 'too big to fail' banks, EU governments implemented bailout measures between 2007 and 2009. These bailouts followed an intergovernmental logic and were not coordinated between EU member states; the efficiency of their responses varied significantly. The main reason for the lack of a coordinated supranational response mirrors the battle of ideas underlying the creation of the euro area: German negotiators argued that, in the absence of a common economic government, the fiscal responsibility for the bailouts remained, and should be decided at the national level (Woll, 2014).

These rescue packages came at a heavy price for EU taxpayers: their impact on public debt between 2008 and 2015 is estimated at 4.8% of the GDP of the European Union (Millaruelo & Del-Rio, 2017). Moreover, the banking crisis morphed into a full-fledged economic crisis as banks shrank their credit lines to the real economy, which led to business foreclosures, GDP loss and higher unemployment. In reaction, EU states became 'Keynesian for a year' by stimulating their economy and supporting counter-cyclical economic measures, which increased member states' deficits and debt levels (Blyth, 2013). The extent of this economic support varied according to the economic strength of euro area countries: while the size of the German stimulus was 2% of its GDP, the Italian stimulus was less than 0.1% of its GDP (Tooze, 2018, p.285). In short, the causes of the GFC followed a classic 'boom and bust' pattern: the lucrative but risky business models of financial institutions in general, and the universal European banks in particular, fuelled the US subprime speculative bubble. Then, when the financial crash materialised, domestic political authorities had no choice but to bail out their banking systems, which had become 'too big to fail'. In turn, bailout costs and counter-cyclical measures aggravated deficits and raised the levels of public debt and deficit, which used to be broadly in line with the rules of the Stability and Growth Pact (SGP) before 2007 (Baldwin & Giavazzi, 2015).

Yet, despite these financial roots, the crisis started to be framed as a budgetary and fiscal crisis by core euro area powers from 2010 onwards (Blyth, 2013). In October 2009, the newly elected Greek government announced that previous administrations masked the extent of its public deficit, which reached 12.7% of its GDP. Soon enough, it became clear that, because of structural problems and the impact of the crisis, Greece would not be able to repay its debt at sustainable interest rates; in other words, the country was insolvent (Tooze, 2018, p. 334). While the standard procedure for insolvent countries consists of finding an agreement with creditors to restructure the outstanding debt (usually against the implementation of structural reforms), this option was quickly barred by French and German representatives as well as the ECB (Fontan & Saurugger, 2019). The main reason for this refusal lies in the balance sheets of French and German banks, which were heavily exposed to the Greek debt following their investments in the euro area periphery in the previous 'boom' years (Thompson, 2015). Since restructuring Greek debt would have involved a new round of bank recapitalisation in the core countries of the euro area, at a high political cost, this option was quickly sidelined by core euro area powers, even though the amount of Greek sovereign debt was less than 1.5% of the euro area GDP (Roos, 2019, p. 237).

Instead, on 3 May 2010, euro area countries provided €120 billion of bilateral financial loans to the Greek government, whose disbursement was conditional on the implementation of stringent austerity measures, written down in a Memorandum of Understanding (MoU). So-called 'Troika' expert groups, bringing together IMF, ECB and European Commission agents, were sent to Greece to watch over the implementation of austerity measures. With this agreement, euro area leaders replicated the template of the 'Vienna Initiative', which was implemented in Central and Eastern Europe in late 2008 and early 2009 (Lütz & Kranke, 2014; Tooze, 2018). Indeed, when Romania, Latvia and Hungary were on the brink of collapse following a sudden reverse capital flight, they asked for financial assistance from the EU and the IMF. In reaction, the EU and the IMF offered credit lines to these countries against the implementation of deep austerity cuts monitored by 'Troika' expert groups and the promise not to devalue their currency.

This policy answer is in line with the dominant framing of the crisis, which underlined that the peripheral countries of the euro area took advantage of the single currency for running high levels of public spending instead of improving the competitiveness of their economies. In turn, the difficulties encountered by peripheral countries in refinancing their debt at sustainable rates is only the outcome of the loss of market confidence in the soundness of their economies. The fact that the financial rescue comes attached with austerity measures is in line with this framing. As peripheral countries cannot regain financial markets' confidence without the financial guarantees of core countries, the latter developed this narrative about the causes of the crisis, and therefore their policy solutions, without much challenge.

More generally, this framing also helped to promote crisis solutions that were consistent with ordo-liberal ideas (Matthijs & McNamara, 2015; Matthijs, 2016). If the crisis was diagnosed as being caused by the structural imbalances in the euro area and banks' risky business models, supranational debt pooling ('eurobonds') and a re-regulation of the banking system could have been easily promoted as 'natural' policy solutions to the crisis. Eurobonds proposals were discussed when the financial pressure on euro area peripheral economies started to deepen in early 2010, but they were quickly dismissed by German elites who worried about moral hazard, in line with their previous rebuttals of joined debt issuance proposals. Conversely, framing the crisis as caused by the fiscal profligacy of euro area peripheral countries gave more weight to the arguments of the ordo-liberal economists who lamented about debt sustainability issues and the breach of the SGP rules during the first years of the crisis. For example, participants in the Eurogroup 'last-chance' summits, which took place during multiple weekends between 2010 and 2015, acknowledged that the ECB emphasis on structural reforms and debt sustainability before the crisis increased the recognition of its expertise during the crisis summits (Fontan, 2018). In turn, this increased expert authority allowed central bankers to use the crisis as a window of opportunity as they persuaded elected policymakers to enact the economic reforms (flexibilisation of labour markets, more stringent budgetary rules) for which they had been asking for a decade.

In sum, while the crisis was mainly caused by the risky activities of banks, which triggered macroeconomic imbalances in the euro area, core countries (France, Germany) and euro area institutions (the Eurogroup, the European Commission and the ECB) managed to frame it as a fiscal, budgetary and competiveness crisis, caused by reckless borrowing in the euro area periphery. This framing provided justifications for the implementation of structural reforms and austerity measures against the provision of financial loans in the periphery. In other words, the initial framing of the crisis exposed a clear victory of the partisans of fiscal rules in their battle of ideas against the proponents of more budgetary integration.

Between Austerity and Stabilisation Measures

Euro area negotiators quickly realised that the mechanisms set up to stabilise Greece were not enough to dispel concerns about the sustainability of the euro area institutional design. The increasing spreads[5] between the core and peripheral countries made it clear that financial contagion would only stop if there were credible stabilising mechanisms in the euro area (Gabor & Ban, 2016). Against this background, on 7 May 2010, Jean-Claude Trichet, the ECB president at the time, warned the euro area heads of state that if they did not find a common rescue solution in the next few days, the financial stress on euro area peripheral sovereign debt would trigger another banking collapse in Europe (Gocaj & Meunier, 2013). This warning pushed euro area negotiators to agree over the following weekend (7–9 May 2010) on a €440 billion rescue mechanism (the European Financial Stability Facility/EFSF), which completed the announcement of the first ECB asset purchase programme (Securities Market Programme).

However, the provision of the EFSF credit lines and the activation of the ECB purchases were conditional on the implementation of austerity measures, written down in MoUs and overseen by the 'Troika' expert groups. This strategy of 'constructive ambiguity'[6] shows that euro area leaders found a balance between two logics: strengthening the regime of fiscal austerity in Europe and building up stabilisation mechanisms (Crespy & Vanheuverzwijn, 2019). Financial loans conditioned on the implementation of austerity measures written down in MoUs were used in Ireland (2010), Portugal (2011), Spain (2012), Cyprus (2013) and three times in Greece (2010, 2012, 2015).

The implementation of austerity measures in the bailed-out countries varied according to different levels of ideational convergence, coalition building and administrative capacities (Hardiman et al., 2019). In Ireland and Portugal, pro-reform ministers used loan conditionality to pass measures that were not asked for by the 'Troika' but that they had wanted to implement for a long time whereas in Greece, the lack of administrative capacity and the antagonist strategy of the SYRIZA government slowed down reforms (Moury et al., 2021). The economic performances of the countries that had to implement these rescue plans were not uniform either. Whereas the rapid recovery in Ireland was often used as an example of the success of the 'Troika' strategy, it was mostly caused by exogenous factors such as its already existing export growth model (Brazys & Regan, 2017). In Greece, loans were mostly used to repay existing loans rather than to modernise its ailing economic system: only 5% of the funds of the first two bailouts were directed towards its national budget, and Greek growth remained lacklustre (Roos, 2019). In other words, the main aim of the emergency measures taken to 'rescue' the euro area periphery was to stabilise the banking systems of core powers rather than help these struggling countries to regain competitiveness.

These emergency measures were institutionalised, with larger and permanent structures being built along these initial lines (Braun, 2015): the EFSF was replaced by the European Stability Mechanism (ESM) in 2013 while the ECB under Mario Draghi claimed that it would do 'whatever it takes' to stabilise the euro in 2012 and activated large-scale asset purchases in 2015 (quantitative easing). More generally, the double logic of austerity measures and stabilisation mechanisms shaped the reforms of the euro area between 2010 and 2015. On the one hand, fiscal surveillance was strengthened with the implementation of the European Semester and the Treaty on Stability, Coordination and Governance (TSCG) in 2010 and 2012, respectively. On the other hand, stabilisation mechanisms were improved with the creation of the Banking Union in 2014 and the establishment of the European Fund for Strategic Investments in 2015. These two strands of reform were deeply intertwined during the negotiations. For example, France accepted the TSCG because it was part of a Franco-German compromise whereby Germany accepted the creation of the Banking Union (Fontan & Saurugger, 2019). Germany dictated the pace of reforms as it reluctantly agreed on stabilisation mechanisms and made it clear that they should be tied to stricter fiscal rules (Howarth & Schild, 2021).

This combination reflects well the sets of incentives and constraints of core and peripheral countries. On the one hand, core countries needed to stabilise the euro area peripheral sovereign debt to avoid a collapse of their banking system and, ultimately of the single currency itself. However, core euro states' negotiators were constrained by domestic factors: their electoral constituencies refused debt mutualisation and fiscal transfers. This refusal was driven by long-standing positions against a 'transfer union' and by the framing of the euro area crisis, which highlighted the so-called fiscal profligacy of peripheral states. On the other hand, peripheral countries tried to avoid the implementation of austerity measures because of their large social, economic and political costs (Stuckler & Basu, 2013). Yet, they did not have much room for manoeuvre as the euro area credit lines and the ECB interventions quickly became their only way to refinance themselves at sustainable interest rates. From this perspective, the combination of austerity and stabilisation mechanisms made political sense, albeit it was self-defeating from an economic point of view because austerity measures prevented a fast and strong economic recovery in peripheral countries (Schelkle, 2013; Matthijs & Blyth, 2018).

The Political Impact of the Response to the Euro Area Crisis

The initial framing and the political response to the crisis led to a 'culturalisation' of the economic situation of the peripheral states, which obscured the complex financial mechanisms that caused the financial imbalances to the benefit of a moral understanding of the crisis (Dyson, 2014). This 'culturalisation' is driven by scapegoating discourses, which pin the responsibility of the crisis on the 'moral' behaviour of citizens living in the euro area periphery (Mylonas, 2012). These discourses were performed by political elites in both core and peripheral countries. On the one hand, elites in creditor countries promoted financial loans as an 'act of solidarity' while justifying austerity as a necessary means to restore economic competitiveness in the euro area periphery after years of fiscal profligacy (Closa & Maatsch, 2014; Wallascheck, 2020). For example, Jeroen Dijsselbloem, president of the Eurogroup, claimed that the 'countries of the North have shown solidarity with the countries affected by the crisis ... but you also have obligations. You cannot spend all the money on drinks and women and then ask for help.'[7] On the other hand, domestic elites in peripheral countries were caught between a rock and a hard place, as they needed to legitimise unpopular austerity decisions that symbolised a loss of sovereignty. To do so, they depoliticised the crisis resolution process by framing austerity as a 'remedy' to heal their 'sick' economies (Borriello, 2017). In turn, the 'culturalisation' of the crisis constrained the room for manoeuvre of negotiators during the crisis resolution process as domestic constituencies became increasingly polarised against each other and increasingly refused austerity measures or stabilisation mechanisms (Crespy & Schmidt, 2014).

Moreover, the institutionalisation of the euro area response to the crisis led to political resistance in euro area states as citizens felt that their demands and interests had not been respected. In the periphery, citizens were protesting against the framing of the crisis and the imposition of austerity measures, which caused democratic and societal damage, in addition to a loss of national sovereignty (della Porta & Parks, 2016). In addition, plaintiffs in Italy, Spain and Portugal challenged the austerity measures in front of their constitutional courts, albeit with mixed success: the Portuguese court was the only one to declare many of the austerity measures written down in the MoUs illegal (Saurugger & Fontan, 2019). In core countries, such as Germany and the Netherlands, citizens were worried about the risks of moral hazard and inflation that were linked to the stabilisation mechanisms and the ECB asset purchase programmes. These concerns stemmed directly from the historical construction of German preferences about the EMU (see above, 'The history of the battle of ideas and the origins of EMU imbalances'). In fact, a group of German ordo-liberal activists challenged every ECB asset purchase programme and stabilisation mechanism in front of the Federal Constitutional Court (de Cabanes & Fontan, 2019). Their legal challenges were in line with previous opposition to the creation of the EMU and strongly informed by ordo-liberal principles.

Finally, the measures taken to answer the euro area crisis had strong political consequences in both core and peripheral states. Indeed, the politics of conditionality attached to the financial loans have undermined incumbent governments to the benefit of protest parties (Hopkin, 2020). For example, euro area leaders and the ECB forced Silvio Berlusconi, the former Italian prime minister, to resign in October 2011 because he did not satisfactorily implement the conditionality measures attached to the ECB purchases of its sovereign debt, and he was quickly succeeded by Mario Monti, a former European commissioner (Fontan, 2018). This event shook up the Italian political system and influenced the outcome of the 2013 elections, which paved the way for the electoral rise of the *Movimento 5 Stelle* and the *Lega* (Chiaramonte, 2014). Conversely, in core euro area countries, governments were challenged by protest parties, which complained about the implementation of stabilisation mechanisms. For example, the far-right party, Alternative für Deutschland, was created in the aftermath of the creation of the ESM and the ECB's asset purchase programmes (Grimm, 2015).

In sum, the initial framing of the euro area crisis obfuscated the financial roots of the macro-economic imbalances and put the spotlight on the fiscal and budgetary troubles of peripheral countries, which were caused mainly by the bailouts of their banking systems in 2008–2009. This framing was key to legitimising the political answer to the crisis, which consisted in a simultaneous strengthening of stabilisation mechanisms and fiscal discipline, rather than building up joint-debt mechanisms. Both the framing and the solutions adopted to solve the crisis reflect an asymmetrical power balance in the battle of ideas that took place between euro area countries. Indeed, core countries managed to rule out policy options that were not in line with their interests (debt restructuring, eurobonds, fiscal transfers) and forced austerity measures in the periphery. However, the transnational activities of the European banking system and the strength of market pressures also forced core countries to agree on the creation of new stabilisation mechanisms that were necessary for the survival of the euro area. In other words, the battle of ideas during the euro area crisis did not lead to a radical overhaul of the initial economic paradigm (Schmidt & Thatcher, 2013). Rather, pre-existing tropes (moral hazard, fears of fiscal profligacy) were activated to legitimise the strengthening of fiscal rules while strong conditionality was attached to the activation of stabilisation mechanisms.

CONCLUSION. THE RECOVERY AND RESILIENCE FACILITY: THE EU'S HAMILTONIAN MOMENT?

When the Covid-19 pandemic struck the European continent in March 2020, after months of complacency by Western elites, national economies went into lockdown and regular economic activity was heavily disrupted as both supply and demand shocks were looming. Tensions started to appear between euro area countries because of their unequal economic capacities: in the early stages of the crisis, Germany was able to commit a bigger portion of its GDP in fiscal measures and guarantees than Italy and Spain. European leaders (EU institutions and national governments) feared that this differentiation could increase risks of a break-up of the euro area and political backlash in peripheral countries and started to discuss again the possibility of joint-debt instruments to finance the relief measures. These discussions led to a Franco-German proposal on 18 May 2020, in which the European Commission would raise €500 billion on the markets, in the names of EU countries, and reallocate the funds to the most affected countries.[8]

Initial reactions to this proposal mirrored the fault lines of the euro crisis resolution: Dutch leaders warned about risks of moral hazard and performed 'culturalisation' discourses against Italian 'mismanagement' and an alliance of four self-proclaimed 'frugal' countries (Austria, Denmark, Netherlands and Sweden) blocked the Franco-German proposal. However, a set of concessions made to these countries during the MFF negotiations cleared the path for the Recovery and Resilience Facility (RFF), which will raise €312 billion of joint debt on the markets. Initial projections reveal that grant distribution under the RFF will favour the countries with a limited economic capacity to respond to the crisis. In other words, the EU states crossed their Rubicon as they overcame decades of disagreement on joint-debt instruments, which assume a redistributive dimension between EU countries.

What explains this change and what is its extent? While further empirical research is needed to answer these questions precisely, we propose here three lines of preliminary observations. First, the 'enabling' element of the RFF is, without a doubt, the reversal of German policy preferences (Crespy & Schramm, 2021). Multiple elements can explain this policy turn: since the 2020 crisis was caused by the exogenous outbreak of a global pandemic, the 'moral hazard' and 'fiscal profligacy' tropes could not be easily mobilised to justify the lack of a common EU response. Moreover, learning effects may have occurred as German leaders realised that the strong conditionality and austerity measures created a political backlash and put hostile leaders in power. Furthermore, the change of finance minister might have been conducive to this change, since the social democrat Olaf Scholz succeeded the conservative Wolfgang Schäuble (Karremans, 2020). Second, the ECB faced new policy challenges because of the macroeconomic consequences of the austerity regime that was imposed during the euro crisis. In particular, inflation in the euro area remained below the ECB target despite the large amounts of liquidity injected by the ECB in financial markets (Van Doorslaer & Vermeiren, 2021). This pushed the ECB, which was one of the main proponents of stringent fiscal rules during the euro area crisis, to reverse its policy stance and encourage expansionary fiscal policies for all member states.[9] Third, it is too early to assess the extent of change. The RFF is supposed to be temporary and it has a modest size in light of the gravity of the crisis and in comparison with federal budgets in other currency areas. Moreover, it remains unclear what conditionality will be attached to the RFF, as grant distribution should be tied to the recommendations of the Commission during the European Semester process.

NOTES

1.   The 'economic miracle' refers to the fast economic expansion of West Germany after World War Two.

2.	The *dirigiste* approach was central to the functioning of the Common Agricultural Policy (CAP) whereas ordo-liberals had a prominent role in competition policy.
3.	The empty chair crisis occurred when French President Charles de Gaulle asked French representatives to leave the meetings of the Council of Ministers in 1965.
4.	Mundell's (1961) 'impossible trinity' theorises this dilemma: a country cannot combine at the same time fixed or stable exchange rates with a sovereign monetary policy and free capital movement.
5.	Here, spreads refer to the difference of interest rates between the German sovereign bonds and peripheral states' sovereign bonds. The widening of the spread is an indicator of the increasing lack of confidence of market operators in the ability of peripheral countries to repay their debt.
6.	This strategy aims to curb risks of moral hazard by attaching strong conditionality to the disbursement of loans.
7.	Silvia Amaro, 'Dijsselbloem under fire after saying southern Europe wasted money on "drinks and women"'. CNBC, 22 March 2017 (www.cnbc.com/2017/03/22/dijsselbloem-under-fire-after-saying-southern-europe-wasted-money-on-drinks-and-women.html).
8.	Sam Fleming, Victor Mallet and Guy Chazan, 'Germany and France unite in call for €500bn Europe recovery fund?' *Financial Times*, 18 May 2020 (www.ft.com/content/c23ebc5e-cbf3-4ad8-85aa-032b574d0562).
9.	Isabel Schnabel, 'Unconventional fiscal and monetary policy at the zero lower bound', Keynote speech at the European Fiscal Board 3rd annual conference (www.ecb.europa.eu/press/key/date/2021/html/ecb.sp210226~ff6ad267d4.en.html).

REFERENCES

Baldwin, R., & Giavazzi, F. (2015). *The Eurozone Crisis: A Consensus View of the Causes and a Few Possible Remedies*, Centre for Economic Policy Research (www.voxeu.org/content/eurozone-crisis-consensus-view-causes-and-few-possible-solutions).

Blyth, M. (2013). *Austerity: The History of a Dangerous Idea*, Oxford University Press.

Bonefeld, W. (2012). 'Freedom and the strong state: on German ordoliberalism'. *New Political Economy*, 17(5), 633–656.

Borriello, A. (2017). '"There is no alternative": how Italian and Spanish leaders' discourse obscured the political nature of austerity'. *Discourse & Society*, 28(3), 241–261.

Braun, B. (2015). 'Governing the future: the European Central Bank's expectation management during the Great Moderation'. *Economy and Society*, 44(3), 367–391.

Brazys, S., & Regan, A. (2017). 'The politics of capitalist diversity in Europe: explaining Ireland's divergent recovery from the euro crisis'. *Perspectives on Politics*, 15(2), 411–427.

Canihac, H. (2021). 'Programming the Common Market: the making and failure of a '*dirigiste*' Europe, 1957–1967'. *Contemporary European History*, 30(3), 383–397.

Chiaramonte, A. (2014). 'The elections of 2013: a tsunami with no winners'. *Italian Politics*, 29(1), 45–63.

Closa, C., & Maatsch, A. (2014). 'In a spirit of solidarity? Justifying the European Financial Stability Facility (EFSF) in national parliamentary debates'. *JCMS: Journal of Common Market Studies*, 52(4), 826–842.

Crespy, A., & Schmidt, V. (2014). 'The clash of titans: France, Germany and the discursive double game of EMU reform'. *Journal of European Public Policy*, 21(8), 1085–1101.

Crespy, A., & Schramm, L. (2021). 'Breaking the budgetary taboo: German preference formation in the EU's response to the Covid-19 crisis'. *German Politics*, 1–22.

Crespy, A., & Vanheuverzwijn, P. (2019). 'What "Brussels" means by structural reforms: empty signifier or constructive ambiguity?' *Comparative European Politics*, 17(1), 92–111.

de Cabanes, A., & Fontan, C. (2019). 'La Cour de Justice face à Gauweiler: La mise en récit de l'indépendance de la BCE'. In A. Bailleux, E. Bernard & S. Jacquot (eds), *Les Récits judiciaires de l'Europe*, Bruylant, 169–191 (https://dial.uclouvain.be/pr/boreal/object/boreal:222654).

de Waele, J.-M., Escalona, F., & Vieira, M. (eds) (2013). *The Palgrave Handbook of Social Democracy in the European Union*, Palgrave Macmillan.

della Porta, D., & Parks, L. (2016). 'Social movements, the European crisis, and EU political opportunities'. *Comparative European Politics*, 1–18 (https://doi.org/10.1057/s41295-016-0074-6).

Dietsch, P., Claveau, F., & Fontan, C. (2018). *Do Central Banks Serve the People?* Polity Press.

Diez, T. (2001). 'Europe as a discursive battleground'. *Cooperation and Conflict*, 36(1), 5–38.

Dyson, K. (1994). *Elusive Union: The Process of Economic and Monetary Union in Europe*, Longman.

Dyson, K. H. F. (2014). *States, Debt, and Power: 'Saints' and 'Sinners' in European History and Integration* (1st edn), Oxford University Press.

Dyson, K., & Featherstone, K. (1996). 'Italy and EMU as a "vincolo esterno": empowering the technocrats, transforming the state'. *South European Society and Politics*, 1(2), 272–299.

Dyson, K. H. F., & Featherstone, K. (1999). *The Road to Maastricht: Negotiating Economic and Monetary Union*, Oxford University Press.

Fontan, C. (2018). 'Frankfurt's double standard: The politics of the European Central Bank during the Eurozone crisis'. *Cambridge Review of International Affairs*, 1–21.

Fontan, C., & Saurugger, S. (2019). 'Between a rock and a hard place: preference formation in France during the Eurozone crisis'. *Political Studies Review*, 18(4), 507–524 .

Gabor, D., & Ban, C. (2016). 'Banking on bonds: the new links between states and markets'. *JCMS: Journal of Common Market Studies*, 54(3), 617–635.

Gocaj, L., & Meunier, S. (2013). 'Time will tell: the EFSF, the ESM, and the euro crisis'. *Journal of European Integration*, 35(3), 239–253.

Grimm, R. (2015). 'The rise of the German Eurosceptic party Alternative für Deutschland, between ordoliberal critique and popular anxiety'. *International Political Science Review*, 36(3), 264–278.

Grossman, E. (2004). 'Bringing politics back in: rethinking the role of economic interest groups in European integration'. *Journal of European Public Policy*, 11(4), 637–654.

Haffert, L., Redeker, N., & Rommel, T. (2021). 'Misremembering Weimar: hyperinflation, the Great Depression, and German collective economic memory'. *Economics & Politics*, 33(3), 664–686.

Hardie, I., & Howarth, D. (2013). *Market-Based Banking and the International Financial Crisis*, Oxford University Press.

Hardiman, N., Spanou, C., Araújo, J. F., & MacCarthaigh, M. (2019). 'Tangling with the Troika: "domestic ownership" as political and administrative engagement in Greece, Ireland, and Portugal'. *Public Management Review*, 21(9), 1265–1286.

Heipertz, M., & Verdun, A. (2010). *Ruling Europe: The Politics of the Stability and Growth Pact*, Cambridge University Press.

Helgadóttir, O. (2016). 'The Bocconi boys go to Brussels: Italian economic ideas, professional networks and European austerity'. *Journal of European Public Policy*, 23(3), 392–409.

Helleiner, E. (1994). *States and the Reemergence of Global Finance: From Bretton Woods to the 1990s*, Cornell University Press.

Hopkin, J. (2020). *Anti-System Politics: The Crisis of Market Liberalism in Rich Democracies*, Oxford University Press.

Howarth, D. J., & Loedel, P. H. (2005). *The European Central Bank: The New European Leviathan?* Palgrave Macmillan.

Howarth, D., & Schild, J. (2021). 'Nein to "Transfer Union": the German brake on the construction of a European Union fiscal capacity'. *Journal of European Integration*, 43(2), 207–224.

Jabko, N. (2006). *Playing the Market: A Political Strategy for Uniting Europe, 1985–2005* (1st edn), Cornell University Press.

Jabko, N. (2010). 'The hidden face of the euro'. *Journal of European Public Policy*, 17(3), 318–334.

James, H. (2012). *Making the European Monetary Union*, Harvard University Press.

Johnston, A., & Regan, A. (2018). 'Introduction: is the European Union capable of integrating diverse models of capitalism?' *New Political Economy*, 23(2), 145–159.

Jonung, L., & Drea, E. (2010). 'It can't happen, it's a bad idea, it won't last: U.S. economists on the EMU and the euro, 1989–2002'. *Econ Journal Watch*, 7(1).

Karremans, J. (2020). 'Political alternatives under European economic governance: evidence from German budget speeches (2009–2019)'. *Journal of European Public Policy*, 28(4), 510–531.

Lemoine, B. (2016). *L'Ordre de la dette: Les infortunes de l'État et la prospérité du marché*, La Découverte.

Lütz, S., & Kranke, M. (2014). 'The European rescue of the Washington Consensus? EU and IMF lending to Central and Eastern European countries'. *Review of International Political Economy*, 21(2), 310–338.

Maes, I. (2004). 'On the origins of the Franco-German EMU controversies'. *European Journal of Law and Economics*, 17(1), 21–39.

Marsh, D. (1992). *The Bundesbank: The Bank That Rules Europe*, Heineman.

Matthijs, M. (2016). 'Powerful rules governing the euro: the perverse logic of German ideas'. *Journal of European Public Policy*, 23(3), 375–391.

Matthijs, M., & Blyth, M. (2018). 'When is it rational to learn the wrong lessons? Technocratic authority, social learning, and euro fragility'. *Perspectives on Politics*, 16(1), 110–126 (https://doi.org/10.1017/S1537592717002171).

Matthijs, M., & McNamara, K. (2015). 'The euro crisis' theory effect: northern saints, southern sinners, and the demise of the eurobond'. *Journal of European Integration*, 37(2), 229–245.

McNamara, K. R. (1998). *The Currency of Ideas: Monetary Politics in the European Union*. Cornell University Press.

Millaruelo, A., & Del-Rio, A. (2017). 'The cost of interventions in the financial sector since 2008 in the EU countries'. *Banco de España Analytical Articles*, 9, 17.

Mourlon-Druol, E. (2012). *A Europe Made of Money: The Emergence of the European Monetary System*, Cornell University Press.

Moury, C., Ladi, S. L., Cardoso, D., & Gago, A. (2021). *Capitalising on Constraint: Bailout Politics in Eurozone Countries*, Manchester University Press.

Mundell, R. A. (1961). 'A theory of optimum currency areas'. *The American Economic Review*, 51(4), 657–665.

Mylonas, Y. (2012). 'Media and the economic crisis of the EU: the "culturalization" of a systemic crisis and *Bild-Zeitung*'s Framing of Greece'. *TripleC: Communication, Capitalism & Critique. Open Access Journal for a Global Sustainable Information Society*, 10(2), 646–671.

Parsons, C. (2002). 'Showing ideas as causes: the origins of the European Union'. *International Organization*, 56(1), 47–84.

Roos, J. (2019). *Why Not Default? The Political Economy of Sovereign Debt*, Princeton University Press.

Saurugger, S., & Fontan, C. (2019). 'The judicialisation of EMU politics: resistance to the EU's new economic governance mechanisms at the domestic level'. *European Journal of Political Research*, 58(4), 1066–1087.

Scharpf, F. W. (1997). 'Economic integration, democracy and the welfare state'. *Journal of European Public Policy*, 4(1), 18–36.

Schelkle, W. (2013). 'Fiscal integration by default'. In P. Genschel & M. Jachtenfuchs (eds), *Beyond the Regulatory Polity?* Oxford University Press, 105–123.

Schmidt, V. A., & Thatcher, M. (eds) (2013). *Resilient Liberalism in Europe's Political Economy*, Cambridge University Press.

Schoeller, M. G., & Karlsson, O. (2021). 'Championing the "German model"? Germany's consistent preferences on the integration of fiscal constraints'. *Journal of European Integration*, 43(2), 191–206.

Stuckler, D., & Basu, S. (2013). *The Body Economic: Why Austerity Kills. Recessions, Budget Battles, and the Politics of Life and Death*, Basic Books.

Thompson, H. (2015). 'Germany and the euro-zone crisis: the European reformation of the German banking crisis and the future of the euro'. *New Political Economy*, 20(6), 851–870.

Tooze, J. A. (2018). *Crashed: How a Decade of Financial Crises Changed the World*, Viking.

Van Doorslaer, H., & Vermeiren, M. (2021). 'Pushing on a string: monetary policy, growth models and the persistence of low inflation in advanced capitalism'. *New Political Economy*, 26(5), 797–816.

Verdun, A. (1999). 'The role of the Delors Committee in the creation of EMU: an epistemic community?' *Journal of European Public Policy*, 6(2), 308–328.

Verdun, A. (2003). 'La nécessité d'un « gouvernement économique » dans une UEM asymétrique: Les préoccupations françaises sont-elles justifiées?' *Politique européenne*, 10(2), 11.

Wallaschek, S. (2020). 'Framing solidarity in the euro crisis: A comparison of the German and Irish media discourse'. *New Political Economy*, 25(2), 231–247.

Warlouzet, L. (2019). 'The EEC/EU as an evolving compromise between French dirigism and German ordoliberalism (1957–1995)'. *JCMS: Journal of Common Market Studies*, 57(1), 77–93.

Weiler, J. H. H. (1995). 'Does Europe need a constitution? Demos, telos and the German Maastricht decision'. *European Law Journal*, 1(3), 219–258.

Woll, C. (2014). *The Power of Inaction: Bank Bailouts in Comparison*, Cornell University Press.

PART II

Policy changes

5. The CAP post-2020 reform and the EU budget process

Peter H. Feindt, Pascal Grohmann and Astrid Häger

INTRODUCTION

The Common Agricultural Policy (CAP) has traditionally been one of the most prominent EU policies. Since the foundation of the European Communities, decision-making on the CAP has been closely intertwined with budgetary considerations at the European level (Ackrill and Kay, 2006). The Treaty of Rome of 1957 devoted a special section to agriculture (Arts 38–47, now Arts 38–44 of the Treaty on the Functioning of the European Union (TFEU)) which stipulated the inclusion of agricultural products into the common market and the establishment of a common agricultural and fisheries policy. This enabled the creation of specific provisions for the internal market for agricultural products and additional policies to achieve the five goals of the CAP stated in Art. 39(1) of the Rome Treaty (now Art. 39(1) TFEU): increase agricultural productivity, ensure a fair standard of living for the agricultural community, stabilize markets, assure availability of supplies, ensure supplies reach consumers at reasonable prices. Consequently, beginning in the early 1960s, a broadening array of agricultural products were folded into a system of product-specific market orders which allowed for a high degree of intervention, in particular through the setting of guaranteed minimum prices for products originating inside the EU, threshold prices for imports, variable import levies, intervention buying and export subsidies (Grant, 1997; Greer, 2005).[1] The main purpose was to provide income support to farmers (Daugbjerg and Swinbank, 2016) and was justified as necessary to achieve the other goals, in particular food security.

While this system was originally expected to pay for itself, in particular through import taxes, it stimulated production, insulated producers from price signals and allowed otherwise uncompetitive producers to stay in the market. The effect was increasing surpluses that triggered intervention buying and necessitated further expenses for stockholding and export subsidies, demanding an ever-larger share of the EU budget (Grant, 1997; Greer, 2005). Throughout the 1980s, the CAP made up around 60 per cent of the entire EU budget (see Figure 5.1), despite various attempts at implementing budget stabilizers. During this period, budgetary concerns were considered the dominant driver for reforms of the CAP (Moyer and Josling, 1990). A series of reforms since 1992 – intended to enable the establishment of the WTO and later the EU Eastern enlargement, besides addressing budgetary issues – have progressively replaced income support through market intervention with direct payments to agricultural producers (Daugbjerg and Swinbank, 2011). Since the beginning of these reforms, the share of the CAP in the overall budget has generally seen a continuous decline while roughly maintaining its nominal size since the Eastern enlargement of 2005/2007. Between 2013 and 2020 the EU spent more than 50 billion euros per year on the CAP, or about 37 per cent of the overall budget (see Figure 5.1).

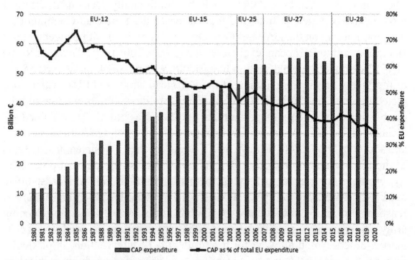

Source: European Commission, 2021.

Figure 5.1   *CAP expenditure in total EU expenditure (current prices), 1980–2020*

As these figures illustrate, negotiations on the overall EU budget and the CAP are closely interlinked by default. As a consequence, policy feedback effects from the CAP have had significant impacts on the trajectory of the EU budget. First and foremost, the CAP provides very visible benefits to eligible farmers in the EU and less visible benefits from significant spill-over effects to landowners and operators upstream and downstream agricultural value chains. These benefits create strong incentives and a common purpose for the formation of interest groups with a focus on their continuation. Accordingly, groups that profit directly or indirectly from the CAP have become a powerful constituency for whom dedicated agricultural ministries and the Directorate General for Agriculture and Rural Development (DG Agri) provide multiple entry points to the EU's multilevel system (creating organizational policy feedback). This agricultural policy community needs a strong CAP budget to pursue its mainly redistributional policy aims, especially since different stakeholders – in particular different subsectors from different member states – compete for the distribution of a limited budget within the CAP (Daugbjerg, 1999). However, while farm income support is enshrined as a policy objective in the TFEU, its political legitimacy – at least in the form provided by the CAP – has come under increasing scrutiny for three reasons:

- the absence of a well-defined policy target (European Court of Auditors, 2018, pp. 38ff.);
- the lack of a link between the intervention and the purported rationale – most of the farm payments are linked to acreage rather than neediness of recipients (European Court of Auditors, 2018, p. 48);
- the lack of efficiency – a significant share of farm payments is passed on to landowners and other market partners (WBAE, 2018, pp. 32f.).

At the same time, other demands on the EU budget have become more urgent. Inside the agricultural policy arena, calls abound to use the available budget to address pressing concerns around the environmental and climate impacts of farming, the welfare of production animals and public health risks from antibiotic use, zoonosis and unhealthy diets (Pe'er et al., 2020). At the same time, new challenges such as migration and the dual climate and digital transformation require investments and compete with the CAP – and even within the CAP – for funds (see Heinelt and Münch, Chapter 1 in this volume). Finally, in times of stretched public budgets – such as caused by the Covid-19 crisis – scrutiny of large policy expenses tends to increase in general.

Against this background, the outcome of the negotiations over the CAP budget and policy design for the funding period 2021–2027 appears as a puzzle. The CAP community managed to deflect cuts to the CAP budget (at least in nominal terms) and to avoid a strong steer to link the farm payments to ambitious outcomes that would effectively support overarching EU aims such as the Green Deal or the digital transformation. Instead, the agreements give ample leeway to member states in the design of their national strategic plans (NSP), which is the envelope policy framework for the national implementation of the CAP. From 2023, member states have significant discretion over various aspects of the direct payments that affect their distribution among different types of producers and can select from a broad menu of policy measures to adopt rural development policies tailored to their preferences.

In the remainder of this chapter, we deploy an interpretive approach to explain this outcome. In doing so, we emphasize the importance of 'struggles over ideas' (Stone, 2002, p. 11) about the cognitive and normative foundations constituting a policy field, which are generated, articulated, deliberated and/or contested in policy discourses. We pay particular attention to competing interpretations of the policy situation, including the problem constructions, causal attributions, moral evaluations and policy prescriptions (cf. Entman, 1993).

We first review the prevalent ideas and discourses that legitimize large EU spending on agriculture before discussing how the specific context of the budget and CAP process for the Multiannual Financial Framework (MFF) 2021–2027 has affected these legitimizing discourses. We then provide a detailed account of the intertwined budget and CAP legislative processes as an ideational struggle between competing discourse coalitions. We finally discuss how the precarious situation of the EU has affected interpretations of the CAP, CAP-related budget struggles and actual CAP policies, and conclude with considerations of why the CAP is still dominantly interpreted as being essential for an EU at the crossroads and why neither the Covid-19 pandemic nor the European Green Deal had major effects on the ideational and policy trajectory of the CAP.

IDEAS AND DISCOURSES LEGITIMIZING LARGE EU SPENDING ON AGRICULTURE

In this section, we deploy a discursive institutionalist perspective (Schmidt, 2018) to explain the historical development of the relation between EU budget processes and CAP decision-making. Since the inception of the CAP, powerful policy discourses have provided cognitive arguments for the relevance of EU spending on agriculture and normative arguments for its compliance with established norms. They have also enabled the communication among the policy community and legitimized large CAP budgets.

Over the course of its development, three distinct discourses have shaped and legitimized the CAP: agricultural productivism, market liberalism and multifunctionalism (Feindt, 2018). They share an interpretation of the agricultural sector as exceptional and as requiring special treatment, albeit for different reasons (Daugbjerg and Feindt, 2017). A *productivist or mercantilist discourse* promoting a 'state-assisted agriculture' (Potter and Tilzey, 2005) became dominant during the negotiations on the formation of the European Economic Community (EEC) in the 1950s and moulded the ideational foundations of the CAP (Knudsen, 2009). It emphasizes the strategic importance and special needs of agricultural producers who contribute to a common good, food security, but suffer from structural income disadvantages which should be addressed through public policy (Coleman, 1998). This theory of a structural farm income problem lies beneath the objectives of the CAP in Arts 38–47 of the Treaty of Rome.

The Treaty of Rome also provided the general framework for budget-making in the European Communities (Ackrill and Kay, 2006). Art. 199 (later Art. 268) of the Treaty on the European Community (TEC) established the balanced budget rule (BBR), later transferred to Art. 310 TFEU. It requires that revenues and expenditures must be balanced. Annual budgets were proposed by the European Commission, discussed by the Assembly (later: European Parliament) and decided by the Council (Ackrill, 2000).

The establishment of the CAP from 1962 immediately affected both revenues and expenditures of the EEC, creating a specific interdependence between sectoral policy aims and budget policy. Intervention purchase, storage and export subsidies required expenses for an expanding range of products with guaranteed prices, while the variable import levy was a major source of revenue (Grant, 1997). However, over time, the intervention logic of the CAP created a goal conflict between farm income support and the BBR. Since guaranteed prices stimulated agricultural production, market prices came under downward pressure. Consequently, expenses for market intervention increased continuously while lower imports reduced revenues from the variable import levy (Ackrill and Kay, 2006). While the EC's traditional own resources, such as customs duties and sugar levies generated from common policies, were initially sufficient for balancing the budget, the effects of the CAP, together with expanded competencies, resulted in an increased need for additional funds.

Due to the high share of the CAP in the overall EU budget, this imbalance repeatedly led to serious budgetary and European integration crises (Ackrill and Kay, 2006, pp. 120–126). The 'empty chair crisis', that is, the French delegation's absence from Council meetings in 1965 and 1966, was preceded by the Commission's attempts under Walter Hallstein to claim the full amount of member states' revenues from internal tariffs to finance common policies, mainly the CAP. The decisions on own resources in 1970 led to heated discussions after the accession of the United Kingdom in 1973, resulting in a formal rebate mechanism for the United Kingdom due to its relatively small agricultural sector. As the CAP experienced a series of budget overruns and its share of the total budget reached more than 70 per cent in the mid 1980s (see Figure 5.1), the EC established rules for financial discipline to avoid a budgetary collapse. After extended negotiations at the highest level, accompanied by intensive farmers' protests, the Fontainebleau Agreement of 1984 included an 'agricultural guideline' limiting the growth rate of CAP expenditures to the growth rate of its own resources. However, neither the Fontainebleau

Agreement nor the CAP's 'stabilizer' reform in the 1988 Brussels Decisions achieved the desired balancing of the budget.

By the mid 1980s, the repeated budget issues, accompanied by reports about system-endemic fraud, had created a sense of crisis surrounding the CAP (Grant, 1997). Tensions with trading partners over border protection and export subsidies, along with reports about negative environmental impacts of agriculture, undermined the ability of the productivist discourse to legitimize the CAP budget, as reflected in a landmark 'Green Paper' by the Commission (1985). The 'state-assisted agriculture' paradigm was first challenged by a *market-liberal discourse*, which is based on cognitive ideas that question the farming sector's need for special treatment and emphasize its ability to compete with other sectors for resources (Coleman et al., 2004). The ensuing normative ideas centre around the role of policymaking in ensuring the functioning of markets, for example, by means of trade liberalization. Market-liberal ideas pose a direct challenge to large public budgets in general, and to a large CAP budget in particular.

The *multifunctionalist discourse* developed in response to the ascent of market-liberal ideas (Erjavec and Erjavec, 2015; Feindt, 2018). Here, cognitive ideas revolve around the notion that agriculture produces not only market-able products such as food and raw materials, but also public goods such as attractive landscapes and diverse habitats. Normative ideas emphasize a duty of farmers to maintain these public goods and act as stewards of the landscape and its ecosystem functions. The policy framework must then enable and remunerate farmers for the provision of public goods, in particular environ-mental, climate and animal protection. Multifunctional ideas can provide new justifications for a significant CAP budget but require fundamental changes in its intervention logic and instrumentation.

The 1992 reform, named after the Irishman Ray MacSharry, EU Commissioner for Agriculture from 1989 until 1993, represented the first step in a series of 'cumulative reinterpretations of the CAP' (Feindt, 2018) which also affected the interlinkages between budget and CAP processes. The MacSharry reform partially replaced income support through market interven-tion with direct income transfers, which were linked to the production of certain agricultural plants and farm animals. This mixture of market liberalization and continuing state support constituted a compromise between market-liberal and productivist ideas (Daugbjerg, 1999; Skogstad, 1998). This semi-liberalization was sufficient to enable an agreement at the Uruguay Round negotiations under the General Agreement on Tariffs and Trade (GATT), which had begun in 1986 and had collapsed in 1990 over disagreement on the protectionist CAP (Daugbjerg, 2017). A budget ceiling and financial discipline mechanisms ensured budgetary predictability. While the CAP's share of the EU budget was slightly reduced to less than 50 per cent, agricultural-productivist ideas still dominated its composition. However, the new instrument – direct transfer payments – made farm income support more visible, which in turn increased the need to justify the use of ample public resources (Daugbjerg, 2003).

For this purpose, the Austrian Franz Fischler, Agriculture Commissioner from 1995 until 2004, strategically augmented the multifunctional agriculture discourse, as in the Cork Declaration on Rural Development in 1996, a land-mark event in forming a broad discourse coalition. To reinforce this strategy, Agenda 2000, adopted in 1999, created an 'Integrated Rural Development Policy' (IRDP), mostly through repackaging existing programmes which shared co-financing arrangements between the EU and member states. In 2005, this 'second pillar' of the CAP was constituted as a distinct finan-cial mechanism, the European Agricultural Fund for Rural Development (EAFRD), which went into operation in 2007 and finances the EU's contri-bution to member states' rural development programmes (RDPs).[2] Otherwise, Agenda 2000 continued the reform path of the MacSharry reform (Ackrill, 2000) through further reduction of intervention prices, thereby reflecting market-liberal ideas, and increased support via direct income transfers, now called direct payments, following agricultural productivism (Feindt, 2018).

At the same time, the dynamics of EU budget discussions changed against the backdrop of the projected Eastern enlargement. While EU expenditure ceilings had grown in the first two five-year financial perspectives, which had to be established after 1988 and set the annual budgets for the policy areas, they stagnated at 1.27 per cent of GNI in 1999 (Ackrill and Kay, 2006). Accordingly, budget debates revolved around maintaining or even cutting budget ceilings, which made the Agenda 2000 reform 'a case of budget con-straining the CAP' (Ackrill, 2000, p. 17).

The Fischler reform of 2003 bundled the various product-related direct payments into a 'Single Farm Payment' which was largely decoupled from production and based on historical payment levels – a further liberalization of markets while maintaining income support. 'Cross-compliance' rules – an expression of multifunctional ideas – tied their receipt to compliance with EU Directives in the areas of health, the environment and animal welfare, as well as new rules of good agricultural and ecological practice (Swinbank and Daugbjerg, 2006). Legally, cross-compliance responded to new 'horizontal' obligations in the reformed Treaty that all EU policies should contribute to sus-tainable development and high levels of environmental, animal and consumer protection (Art. 11 and Art. 114(3) TFEU). Politically, cross-compliance served to buffer the legitimacy of farm payments by linking them in a visible manner to the provision of public goods.

The following mid-term 'Health Check' of 2008 was not linked to major budget decisions. It mainly extended the established reform path to further sectors and introduced funding to address 'new challenges', following multifunctionalist ideas: climate change, biodiversity, water management, and – in a productivist response to an ongoing milk price crisis – support for dairy farmers. Budgetary leeway was increased because high world-market prices for farm products allowed the reduction of spending on export subsidies and intervention purchases (Daugbjerg and Swinbank, 2011).

The 2013 Ciolos reform of the CAP for the period 2014–2020 was the first under the new institutional rules of the Lisbon Treaty, which altered the link between the budget process and CAP decision-making (Benedetto, 2013). Art. 312 TFEU requires the adoption of a Multiannual Financial Framework (MFF) for a period of at least five years (para. 1) that determines annual ceilings for categories of expenditure which correspond to 'the Union's major sectors of activity' (para. 3). The MFF shall be adopted as a regulation, with unanimity in the Council after consent from the Parliament by a majority of its members (para. 2).[3] Decision-making on the CAP for the first time followed the ordinary legislative procedure with co-decision of the Parliament (Art. 43(2) TFEU).[4]

Negotiations on the CAP 2014–2020 and on the MFF took place simultaneously, with important implications for the outcome (Matthews, 2015). First, the MFF negotiations were marked by the aftermath of the financial crisis 2007/2008 and the ensuing austerity agenda. This created strong pressure to create a narrative that could legitimize the continuation of a large CAP budget. Defying expectations of significant cuts to the CAP budget, the nominal level of expenses was generally defended and the decline in the CAP's budget share corresponded to the long-term trend (Greer, 2013). Second, the tandem negotiations led to a delay in the process, as the EP, now with co-decision powers, refused to adopt any decisions on the CAP until the expenditure ceilings had been established as part of the MFF. As a result, there was no condensed negotiation window, which favoured status quo positions over radical reformist views (Greer, 2017). Third, some aspects of the CAP were integrated into the MFF negotiations, such as on partial convergence of direct payments across member states or the introduction of 'greening requirements' for 30 per cent of the direct payments. While this fixed the general policy architecture, determining the relevant details was left to the ordinary legislative process, with leading roles of the Commission's Directorate-General for Agriculture and Rural Affairs (DG Agri), the Agriculture Council and the EP's Committee on Agriculture (COMAGRI). In these arenas, productivist ideas were still particularly strong (Roederer-Rynning, 2015), dominating coordinative discourse and favouring status quo interests. As a result, the attempt to use the budget process as leverage to achieve a 'greening' of the CAP failed (Hart, 2015). Ample use of multifunctionalist ideas in communicative discourse was widely criticized as 'greenwashing' (Alons, 2017).

THE CONTEXT OF THE BUDGET AND CAP PROCESS FOR THE PERIOD 2021–2027

Negotiations about the CAP for the funding period 2021–2027 took place against a background of increased politicization and uncertainty. A generally increasing politicization of EU policies has been driven by issue salience, actor expansion and actor polarization (Grande et al., 2016). These dynamics are also at work in the CAP. However, the politicization dynamics surrounding the CAP differ from those affecting other EU policy areas. Here, politicization is driven less by struggles over the level of European integration, national identity and mutual solidarity (cf. Münch, Chapter 8 in this volume) than by an intensification of the long-standing struggle between the competing discourse coalitions – agricultural productivism, market liberalism and multifunctionalism – indicating a high degree of politicization (Feindt et al., 2021). In addition, the political cleavage between rural and urban areas regained political significance during the 2010s with the rise of right-wing populist movements that feed on rural decline and resentment against 'urban elites', sentiments that have been addressed and reinforced by electoral strategies of conservative and right-wing parties (Mamonova and Franquesa, 2020; Sheingate and Greer, 2021).

Preparations for the CAP for the funding period 2021–2027 started in 2017 in a context characterized by relatively flush public budgets and a consensus to increase the EU budget. The broader discourse emphasized the importance of 'new challenges' to the EU, often implying that budgets should be shifted from old priorities like farm support to new priorities such as migration, innovation and growth (see Heinelt and Münch, Chapter 1 in this volume). However, several factors reinforced the productivist discourse. First, a destabilizing international context – the Russian annexation of Crimea, Brexit and Trumpism (accompanied by predictions of 'the end of the West') – provided discursive opportunities to highlight the importance of domestic production for ensuring food security. The Russian import embargo of farm products from the EU hit many agricultural producers hard since the loss of export markets – despite legal and illegal workarounds – increased domestic supply and created structural downward pressure on farm gate prices (European Parliament, 2017). The spread of swine flu from East to West led major importers, in particular China, to close their markets to pig products from the affected countries (Bellini, 2021).

Simultaneously, the multifunctional discourse was reinforced by the EU's commitment to reduce its greenhouse gas emissions under the Paris Agreement and broader societal pressure to address climate change, epitomized by the Fridays for Future movement. From 2017 onwards, the contribution of intensive farming practices to biodiversity loss became a key topic in CAP debates (Pe'er et al., 2020).

Conflicts between 'winners' and 'losers' of globalization (Kriesi, 2014) play an important part in the agricultural policy of the EU. On which side an individual farmer is positioned depends mainly on the sector and the location of the farm, which determine the production possibilities and competitiveness. 'Winners' and 'losers' of globalization are therefore spatially clustered at the level of agricultural regions. The ensuing conflicts between different national and regional interests have shaped the politics of the CAP since its inception. For example, the struggle between Germany and France over the setting of the intervention price for wheat in the 1960s carried on for years and involved the highest level of governance (Ackermann, 1970; Knudsen, 2009; Tracy, 1989). Since the early 1990s, the balance has tilted towards the more competitive sectors and regions, at least in the area of the agricultural market orders. The liberalization steps since the MacSharry reform have removed much of the border protection that agricultural producers in the EU had enjoyed. Internal market prices were increasingly aligned with global market prices. In the dairy sector, milk quotas were phased out by 2015 with the expectation of growing export markets, which, however, did not materialize. As a result, the liberalization of agricultural markets produced fewer 'winners' and more 'losers' than predicted.

The policy changes in favour of competitive agricultural sectors and regions were balanced by changes to the system of direct payments and the introduction of new types of state aid. The MacSharry reform had introduced direct payments to compensate for lower market prices. A complicated and differential system meant that farms in more productive locations tended to receive higher direct payments. The Fischler reform not only decoupled the direct payments from production, but also required that direct payments within member states should converge towards a unitary national 'basic premium', benefitting farms in less productive areas. The Cioloş reform provided further flexibility to pay higher premiums for smaller farms and reduce payments for very large farms. Similarly, the programmes for extensive agriculture, which have been introduced since 1992 and mostly benefit less-competitive regions, can also be seen as an attempt at balancing the regional distribution of the benefits from the CAP. However, the territorial impacts of the CAP are varied, often indirect and complex (Shucksmith et al., 2005).

Although the 'populist challenge' (Kriesi, 2014) has not openly and directly affected the CAP, it constitutes an important context factor for the CAP reform debate between 2017 and 2021. Right-wing and authoritarian populism has been particularly successful in rural and peripheral areas, fuelled by a general sense of disenfranchisement and alienation from the established political system, which has become manifest in many rural areas in Europe and beyond

(Scoones et al., 2021). Rural populations affected by the loss of local employment or its replacement with often precarious seasonal or migrant workers, the accumulation of land and other rural assets by corporate and financial institutions and the decline of state-funded infrastructure have often turned to political forces that exploit sentiments of frustration and deprivation by blaming 'urban', 'cosmopolitan' or 'foreign' elites (Mamonova and Franquesa, 2020).

Many of the problematic economic developments in rural areas have been facilitated by the liberalization of the common market. The CAP has been developed as the one major EU policy that has provided support for rural areas in Europe, along with those parts of the structural funds that have targeted disadvantaged rural areas. While the CAP support formally targets mostly farms and farmers, a large and increasing share of the payments has spilled over to other rural groups, in particular landowners. Calls for a reduced CAP budget or a redistribution within the CAP away from farm income support to other purposes that align more with the priorities of urban voters are easily framed as attacks on the rural population. Understandably, many policymakers in Brussels were hesitant to unleash another rural protest movement by proposing a major reform of the CAP. The perceived threat of triggering a protest movement like the 'yellow vests' in France was repeatedly cited as a reason against major CAP reform.[5]

The European integration project has become a target of rural populist sentiment. European policymakers are easily framed as 'cosmopolitan elites' alienated from local population. The often technocratic and complex character of policymaking in the EU, which has been a characteristic of the CAP for a long time (Grant, 1997), seems to confirm the alleged alienation of the 'political elites' from 'common people'. Right-wing populist and conservative parties have used the politicization of technical aspects of public policy such as clean water regulation to mobilize farmers for electoral purposes (Sheingate and Greer, 2021). In agricultural policy, rural populism plays out in ambiguous ways. As Sheingate and Greer (2021) emphasize, 'there is a rural dimension to right-wing populism that depends on the traditionally conservative political orientation of farmers. This fact points to an enduring, if peculiar, feature of agricultural politics: farmers remain sceptical of government, even though many continue to benefit greatly from its protections' (Sheingate and Greer, 2021). This ambivalence also plays out in the politics of the CAP budget: farmers and their interest groups fight for a large CAP budget but against associated regulations of their farming practices. They appreciate the EU as a political venue that ensures continued financial support and detest it as the source of 'intrusive' regulation. Populist resentment among farmers can be mobilized against a reduction in the CAP budget (less integration) and against stricter regulations (more integration).

THE INTERTWINED BUDGET AND LEGISLATIVE PROCESS FOR THE CAP AS IDEATIONAL STRUGGLE

Official preparation for the legislative proposals for the CAP 2021–2027 started with an online consultation by the European Commission which was open from February to May 2017. More than 60,000 responses revealed different priorities between farmers and non-farmers, but also broad support for rural development measures and a sceptical assessment of the CAP's effectiveness in addressing the main challenges among both groups (European Commission and ECORYS, 2017). Response patterns by farmers resonated with the productivist discourse, responses by non-farmers mostly with the multifunctionality discourse.

On 29 November 2017, the Commission published its Communication 'The Future of Food and Farming' (European Commission, 2017), which outlined a 'goal-oriented CAP' with a 'new delivery model' that would ensure that all CAP expenditures demonstrably contribute to achieving the overarching objectives. The document displays the Commission's well-established hybrid discourse, which combines elements of the three main CAP discourses (Erjavec and Erjavec, 2015), but introduces resilience as a new key concept, albeit in weak and generic terms.

On 2 May 2018, the Commission presented the legislative proposals for the MFF 2021–2027 (European Commission, 2018b), accompanied by the Communication, 'A Modern Budget for a Union that Protects, Empowers and Defends' (European Commission, 2018a). It proposed an overall reduction of the CAP budget in real terms by 15 per cent with over-proportional cuts of about 20 per cent in pillar 2, while expenditures for direct payments would be reduced by about 11 per cent. This would shrink the CAP's share in the overall budget to 30 per cent. Article 2 of the proposed regulation emphasized flexibility between the CAP pillars.

The legislative proposals for the CAP were published a few weeks later, on 1 June 2018 (COM 2018/392 final). In particular, the Commission proposed the introduction of 'eco-schemes' which would make parts of the direct payments conditional on the adoption of environmentally and climate-friendly management practices. Member states would be required to develop an NSP, based on a situational and need analysis, that demonstrates how each intervention in both pillars would contribute to the achievement of nine strategic goals. While the Commission maintained its hybrid discourse, it now introduced the resilience of Europe's farming and food systems as a new guiding principle.

The financial proposals were met with fierce critique from farm interest groups, environmental NGOs and the other EU institutions, albeit for different reasons. The European Economic and Social Committee complained that 'the proposed cuts … in planned commitments for the common agricultural policy (CAP) … will make it impossible to implement a model of sustainable rural development'.[6] The Committee of the Regions criticized that 'the financing of additional priorities is to be at the expense of existing EU policies with proven EU added value, such as the Cohesion Policy, the Common Agricultural Policy and, in particular, rural development policy'.[7] It called for a share of 5 per cent of the entire EU budget for rural development (recital 27). The Parliament, in its resolution P8_TA(2018)0449 of 14 November 2018, declared 'its opposition to any reduction in the level of long-standing EU policies enshrined in the Treaties, such as cohesion policy and the common agricultural and fisheries policies' (recital 4) and requested to 'maintain the financing of the common agricultural policy (CAP) for the EU-27 at the level of the 2014–2020 budget in real terms while budgeting the initial amount of the agricultural reserve' (recital 17, item xvi).[8]

The legislative process stalled in the run-up to the elections to the European Parliament in May 2019. While COMAGRI adopted a status quo-oriented resolution, numerous MEPs submitted further amendments. The Parliament did not manage to integrate more than 1,000 amendments into a consolidated proposition for a floor vote, indicating an inability to consolidate a multiplicity of ideas and demands into a coherent discourse. As a result, the outgoing Parliament failed to adopt a position.

The elections in May 2019 ushered in significant changes. For the first time, the combined share of seats for the conservatives (EPP) and the socialists and social democrats (S&D) fell below 50 per cent. Liberal (Renew Europe) and green parties made significant gains. While Eurosceptic populists were still far away from a blocking minority, EP decision-making started to rely on more floating coalitions (Crum, 2020). At 50.6 per cent, EU-wide voter turnout was the highest since 1994 (+ 7.53 per cent in comparison with 2014), but the rise in turnout was unevenly distributed among member states (de Wilde, 2020, p. 45). The most mobilizing policy issues, based on Eurobarometer and survey data (Braun and Schäfer, 2021), were climate change and the environment (Denmark, France, Luxembourg, the Netherlands, Austria, Sweden, Finland), economy and growth (Portugal, Spain, Ireland, United Kingdom, Italy, Slovenia, Croatia, Hungary, Greece, Romania, Poland, Lithuania, Latvia, Estonia, Cyprus), European integration (Czech Republic, Slovakia) and immigration (Bulgaria), indicating a strong cleavage between pro-environmental and pro-growth discourses, with potentially high relevance for the CAP.

In October 2019, the newly elected Parliament confirmed the demand that the CAP budget should be maintained at previous levels in real terms, called for continuation of the negotiations and a contingency MFF if the current MFF needed to be extended.[9]

The difficult formation of the new Commission re-established a strong role for the Council after the rejection of the top two electoral candidates, Weber and Timmermans (de Wilde, 2020, p. 37). Surprise candidate Ursula von der Leyen 'satisfied the conservative majority and addressed Central European concerns against Timmermans' (Heidbreder and Schade, 2020). She was elected by the Parliament on 16 July, with a slim majority, taking 383 out of 751 votes (374 needed), missing about 100 MEPs from the EPP-S&D coalition and depending on votes from the Polish Law and Justice Party and the Italian populist Cinque Stelle party. During the hearings, her positions on the CAP remained generic.

After rejection of several candidates during the hearings, the Commission was approved by Parliament on 27 November 2019 and took office on 1 December 2019. The new Commissioner for Agriculture and Rural Development, Janusz Wojciechowski, a member of the Polish Law and Justice Party and long-standing vice chair of COMAGRI, signalled a status quo-oriented and productivist position towards CAP reform.

In late 2019, the negotiations started to move again when the Finnish presidency presented a new proposal for the MFF which would keep the CAP budget nominally constant at the level of the previous seven-year period and reduce the cuts in the second pillar, marking significant gains for the proponents of the status quo. However, during the Croatian presidency, in the first half of 2020, Council negotiations on the CAP made little progress. Instead, the policy context was shaken up by two developments.

In the first development, the new Commission caused general surprise with a stream of climate and environment-oriented initiatives. The 'European Green Deal' (European Commission, 2019), presented on 11 December 2019, established an explicit link between economic growth and prosperity and the protection of the environment – a return to discourses prevalent in the second Barroso Commission (Burns, 2021, p. 87; Burns, Eckersley, and Tobin, 2020; see also Bornemann, Chapter 7 in this volume). It confirmed the EU's commitment to carbon neutrality by 2050, proposed a just transition fund (to generate buy-in from Eastern European states), a climate law and sectoral policies to support and achieve carbon neutrality, for example, in the energy, building, transport, business and agriculture sectors. The proposal for a European climate law (later Regulation (EU) 2021/1119) was tabled on 4 March 2020. On 20 May 2020, the Commission presented its EU Biodiversity Strategy for 2030 (European Commission, 2020b) and the Farm to Fork Strategy (European Commission, 2020a). The Commission's initiatives clearly affected the discourse around the CAP. This was accompanied by a reorganization within the Commission, which tasked Vice President Frans Timmermans with ensuring that the Green Deal would be implemented in Union policies, including the CAP. This could also be understood as an attempt to open up the closed policy networks that have dominated CAP negotiations for decades.

The second development was triggered by the Covid-19 pandemic, which started to hit Europe in February 2020 and prompted calls for unprecedented stimulus spending. On 21 April 2020, Council President Charles Michel and Commission President von der Leyen presented a 'joint roadmap for recovery'.[10] Importantly, the CAP is mentioned in this document as an area for financial investment: 'This means investing massively in the Green and Digital transitions and the circular economy, alongside other policies such as cohesion and the Common agricultural policy' (p. 4). On 27 May 2022, the Commission published its 'recovery plan', which combined an increased volume for the MFF with the creation of a new 'recovery instrument', now called 'NextGeneration EU' (NGEU). On 23 June 2020, the environmental ministers pointed out that the approach to the Covid-19 recovery should be guided by the EU Green Deal, a remark with clear relevance to the CAP.

In a parallel movement, efforts were made to secure continuation of farm payments in the absence of a new legislative framework. Since early 2020 it had been clear that the new CAP could not be adopted and implemented by January 2021. In response to the stalled CAP negotiations and the accelerating negotiations of a large financial package, the Parliament once again demanded a contingency MFF, with a particular view to securing CAP payments beyond the end of 2020.[11] A consensus emerged that the current rules should be extended by two years (up to 31 December 2022). This became law only in late December 2020 with the publication of Regulation (EU) 2020/2220, which also included some minor changes and rules on the use of the additional NGEU funds.

The German presidency in the second half of 2020 made finalizing the CAP negotiations a priority. As demanded by the Parliament, the MFF had to be settled first. After four days and four nights of negotiations – one of the longest EU summits ever – the Council agreed on the MFF 2021–2027 and the recovery fund NGEU (with an overall amount of €390 billion in grants and €360 billion in loans). The MFF set the CAP budget for 2021 at €336.4 billion in constant 2018 prices, of which €258.6 billion was allocated to the European Agriculture Guarantee Fund (EAGF) and €77.8 billion to the EAFRD. This meant a reduction of 10 per cent in the first pillar and 19 per cent in the second pillar compared to the funding period 2014–2020, mostly reflecting the departure of the United Kingdom from the EU. The CAP budget constitutes about 32 per cent of the MFF. The losses in the EAFRD were partly compensated by the inclusion of almost €8.1 billion in the NGEU as a top-up to rural development programmes in 2021 and 2022.[12] This amount was, however, much less than the €15 billion for rural development proposed by President Charles Michel on 17 July 2020.[13] With Poland and Italy being the top recipients, the distributional shares among member states deviated from those of the EAFRD funds in the MFF.[14]

The resolution of the Parliament of 23 July 2020 in response to the Council agreement deplores insufficient funding in various policy areas, but does not mention the CAP, an indication that the agricultural policymakers in the EP were comparatively happy with the outcome.[15]

Negotiations on the CAP now moved on. The Agriculture Council adopted its position, after a two-day meeting, in the early hours of 21 October 2020.[16] The most surprising element was an agreement that member states should be required to allocate at least 20 per cent of their EAGF budget (pillar 1) to eco-schemes and at least 30 per cent of their EAFRD spending to environment and climate-related measures. The original proposal by then Agriculture Commissioner Hogan had included no mandatory environmental budget nor a minimum budget share for eco-schemes. According to participants, Germany, France and the Scandinavian countries were pressing for a higher share. When the meeting was close to breaking up at 2.30 a.m., Agriculture Commissioner Janusz Wojciechowski reportedly suggested settling on a 10 per cent share.[17] The German presidency therefore considered the outcome a major achievement and a 'system change'.[18] The compromise included a two-year 'learning phase' in 2023 and 2024 that allows for flexibility in the implementation of the eco-schemes. Furthermore, member states can count support for young farmers of up to 2 per cent of the EAGF and any environmental spending above 30 per cent of their second pillar budget against their eco-scheme obligation. Additionally, the Council proposed more ambitious environmental requirements, now called 'enhanced conditionality', for the receipt of direct payments, and an option for member states to reduce payments above €60,000 per recipient.

In direct response, the European Parliament adopted its position on 23 October 2020.[19] The new Parliamentarians had picked up the amendments that had already been adopted by COMAGRI and the Committee on the Environment before the election. The English version of the three resolutions now contained 646 pages of proposed amendments. The Parliament, in particular, required the inclusion of a 'social conditionality' into the conditions for direct payment, making the capping of direct payments mandatory, and setting the minimum amount for eco-schemes at 30 per cent of direct payments. On 17 December 2020, the Parliament adopted its position on the MFF in response to the Council.[20] It welcomed the agreement on the MFF and highlighted the binding minimum share of 30 per cent for climate-related spending and 7.5 per cent (from 2024, 10 per cent from 2026) for biodiversity-related spending, without explicit mention of the CAP.

The positions of the Council and the Parliament set the stage for the trilogue negotiations on the CAP which were mostly conducted under the Portuguese presidency in the first half of 2021. The negotiations addressed a number of highly technical and administrative issues which are nevertheless significant for potential effects on farm income and the attractiveness of the voluntary programmes to enhance land management practices, in particular the conditionality rules for the area-based direct payments and the list of eco-scheme practices. Other aspects related to the details of the 'new delivery model', in particular the monitoring, compliance and indicator system, but also rules for market intervention. A less prominent but significant point was the rules for recognition of expenses as climate- or biodiversity-related.

An unusual feature was the repeated interventions by Commission Vice President Timmermans, who felt that CAP negotiators would not sufficiently address the Green Deal requirements. Timmermans even threatened that the 2018 Commission Proposal would be withdrawn, which Commission President von der Leyen quickly ruled out.[21] Timmermans later complained that 'the agricultural ministers – and I have experienced this personally – have this attitude: Timmermans, what are you doing here? This is our shop. Stay out of here.'[22]

The trilogue negotiations were finalized on 25 June 2021.[23] The final stages were conducted as a 'super-trilogue', which meant that only the Portuguese presidency and the Parliament's representatives participated, so that member states no longer had direct access.[24] The EP delegation was chaired by the head of COMAGRI, Norbert Lins (EPP, Germany). The delegations on strategic plans, horizontal regulation and common market organization were chaired by Peter Jahr (EPP, Germany), Ulrike Müller (Renew Europe, Germany) and Eric Andrieu (S&D, France) respectively. Overall, this secured a strong influence, not just from the three main factions, as well as German and French perspectives, but also from producer-oriented ideas with moderate adoption of environmental and social concerns. The compromise was confirmed in the Council on 28 June 2021. The minimum budget share for eco-schemes was set at 25 per cent of the national amount for direct payments. Member states must dedicate up to 3 per cent (previously 2 per cent) of direct payments to support young farmers[25] and at least 10 per cent to support small farms. This can take the form of a 'redistribution premium' of up to 12 per cent (previously 7 per cent) of direct payments. The Parliament succeeded in adding a 'social conditionality', which means that recipients of farm aid would have to comply with elements of European social and labour law. As part of the environmental conditionality, farms must dedicate at least 3 per cent of their arable land to biodiversity and non-productive elements. Further support can be provided via eco-schemes to increase this share to 7 per cent.

The legislative details were elaborated over summer 2021. The three final pieces of legislation – Regulation (EU) 2021/2115 on strategic plans, Regulation (EU) 2021/2116 on the financing, management and monitoring

of the CAP (Horizontal Regulation), and Regulation (EU) 2021/2117 amend-
ing the Common Market Organisation – were adopted by Parliament on 23
November 2021 and by the Council on 2 December 2021 and published in the
Official Journal on 6 December 2021.[26] In Parliament, the three regulations
were backed by most conservative, liberal and centre-right members, with
opposition mostly from centre-left and green members.[27]

Member states were supposed to submit their NSPs by 1 January 2022. The
Commission is tasked with checking the compatibility of the NSP with the
regulation and the Green Deal. But the latter was not part of the legislation, and
it was hence unclear how strictly this check would be carried out.[28]

DISCUSSION AND CONCLUSION

The relationship between EU agricultural and budget policies is marked by the
heritage of a policy trajectory that originated in the early days of the European
Community. After its establishment in the 1960s, the CAP soon required an
increasing share of the EU budget. Building on productivist ideas that emphasize the exceptional character of agriculture, an extensive system of market
interventions was created. Expectations that this system would pay for itself
were soon undermined by its success. The ensuing costs created major budget
crises throughout the 1980s. Since the establishment of the MFF, the CAP
had to become financially more predictable. This was enabled by the 1992
MacSharry reform which started to replace income support for farmers through
market interventions with direct payments. Their visibility created a need for
justification, particularly against the background of the rise in market-liberal
ideas in the 1980s and 1990s. The Commission therefore played an active
role in the articulation and diffusion of a multifunctional agriculture discourse
which updated the reasoning why the farm sector needed public support, as
epitomized in the Cork Declaration of 1996 and the creation of the EAFRD as
a second pillar of the CAP in 1999. Since the Fischler reform in 2003, the CAP
linked the major part of the farm payments to regulations about environmental,
consumer and animal protection. Decoupling the payments from production
also strengthened market signals in line with market-liberal ideas. As a result,
the CAP constituted a mix of policies that combined ideational elements of
productivist, market-liberal and multifunctional agricultural discourses, which
the Commission combined into a hybrid discourse that proved instrumental in
creating flexibility for policy coordination, justification and adaptation.

In the run-up to the negotiations about the CAP post 2020, this model faced
major challenges. Evidence mounted about the lack of transfer efficiency and
environmental effectiveness of the CAP payments. The farm sector also came
under scrutiny as a source of greenhouse gas emissions. All this contributed
to a growing sense of policy failure. Brexit, removing a big net contributor

from the EU, further increased pressure on the CAP budget. In response, the Commission proposed its 'new delivery model' as a signal that the CAP expenditures would demonstrably contribute to EU policy goals, while the Commission's first MFF proposal foresaw a significant reduction of CAP spending in real terms and as a share of the overall EU budget.

The ensuing process demonstrated, first, the power of the agricultural policy community in the budget process; second, the continuing dominance of long-established, producer-centred discourses among CAP policymakers; and third a distributive bargaining game at various levels. The first point becomes clear in the responses from the Parliament and the member states to the first Commission proposal for the CAP. The proposed cuts to CAP budgets were broadly deplored and partly reversed in several steps, with the MFF proposal from the Finnish presidency as an important milestone. An agreement on the MFF was clearly out of reach until the interests of member states and constituencies that greatly benefit from the CAP were satisfied. Notably, the long duration and large volumes of the CAP were itself invoked as reasons for a continuation of a large CAP budget.

The second point becomes visible throughout the process. The first MFF proposal from the Commission allocated the proposed cuts to the CAP budget over-proportionally to the second pillar, which contains the 'multifunctional' element of the CAP, which left more room for the direct payments to producers in the first pillar. Attempts to increase the CAP budget were then focused on restoring the share of the second pillar in the CAP, which had the advantage of greater appeal to non-agricultural policymakers. This relates to the third point: the distributional bargaining at the level of the entire EU budget requires arguments that demonstrate the CAP's value to the EU in comparison to other policy areas, while distributional bargaining within the CAP community affects the distribution of funds to either productivist or multifunctional or competitiveness- and innovation-oriented purposes. Hence, proponents of productivism have to persuade the broader policy community that direct income support for farmers creates more value for the European Union than support for sustainable farming practices or new agricultural value chains, for example. It is likely that the rural protests in many member states made conservative, liberal and social democratic policymakers hesitant to reduce transfer payments to an influential rural constituency for fear of fanning the flames among right-wing populists, although this point deserves further inquiry. It is at least plausible that a strong and productivist CAP was seen as providing electoral value, or at least reducing electoral risks, to incumbents in the Council and the Parliament. In this constellation, member states' positions were constructed as a mixture of ideational positions, financial net-payer positions and electoral considerations.

It is significant that two major exogenic shocks – the Covid-19 pandemic and the European Green Deal – had little effect on the CAP's ideational and policy path dependence and its budget. The explanation is clear: the institutional and political opportunity structures in the EU strongly favour the continuation of established policies over policy change. The majority of actors in the triangle of GD Agri, COMAGRI and the Agriculture Council embrace agricultural exceptionalism and productivist ideas. A relatively high degree of internal coherence and coordination enables this policy community to develop strategic leverage. The refusal to finalize the legislative proposals for the CAP post 2020 until the budget had been settled created enormous pressure on the budget negotiations, given the importance of CAP payments for rural constituencies. The hiatus in the budget negotiations was skilfully exploited to extend the existing rules by two years, which was probably the best outcome for status quo-oriented farms and business models since it delayed the introduction of potentially more ambitious environmental conditions. On the other hand, the meagre share of NGEU payments that went into rural development policies might indicate a limited ability of the agricultural policy community to capitalize on unforeseen developments.

The limited effect of the European Green Deal, for which the CAP reform was probably the first hard test, is equally ambivalent. Attempts by Vice President Timmermans to open up the process remained largely unsuccessful. The Green Deal ambition was watered down through a sequence of incremental strategies. Most importantly, the climate budgeting tools were seriously compromised by questionable decisions, in particular the categorization of 40 per cent of direct payments and of payments for less-favoured areas as climate-relevant. It is currently unclear how clearly the Commission can and will evaluate the complementarity of the NSP with the Green Deal, the Farm to Fork Strategy and the Biodiversity Strategy, particularly since these are not part of the legislative proposals. This, however, opens up the possibility that urgent challenges related to climate change and biodiversity are not properly addressed, with negative long-term consequences.

A less visible element of agricultural exceptionalism in the linked CAP and budget process is that significant parts of the political decisions were allocated to administrative processes which mostly take place in agriculture departments. This particularly applies to the detailed elaboration of the eco-schemes, the development of NSPs and their approval by the Commission. This points to the importance of the discourses that shape strategy development and legislative implementation by administrators and implementers, an area that deserves further research.

Overall, the relationship between the MFF and CAP processes for the budget period 2021–2027 reveals a strong but diminishing influence of the agricultural policy community and its strongly productivist ideas and discourses on the budget process. A relatively united CAP community – with strongholds in COMAGRI and the Agriculture Council – was able to hold out until they received the desired budget and the policy space to maintain producer-oriented policies. However, this could not stop the continuous decrease of the CAP share in the overall budget. In the context of the Recovery Fund, the CAP budget looks even less prominent, shrinking to about 20 per cent of the overall combined financial volume of the MFF and NGEU.

The hybrid CAP discourse, which combines elements of productivist, market-liberal and multifunctionalist discourses, has helped actors to legitimize their positions and the overall outcome to very diverse audiences, and even to absorb the European Green Deal and the Farm to Fork Strategy. However, this discourse also gave licence to a watering down of the Green Deal that makes it unlikely that climate and biodiversity issues will be effectively addressed. Similarly, worries over a populist wave in rural areas led to hesitation to reduce support for rural areas in the form of farm subsidies. But it remains questionable how effectively the CAP 2023–2027 (after the extension of the previous CAP by two years) will address the underlying frustrations about declining infrastructure, health care and opportunities, and thereby the urban–rural cleavage.

NOTES

1. In 2013, the product-specific market organizations were subsumed under one common market organization for agricultural products, see Regulation (EU) No 1308/2013 of the European Parliament and of the Council of 17 December 2013 establishing a common organisation of the markets in agricultural products and repealing Council Regulations (EEC) No 922/72, (EEC) No 234/79, (EC) No 1037/2001 and (EC) No 1234/2007.
2. Council Regulation (EC) No 1698/2005 of 20 September 2005 on support for rural development by the European Agricultural Fund for Rural Development (EAFRD).
3. Previously, multiannual financial frameworks had the form of interinstitutional agreements.
4. Notably, the Parliament is not involved in the adopting 'measures on fixing prices, levies, aid and quantitative limitations' (Art. 42(3) TFEU).
5. Personal communication with policymakers in Brussels and Berlin.
6. Opinion of the European Economic and Social Committee on 'Communication from the Commission to the European Parliament, the European Council, the Council, the European Economic and Social Committee and the Committee of the Regions. A Modern Budget for a Union that Protects, Empowers and Defends. The Multiannual Financial Framework for 2021–2027' (2018/C 440/18), adopted 19 September 2018, https://eur-lex.europa.eu/legal-content/EN/TXT/PDF/?uri=CELEX:52018AE2072&from=EN.
7. Committee of the Regions 131st COR Plenary Session and Opening Session of the Week, 8.10.2018–10.10.2018. Opinion of the European Committee of

the Regions — The Multiannual Financial Framework package for the years 2021–2027 (2018/C 461/10), recital 4.

8. Interim report on the Multiannual Financial Framework 2021–2027 – Parliament's position with a view to an agreement European Parliament resolution of 14 November 2018 on the Multiannual Financial Framework 2021-2027 – Parliament's position with a view to an agreement (COM(2018)0322 – C8-0000/2018 – 2018/0166R(APP)).

9. European Parliament resolution P9_TA(2019)0032 Multiannual Financial Framework 2021–2027 and own resources: time to meet citizens' expectations, adopted 10 October 2019, www.europarl.europa.eu/doceo/document/TA-9-2019 -0032_EN.html, last accessed 5 July 2022.

10. European Commission and European Council, 'A Roadmap for Recovery. Towards a more resilient, sustainable and fair Europe', www.consilium.europa .eu/media/43384/roadmap-for-recovery-final-21-04-2020.pdf, last accessed 15 March 2022.

11. European Parliament resolution P9_TA(2020)0065. A safety net to protect the beneficiaries of EU programmes: setting up an MFF contingency plan, adopted 13 May 2020.

12. European Council (n.d.): 'Infographic – Multiannual financial framework 2021–2027 and Next Generation EU', available at www.consilium.europa.eu/en/ infographics/mff2021-2027-ngeu-final/, last accessed 15 March 2022.

13. European Council (n.d.): 'Infographic – Proposal for an EU recovery plan – key features', available at www.consilium.europa.eu/en/infographics/mff-recovery -negobox/, last accessed 5 July 2022.

14. For the distribution see European Commission (n.d.): 'NGEU Breakdown of European Agricultural Fund for Rural Development per Member State (current prices)', available at https://ec.europa.eu/info/sites/default/files/about_the _european_commission/eu_budget/eafrd_-_ngeu_current_0_0.pdf, last accessed 15 March 2022.

15. European Parliament resolution P9_TA(2020)0206 of 23 July 2020 on the conclusions of the extraordinary European Council meeting of 17–21 July 2020 (2020/2732(RSP).

16. 12148/1/20 REV 1, ST 12148 2020 ADD 1 – NOTE and ST 12148 2020 INIT – NOTE, available at www.consilium.europa.eu/en/press/press-releases/2020/10/ 21/council-agrees-its-position-on-the-next-eu-common-agricultural-policy/, last accessed 15 March 2021.

17. Personal communication with several members of the German Federal Ministry of Food and Agriculture, November and December 2020.

18. German Federal Ministry of Food and Agriculture, Press Release 206/2020, 21 October 2021, available at www.bmel.de/SharedDocs/Pressemitteilungen/DE/ 2020/206-kl-eu-agrarrat-luxemburg.html, last accessed 15 March 2021.

19. European Parliament resolution P9_TA(2020)0287 Common agricultural policy – support for strategic plans to be drawn up by Member States and financed by the EAGF and by the EAFRD; resolution P9_TA(2020)0288 Amendments adopted by the European Parliament on 23 October 2020 on the proposal for a regulation of the European Parliament and of the Council on the financing, management and monitoring of the common agricultural policy and repealing Regulation (EU) No 1306/2013 (COM(2018)0393 – C8-0247/2018 – 2018/0217(COD)); resolution P9_TA(2020)0289 Common agricultural policy – amendment of the CMO and other Regulation.

20. European Parliament resolution P9_TA(2020)0360 of 17 December 2020 on the Multiannual Financial Framework 2021–2027, the Interinstitutional Agreement, the EU Recovery Instrument and the Rule of Law Regulation (2020/2923(RSP).
21. EU Observer: 'Timmermans "disappointed" with ongoing CAP reform', 16 November 2020, https://euobserver.com/green-deal/150068, last accessed 15 March 2022.
22. Deutschlandfunk: Interview with Frans Timmermans, 26 June 2021, www.deutschlandfunk.de/gemeinsame-agrarpolitik-was-die-eu-agrarreform-bringen-soll-100.html, authors' transcription and translation.
23. European Council: 'Political agreement on new Common Agricultural Policy: fairer, greener, more flexible', Press release, 25 June 2021, available at https://ec.europa.eu/commission/presscorner/detail/en/IP_21_2711, last accessed 15 March 2022.
24. Personal communication with members of the German Federal Ministry of Food and Agriculture, summer 2021.
25. Annex XII to Regulation (EU) 2021/2115 contains specific amounts for each member state.
26. Official Journal of the European Union, L 435, 6 December 2021, available at https://eur-lex.europa.eu/legal-content/EN/TXT/?uri=OJ:L:2021:435:TOC, last accessed 15 March 2022.
27. 'The "Strategic plans regulation" was adopted with 452 votes in favour, 178 against and 57 abstentions, the "Horizontal regulation" with 485 votes in favour, 142 against and 61 abstentions and the "Common market organisation regulation" with 487 in favour, 130 against and 71 abstentions.' European Parliament: 'Common Agricultural Policy reform gets final approval from MEPs', Press release, 23 November, available at www.europarl.europa.eu/news/en/press-room/20211118IPR17613/common-agricultural-policy-reform-gets-final-approval-from-meps, last accessed 15 March 2022.
28. Personal communication with members of the German Federal Ministry of Food and Agriculture, autumn 2021.

REFERENCES

Ackermann, P. (1970). *Der Deutsche Bauernverband im politischen Kräftespiel der Bundesrepublik: Die Einflußnahme des DBV auf die Entscheidung über den Europäischen Getreidepreis*, Tübingen: Mohr.

Ackrill, R. (2000). 'The European Union Budget, the Balanced Budget Rule and the Development of Common European Policies'. *Journal of Public Policy* 20(1): 1–19, https://doi.org/10.1017/S0143814X00000738.

Ackrill, R. and Kay, A. (2006). 'Historical-Institutionalist Perspectives on the Development of the EU Budget System'. *Journal of European Public Policy* 13(1): 113–133, https://doi.org/ 10.1080/13501760500380775.

Alons, G. (2017). 'Environmental Policy Integration in the EU's Common Agricultural Policy: Greening or Greenwashing?' *Journal of European Public Policy* 24(11): 1604–1622, https://doi.org/10.1080/13501763.2017.1334085.

Bellini, S. (2021). 'The Pig Sector in the European Union', in L. Iacolina, et al. (eds), *Understanding and Combatting African Swine Fever: A European Perspective*, Wageningen: Wageningen Academic Publishers, 183–195.

Benedetto, G. (2013). 'The EU Budget after Lisbon: Rigidity and Reduced Spending?' *Journal of Public Policy* 33(3): 345–369, https://doi.org/10.1017/S0143814X13000172.

Braun, D. and Schäfer, C. (2021). 'Issues that Mobilize Europe. The Role of Key Policy Issues for Voter Turnout in the 2019 European Parliament Election'. *European Union Politics* 23(1): 120–140, https://doi.org/10.1177/14651165211040337.

Burns, C. (2021). 'Environment and Climate 2050', in C. Damro, E. Heins and D. Scott (eds), *European Futures: Challenges and Crossroads for the European Union of 2050*, New York, NY: Routledge, 77–92.

Burns, C., Eckersley, P., and Tobin, P. (2020). 'EU Environmental Policy in Times of Crisis'. *Journal of European Public Policy* 27(1): 1–19, https://doi.org/10.1080/13501763.2018.1561741.

Coleman, W.D. (1998). 'From Protected Development to Market Liberalism: Paradigm Change in Agriculture'. *Journal of European Public Policy* 5(4): 632-651, https://doi.org/10.1080/13501769880000061.

Coleman, W.D., Grant, W., and Josling, T. (2004). *Agriculture in the New Global Economy*, Cheltenham, UK and Northampton, MA, USA: Edward Elgar Publishing.

Commission of the European Communities (1985). 'Perspectives for the Common Agricultural Policy'. Communication from the Commission to the Council and the Parliament, COM(85), 333 Final, Brussels.

Crum, B. (2020). 'Party Groups and Ideological Cleavages in the European Parliament after the 2019 Elections', in S. Kritzinger, C. Plescia, K. Raube, J. Wilhelm and J. Wouters (eds), *Assessing the 2019 European Parliament Elections*, New York, NY: Routledge, 54–65.

Daugbjerg, C. (1999). 'Reforming the Cap: Policy Networks and Broader Institutional Structures'. *JCMS: Journal of Common Market Studies* 37(3): 407–428, https://doi.org/10.1111/1468-5965.00171.

Daugbjerg, C. (2003). 'Policy Feedback and Paradigm Shift in EU Agricultural Policy: The Effects of the MacSharry Reform on Future Reform'. *Journal of European Public Policy* 10(3): 421–437, https://doi.org/10.1080/1350176032000085388.

Daugbjerg, C. (2017). 'Responding to Non-Linear Internationalisation of Public Policy: The World Trade Organization and Reform of the Cap 1992–2013'. *JCMS: Journal of Common Market Studies* 55(3): 486–501, https://doi.org/10.1111/jcms.12476.

Daugbjerg, C. and Feindt, P.H. (2017). 'Post-Exceptionalism in Food and Agricultural Policy: Transforming Public Policies'. *Journal of European Public Policy* 24(11): 1565–1584.

Daugbjerg, C. and Swinbank, A. (2011). 'Explaining the "Health Check" of the Common Agricultural Policy: Budgetary Politics, Globalisation and Paradigm Change Revisited'. *Policy Studies* 32(2): 127–141, https://doi.org/10.1080/01442872.2010.541768.

Daugbjerg, C. and Swinbank, A. (2016). 'Three Decades of Policy Layering and Politically Sustainable Reform in the European Union's Agricultural Policy'. *Governance* 29(2): 265–280.

de Wilde, P. (2020). 'The Fall of the Spitzenkandidaten. Political Parties and Conflict in the 2019 European Elections', in S. Kritzinger, C. Plescia, K. Raube, J. Wilhelm and J. Wouters (eds), *Assessing the 2019 European Parliament Elections*, New York, NY: Routledge, 17–53.

Entman, R. (1993). 'Framing: Toward Clarification of a Fractured Paradigm'. *Journal of Communication* 43(4): 51–58.

Erjavec, K. and Erjavec, E. (2015). '"Greening the CAP" – Just a Fashionable Justification? A Discourse Analysis of the 2014–2020 CAP Reform Documents'. *Food Policy* 51: 53–62.

European Commission (2017). 'The Future of Food and Farming', COM(2017) 713 Final.

European Commission (2018a). 'A Modern Budget for a Union That Protects, Empowers and Defends. The Multiannual Financial Framework for 2021–2027'. Communication from the Commission to the European Parliament, the European Council, the European Economic and Social Committee and the Committee of the Regions, COM(2018) 321 Final.

European Commission. (2018b). 'Proposal for a Council Regulation Laying Down the Multiannual Financial Framework for the Years 2021 to 2027', COM(2018) 322 Final.

European Commission (2019). 'The European Green Deal'. Communication from the Commission to the European Parliament, the European Council, the Council, the European Economic and Social Committee and the Committee of the Regions, COM(2019) 640 Final.

European Commission (2020a). 'A Farm to Fork Strategy for a Fair, Healthy and Environmentally-Friendly Food System'. Communication from the Commission to the European Parliament, the Council, the European Economic and Social Committee and the Committee of the Regions, COM/2020/381 Final.

European Commission (2020b). 'EU Biodiversity Strategy for 2030 Bringing Nature Back into Our Lives'. Communication from the Commission to the European Parliament, the Council, the European Economic and Social Committee and the Committee of the Regions, COM/2020/380 Final, Brussels.

European Commission (2021). 'Common Agricultural Policy: Key graphs & figures. CAP expenditure in the total EU expenditure', available at https://ec.europa.eu/info/sites/default/files/food-farming-fisheries/farming/documents/cap-expenditure-graph1_en.pdf, last accessed 15 March 2022.

European Commission and ECORYS (2017). 'Modernising and Simplifying the Common Agricultural Policy. Summary of the Results of the Public Consultation'. Brussels: European Commission, available at https://ec.europa.eu/agriculture/sites/agriculture/files/consultations/cap-modernising/summary-public-consul.pdf, last accessed 31 August 2018.

European Court of Auditors (2018). 'Basic Payment Scheme for Farmers – Operationally on Track, but Limited Impact on Simplification, Targeting and the Convergence of Aid Levels'. Special Report 2018/10, Brussels, available at www.eca.europa.eu/en/Pages/DocItem.aspx?did=45158, last accessed 14 January 2022.

European Parliament (2017). 'Russia's and the EU's Sanctions: Economic and Trade Effects, Compliance and the Way Forward', Brussels, available at www.europarl.europa.eu/thinktank/en/document.html?reference=EXPO_STU(2017)603847, last accessed 15 March 2022.

Feindt, P.H. (2018). 'EU Agricultural Policy', in H. Heinelt and S. Münch (eds), *Handbook of European Policy: Formulation, Development and Evaluation*, Cheltenham, UK and Northampton, MA, USA: Edward Elgar Publishing, 115–133.

Feindt, P.H., Schwindenhammer, S., and Tosun, J. (2021). 'Politicization, Depoliticization and Policy Change: A Comparative Theoretical Perspective on Agri-Food Policy'. *Journal of Comparative Policy Analysis: Research and Practice* 23(5–6): 509–525, https://doi.org/10.1080/13876988.2020.1785875.

Grande, E., Hutter, S., Kerscher, A., and Becker, R. (2016). 'Framing Europe: Are Cultural-Identitarian Frames Driving Politicization?', in S. Hutter, E. Grande and H.-P. Kriesi (eds), *Politicizing Europe. Integration and Mass Politics*, Cambridge: Cambridge University Press, 181–206.

Grant, W. (1997). *The Common Agricultural Policy*, New York: St. Martins.

Greer, A. (2005). *Agricultural Policy in Europe*, Manchester: Manchester University Press.

Greer, A. (2013). 'The Common Agricultural Policy and the EU Budget: Stasis or Change?' *European Journal of Government and Economics* 2(2): 119–136.

Greer, A. (2017). 'Post-Exceptional Politics in Agriculture: An Examination of the 2013 Cap Reform'. *Journal of European Public Policy* 24(11): 1585–1603, https://doi.org/10.1080/13501763.2017.1334080.

Hart, K. (2015). 'The Fate of Green Direct Payments in the Cap Reform Negotiations', in J. Swinnen (ed.), *The Political Economy of the 2014–2020 Common Agricultural Policy. An Imperfect Storm*, Brussels/London: Centre for European Policy Studies (CEPS)/Rowman and Littlefield International, 245–276.

Heidbreder, E.G. and Schade, D. (2020). '(Un)Settling the Precedent: Contrasting Institutionalisation Dynamics in the Spitzenkandidaten Procedure of 2014 and 2019'. *Research & Politics* 7(2): 2053168020925975. https://doi.org/10.1177/2053168020925975.

Knudsen, A.-C.L. (2009). *Farmers on Welfare. The Making of Europe's Common Agricultural Policy*, Ithaca and London: Cornell University Press.

Kriesi, H. (2014). 'The Populist Challenge'. *West European Politics* 37(2): 361–378, https://doi.org/10.1080/01402382.2014.887879.

Mamonova, N. and Franquesa, J. (2020). 'Right-Wing Populism in Rural Europe. Introduction to the Special Issue'. *Sociologia Ruralis* 60(4): 702–709, https://doi.org/10.1111/soru.12306.

Matthews, A. (2015). 'The Multi-Annual Financial Framework and the 2013 Cap Reform', in J. Swinnen (ed.), *The Political Economy of the 2014–2020 Common Agricultural Policy. An Imperfect Storm*. Brussels/London: Centre for European Policy Studies (CEPS)/Rowman and Littlefield International, 169–192.

Moyer, H.W. and Josling, T.E. (1990). *Agricultural Policy Reform: Politics and Process in the EC and the USA*, Brighton: Harvester Wheatsheaf.

Pe'er, G., Bonn, A., Bruelheide, H., Dieker, P., Eisenhauer, N., Feindt, P.H., Hagedorn, G., Hansjürgens, B., Herzon, I., Lomba, Â., Marquard, E., Moreira, F., Nitsch, H., Oppermann, R., Perino, A., Röder, N., Schleyer, C., Schindler, S., Wolf, C., Zinngrebe, Y., and Lakner, S. (2020). 'Action Needed for the EU Common Agricultural Policy to Address Sustainability Challenges'. *People and Nature* 2(2): 305–316, https://doi.org/10.1002/pan3.10080.

Potter, C. and Tilzey, M. (2005). 'Agricultural Policy Discourses in the European Post-Fordist Transition: Neoliberalism, Neomercantilism and Multifunctionality'. *Progress in Human Geography* 29(5): 581–600, https://doi.org/10.1191/0309132505ph569oa.

Roederer-Rynning, C. (2015). 'COMAGRI and the "CAP after 2013" Reform: In Search of a Collective Sense of Purpose', in J. Swinnen (ed.), *The Political Economy of the 2014–2020 Common Agricultural Policy: An Imperfect Storm*. London: Rowman and Littlefield, 331–356.

Schmidt, V.A. (2018). 'The Role of Ideas and Discourse in European Integration', in H. Heinelt and S. Münch (eds), *Handbook of European Policies. Interpretative*

Approaches to the EU, Cheltenham, UK and Northampton, MA, USA: Edward Elgar Publishing, 35–54.

Scoones, I., Edelman, M., Borras Jr, S.M., Forero, L.F., Hall, R., Wolford, W., and White, B. (eds), (2021). *Authoritarian Populism and the Rural World*, Milton Park: Routledge.

Sheingate, A. and Greer, A. (2021). 'Populism, Politicization and Policy Change in US and UK Agro-Food Policies'. *Journal of Comparative Policy Analysis: Research and Practice* 23(5–6): 544–560, https://doi.org/10.1080/13876988.2020.1749518.

Shucksmith, M., Thomson, K.J., and Roberts, D. (eds), (2005). *The Cap and the Regions: The Territorial Impact of the Common Agricultural Policy*, Wallingford: CABI Publishing.

Skogstad, G. (1998). 'Ideas, Paradigms and Institutions: Agricultural Exceptionalism in the European Union and the United States'. *Governance* 11(4): 463–490, https://doi.org/10.1111/0952-1895.00082.

Stone, D.A. (2002). *Policy Paradox: The Art of Political Decision Making*, New York: W.W. Norton.

Swinbank, A. and Daugbjerg, C. (2006). 'The 2003 CAP Reform: Accommodating WTO Pressures'. *Comparative European Politics* 4(1): 47–64, https://doi.org/10.1057/palgrave.cep.6110069.

Tracy, M. (1989). *Government and Agriculture in Western Europe 1880–1988*, New York/London: Harvester Wheatsheaf.

WBAE – Scientific Advisory Board on Agricultural Policy, Food and Consumer Health Protection (2018). 'For an EU Common Agricultural Policy Serving the Public Good after 2020: Fundamental Questions and Recommendations'. Report of the Scientific Advisory Board on Agricultural Policy, Food and Consumer Protection at the Federal Ministry of Food and Agriculture, Berlin: BMEL, available at www.bmel.de/SharedDocs/Downloads/EN/_Ministry/AgriculturalPolicyafter2020-report.pdf, last accessed 15 January 2022.

6. The 2021 reform of EU cohesion policy in context of the negotiations on the Multiannual Financial Framework

Wolfgang Petzold

In 1986, the foundations of what was coined EU cohesion policy were laid down by the Single European Act and subsequent regulations. Ever since, six reforms in 1993, 1999, 2006, 2013 and 2021 kept the key beliefs underpinning the policy's scope and budget surprisingly unchanged despite manifold challenges. In this chapter, a brief look at these reforms and their respective contexts is taken, arguing that the most recent one in particular may open new avenues for a more radical policy change. More specifically, it will be shown that while existing institutional settings have favoured path-dependency of EU cohesion policy, pressure on its future redesign may stem from the delivery mechanism of the new Recovery and Resilience Facility.

EU COHESION POLICY AND ITS MULTILAYERED REFORMS

Against the background of existing EU funds, the European Social Fund since 1958, the European Agriculture Guidance and Guarantee Fund since 1962 and the European Regional Development Fund since 1975, the 1986 reform of the Treaty establishing the European Community set the objective to promote 'economic and social cohesion' and to reduce 'disparities between the levels of development of the various regions and the backwardness of the least favoured regions'. In the same year, the Council of the EU adopted a set of five regulations on common general provisions, coordination and implementation of each of the three funds, laying down some key principles of EU cohesion policy, which have remained in place ever since, including:

– *concentration* on a limited number of objectives with the focus on the least developed regions;

– *multi-annual programming* based on analysis, strategic planning and evaluation;
– *additionality* ensuring that member states do not substitute EU expenditure for national expenditure;
– *partnership* in the design and implementation of programmes involving national, sub-national and EU actors, the social partners and non-government organisations, ensuring ownership and transparency of the interventions.

The overview in Table 6.1 shows how these principles and the funds and instruments developed over the subsequent five reforms.

All reforms of cohesion policy have been closely linked to negotiations concerning the EU's Multiannual Financial Frameworks. Taking a decision on the latter still requires unanimity in the Council with no veto option for the European Parliament. The Lisbon Treaty has put the two institutions on equal footing as regards the regulations governing cohesion policy funds and instruments under the ordinary legislative procedure and qualified majority voting in the Council. At the same time, negotiations on the overall allocation of cohesion policy funds, the eligibility of regions, thematic concentration, co-financing rates, etc., remain dependent on member states reaching a unanimous agreement in both the Council and in the European Council – a situation that leads to complex, double-track negotiations in and between the two law-making institutions. Final consensus usually comes as a package deal and includes agreements on other EU policies based on compromises and side payments. However, such bargaining processes are framed by dominant or even shared perceptions of what policy choices are feasible and appropriate, which are expressed in particular narratives (Heinelt and Petzold, 2018).

Moreover, cohesion policy reforms have been context-bound, open and flexible in order to address wider policy objectives or agendas set by an ever-closer and ever-larger European Union, as shown in Table 6.2. Despite regular criticism as regards its complexity and delayed implementation, EU cohesion policy's flexibility has most likely not only helped to keep its relative share of the EU budget in the order of about one-third but also to experience mostly less significant cuts when one compares the initial proposals of the total EU budget with those for cohesion policy allocations.

Looking into the reasons for such success, scholars have argued that EU cohesion policy and its reforms provide the various players at EU, national and regional level with a loosely coupled but coherent multilevel system, which is characterised by the sequencing of decisions, the separation of decision-making and different implementation arenas (Bachtler and Mendez, 2007, 2020; Bachtler and Polverari, 2017; Bachtler et al., 2013, 2016; Heinelt and Lang, 2011; Heinelt et al., 2003; Manzella and Mendez, 2009; Mendez,

Table 6.1   EU cohesion policy 1989–2027: objectives, funds and geographical coverage

1989–1993	1994–1999	2000–2006	2007–2013	2014–2020	2021–2027
Objective 1: development and structural adjustment of regions where development is lagging behind, i.e. where the GDP per head is less than 75% of EU average (ERDF, ESF, EAGGF, FIFG: as of 1994)			Convergence, regions with a GDP < 75% of EU average (ERDF, ESF)	Investment in jobs and growth – with 11 thematic objectives (ERDF, ESF) covering – Less-developed regions (< 75% of EU average) – transition regions with 75–90% of EU average – more-developed regions with > 90% of EU average	Investment in jobs and growth – with 5 policy objectives (ERDF, ESF+, CF, JTF) covering – less-developed regions (< 75% of EU average) – transition regions with 75–100% of EU average – more-developed regions with > 100% of EU average – European Urban Initiative
		Phasing-out and -in regions, i.e. former regions with a GDP < 75%			
Objective 2: converting the regions, frontier regions or parts of regions seriously affected by industrial decline (ERDF, ESF)	Objective 2: converting the regions or parts of regions seriously affected by industrial decline (ERDF, ESF)	Objective 2: supporting the economic and social conversion of areas facing structural difficulties (ERDF, ESF)	Regional competitiveness and employment for all EU regions with a GDP > 75% of EU average (ERDF, ESF)		
Objective 3: combating long-term unemployment (ESF)	Objective 3: combating long-term unemployment and facilitating occupational integration (ESF)	Objective 3: supporting the adaptation and modernisation of policies and systems of education, training and employment (ESF)			
Objective 4: occupational integration of young people (ESF)	Objective 4: adapting the workforce to industrial changes (ESF)				

1989–1993	1994–1999	2000–2006	2007–2013	2014–2020	2021–2027
Objective 5b: promotion of rural areas (EAGGF, ERDF, ESF)	Objective 5b: development and structural adjustment of rural and fisheries areas (EAGGF, ERDF, ESF, FIFG)			Objectives of the reformed common agricultural (EAFRD) fisheries policies (EMFF)	Objectives of the reformed common fisheries policy (EMFAF)
	Objective 6: regions with an extremely low population density				
Support for investment in transport and environmental infrastructure for countries with a GNI below 90% of the EU average (CF)					
					Support for regions with a carbon- or fossil-fuels intensive economy (JTF)
16 Community Initiatives (ERDF, ESF, EAGGF)	13 Community Initiatives (ERDF, ESF, EAGGF, FIFG)	4 Community Initiatives (ERDF, ESF, EAGGF)	European Territorial Cooperation/Interreg (ERDF)		

Notes: ERDF: European Regional Development Fund; ESF: European Social Fund; CF: Cohesion Fund; EAGGF: European Agricultural Guarantee and Guidance Fund; EAFRD: European Agricultural Fund for Rural Development; FIFG: Financial Instrument for Fisheries Guidance; EMFF: European Maritime and Fisheries Fund; EMFAF: European Maritime, Fisheries and Aquaculture Fund; JTF: Just Transition Fund.
Source: Author's own elaboration.

Table 6.2   *The reforms of EU cohesion policy: context, narratives, budget*

Period	EU context	Policy shifts and narratives	EU cohesion policy share of MFF/EU GNI (in %)	Cuts*: total MFF/EU cohesion policy (in %)
1989–1993	Budget crisis, single market programme '1992', from EU9 to EU12	Multi-annual programming, common objectives and principles for different funds including definition of target regions	25.5/0.3	3/2.5
1994–1999	EMU preparation, Maastricht Treaty, from EU12 to EU15	Cohesion Fund	33.1/0.4	8.5/8.8
2000–2006	'Agenda 2000', from EU15 to EU25	Effectiveness, decentralisation, concentration, capping, 'audit explosion'	30.2/0.38	3/7
2007–2013	'Lisbon Strategy', 'Sapir report' (2003), financial crisis, from EU25 to EU28	Alignment with broader EU strategy, evidence-based, academic debate	35.8/0.4	15.4/8.7
2014–2020	'Europe 2020', economic crisis, European Semester	Place-based approach; ex ante and macro-economic conditionalities	29.4**/0.3	8/4
2021–2027	Brexit, White Paper (2017), 'rule-of-law' debate, pandemic, 'NextGenerationEU', from EU28 to EU27	Simplification, results-orientation, conditionality regulation, Just Transition Fund, competition with Recovery and Resilience facility, differentiation, European Semester	30.8/0.35	5.4/0

Notes: * Comparison of cuts in % of total MFF and cohesion policy allocations: initial proposal by the European Commission vs final agreement between Council and EP.
** Percentage of the total for EU27 with the EDF included.
Source: Author's own elaboration.

2013; Piattoni and Polverari, 2016). By granting a certain level of discretion to all stakeholders involved, EU cohesion policy reforms appear to feed the debate, thus reaffirming and fine-tuning institutional positions in response to varying and changing political contexts. Over more than three decades, an EU cohesion policy community has emerged, with loosely connected debates on 'spatial justice', urban and rural development, social inclusion and labour market policies. To them, cohesion policy provides a transnational arena for discussion framed by a common terminology and sets of rules and beliefs, which have developed over time through interactive discourse and are captured by particular narratives.

UNDERSTANDING THE 2021 REFORM: THE POSITIONING OF THE EU INSTITUTIONS

The European Commission

In order to understand the most recent reform of EU cohesion policy, it is helpful to look into the previous period, 2014–2020, and its dynamics. Ahead of the legislative process laying down the provisions for that period, the European Commission supported a far-reaching debate involving academics and international institutions about cohesion policy's added value, priorities and the institutional setting, which culminated in April 2009 in the presentation of what was called the 'Barca Report' – named after the then-Director-General of the Italian Ministry for Economic and Financial Affairs, Fabrizio Barca (Barca, 2009). In addition to providing a critical appraisal of EU cohesion policy, the report set out some reform options and a politically motivated subtext to protect and re-legitimise the policy in the face of growing criticism about its rationale and effectiveness. It did so by arguing that cohesion policy was making a distinct contribution to the EU's growth and jobs agenda, by presenting territorial disparities as 'untapped potential' and by claiming that economic integration needed to be accompanied by 'place-based' policies to counteract the imbalances resulting from the 2008/2009 crisis.

Discussions about 'place-based' vs 'space-blind' economic development were also held by international organisations such as the Organisation for Economic Co-operation and Development and the World Bank. While the former regularly advocated integrated development approaches involving multilevel governance and coordination among relevant stakeholders (Organisation of Economic Development and Co-operation, 2009), the latter challenged the assumption that economic activities must be spread geographically to benefit the most poor and vulnerable and favoured instead economic integration through the mobility of people, products and ideas in its *World*

Development Report 2009: Reshaping Economic Geography (World Bank, 2009).

For the 2014–2020 period, the five European Structural and Investment Funds had been put under a common regulatory and strategic umbrella while preserving a number of fund-specific provisions. Furthermore, the legislative framework was complemented by a set of 22 delegated and implementing acts – not counting legal acts relating to the control of measures under the Common Agricultural Policy and an additional 17 delegated and implementing acts applicable to the European Maritime and Fisheries Fund. The total legislative package consisted of more than 800 pages representing a significant increase compared to the previous period.

It appears that the 2013 reform of EU cohesion policy provided the three EU decision-making institutions, the European Parliament, the Council of the EU and the European Commission, with arenas for discussion, in which existing and new policy narratives and options could be tested and combined with normative values. Moreover, existing links with the EU's overarching Europe 2020 strategy were reinforced and compliance with other EU policies at member state and regional level were strengthened by the new conditionality rationale. With regard to implementation, the price paid included an increased administrative burden and reduced flexibility for national and regional players. Finally, the reform process remained embedded in the overarching *juste retour* logic deriving from the unanimity rule in the Council on the EU Multiannual Financial Framework and the limited influence of the European Parliament on it (Heinelt and Petzold, 2018; Petzold, 2013).

Reflections about the post-2020 reform of EU cohesion policy were launched in August 2015 by a speech given by the then-Commissioner for Regional Policy, Corinna Crețu, who introduced 'ten key questions' into the reform debate. These addressed issues such as the relationship between competitiveness and cohesion, the situation of lagging regions, which are not converging towards the EU average despite decades of national and EU support, the question of whether advanced regions should still receive cohesion funds, the role of financial instruments, the relationship between EU priorities and the policy's territorial focus, challenges related to energy security and migration, the urban dimension, simplification and the quality of institutions, the funds' allocation and the indicators underpinning it and finally the policy's integration into the EU's economic governance and reform agenda (Crețu, 2015). In parallel, a series of studies, most prominently one on 'lagging regions', as well as a High Level Group for Simplification of the structural funds, were launched (European Commission, 2017a; European Commission, 2015). Such reflections were embedded in the debate on the future of Europe, which the then-President of the European Commission, Jean-Claude Juncker, had launched after the referendum of June 2016, which resulted in the United

Kingdom leaving the European Union. The subsequent 'White Paper on the Future of Europe' was presented by the European Commission in March 2017 (European Commission, 2017b) and a reflection on the future of EU finances in June (European Commission, 2017c). The latter set the tone for the proposal of the Multiannual Financial Framework post 2020 towards the background of five future scenarios, of which four suggested a reduction of cohesion funding.

In September 2017, an internal paper of the European Commission spelled out the details of different future scenarios for EU cohesion policy post 2020 and identified areas for the policy's improvement such as reducing overlaps and competition among policies and funding instruments, reducing uncertainty and administrative burden for beneficiaries by aligning the rules for similar interventions, reducing complexity of the legal framework, addressing complexity of management, control and audit systems, reporting and monitoring, improving flexibility to respond to new challenges and supporting administrative capacity-building and institutional reforms. In quantitative terms, the paper presented three scenarios with a reduction of the financial envelope for cohesion policy of either 26% – with funding exclusively for less-developed regions – or 39% with funding only available for cohesion countries. The third, zero-increase scenario, was based on the current policy design, that is, with different levels of support for all EU regions (European Commission, 2017d).

On 29 May 2018, the European Commission proposed the new set of rules for EU cohesion policy 2021–2027, including the Common Provisions Regulation covering seven funds – the European Regional Development Fund, the Cohesion Fund, the European Social Fund+, the European Maritime and Fisheries Fund, as well as the Asylum, Migration and Integration Fund, the Internal Security Fund and the Border Management and Visa Instrument. On 14 January 2020, the European Commission presented an amended proposal of the Common Provisions Regulation in order to embed the Just Transition Fund as a new fund under cohesion policy.

The European Parliament

The positioning of the European Parliament on the reform of EU cohesion policy started as early as June 2017 with the adoption of a Resolution on 'Building blocks for post-2020 EU cohesion policy', which emphasised the need for simplification and synergies between different EU funds, a clear legislative framework and avoiding delays of programme delivery in the new period (European Parliament, 2017). The 2019 elections to the European Parliament brought its negotiations with the Council to a halt between April and September (European Parliament, 2021). The European Parliament's 'building blocks' for reform highlighted issues such as simplification and synergies between different EU funds, the need for early preparation, a clear legislative framework and better communication, as well as the importance of innovative low-carbon local development, a strong 'urban dimension' and the integration of migrants.

At the European Parliament, the Committee on Regional Development took the lead on the legislative proposal made by the European Commission in May 2018. The draft report was voted on in February 2019 and included a number of amendments, which were adopted by the plenary in March 2019. Following intensive discussions with the Council and the European Commission in 2019 and 2020, the European Parliament adopted the final version of the cohesion policy regulations in June 2021.

The Council of the EU

Between the proposal on the regulatory framework of EU cohesion policy in May 2018 and its publication in June 2021, seven presidencies of the Council of the European Union – Bulgaria and Austria in 2018, Romania and Finland in 2019, Croatia and Germany in 2020, and Portugal in 2021 – were involved in the negotiations. Inside the Council, works on the proposals on the Common Provisions Regulation, the ERDF, the Cohesion Fund, the ESF+, and the Just Transition Fund were dealt with by the 'Working Party on Structural Measures',[1] which informed the meetings of the General Affairs Council on cohesion policy and the informal meetings of the ministers responsible for cohesion policy. While the latter two usually meet at ministerial level once or twice during a presidency's term, the Working Party holds its meetings almost weekly as soon as new regulations are tabled and had more than 100 formal gatherings between May 2018 and June 2021.

In April 2018, the Council had adopted conclusions on the implementation and delivery of cohesion policy after 2020 in response to a report of the European Commission on the implementation of the structural funds since 2014 (European Commission, 2017e). In its conclusions, the Council stated the need for a proportionate management system, simplified legislation and flexible programming, smooth transition between programming periods, and the optional use of financial instruments, and highlighted the 'territorial approach' including community-led local development, cross-border cooperation and the urban dimension of cohesion policy (Council of the EU, 2018).

In June 2018, the Working Party had agreed to divide the negotiations on the Common Provisions Regulation into eight thematic blocks with the objective of agreeing upon partial mandates for the negotiations with the European Parliament. These blocks concerned (1) programming and strategic planning; (2) enabling conditions and performance framework; (3) monitoring, evaluation, communication and visibility; (4) financial support from the funds; (5) management and control; (6) financial management; (7) definitions and other provisions such as delegation of power, implementing, transitional and final provisions; and (8) financial framework and all other provisions with budgetary implications or of a horizontal nature such as the transfers of financial allocations between funds and to other instruments, co-financing rates, and decommitment rules. While the Working Party dealt with blocks 1 to 7, all issues of block 8 were excluded from their discussions and remained subject to the development of the 'negotiating box' for the European Council including through the Ad hoc Working Party on the Multiannual Financial Framework.

During the Austrian presidency, the Working Party on Structural Measures had broadly agreed on blocks 1 and 5, while blocks 2, 3, 4, 6 and 7 were in its focus during the Romanian presidency. The Permanent Representatives Committee subsequently agreed on partial negotiation mandates for these blocks and invited the European Parliament to three 'political trilogues' in spring 2019 and another four such trilogues between September and December 2019. On 13 December 2019, the Permanent Representatives Committee endorsed a progress report on the negotiations and the state of play of blocks 1, 2 and 5, including a table highlighting agreement, differences and possible compromises on particular articles between the European Commission proposals, the amendments suggested by the European Parliament, and the Council position (Council of the EU, 2019).

On the Multiannual Financial Framework and financial aspects of cohesion policy, the European Council had its first exchanges in December 2018 and discussed a draft 'negotiating box' in June 2019, which was updated in December and included figures for the first time. European Council President Charles Michel presented a new 'negotiating box' for the subsequent European Council meeting in February 2020, which remained inconclusive. Following the in-principle agreement between the European Council and the European Parliament in April on the 'roadmap to recovery', the European Commission's revision of its proposal for the Multiannual Financial Framework was presented on 27 May 2020. Before the final agreement of the European Council was achieved on 21 July, a new 'negotiating box' had been tabled on 10 July (see Becker, Chapter 2 in this volume; European Parliament, 2021). More than a quarter of the text of the European Council's conclusions on the Multiannual Financial Framework and 'Next Generation EU' funds – 18 of the 65 pages – refer to cohesion policy. Beyond financial means by goal and fund, allocation methods, upper and lower ceilings of national support, the so-called capping and safety net levels, the conclusions also refer to the categories of regions, related co-financing rules, annual pre-financing rates, decommitment provisions and other details (European Council, 2020). They impact on the cohesion policy regulations and so bypass the rule of co-decision applicable to these, as the European Parliament has repeatedly argued (European Parliament, 2021).

Other EU Institutions and Bodies

As with previous reforms, other EU institutions have commented on the reform process of EU cohesion policy according to their role and their means. Among them, the European Committee of the Regions has been most active. Traditionally, the latter has been vocal on maintaining and deepening the partnership principle and the place-based approach of the policy. During the recent reform, it has federated numerous stakeholders through the so-called 'Cohesion Alliance', a consortium of almost 300 regions, cities and counties as well as 50 European and national associations representing the former, which signed a declaration in 2017 favouring a more prominent role for regions and cities in the policy's design and implementation, among others. Moreover, the European Committee of the Regions has given more support to the 'all-regions-in' approach and flexibility in and simplification of the funds' management through a longer expenditure period (n+3) and higher co-financing rates (European Committee of the Regions, 2021). Recently, the Committee has also published reflections on 'cohesion as a fundamental value' claiming that its principles of 'territorial justice' and 'multi-level governance' should also be respected by other EU policies (European Committee of the Regions, 2021).

The other advisory body to the EU institutions, the European Economic and Social Committee, presents the views of the social partners and civil society and has, for example, argued in favour of EU cohesion policy as a means to 'bring Europe closer to the citizens' and to tackle disparities between regions and inequality between people. It has also supported simplification and flexibility of the policy's management (European Economic and Social Committee, 2020).

Finally, the European Court of Auditors has issued several reports during the reform process. Beyond addressing the regularity of cohesion policy spending and potential cost savings, the Court has reflected on the policy's governance and its delayed implementation, performance-based financing, European Territorial Cooperation and financial instruments (European Court of Auditors, 2017, 2021a–c).

EU COHESION POLICY 2021–2027

While the political agreement between the European Parliament, the Council of the EU and the European Commission on the Regulations governing cohesion policy funds and instruments was achieved in December 2020, negotiations between the three EU institutions on technical details continued in spring 2021, delaying the publication of the legal framework for the 2021–2027 period until June 2021 (European Commission, 2021a). A total of 37 months after the initial proposal had been made, the 700 pages of the five EU regulations in question – on the common provisions for all funds, the European Regional Development Fund and the Cohesion Fund, the European Social Fund+, the Just Transition Fund and European Territorial Cooperation/ Interreg – represent almost as much as the volume of legal provisions of the previous period. In a nutshell, the design of EU cohesion policy between 2021 and 2027 looks as follows:

– The funds and instruments: including the new Just Transition Fund, which was added in 2020 to the initial proposal of 2018, there will now be four cohesion policy funds and instruments, while a fifth one, the European Maritime Fisheries and Aquaculture Fund, remains loosely coupled and a sixth one, the European Agricultural Fund for Rural Development has left the camp (again). This, together with the ESF+ now being linked to the implementation of the European Pillar of Social Rights, and all the remaining funds referring more strongly to the European Semester process, one could read the reform's result as if cohesion policy is moving away from its territorial, multilevel approach to one that is more rooted in the idea of member states' compliance rules and agendas set at EU level on economic governance and the conditionality of transfers.
– The objectives: the ERDF, the ESF+, the Cohesion Fund (and the EMFAF) will support five policy objectives. These will focus on green and digital transition, a more connected, inclusive and social Europe, and a Europe that is closer to its citizens. Specific spending targets are established for reaching the climate targets for the ERDF (30%) and the Cohesion Fund (37%).
– The financial allocation: with almost €380 billion allocated to EU cohesion policy, the share of funds and instruments compared to the total MFF now stands at almost 31% – about the level it had been in the previous period and one percentage point above the initial proposal of May 2018. Almost 85% of the resources will be concentrated on less-developed or transition regions and countries receiving support from the Cohesion Fund. At the level of the member states, allocations in real terms will be reduced by about 10% on average or between 5% and 24% for 14 countries while the remainder will see no change or increases of up to 8% compared to 2014–2020.
– Geographical and thematic concentration: the categories of EU regions between less-developed (with a GDP/GNI below 75% of the EU average), transition regions (75–100%) and more developed regions (> 100%) remain more or less unchanged – except that the upper margin of GDP for transition regions was slightly increased from 90% to 100% compared to the previous period. Thematically, all regions and member states must

Table 6.3   EU cohesion policy 2021–2027: funds, goals and geographical concentration (in € billion, current prices)

	ERDF	ESF+	Cohesion Fund	Just Transition Fund	Total	in %
Total	*225.26*	*98.16*	*36.61*	*19.24*	*379.26*	*100.00*
Goal 'Investment in jobs and growth' *					313.16	82.57
– less-developed regions					226.96	59.84
– transition regions					53.55	14.12
– more-developed regions					30.49	8.04
– outermost and sparsely populated regions					2.16	0.57
Goal 'European Territorial Cooperation – Interreg'	9.04					2.38
– less-developed regions	6.53					1.72
– transition regions	1.65					0.43
– more-developed regions	0.55					0.15
– outermost and sparsely populated regions	0.32					0.08
EU initiatives					1.21	0.32
– Interregional Innovation Investments	0.56					0.15
– European Urban Initiative	0.45					0.12
– ESF transnational cooperation		0.20				0.05
Member states with a GNI <90% of EU average			36.61			9.65
Regions with a carbon or fossil fuels intensive economy				19.24		5.07
in %	*59.39*	*25.88*	*9.65*	*5.07*	*379.26*	*100.00*

Notes: * Allocations for the ERDF and ESF+ together.
Source: European Commission, 2022c.

concentrate the support on 'a more competitive and smarter Europe' and 'a greener, low-carbon transition, net zero carbon economy' to different degrees (European Commission, 2021a); more developed regions and member states must concentrate at least 85% of their ERDF and Cohesion Fund allocation to these objectives, transition regions, 70% and less-developed regions, 55%. Moreover, at least 8% of regional or national allocations must be earmarked to urban development that will be delivered through local development partnerships, an increase by two percentage points compared to the European Commission's proposal of May 2018. Table 6.3 and Figure 6.1 provide more detail.

– Management of funds and instruments: while the set of rules related to the funds' management remain largely unchanged compared to the previous period – with slight simplifications as regards, for example, the inclusion of delegated acts, the abolition of the performance reserve, simplified audit provisions and higher grades of flexibility for transfers between funds during the implementation – some changes introduced by the European Parliament and the Council are significant. For example, the co-financing rates from the EU funds have been increased and now vary between 40% for more developed regions, 60% vs 55% proposed for transition regions and 85% vs 70% proposed for less-developed regions. Compared to 2014–2020, these rates are now also 5 and 10 percentage points higher for less-developed and transition regions respectively, while they are 10 percentage points lower for more-developed regions. In addition, the 'n+2' rule, referring to the last payments to be made at the latest two years after

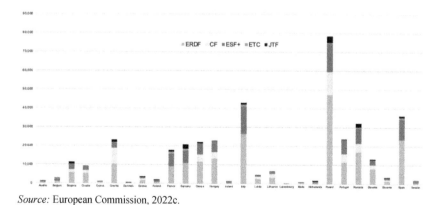

Source: European Commission, 2022c.

Figure 6.1   *EU cohesion policy funds 2021–2027 (in € million by member state, current prices)*

the programming period and suggested by the European Commission to speed up spending, has become 'n+3' again – as was the case between 2014 and 2020.

Implementation of the 2021–2027 cohesion policy has been slow: by March 2022, only half of the national partnership agreements had been introduced and just a quarter of the 400 national and regional operational programmes had been received by the European Commission.

THE RECOVERY AND RESILIENCE FACILITY: THE EU COHESION POLICY'S SILENT REFORM?

Following the outbreak of COVID-19 in Europe in spring 2020, the first EU measures to counterbalance the economic crisis resulting from the pandemic were taken in mid March by the European Central Bank through the Pandemic Emergency Purchase Programme, and by the 'pandemic crisis support' under the European Stability Mechanism in May (see, for more detail, Becker, Chapter 2 in this volume). On 18 May 2020, the governments of France and Germany proposed that the European Commission should establish a 'Recovery Fund' in the order of €500 billion, which it would borrow on financial markets and incorporate in the EU budget, while the Spanish government had suggested such an instrument at the level of €1,000 billion. The European Commission presented its proposal of a 'Next Generation EU' plan worth €750 billion on 27 May 2020. Following the European Council's agreement of 21 July 2020 and the political agreement with the European Parliament in December, the regulation on the Recovery and Resilience Facility entered into force on 19 February 2021 (European Commission, 2021b). Interestingly, the legal basis of the facility is Article 175(3) of the Treaty on the Functioning of the European Union, which suggests 'specific actions' to be taken in 'accordance with the ordinary legislative procedure' while referring to economic, social and territorial cohesion and Article 174 of the same Treaty. The total amount available for the member states between 2021 and 2026 finally amounts to €723.8 billion, of which €385.8 billion is in the form of loans and €338 billion is grants. The split between member states is built on population figures, the fall of national GDP in 2020 and 2021 and unemployment rates. National recovery and resilience plans must refer to policy areas in six pillars:

– green transition;
– digital transformation;
– smart, sustainable and inclusive growth, including economic cohesion, jobs, productivity, competitiveness, research, development and innovation,

and a well-functioning internal market with strong small and medium-sized enterprises (SMEs);
–   social and territorial cohesion;
–   health, and economic, social and institutional resilience, with the aim of, inter alia, increasing crisis preparedness and crisis response capacity;
–   policies for the next generation, children and the youth, such as education and skills.

Member states must earmark at least 37% of their allocation to green transition and 20% to digital transformation. Moreover, planning and implementation of the Facility is strongly linked to the recommendations made to member states as part of the European Semester process.

Implementation of the Facility was fast: by summer 2021, the majority of member states had submitted their recovery and resilience plans. By the end of January 2022, 22 out of 26 national plans had been adopted by a Council decision and payments in the order of €56 billion had been executed (European Commission, 2022a). Table 6.4 provides a basic comparison of scope, volume and governance of EU cohesion policy and the Recovery and Resilience Facility.

Several scholars have commented critically on the Facility's design by pointing to the problem of additionality (Corti et al., 2022), conditionality and EU values (Blauberger and van Hüllen, 2021), questioning its effectiveness to achieve compliance with national reforms suggested by the European Semester (Bekker, 2021), its 'spatial blindness' (Crescenzi et al., 2021), its complementarity and coherence with cohesion policy funds (Ferry and Kah, 2021) and its role in the EU's economic governance architecture (Verdun and Vanhercke, 2021).

EU COHESION POLICY 2021–2027 AND BEYOND: FLEXIBLE OR FRAGMENTED?

As has been shown, during the design, decision and implementation phases, governance of EU cohesion policy is dependent on players with different interests and resources. There is little room for them to manoeuvre because of the 'shadow' cast by unanimity, which is required at the Council in relation to the Multiannual Financial Framework. Furthermore, their room for manoeuvre is limited by the policy's path-dependency, which frames its design and governance. Such principles and overarching strategies represent discursively constructed limitations of what seems feasible and appropriate. Negotiations and their results indicate the following lessons learned:

Table 6.4   2021–2027 EU cohesion policy funds and the Recovery and Resilience Facility

	Cohesion policy funds	Recovery and Resilience Facility
Legal basis	Art. 177 TFEU	Art. 175(3) TFEU
EU institutions deciding	European Parliament, Council of the EU	European Parliament, Council of the EU
Total allocation (in current prices)	€379.3 billion (grants)	€732.8 billion (grants and loans)
Indicators used to calculate the allocation by region/country	Data at NUTS 2 level including population, GDP/GNI 2015–2017, labour market, etc., capping and safety nets apply at national levels	Data at national level including population, fall of GDP in 2020/21, unemployment rate 2015–2019; capping applies
Number of regulations and their volume (pages)	5/708	1/58
Thematic priorities	Five policy objectives and thematic priorities by fund; depending on the category of regions between 55% and 85% to be earmarked for green and digital transition, at least 30% of the total for climate action	Six pillars: at least 37% of the total to be earmarked for climate objectives, 20% for digital transition
Conditionality provisions	'Enabling conditions', linked to the European Semester	Adoption of programmes and payments dependent on reforms suggested by the European Semester
Management	Shared management, 27 national partnership agreements, 400 national or regional programmes, decided by the European Commission	Direct management, 27 national plans decided by the Council of the EU, no or little involvement of subnational entities

Source: Author's own elaboration.

- The longest-ever negotiations of the legislative package have taken 37 months from the initial Commission's proposal in May 2018 to the adoption by Council and European Parliament in June 2021.
- The total EU budget for 2021–2027 is slightly below the level of the previous one in terms of EU GNI if one only counts the Multiannual Financial Framework – but is about 1.5 times the previous amount if the allocation for 'Next Generation EU' is factored in.
- Dynamics within and between the EU institutions have been embedded in their long-term orientations and the legal setting, requiring double-track negotiations, the net payers vs beneficiaries debate, etc.
- Changing narratives during the negotiation process have led to a higher level of the policy's politicisation due to parallel events such as Brexit, the pandemic and first-time borrowing through the EU budget, of the rule-of-law conditionality and the European Green Deal (on the relevance of the ideas behind the European Green Deal, see Bornemann, Chapter 7 in this volume).
- New rules, funds, instruments and time frames will possibly result in a rather complex, if not fragmented, implementation for all actors involved.

In the context of the 2021 reform, flexibility has taken three forms: first, the European Parliament and the member states have achieved a couple of amendments to the initial proposal made by the European Commission, which will serve a more flexible management of the funds, for example, as regards the move from the n+2 to the n+3 rule, higher co-financing rates and thematic concentration of the funds now left to the member states. Second, changes suggested in 2019 by the new European Commission and the new European Parliament and the political priorities set for the 2019–2024 period, notably the European Green Deal, led to increased earmarking for climate action in the EU budget and the introduction of the Just Transition Fund, now part of EU cohesion policy. Third, the flexible response to the pandemic through new instruments has proven to be rapid as regards the legislative procedure and the execution of funds (Bachtler and Mendez, 2021; Conference of Peripheral and Maritime Regions, 2020).

The 2021 reform of EU cohesion policy has confirmed its role as a facilitator of transition and compromise despite conflicting positions and narratives on how to address inequalities between places and people in an 'ever closer' EU. However, it appears that a stronger link to the European Semester process and 'conditional investment' have replaced the 'place-based narrative', which has been the leitmotif of the 2013 reform (Bachtler and Mendez, 2020; Mendez, 2013) with the rule-of-law mechanism now being applied to the EU budget as a whole. In parallel, the reform has also led to a more fragmented delivery of funds and instruments, with ideas of 'territorial justice between the places and the people of the EU' losing ground while those suggesting member states' compliance with other policies gain ground.

Moreover, the reform appears to have put cohesion policy funds and the Recovery and Resilience Facility in competition. It reopens the debate on whether addressing disparities between the regions of the EU can be better achieved through direct transfers into national budgets accompanied by reforms than through complex multilevel implementation arrangements.

As regards the future of cohesion policy post 2027, the European Commission's Eighth Report on Economic, Social and Territorial Cohesion (European Commission, 2022b) suggests focusing the debate on three headings including addressing new drivers of disparities, strengthening the role of regions and developing the tools 'to deliver cohesion towards 2050'. As 'new drivers of disparities', the report identifies the needed carbon neutral transition towards a circular economy, the risks of technological change and asymmetric shocks linked to globalisation, demographic change and the pressure on democracy and its values.

A 'strengthened role for regions', so the report says, should be underpinned by new economic perspectives for less-developed and peripheral regions, embedding innovation in all regions, increasing cross-border and inter-regional cooperation, strengthening urban–rural links and the role of smaller cities and towns and addressing the needs of left-behind places. Finally, as regards the 'tools to deliver cohesion towards 2050' the report proposes to increase the effectiveness of place-based policies through local or regional plans supporting smart specialisation, just transition and integrated territorial development. Moreover, streamlining the access of beneficiaries to cohesion policy instruments should be pursued, unlocking public and private investment for the green, digital and demographic transitions, investing in people throughout their life and enhancing complementarities with other EU policies. With regard to the latter aspect, the report suggests introducing a new principle, 'do no harm to cohesion', to prove that policies will not hamper the convergence process or contribute to regional disparities.

Launched by a large-scale political event in March 2022, it can be expected that the debate about cohesion policy's design will intensify after the next elections to the European Parliament in May 2024, along with the discussion about the EU's next Multiannual Financial Framework post 2027.

NOTE

1.   As of June 2021, the Working Party was merged with the one on outermost regions and became the 'Working Party on Structural Measures and Outermost Regions'.

REFERENCES

Bachtler, J., & Mendez, C. (2007). 'Who governs EU cohesion policy? Deconstructing the reforms of the Structural Funds'. *Journal of Common Market Studies*, 45(3), 535–564.

Bachtler, J., & Mendez, C. (2020). 'Cohesion and the EU budget: is conditionality undermining solidarity?' In R. Coman, A. Crespy, & V.A. Schmidt (eds), *Governance and Politics in the Post-Crisis Union*, Cambridge: Cambridge University Press, 121–139.

Bachtler, J., & Mendez, C. (2021). 'Recovery and cohesion: ambitious objectives, challenging implementation', European Regional Policy Research Consortium Report 21/2, Glasgow and Delft: European Policies Research Centre.

Bachtler, J., & Polverari, L. (2017). *Building Blocks for a Future Cohesion Policy. First Reflections*, Brussels: European Parliament, Policy Department for Structural and Cohesion Policies. Research for REGI Committee.

Bachtler, J., Mendez, C., & Polverari, L. (2016). 'Ideas and options for cohesion policy post-2020'. IQ-Net Thematic Paper, 38(2), Glasgow: European Policies Research Centre.

Bachtler, J., Mendez, C., & Wishlade, F. (2013). *EU Cohesion Policy and European Integration. The Dynamics of EU Budget and Regional Policy Reform*, Aldershot: Ashgate.

Barca, F. (2009). 'An Agenda for a Reformed Cohesion Policy. A place-based approach to meeting European Union challenges and expectations'. Independent Report prepared at the request of Danuta Hübner, Commissioner for Regional Policy, Brussels.

Bekker, S. (2021). 'The EU's Recovery and Resilience Facility: a next phase in EU socioeconomic governance?' *Politics and Governance*, 9(3), 175–185.

Blauberger, M., & van Hüllen, V. (2021). 'Conditionality of EU funds: an instrument to enforce EU fundamental values?' *Journal of European Integration*, 43(1), 1–16.

Conference of Peripheral and Maritime Regions (2020). '"Next Generation EU" – a threat to Cohesion Policy?' Technical note, 16 December 2020, Brussels and Rennes, https://cpmr.org/wpdm-package/next-generation-eu-a-threat-to-cohesion-policy-december-2020/?wpdmdl=27908&ind=1608103449422 (last accessed 15 March 2022).

Corti, F., Gros, D., Ruiz, T., Liscai, A., Kiss-Galfalvi, T., Gstrein, D., Herold, E., & Dolls, M. (2022). 'The Recovery and Resilience Facility: A springboard for a renaissance of public investments in Europe?' Recovery and Resilience Reflection Papers No 6, Brussels: Centre of European Policy Studies.

Council of the EU (2018). 'Delivery and implementation of cohesion policy after 2020, Conclusions of the General Affairs Council', 12 April 2018, www.consilium.europa.eu/en/press/press-releases/2018/04/12/delivery-and-implementation-of-cohesion-policy-post-2020-council-adopts-conclusions/ (last accessed 14 March 2022).

Council of the EU (2019). 'Cohesion policy legislative package 2021–2027 – Common Provisions Regulation', Progress Report by the General Secretariat of the Council (14962/19), 13 December 2019.

Crescenzi, R., Giua, M., & Sonzogno, G.V. (2021). 'Mind the clock: an evidence-based assessment of the implementation of Next Generation EU'. *Journal of Policy Modeling*, 43(2), 278–297.

Crețu, C. (2015). 'An agenda for the reform of EU cohesion policy post-2020', speech given at the fifth annual conference of the European Regional Science Association (ERSA), Lisbon, 28 August 2015.

European Commission (2015). 'Decision of 10 July 2015 setting up the High Level Group of Independent Experts on Monitoring Simplification for Beneficiaries of the European Structural and Investment Funds', COM(2015)4806 final.

European Commission (2017a). 'Competitiveness in low-income and low-growth regions – The lagging regions report', SWD(2017)132 final.

European Commission (2017b). 'White Paper on the future of Europe. Reflections and scenarios for the EU27 by 2025', COM(2017)2025.

European Commission (2017c). 'Reflection paper on the future of EU finances', COM(2017)358.

European Commission, DG REGIO (2017d). 'Cohesion policy programmes (ERDF and Cohesion Fund only), preparation of the post-2020 MFF programmes', concept paper (not published), 18 September 2017.

European Commission (2017e). 'Strategic report 2017 on the implementation of the European Structural and Investment Funds', COM(2017)755 final, Brussels.

European Commission (2021a). Regulations on the Just Transition Fund (EU 2021/1056), the ESF+ (EU 2021/1057), the European Regions Development Fund and the Cohesion Fund (EU 2021/1058), European Territorial Cooperation (EU 2021/1059) and on Common Provisions (EU 2021/1060). *Official Journal L* 231, 30 June 2022.

European Commission (2021b). Regulation (EU) 2021/241 of the European Parliament and the Council of the EU establishing the Recovery and Resilience Facility. *Official Journal L* 57, 18 February 2021.

European Commission (2022a). 'Report from the Commission to the European Parliament and the Council on the implementation of the Recovery and Resilience Facility', COM(2022)75 final, 1 March 2022.

European Commission (2022b). 'Cohesion in Europe towards 2050'. Eighth Report on Economic, Social and Territorial Cohesion.

European Commission (2022c). 'Cohesion Policy 2021–2027', https://ec.europa.eu/ regional_policy/en/2021_2027/ (last accessed 8 March 2022).

European Committee of the Regions (2021). 'Shaping EU cohesion policy. How the CoR's opinions contributed to the legislative framework 2021–2027', https://cor .europa.eu/en/events/Documents/COTER/Shaping%20EU%20Cohesion%20policy %20-%20how%20the%20CoR%E2%80%99s%20opinions%20contributed%20to %20the%20legislative%20framework%20for%202021-2027.pdf (last accessed 14 March 2022).

European Council (2020). 'Special Meeting of the European Council (17, 18, 19, 20 and 21 July 2020) – Conclusions', www.consilium.europa.eu/media/45109/210720 -euco-final-conclusions-en.pdf (last accessed 14 March 2022).

European Court of Auditors (2017). 'The Commission's negotiation of 2014–2020 Partnership Agreements and programmes in Cohesion: spending more targeted on Europe 2020 priorities, but increasingly complex arrangements to measure performance'. Special Report No 2.

European Court of Auditors (2021a). 'Performance-based financing in cohesion policy'. Special Report No 24.

European Court of Auditors (2021b). 'Interreg cooperation: The potential of the European Union's cross-border regions has not yet been fully unlocked'. Special Report No 14.

European Court of Auditors (2021c). 'Financial instruments in cohesion policy at closure of the 2007–2013 period'. Special Report No 6.

European Economic and Social Committee (2020). *Cohesion policy as fundamental pillar for bringing the EU closer to its citizens and for reducing disparities among EU regions and inequalities among people – The views of organised civil society for the programming period 2021–2027*, Brussels: EU Publications.

European Parliament (2017). 'Building blocks for a post-2020 EU Cohesion policy, Resolution of 13 June 2017 (2016/2326(INI))'. *Official Journal C* 331, 41–49.

European Parliament (2021). *The role of the European Council in negotiating the 2021–27 MFF. Continuity and change in the politics of the EU's latest seven-year financial settlement*. Brussels: European Parliament Research Service.

Ferry, M., & Kah, S. (2021). 'Pursuing positive interactions – within Structural Funds and with the RRF', report for the 50th Q-Net Conference on 21 June 2021, Delft: European Policies Research Centre.

Heinelt, H., & Lang, A. (2011). 'Regional actor constellations in EU cohesion policy: differentiation along the policy cycle'. *Central European Journal of Public Policy*, 5(2), 4–28.

Heinelt, H., & Petzold, W. (2018). 'The structural funds and EU cohesion policy'. In H. Heinelt & S. Münch (eds), *Handbook of European Policies, Interpretive Approaches to the EU*, Cheltenham, UK & Northampton, MA, USA: Edward Elgar Publishing, 134–155.

Heinelt, H., Kopp-Malek, T., Lang, J., & Reissert, B. (2003). 'Policy-making in fragmented systems: how to explain success?' In B. Kohler-Koch (ed.), *Linking EU and National Governance*, Oxford and New York: Oxford University Press, 135–153.

Manzella, G. P., & Mendez, C. (2009). *The Turning Points of EU Cohesion Policy*. Luxembourg and Strathclyde: European Investment Bank and the European Policies Research Centre at the University of Strathclyde.

Mendez, C. (2013). 'The post-2013 EU cohesion policy reform and the place-based narrative'. *Journal of European Public Policy*, 20(5), 639–659.

Organisation for Economic Co-operation and Development (2009). *Regions Matter: Economic Recovery, Innovation and Sustainable Growth*, Paris: OECD.

Petzold, W. (2013). 'Conditionality, flexibility, unanimity: the embedded 2013 reform of EU Cohesion Policy'. *European Structural and Investment Funds*, 1(1), 7–14.

Piattoni, S., & Polverari, L. (2016). *Handbook on Cohesion Policy in the EU*, Cheltenham, UK & Northampton, MA, USA: Edward Elgar Publishing.

Verdun, A., & Vanhercke, B. (2021). 'The European Semester as Goldilocks: macroeconomic policy coordination and the Recovery and Resilience Facility'. *Journal of Common Market Studies*, Special Issue 60(1), 204–223.

World Bank (2009). *World Development Report 2009: Reshaping Economic Geography*, Washington DC: World Bank.

7. Sustainabilising Europe in times of crisis? The meta-policy role of the European Green Deal in the context of the COVID-19 pandemic and the negotiations on the EU's Multiannual Financial Framework

Basil Bornemann

INTRODUCTION

Presented by the European Commission in December 2019, the European Green Deal (EGD) is envisioned as the European Union's (EU) new long-term growth strategy. Its ambition is 'to transform the EU into a fair and prosperous society with a modern, resource-efficient and competitive economy' (European Commission, 2019, p. 2). The key objectives of the plan, which consist of various policy-specific goals and measures, are net-zero greenhouse gas emissions by 2050; decoupling economic growth from resource use; preserving the EU's natural capital; and protecting public health from environmental risks. Here, a 'just transition mechanism' is meant to make the transformation inclusive and socially just by technically and financially supporting the economic sectors and regions most significantly affected by this envisaged change. The challenges and ambitions of the EGD can be seen in European Commission's President Ursula von der Leyen referring to the EGD as 'Europe's man on the moon moment' in a press statement before the official announcement in front of the European Parliament (von der Leyen, 2019c). This gives the EGD a historic role not only in the development of European sustainability policy, but also in the development of the EU as a whole (Eckert & Kovalevska, 2021). However, soon after this supposed European moon-landing moment, Europe (and the rest of the world) was brought down to earth. The COVID-19 pandemic led to unprecedented disruptions in social and economic life.

The EGD in the face of the emergent COVID-19 crisis represents an interesting real-life experiment on the tension-filled relation between (long-term) sustainability policy and (short-term) crisis policy or, more precisely, on the crisis-resilience of sustainability policy and sustainability-adeptness of crisis policy. Recently, we have observed a paradoxical pattern here. On the one hand, crises have repeatedly been regarded as triggers and opportunities for sustainability policies. This was evident, for example, in the economic and financial crisis of 2008/2009, when calls for a Green New Deal were voiced in US and European politics. On the other hand, these calls for 'greening' or 'sustainabilisation' out of the crisis have not translated into corresponding policies. On the contrary, there is evidence that existing long-term environmental and sustainability policy ambitions, ideas and programmes have been weakened (Burns et al., 2018, 2020; Gravey & Jordan, 2020). Although no active policy dismantling occurred during the crisis, there are clear indications of a slowing dynamic or inactivity (Skovgaard, 2014). In times of crisis, the here and now begin to dominate political attention while the there and tomorrow fade (see Barbehön, Chapter 3 in this volume).

As with the economic and financial crises, there have been calls in both scientific and policy communities to seize the COVID-19 pandemic as an opportunity for sustainable change, or at least to make crisis management more sustainable. The pandemic provides an opportunity to recognise the downsides of the existing economic development model and use stimulus funds to rebuild jobs and the economy in a way that enables transitioning to a more sustainable future (see, for example, Rosenbloom & Markard, 2020). What has become of these demands in political practice? Can we observe another marginalisation of sustainability policies in the context of the COVID-19 pandemic – or is there a different response? Does the EGD lend itself to greater crisis persistence, or is there even evidence of strengthening sustainability in times of crisis? And if so, why?

To answer these questions, I adopt an interpretive perspective, more specifically discursive institutionalism, which focuses on the role of ideas in interaction processes within institutional settings (Schmidt, 2008, 2018). Although interpretive approaches already contribute to understanding policymaking under 'normal' conditions, including in the EU (Heinelt & Münch, 2018), they take on particular relevance in times of crisis. Crises are 'transformative moments' in which established ideas, beliefs and institutionalised interactions are challenged and new cognitive and normative constructs emerge (Hay, 1999; Schmidt, 2008). The discursive institutionalism approach draws attention to how – under what institutional conditions and through what interactions – ideas gain traction and shape policymaking in times of crisis.

Building on this approach, the main focus of this chapter is on a set of sustainability-oriented ideas that underlie the EGD in its role as a meta-policy and the ways in which these ideas promote a 'sustainabilisation' of policy-making within the EU's institutional framework during crises. Of particular interest are the negotiations on the EU's Multiannual Financial Framework (MFF), which were temporarily suspended at the beginning of the crisis before being resumed and refocused on crisis recovery. I argue that the COVID-19 pandemic provided the European Commission with the opportunity to place the EGD at the centre of European policymaking of the MFF and the related crisis recovery programme. In doing so, the EGD's ideational structure proved particularly functional in dealing with the uncertainties of the pandemic. The EGD, receiving financial backbone through the MFF, was strengthened during the crisis, and it has even become an important foundation of the European crisis recovery policy.

I begin with a brief recap of the development of European sustainability policy to contextualise the making of the EGD, as well as its basic structure and elements, which characterise it as a meta-policy. From an interpretive perspective, I then reconstruct five core ideas of sustainability governance – an extensive, integrative, transformative, inclusive and reflexive orientation – that underlie the EGD and make it a sustainability-oriented meta-policy. I then turn to the implementation of the EGD, showing that the EGD not only demonstrated remarkable perseverance during the COVID-19 crisis, but also became an important reference point in the resumed negotiations on the MFF and European crisis recovery strategy. Thus, rather than being weakened during the crisis, the EGD moved to the centre of European policy, where it became an effective sustainability-oriented meta-policy. I argue that the EGD's role can be attributed to a combination of its political significance for the European Commission and its ideational structure, which provided a suitable interpretive framework helping to weather turbulent times in European policymaking in the EU's intergovernmental arm, that is, the European Council. I conclude with general considerations on the potential of sustainability-oriented meta-policies, such as the EGD, to sustainabilise policymaking in times of crisis.

THE DEVELOPMENT OF EUROPEAN SUSTAINABILITY POLICY

The EGD stands in a long tradition of European environmental and sustainability policy (Eckert & Kovalevska, 2021). Environmental policy has been at the core of the European integration project since the 1980s. Harmonising environmental norms and regulations was seen as a crucial element of the single market agenda, which aimed to establish an economic level playing field across the EU. The 1980s and early 1990s saw a significant expansion in environmental policy activities (Weale, 1996; Weale et al., 2002). Driven by environmentally ambitious member states, which elevated their own ambitious environmental policies to the EU level (Jordan & Liefferink, 2004), the EU replaced the US as a leader in environmental and consumer protection and risk regulation in the early 1990s (Vogel, 2003).

In the late 1990s and early 2000s, it was primarily the European Commission that drove and developed the discourse and terminology of environmental protection and sustainability, seeking to integrate environmental concerns into economic and development policy. Especially after the US withdrawal from the Kyoto Protocol, the European Commission was eager to have the EU take a leading role in international climate policy and sustainable development (Fleming & Mauger, 2021; Oberthür & Dupont, 2021). A case in point is the European Sustainable Development Strategy, adopted in 2001 (European Commission, 2001), the development of which was largely driven by the European Commission to position the EU as a pioneer and standard-setter of sustainability policy at the World Summit on Sustainable Development in Johannesburg in 2002 (Lightfoot & Burchell, 2005). In turn, this leadership ambition has been an important legitimising basis for the European integration process (Haas & Jürgens, 2021; Weale et al., 2002).

After a phase of dynamic enlargement and deepening, the EU repeatedly and persistently entered troubled waters in the late 2000s. The onset of the global economic and financial crisis, combined with lingering institutional decision-making and legitimacy problems, which became particularly visible during the crisis, caused the popularity of the European project to wane (Serricchio et al., 2013), leading to strong EU-critical movements and increasing disintegration dynamics, which were to culminate in Brexit. In this phase, there were also clear signs that the once ambitious environmental policy aspirations were stalling or even being scaled back (Gravey & Jordan, 2020; Steinebach & Knill, 2017). In a context in which former green pioneers were no longer willing or able to lead, the EU seemed to have lost its claim to international environmental leadership (Wurzel et al., 2016).

However, even during this crisis, there were attempts – especially on the part of the European Commission – to launch ambitious sustainability-oriented policy strategies. For example, with the programme 'Europe 2020: A European Strategy for Smart, Sustainable and Inclusive Growth' (European Commission, 2010), the Barroso II Commission (2010–2014) attempted to continue the process of cross-policy and long-term governance that started with the European Sustainable Development Strategy in 2001, while linking it more closely to economic growth. This strategic reorientation of environmental policy as a sustainability-oriented economic growth policy is reflected in the 'Roadmap to a Resource-Efficient Europe' (European Commission, 2011), which identified the prospects for a green growth strategy as a means of overcoming the crisis. The Juncker Commission (2014–2019) continued to work towards a sustainability-oriented growth policy. In 'An EU Action Plan for the Circular Economy' (European Commission, 2015), the Commission proposed a transition to a different, 'sustainable' economy. In the 'European Strategy for Plastics in a Circular Economy' (European Commission, 2018), the European Commission described its global leadership in transitioning to the plastics of the future and its focus on transforming the EU economy into a modern, low-carbon, resource- and energy-efficient one.

Overall, these overarching strategies signal a fundamental paradigm shift towards a green growth model (Munta, 2020); they reflect persistent and increasingly urgent calls for a fundamental societal shift towards sustainability, as expressed, for example, in the UN 2030 Agenda. Politically, however, they have remained relatively marginal. Commission-driven strategies have received only rudimentary political support from other European institutions. In particular, the European Council has been eager to regain and nationalise economic steering capabilities in the post-Maastricht era (Bickerton et al., 2015). The marginal positioning of sustainability strategies on the European political agenda became particularly evident in times of crisis. Contrary to what the Commission envisaged, the Europe 2020 strategy, for example, hardly played a policy-guiding role in addressing the economic, financial and euro crises. Thus, the strategy was perceived as too long term and not sufficiently responsive to the short-term demands of the crisis.

In recent years, we have observed divergence between environmental aspirations both on the global and European level and the reality on the ground in member states. Climate policy is a particularly pertinent case. On the one hand, the EU began to see itself as a driver of international climate policy, especially after the failure of the Conference of the Parties 2009 in Copenhagen (Fleming & Mauger, 2021). The EU's climate mitigation targets have been at the forefront internationally and have served to underpin EU international climate leadership. On the other hand, EU domestic climate policies have been insufficient to achieve the Paris Agreement's temperature target of limiting the increase of global temperature to 2 or even 1.5 degrees Celsius (Dupont et al., 2020).

These gaps became increasingly apparent when in 2018 the climate issue became more politicised due to multiple reasons, such as heatwaves and the mobilisation of the Fridays-for-Future movement. In November 2018, the Commission – building on the IPCC's Special Report on the impacts of global warming of 1.5 degrees Celsius – published a communication calling for the EU to pursue climate neutrality for 2050 (Dupont et al., 2020). This became an important normative reference point for the EGD.

THE MAKING OF THE EUROPEAN GREEN DEAL

The EGD was presented to the public on 11 December 2019 by the newly appointed European Commission under President Ursula von der Leyen. However, it had already taken shape during her application process, thus playing a key role in her approval by the European Parliament (EP). In fact, after her nomination by the European Council in July 2019, the then Commission President-designate Ursula von der Leyen made the EGD, including the goal of Europe becoming the first climate-neutral continent, a key plank of her election campaign. As such, the EGD took a central role in her opening statement in the European Parliament plenary session on 16 July 2019 (von der Leyen, 2019b).

Von der Leyen's proposal did not emerge in a vacuum. Rather, in her application programme, 'My Agenda for Europe. A Union that Strives for More' (von der Leyen, 2019a), she indicates that the EGD is 'inspired' by the European Council's new strategic agenda 2019–2024 (European Council, 2019), as well as by extensive consultations and 'my discussions with the political groups in the European Parliament' (von der Leyen, 2019a, p. 4).

These consultations apparently led her and her campaign team to utilise bold historical references: the New Deal policy of US President Franklin D. Roosevelt, which he had formulated at the beginning of the 1930s as a progressive countermodel to the timidly preserving Hooverian status quo policy and which shaped American politics in the form of a Keynesian economic policy until far into the 1970s (Brüggen, 2001). Since then, the term 'New Deal' has stood for a policy of concerted progressive social change supported by various political camps. New Deal policy does not focus on individual policy areas but is decidedly geared towards systemic, infrastructural change that encompasses numerous political and social areas. It is about nothing less than a comprehensive societal transformation that reshuffles the cards (in terms of existing societal relationships) to overcome current path dependencies and entrenchments (Bloomfield & Steward, 2020; Brand, 2009; Mastini et al., 2021).

The reverberations of the historical New Deal model are far from coincidental, but distinctions are made at the conceptual level, carrying implications for the content of the EGD. First, there is no talk of a *new* deal. Haas and Jürgens suggest that this omission is intentional and is due to the fact that the concept of the New Deal had been taken up by progressive forces within the US Democratic Party to lend weight to their demands for a redistribution of income and wealth, as well as a strengthening of the public sector – demands that are not found in the EGD in this way (Haas & Jürgens, 2021). Second, the word *European* marks a cultural difference and refers to a specific approach to deal-making characterised by complex multilevel negotiations. Finally, the reference to *green* makes a connection to earlier concepts of a large-scale ecologically oriented reform policy, which have been the subject of discussion for some years in various contexts under the term Green New Deal (Lehndorff, 2021; Mastini et al., 2021; Simonis, 2020).

Apart from the discussions that took place in Germany, especially in the late 1980s and early 1990s by the Greens and Social Democrats in preparation for a longer-term strategic alliance (Brüggen, 2001), the discussion of a Green New Deal emerged in the wake of the economic and financial market crisis of 2007/2008 (Bloomfield & Steward, 2020). In the US, progressive Democrats, around the young Congresswoman Alexandra Ocasio-Cortez, promoted a Green New Deal to overcome the severe economic consequences of the financial and economic crisis. At the international level, the idea of a Green New Deal has been taken up by the UN Environment Programme but with a rather neoliberal orientation (Brand, 2009).

In the European context, the discussion of a Green New Deal originated within the Green New Deal Group of the New Economics Foundation, an organisation close to the Greens. Here, a strong orientation towards the idea of ecological modernisation dominated, that is, towards global environmental management based on continued 'green' technological progress and efficiency revolution, here relying on growth, technology and control optimism. From the critics' point of view, the Green New Deal is hardly suitable as an orientation for a 'radical reform policy' (Brand, 2009, p. 477, translation by the author). Rather, it is a 'reconciliation formula' that 'postulates fundamental changes' but without 'challenging existing social power relations and without questioning the imperial mode of living' (Brand, 2009, p. 480, translation by the author). Thus, this political transformation project mutated into a rather technocratic ecological modernisation programme, which, in contrast to the Rooseveltian New Deal of the 1930s, was supported less by a progressive constellation of forces than by technological and control optimism (Brand, 2009; Redaktion, 2021; Zeller, 2021). Despite all the tempering of radical components, the breakthrough of a Green New Deal policy did not happen for the time being and European and national crisis management policies remained in a mode of austerity-oriented recovery (Bloomfield & Steward, 2020).

However, in terms of concept and content, the idea of a Green Deal policy was in place. A specific political constellation at the end of the Juncker Commission helped it enter the policy agenda (Munta, 2020). During these times, the perception of a continuing need for reform dominated, resulting from the financial and economic crisis. Because there was also a realisation that this need for reform could hardly be realised at the institutional level, attention turned to a large-scale and comprehensive policy programme that – as the successor to the Europe 2020 strategy – would serve as the basis for shaping policy at the European level (Munta, 2020).

The need for such a programme was nurtured with the view of culminating sustainability policy developments at the international level, namely the 2030 Agenda and the Paris Agreement, as well as increasingly critical voices from the scientific community. Finally, dissatisfaction and the need for change were articulated in increasing political pressure on the streets, first in the yellow vest protests and in the rise of populism and then in the climate movement. Whereas the climate protests pointed to a comprehensive need for action on climate policy, populist countermovements highlighted the limits of transformation, pointing to the potentially disruptive social consequences of ambitious climate policy.

These political developments provided the background for the 2019 European elections, which saw significant gains in votes and mandates for liberal, green and right-wing populist parties and significant losses in votes and mandates for the two (previously and still) strongest party groupings: the conservatives and social democrats. The election of a new Commission president was also overshadowed by a failed top candidate process. Instead of one of the top candidates being nominated by the parties before the election, after negotiations, the European Council proposed Ursula von der Leyen, then the German Minister of Defence, to the EP for election. There, she faced the challenge of organising a cross-party majority (Munta, 2020).

Given the balance of power in the EP, this meant that the Commission president-designate had to win over not only conservative forces but also members of the social democratic and liberal and green factions. At the same time, she had to move within the new strategic guidelines of the European Council, in which climate protection and a transformative industrial policy would play a central role (Bloomfield & Steward, 2020, p. 770; Thieme & Galariotis, 2020). To this end, in line with European negotiating logic, a comprehensive political package lent itself to the specific ideas and interests of the various parties in the form of an implicit coalition agreement (Bloomfield & Steward, 2020; Skjærseth, 2021). Appointing the socialist Frans Timmermans to manage the EGD portfolio 'increased the credibility to the story' and clearly helped generate broad support in the EP (Munta, 2020, p. 8).

Overall, the EGD galvanises the perception of historical transformation, which is necessary in the face of major challenges and requires the collaboration of different political forces. In this respect, the intonation of the EGD can be seen as an attempt to bring together different and partly opposing political forces and camps in the EP and bundle them in a new coalition – while at the same time taking up the strategic guidelines of the European Council.

THE STRUCTURE AND CONTENT OF THE EUROPEAN GREEN DEAL

The EGD was published in the form of a communication from the European Commission to the European institutions (European Commission, 2019). Formally speaking, the EGD is not a binding policy developed by European institutions. It is an action plan of the European Commission based on the president of the European Commission's authority to formulate governing guidelines. Together with five other priorities, the EGD constitutes a 'framework for our common work' (von der Leyen, 2019a, p. 5). Therefore, the EGD can be described as a meta-policy, that is, an overarching second-order policy that orients first-order policymaking processes between institutional actors in different policy areas (Bornemann, 2014). Thus, it is not a policy with direct social steering ambitions, but a comprehensive and strategic policy framework that sets new reform priorities in various existing first-order policy areas and orients policymaking through a set of cognitive and normative ideas. This interpretation is supported by the view that the EGD does not represent a new policy as such but '*adds a new layer of ambition onto EU policies* to transform the EU into a decarbonised, resource-efficient, green and socially fair continent' (Munta, 2020, p. 3, emphasis added). It forms the centrepiece of a new growth paradigm that is slowly taking over at the EU level (Bloomfield & Steward, 2020).

Making Europe the first climate-neutral continent is the overall objective of the EGD, which 'resets the Commission's commitment to tackling climate and environmental-related challenges that is this generation's defining task' (European Commission, 2019, p. 2). Achieving climate neutrality by 2050 requires that European climate policy plans be accelerated, for example, by increasing the EU's 2030 reduction target of greenhouse gas emissions from 40% to at least 50–55%.

Although climate neutrality is the overarching goal, the EGD is not limited to climate policy (Wolf et al., 2021). In fact, it comprises other far-reaching policy goals and means. For example, it refers to the Biodiversity Strategy 2030, which is supposed to make the EU a global leader in international biodiversity; the creation of a more sustainable food system with a comprehensive farm-to-fork strategy; and an ambitious circular economy strategy to recreate the economy and realise a goal of zero environmental pollution.

Supported by massive investments, these objectives provide 'an opportunity to put Europe firmly on a new path of sustainable and inclusive growth' (European Commission, 2019, p. 2). Moreover, the EGD is committed to a 'just and inclusive' transition that puts 'people first' and pays attention to 'the regions, industries and workers who will face the greatest challenges'

(European Commission, 2019, p. 2) – an ambition that manifests in the plan to develop the Just Transition Mechanism (JTM), including the Just Transition Fund (JTF), which is supposed to support the regions and sectors most reliant on coal or heavily polluting fossil fuels and, therefore, structurally affected by the imminent transformation (European Commission, 2019, p. 16).

In terms of concrete actions, the EGD covers the full spectrum of 'all policy levers', including regulation and standardisation, investment and innovation, national reforms, dialogue with social partners and international cooperation (European Commission, 2019, p. 4). A roadmap (in the annexe of the communication on the EGD) specifies the timing of more than 50 key actions for implementing the EGD in seven policy areas, namely climate, energy, industry, mobility, food and agriculture, biodiversity and environmental protection (building and construction is mentioned on the website only). In addition to these domain-specific activities, the roadmap specifies actions for mainstreaming sustainability in all EU policy domains. Another important element is the identification and elimination of existing actions that counter the successful implementation of the EGD. To this end, the European Commission 'will work with the Member States to step up the EU's efforts to ensure that current legislation and policies relevant to the Green Deal are enforced and effectively implemented' (European Commission, 2019, p. 4). Furthermore, a set of actions, such as strengthening Green Deal diplomacy, relates to an area entitled 'the EU as a global leader'. Finally, actions for working together across sectors and levels in the European Climate Pact are outlined (European Commission, 2019, p. 22ff).

THE EUROPEAN GREEN DEAL AS A SUSTAINABILITY-ORIENTED META-POLICY

The Commission's communication on the EGD contains numerous rhetorical references to sustainability and sustainable development. For example, the decisions and investments associated with EGD are seen as an opportunity to overcome 'unsustainable practices' and set Europe on a 'new path of sustainable and inclusive growth' (European Commission, 2019, p. 2). In this way, Europe should fulfil its global leadership role regarding sustainability-oriented transformation. Thus, the EGD is presented as 'an integral part of this Commission's strategy to implement the United Nation's 2030 agenda and the sustainable development goals' (European Commission, 2019, p. 3). The sustainability ambition is also emphasised by the announcement that the 'Commission will refocus the European Semester process of macroeconomic coordination to integrate the United Nations' sustainable development goals, to put sustainability and the well-being of citizens at the centre of economic policy, and the sustainable development goals at the heart of the EU's policymaking and action' (European Commission, 2019, p. 3). These and other explicit references support the view of the EGD as standing in the long tradition of sustainability-oriented policymaking and governance in the EU (Eckert & Kovalevska, 2021; Schepelmann & Fischedick, 2020).

I examine to what extent, beyond these general rhetorical references, a more distinctive sustainability quality can be discerned in the EGD, making EGD a *sustainability-oriented meta-policy* that is to shape European policymaking in a sustainable way. To reconstruct the EGD's sustainability quality, I bring into play specific governance ideas that have become established in the relevant discussion on sustainability governance (Meadowcroft, 2007a; Steurer, 2010) and that have been updated more recently in the context of the UN 2030 Agenda (Bornemann & Christen, 2021). These are cognitive and normative orientations, each of which addresses a specific governing challenge of sustainable development. To the extent that these orientations are present and pronounced in the meta-policy EGD, the latter appears to be prepared, at least in principle, for the challenges of sustainable development, becoming a sustainability-oriented meta-policy. In what follows, I briefly explain the ideas of extensiveness, integration, transformation, inclusion and reflexivity, and how they manifest themselves in the EGD.

Extensiveness

Sustainable development is a universal and pervasive idea; that is, it permeates numerous problem areas and action fields of society. A sustainability-oriented meta-policy that reflects this comprehensive aspiration must cover numerous policy areas that, in turn, are linked to specific societal fields of action. The EGD comes close to this extensive approach in its basic design. As a cross-policy framework, it covers numerous policy areas. In addition to the eight policy areas explicitly mentioned as implementation sites, there is the claim that 'All EU actions and policies will have to contribute to the European Green Deal objectives' (European Commission, 2019, p. 3), with digitalisation policy being explicitly mentioned. Moreover, the EGD is expected to have an impact on other policy areas in the future. For example, it orients the EU's foreign policy and diplomacy: 'By setting a credible example, and following-up with diplomacy, trade policy, development support and other external policies, the EU can be an effective advocate ... to promote and implement ambitious environment, climate and energy policies across the world' (European Commission, 2019, p. 20).

Integration

A key aspiration of the sustainability idea is to embed those problems that were formerly analysed and dealt with separately into more complex problem contexts. Accordingly, sustainability-oriented governance is based on the assumption of particularly complex and interdependent problem constellations that require a highly systemic and integrative approach coordinating and inter-linking specific steering efforts in different policy areas (Bornemann, 2014). This falls into the tradition of New Deal policymaking: triggering fundamental societal change through the combination of multiple interventions in different areas that are somewhat coordinated regarding their objectives.

On paper, there are indications that the EGD is inspired by a systemic–integrative idea (see also Rosamond & Dupont, 2021). EGD communication highlights that the 'challenges are complex and interlinked' and that 'policy response must be bold and comprehensive and seek to maximise benefits for health, quality of life, resilience and competitiveness' (European Commission, 2019, p. 3). Therefore, based on 'policy insights generated by the sustainable transitions community' (as promoted by the European Environment Agency), the EGD challenges the simplistic approach of 'promoting a handful of tech-nology winners as a feasible solution' (Bloomfield & Steward, 2020, p. 774). In contrast, it marks a 'reorientation toward systemic solutions for sustaina-bility transitions' with a 'wider mix of interventions than just market-based instruments' (Bloomfield & Steward, 2020, p. 774).

Through 'intense coordination' between different policy areas and measures, 'synergies across all policy areas' could be exploited (European Commission, 2019, p. 3). The reference to synergy potentials to be leveraged is just as much a classic motif in sustainability thinking as the reference to the conflicts and contradictions that must be systematically addressed: 'While all of these areas for action are strongly interlinked and mutually reinforcing, careful attention will have to be paid when there are potential trade-offs between economic, environmental and social objectives' (European Commission, 2019, p. 4). Thus, to ensure policy coherence, the EGD intends to achieve greater commit-ment and political support for the sometimes conflict-laden cross-fertilisation between different policy sectors (Munta, 2020).

Transformation

Over the past ten years, 'transformation' has become a central idea in sustaina-bility discourse. The 'transformative turn' accentuates the (earlier) insight that sustainable development cannot simply be based on incremental adjustments to social and political practices within existing socio-economic systems (Brand, 2017). Rather, sustainability requires a fundamental change in the configurations and functioning of the systems themselves. Dryzek qualifies the change pattern of sustainability as being imaginative and profound in terms of the envisioned society but still moderate and reform-oriented (instead of radical) in terms of the change strategy (Dryzek, 2013). The transformative ambition, which has been prominently articulated in the 2030 Agenda 'Transforming Our World', also means that sustainable development is no longer just about the Global South catching up. The Global North must fundamentally rethink and adapt its own development and growth model.

The EGD comes with an outspoken transformative ambition geared towards systemic change. For example, the European Commission's communication frames the EGD as 'a new growth strategy that aims to transform the EU into a fair and prosperous society, with a modern, resource-efficient and competitive economy where there are no net emissions of greenhouse gases in 2050 and where economic growth is decoupled from resource use' (European Commission, 2019, p. 2). Bloomfield and Steward (2020, p. 770) argue that '[r]ather than vague talk of a "green revolution" or selective technology hype', the EGD emphasises 'the need to change systems' and offers 'pathways of sustainability transformation' in five key sociotechnical systems – energy, industry, buildings, mobility and food – that are responsible for the overwhelming majority of carbon emissions. Another expression of transformative aspiration is that the EGD's time horizon is particularly long-term, especially in the context of climate policy objectives (with the year 2050 for climate neutrality). At the level of concrete measures, the transformation claim manifests itself in the JTM, which aims to enable transformation through distributional and compensatory measures.

Some critics argue that at best, the EGD envisions a transformation 'light', conceiving transformation merely 'within the existing growth paradigm' but not in terms of a change of that paradigm. In essence, the growth imperative of the EGD turns out to be a 'blind spot' from a sustainability perspective (Pianta & Lucchese, 2020; Schepelmann & Fischedick, 2020; Zeller, 2021). However, it can also be argued that a growth orientation does not per se contradict the transformative claim of sustainable development (Dryzek, 2013).

Inclusion

The insight that governments alone do not hold the exclusive responsibility and capacity to realise sustainable development belongs to the core of sustainability thinking. Sustainability governance should take on all kinds of actors, allowing for their participation in sustainability-oriented problem-solving (Meadowcroft, 2007b). In the wake of the recent 2030 Agenda, this inclusive, participatory ideal has been further strengthened, most prominently emphasised in the aspiration to 'leave no one behind' in the sustainability transformation (Fukuda-Parr & Hegstad, 2019).

The EGD stands clearly in this inclusive tradition of sustainability. In addition to the so-called Climate Pact, which aims to involve all kinds of actors at different levels in future policy processes on the climate transition, the clear commitment to 'leave no one behind' is reflected in the ambition of a 'just and inclusive, people-centred transition', here representing a key overarching component of the EGD that becomes manifest in the JTM (Dupont et al., 2020; Siddi, 2000). With the JTM, the European Commission acknowledges that the transition towards a climate-neutral economy will have economic and social justice impacts, especially in regions that rely on fossil fuel extraction and treatment or on highly carbon-intensive industries. These regions will strongly risk losing their industries and workers' jobs. The JTM endeavours to smooth these expected socio-economic turbulences (Fleming & Mauger, 2021).

Critics have pointed out that the EGD's main inclusion focus is on particular groups, such as workers and unemployed citizens, rather than the people in a particular region as a whole. Thus, solidarity under the JTM would only apply within the identified regions, while there are plenty of justice issues in the energy transition to climate neutrality in all regions of the EU and around the globe. However, there are also indications that recent parliamentary proposals have broadened the scope of consideration to include other groups of actors (Fleming & Mauger, 2021).

Reflexivity

Reflexivity is at the core of sustainability governance. In this context, reflexivity means a combination of strategic and incremental orientation: the embedding of incremental policymaking aiming to address uncertainty in a broader long-term strategic framework. Thus, a reflexive orientation is intended to enable the management of uncertainty through incremental learning while still being committed to long-term visions and goals (Meadowcroft, 2007a). In addition to experience-based improvement of concrete policy measures, reflexivity also means the continuous review of the conditions under which policymaking takes place. Reflexivity means being aware of the implications of the existing institutional and political conditions of governance and shaping them in a targeted way (Beck, 2006).

In terms of its publicly communicated understanding, the EGD exhibits the elements of a reflexive governance approach. The EGD presents a roadmap of key policies for the EU's climate agenda, based on which the Commission has started and will continue to develop legislative proposals and strategies from 2020 onwards (Siddi, 2020). Accordingly, the EGD is not designed as a well-defined and detailed plan but as an 'evolving framework' that outlines the key policies and measures that 'will be updated as needs evolve and the policy responses are formulated' (European Commission, 2019, p. 2).

However, the reflexive elements appear relatively weak. For example, there is no clear procedure for structuring the review and alignment of individual policies. It is not clear whether the announced updating of policies and measures is itself based on a systematic evaluation process. It also remains unclear whether the claim of learning and continuous improvement also includes the institutional and political conditions of action.

Although with certain qualifications, the EGD as a whole can be seen as a meta-policy based on key ideas underlying sustainability thinking and governance. In this respect, the EGD can well be described as a sustainability-oriented meta-policy. The following section explores how this sustainability-oriented meta-policy has been implemented and the extent to which it has contributed to the sustainabilisation of European policymaking.

THE IMPLEMENTATION OF THE EUROPEAN GREEN DEAL IN TIMES OF CRISIS

When the EGD was presented at the end of 2019, the EU was in a phase of relative calm and stability. Although the multiple crises of the previous years – the financial, euro and refugee crises, not to mention the latent legitimacy crisis of the EU (Hutter et al., 2016; Schmidt, 2018) – were not resolved, the economy was in full swing. Indeed, the time seemed ripe to leave behind the long years of crisis management and rethink more fundamentally and strategically the European social and economic model (Munta, 2020). To this end, the EGD was the top priority of the newly elected Commission, and there were swift steps towards implementation, especially in the field of climate policy. For example, a new ambition was expressed in the European Commission's proposal for a climate law to anchor the 2050 climate neutrality target and the proposition of an EU industrial strategy in early March 2020 (Dupont et al., 2020).

These moves to implement the EGD through legislation and strategy have been complemented by attempts to mobilise financial resources for the EGD. As early as January 2020, the Commission presented the Sustainable Europe Investment Plan (European Commission, 2020a), including a concrete proposal for the JTF as a means to implement the JTM (European Commission, 2020b). Even if, according to critics, the plan fell short of what was needed to finance a climate policy turnaround, the JTF contained promising elements that underscored the European Commission's ambition level (CAN, 2020). Importantly, it was also an attempt to link the EGD with the MFF, that is, the European budget. Because the relevant negotiations had already begun during the years of the Juncker Commission, the von der Leyen Commission has had little opportunity to back up its new policy goals, first and foremost the EGD, with financial resources. The MFF negotiations themselves, in which different coalitions of member states faced each other, reached an impasse at the end of 2019 and the beginning of 2020 (see Heinelt & Münch, Chapter 1 in this volume, and Becker, Chapter 2 in this volume). However, after the new Council President, Charles Michel, took over the negotiation mandate, the von der Leyen Commission successfully advocated the inclusion of financing the JTF (€7.5 billion) in the MFF. This was also a step towards overcoming the blockades in the budget negotiations of countries such as Poland, which had been critical of the EGD because of their exposure to the consequences of an ambitious decarbonisation policy (Rietig, 2021, p. 1029).

Shortly thereafter, the COVID-19 pandemic broke out, altering people's lives, policy agendas and political processes. Following rigorous lockdown measures to contain the spread of the virus and prevent the collapse of health systems, many countries experienced severe disruptions in almost all social and economic sectors. Although political processes such as the implementation of the EGD, as well as the ongoing negotiations on the MFF, were initially put on hold (see Becker, Chapter 2 in this volume), political leaders in the member states and the EU institutions quickly realised that an ambitious recovery programme was needed in view of the major economic shocks. The EGD – and in particular its climate policy targets – became important points of reference in the subsequent process (Dupont et al., 2020).

On the one hand, there have been attempts to weaken the EGD, or at least temporarily suspend it during crises (Eckert, 2021). Several member states and organised business interests called for postponement of at least some elements of the EGD and other existing environmental provisions, including stricter greenhouse gas emission standards, the ban on single-use plastics and the reform of the EU emissions trading system (Munta, 2020). For example, as early as March 2020, Czech Prime Minister Milan Babis called for abandonment of the EGD, while Poland suggested a suspension of the planned expansion of the EU emissions trading system (Elkerbout et al., 2020). The European Automobile Manufacturers Association called for an adjustment of the timing of EU regulations, such as CO_2 emission standards, while in April 2020, BusinessEurope requested to delay key climate and environment initiatives (Dupont et al., 2020).

On the other hand, there were early attempts to connect any thoughts about recovery plans with the implementation of the EGD. The Dutch government, for example, promoted a plan for 'green recovery' very early on, floating around ideas on how to ensure that expenditure and investment remain firmly anchored in the EU's push for climate neutrality and a circular economy (Munta, 2020). This suggestion was picked up by a group of 17 environmental ministers who insisted on making the EGD a central reference point of the

EU's recovery policy. Also, non-governmental organisations, interested businesses and many policymakers rebuffed the attacks on the EGD and, supported by international organisations such as the International Energy Agency, argued that the necessary stimulus programmes represented a unique opportunity to leverage the transition to a climate-resilient economy (Dupont et al., 2020).

Although it is too early to assess the actual effects of these political struggles and the COVID-19 crisis more generally on EGD implementation (Eckert, 2021), initial observations suggest a mixed picture leaning towards the positive side overall. On the negative side, the EGD clearly lost its political primacy to issues such as health and economic recovery, and policymaking shifted, at least temporarily, from strategic considerations to crisis management. Also, in terms of timing, the COVID-19 crisis disrupted the Commission's ambitious work on the EGD. Many key initiatives from the EGD were significantly postponed, including the Farm-to-Fork Strategy and the EU Biodiversity Strategy for 2030 (Munta, 2020). In the recent reform of the Common Agricultural Policy (CAP) in early summer 2021, which is undoubtedly a key European policy area, EGD objectives played only a minor role (Pantzer, 2021), despite declared attempts by the Commission to bring in the EGD and efforts to communicate the CAP as being aligned with the EGD (European Commission, 2021a).

However, there are also signs of a remarkable persistence of the EGD and even a strengthening of it, which plays out on three levels: discourse, policy ambitions and financial resources. First, the EGD has become a central argumentative reference point in the discourse about the European crisis recovery policy (Rosamond & Dupont, 2021). The European Commission began to present the EGD as a forward-looking way out of the crisis: '[Now is] our chance to shape our economies differently and make them more resilient', von der Leyen states in a video message from May 2020 (Redaktion, 2021). Consequently, the Commission assigned the EGD and the idea of making Europe more sustainable, resilient and better prepared for the challenges and opportunities of the green and digital transformation an important role in the proposal for a regulation establishing the Recovery and Resilience Facility (European Commission, 2020c). Indeed, these references prevailed in the policy process between the EP and Council and can be found in the regulations finally adopted by the EP and Council (EU, 2021). More broadly, recent research shows how the Council has given the EGD and its key concepts an increasingly central position in its various decisions and statements related to the COVID-19 recovery (Rosamond & Dupont, 2021).

Second, there are increasing signs that European climate policy ambitions have been raised during the COVID-19 pandemic. For example, as envisaged in the EGD, the 2030 reduction target for achieving climate neutrality by 2050 and corresponding additional measures were adopted during the crisis

(Fleming & Mauger, 2021). In September 2020, the Commission had already proposed increasing the 2030 emission reduction target to at least 55% through the Climate Law (European Commission, 2020d), with the EP even advocating a further strengthening to 60%. At the European Council meeting on 10–11 December 2020, a reduction target of 55% was finally adopted.

Third, there is evidence that 'post-COVID economic recovery planning has put fiscal backbone into the European Green Deal' (Bloomfield & Steward, 2020, p. 774). In their joint roadmap for a European recovery plan presented in mid April 2020, Council President Michel and Commission President von der Leyen have already emphasised that European crisis recovery should aim at a green and digital transition, explicitly mentioning the EGD as being 'essential as an inclusive and sustainable growth strategy in this respect' (President of the European Commission & President of the European Council, 2020, p. 4). Moreover, they announced that the MFF, together with additional recovery funds (later adopted under the name 'NextGenerationEU'), should become a key crisis management tool that should make Europe greener, more digital and more resilient and 'allow Europe to make the most of the first-mover advantage in the global race to recovery' (President of the European Commission & President of the European Council, 2020, p. 3). Subsequently, the Council instructed the Commission to present a new draft for the MFF and a proposal for a recovery fund. This relaunch of the MFF negotiations gave the Commission the opportunity to financially underpin the EGD (see Becker, Chapter 2 in this volume; Eckert, 2021).

For example, the Commission tried to increase funding for the JTF and was at least partially successful. Although it could not push through its proposed target of €40 billion (which would have meant an increase of €32.5 billion over the pre-crisis level of €7.5 billion), the Commission was able to mobilise an additional €10 billion of fresh money for the JTF from the EU NextGeneration Plan (Fleming & Mauger, 2021). In addition to linking crisis-related special funds to the EGD, the climate policy component of the MFF was strengthened during newly launched negotiations. In the previous MFF 2014–2020, the Commission had already succeeded in earmarking 20% of the EU budget for spending in favour of climate action (Rietig, 2021). The mainstreaming target of 25% proposed at the beginning of the negotiations for the MFF 2021–2027 in 2018 by the then Juncker Commission was adjusted to 'at least 25%' in the resumed negotiations in May 2020. In addition, substantial parts of the NextGenerationEU stimulus fund also served climate mainstreaming and greening. After intense negotiations between the Council and Parliament, the MFF and NextGenerationEU were adopted in December 2020 at the height of the second wave of the COVID-19 crisis in Europe. The overall package stipulates that at least 30% (€547 billion) of the 2021–2027 multiannual budget and the NextGenerationEU programme be allocated to 'climate-relevant spending', meaning that the spending must effectively contribute to the green transformation or to addressing related challenges (Fleming & Mauger, 2021; Rietig, 2021). Thus, despite the crisis, it was possible to bolster the EGD with substantial funding and increase spending on climate mainstreaming and greening, not only compared with previous crises – the post-2008 European Economic Recovery Programme allocated only 2% of its €200 billion budget to climate and energy spending (Elkerbout et al., 2020, p. 1103) – but also with pre-crisis levels.

Overall, there is growing evidence that the EU's crisis response has strengthened previous policy trends and thereby enhanced rather than diminished the prospects for the implementation of the EGD (Dupont et al., 2020, p. 1103; Eckert, 2021). Certain drawbacks notwithstanding, the EGD has so far weathered the COVID-19 crisis well. It has established itself as a sustainability-oriented meta-policy guiding policy action in various areas, particularly climate policy, even under the conditions of an unprecedented pandemic crisis. The EGD also became an important conceptual reference point in the debates and decisions on the MFF and European recovery programme, in turn strengthening the financial backbone of the EGD.

This experience is in marked contrast to previous EU responses to crises, particularly the economic and financial market crisis of 2008/2009, where environmental and climate policies were relegated to the background, leading to stagnation and delays in the development and implementation of sustainability-oriented policies (Dupont et al., 2020; Gravey & Jordan, 2020). Compared with previous crises, there was no significant setback but instead a strengthening of sustainability ambitions. In the following, I explore *how* the EGD was able to sustainabilise European policymaking in times of crisis.

THE SUSTAINABILITY ORIENTATION OF THE EUROPEAN GREEN DEAL AS A CONDITION OF ITS EFFECTIVENESS?

As described above, the earlier idea of a Green New Deal emerged during the financial and economic crisis of 2008/2009. However, the respective suggestions did not find their way into the policy agenda. At the time, it was not possible to effectively anchor the corresponding concepts in the political agenda and translate them into concrete policy. By contrast, the EGD was already in place before the COVID-19 pandemic and unfolded its full political impact during the course of crisis policymaking.

The EGD was formulated as the new overarching European reform programme at a time when European politics was about to leave behind the continued crisis management mode of previous years and turn to a long-term and strategic reorientation of European policy under the impression of rising populism and climate protests. In doing so, the EGD was also embedded in political logic from the very beginning. It was a programmatic offer by the Commission President-designate von der Leyen to address major political concerns voiced on the streets, to win the support of a broad spectrum of political forces in a more diversified EP for her own election and to adhere to the programmatic guidelines of European policy established by the European Council.

The fact that the EGD was launched as a politically embedded strategic core project of the Commission before the beginning of the COVID-19 crisis is an important condition for its persistence and policy relevance throughout the crisis (Dupont et al., 2020; Wolff & Ladi, 2020). The coincidence of the crisis and the MFF negotiations then opened a window of opportunity for the Commission to keep the EGD at the top of the agenda and even provide it with additional financial leverage (Becker, Chapter 2 in this volume). Accordingly, Dupont et al. (2020) conclude that the Commission's entrepreneurship and strong politicisation of climate change led to a strengthening of the EGD – and climate policy in particular – in the EU's crisis response, rather than sidelining it, as had occurred in the past (see also Eckert, 2021). Proclaimed a historic moon landing moment just before the crisis, the EGD allowed the Commission to show leadership and govern in turbulent times based on its own broadly supported and politically and institutionally entrenched meta-policy framework.

However, the timing, symbolic charge, and political entrenchment of the EGD primarily explain its continued relevance *to the Commission* (or the supranational arm of the EU more generally). The fact that the EGD has also remained an important reference point in the intergovernmental arm of the EU, that is, the European Council (Rosamond & Dupont, 2021), requires consideration of additional factors. Previous research has shown that, in particular, the European Council tends to marginalise and weaken climate policy proposals in times of crisis. Divergences between EU member states' preferences have historically blocked or delayed policy action during external turbulence, such as after the financial and economic crisis (Burns, 2019; Dobbs et al., 2021; Rosamond & Dupont, 2021).

Drawing on discursive institutionalism (Schmidt, 2008, 2018), I argue that the persistence and growing importance of the EGD, even in the intergovernmental context, can be explained by its particular ideational foundation and the way these underlying ideas were mobilised by the Commission to become important frames for interpreting the COVID-19 crisis and orienting crisis response policies. The sustainability-oriented ideas underlying the EGD made it a particularly convincing and viable ideational basis for crisis policy in an institutional environment characterised by increasingly divergent interests. As a sustainability-oriented meta-policy, the EGD brings to bear a set of ideas that proved to be particularly connectable and conducive to collective interpretation and management of the COVID-19 crisis; they provided a helpful interpretive horizon for navigating emerging uncertainties and conflicts through turbulent times, especially in the intergovernmental negotiations on the MFF 2021–2027 and the NextGenerationEU, thus keeping the EGD at the centre of European policymaking. It is thanks to its ideational structure that the EGD was not sidelined during the crisis but became an important orientation framework for European policymaking.

First, the extensive scope of the EGD, covering a wide range of themes related to multiple policy areas, proved to be a particularly useful interpretive structure for addressing the experience of a comprehensive COVID-19 crisis. It quickly became clear that the crisis itself and long-term consequences and impacts associated with it would affect all sectors of society. Although the policy programmes envisioned in the EGD do not cover all crisis-relevant policy areas, its comprehensive structure provides numerous thematic points of contact and links for thinking about crisis management policies. Because of its breadth, it also offers multiple touchstones for different interests and ideas, thus providing a framework for finding compromises and common solutions. Because of this broad connectivity, there were numerous opportunities to link crisis management and MFF negotiations with the objectives and themes of the EGD. Indeed, the EGD – or individual themes from it – prevailed on the policy agenda of European institutions and, in particular, the European Council (Rosamond & Dupont, 2021).

The systemic–integrative orientation of the EGD seems to be similarly compatible. The EGD provides a systemic framework that not only encompasses numerous problem and policy areas in its own right (i.e. extensiveness), but also relates and links them to each other. This systemic–integrative approach proved particularly compatible with the COVID-19 crisis and coordination of corresponding crisis management policies because it provided a suitable, resonant space for what was soon perceived as a whole-system crisis and the resulting need for integrative responses. Thus, the systemic crisis encountered a policy framework providing a suitable interpretive framework for dealing with it in a systemic–integrative way (Rosamond & Dupont, 2021).

The transformative claim of the EGD, that is, the idea of the necessity of profound social change to enable a 'fair and prosperous society, with a modern, resource-efficient and competitive economy' (European Commission, 2019, p. 2), corresponds with the experience of the vulnerability of existing systems and expectations arising in the wake of the COVID-19 crisis that there cannot be a simple return to normality. The recognition of the crisis as a critical turning point in societal development underlined the need for a transformative crisis policy that, instead of short-term symptom control, addresses basic socio-economic structures to help build 'a greener, more digital and more resilient Europe' (European Commission, 2021b, p. 2).

The inclusive approach of the EGD, which most prominently manifests in the JTM, was an essential moment for overcoming interest conflicts between member states, even before the crisis began. For example, the JTM and expected financial support for regions that are particularly vulnerable to decarbonisation served as an essential factor in getting Poland – because of its coal-intense energy system a significant opponent of ambitious decarbonisation goals – on board with a more ambitious climate policy. In the face of the COVID-19 crisis, the financial capacity of the JTM was further expanded, hence affirming the inclusive orientation of the EGD. Inclusion also became a key point of the European crisis recovery programme, as, for example, expressed in strong rhetorical references to European solidarity and inclusion as core principles in the joint roadmap for recovery (President of the European Commission & President of the European Council, 2020) and, ultimately, the agreement on issuing European Coronabonds. The inclusive orientation of the EGD was not only key in preventing conflicts of interest and mobilising European solidarity in the crisis: it was also strengthened and expanded in the crisis.

Finally, the EGD's reflexive design, which combines long-term strategic planning with a short-term incremental approach, proved particularly adaptable and resilient during the COVID-19 crisis. This approach allowed for flexibility and adaptability in EGD-related policymaking, which enabled the EGD to be sustained during crises. Instead, different elements of the EGD could be selectively activated, depending on the situation. Also, the long-term perspective of the EGD opens up an important collective orientation framework for coping with turbulence.

Overall, the EGD came to function as an extensive, integrative, transformative, inclusive and reflexive meta-policy shaping the collective interpretation and management of the COVID-19 crisis in the context of the MFF and the NextGenerationEU negotiations. However, it cannot be assumed that the EGD is effective on its own. Rather, it is the European Commission that has pushed the EGD as an interpretive framework for collective navigation through the turbulence of the COVID-19 crisis in the European Council. In the institutional framework of the EU, the Commission played the role of a meta-governor, as it were, shaping the policy process in the Council via the sustainability-oriented ideas underlying the meta-policy of the EGD.

CONCLUSION

Even if it remains too early for a conclusive assessment (Eckert, 2021), with some optimism, the EGD appears to be a turning point in the historical development of European sustainability policy, elevating it to a new level. Whereas previous sustainability strategies have often remained toothless as they were detached from the intergovernmental arm of the EU, the EGD appears to be a meta-policy with considerable potential to render European policy sustainable. Declaring the EGD to be the core project of its legislature and mobilising symbolic references to New Deal policies and the 'moon landing', the European Commission framed the EGD as a turning point in sustainability policy even before the COVID-19 crisis, while the latter can be interpreted as a confirmation and reinforcement of this turn (Dupont et al., 2020). Even though the EGD lost its primacy on the policy agenda, being replaced by health and economic issues and crisis management when the pandemic broke out, the EGD began to serve as an effective sustainability-oriented meta-policy. Both the fact that the climate policy ambitions enshrined in the EGD were translated into concrete policy during the COVID-19 pandemic, and that the EGD was provided with unprecedented resources through the MFF and the next generation, can be seen as evidence of a 'sustainabilisation' of European policymaking during the crisis.

The case of the EGD sheds light on the conditions and mechanisms of effective sustainability-oriented meta-policy strategies in the European context, as well as on the relationship between crisis and sustainability policy in the complex fabric of European governance. In light of the experience with the economic and financial crisis of 2008/2009, the European institutions hardly seem to be in a position to develop a comprehensive, sustainability-oriented crisis response policy. Instead, existing environmental and sustainability policies tend to be marginalised in the crisis. However, the example of the EGD shows that an overarching and sustainability-oriented meta-policy can indeed make a difference. Such a meta-policy can not only endure in times of crisis, but its impact can even be leveraged. The prerequisite for this seems to be that it already exists before the crisis, that it has a central political significance for the Commission, which the latter is willing to enact, and that its ideational orientation proves to be a supportive interpretive scheme for dealing collectively with the turbulence and uncertainties of the crisis, especially in the intergovernmental arm of the EU.

In the future, it will be interesting to see whether and to what extent the EGD will continue to serve as a sustainability-oriented meta-policy after the COVID-19 pandemic and in dealing with other crises, such as the emerging rule of law crisis or upcoming economic, energy and humanitarian crises induced by the war in Ukraine.

REFERENCES

Beck, U. (2006). 'Reflexive governance: politics in the global risk society'. In J.-P. Voss, D. Bauknecht & R. Kemp (eds), *Reflexive Governance for Sustainable Development*, Edward Elgar Publishing, 31–56.

Bickerton, C. J., Hodson, D., & Puetter, U. (2015). 'The new intergovernmentalism: European integration in the post-Maastricht era'. *JCMS: Journal of Common Market Studies*, 53(4), 703–722, https://doi.org/10.1111/jcms.12212.

Bloomfield, J., & Steward, F. (2020). 'The politics of the Green New Deal'. *Political Quarterly*, 91(4), 770–779, https://doi.org/10.1111/1467-923X.12917.

Bornemann, B. (2014). *Policy-Integration und Nachhaltigkeit: Integrative Politik in der Nachhaltigkeitsstrategie der deutschen Bundesregierung* (2nd edn), Springer VS.

Bornemann, B., & Christen, M. (2021). 'A new generation of sustainability governance: potentials for 2030 Agenda implementation in Swiss Cantons'. *Politics and Governance*, 9(1), 187–199, https://doi.org/10.17645/pag.v9i1.3682.

Brand, K.-W. (ed.) (2017). *Die sozial-ökologische Transformation der Welt: Ein Handbuch*, Campus Verlag.

Brand, U. (2009). Schillernd und technokratisch: Grüner New Deal als magic bullet in der Krise des neoliberal-imperialen Kapitalismus? *PROKLA. Zeitschrift für kritische Sozialwissenschaft*, 39(156), 475–481. https://doi.org/10.32387/prokla.v39i156.426.

Brüggen, W. (2001). 'Grüner New Deal'. In W. F. Haug (ed.), *Historisch-kritisches Wörterbuch des Marxismus, Band 5*, Argument, 1062–1070.

Burns, C. (ed.) (2019). *The Impact of the Economic Crisis on European Environmental Policy* (1st edn), Oxford University Press.

Burns, C., Eckersley, P., & Tobin, P. (2020). 'EU environmental policy in times of crisis'. *Journal of European Public Policy*, 27(1), 1–19, https://doi.org/10.1080/13501763.2018.1561741.

Burns, C., Tobin, P., & Sewerin, S. (eds) (2018). *The Impact of the Economic Crisis on European Environmental Policy*, Oxford University Press, https://doi.org/10.1093/oso/9780198826958.001.0001.

CAN (2020). 'Sustainable Europe Investment Plan and a Just Transition Mechanism: Short on climate neutrality'. Briefing Paper. Climate Action Network, Europe, https://caneurope.org/content/uploads/2020/03/Just-Transition-and-Sustainable-Europe-Investment-Plan-Briefing-CAN-Europe-March-2020.pdf.

Dobbs, M., Gravey, V., & Petetin, L. (2021). 'Driving the European Green Deal in turbulent times'. *Politics and Governance*, 9(3), 316–326, https://doi.org/10.17645/pag.v9i3.4321.

Dryzek, J. S. (2013). *The Politics of the Earth: Environmental Discourses* (3rd edn), Oxford University Press.

Dupont, C., Oberthür, S., & von Homeyer, I. (2020). 'The Covid-19 crisis: a critical juncture for EU climate policy development?' *Journal of European Integration*, 42(8), 1095–1110, https://doi.org/10.1080/07036337.2020.1853117.

Eckert, E., & Kovalevska, O. (2021). 'Sustainability in the European Union: analyzing the discourse of the European Green Deal'. *Journal of Risk and Financial Management*, 14(2), 80, https://doi.org/10.3390/jrfm14020080.

Eckert, S. (2021). 'The European Green Deal and the EU's regulatory power in times of crisis'. *JCMS: Journal of Common Market Studies*, 59(S1), 81–91, https://doi.org/10.1111/jcms.13241.

Elkerbout, M., Egenhofer, C., & Ferrer, J. N. (2020). 'The European Green Deal after Corona: Implications for EU climate policy'. CEPS Policy Insights, No 2020-06, 12.

EU (2021). Regulation (EU) 2021/241 of the European Parliament and of the Council of 12 February 2021 establishing the Recovery and Resilience Facility. OJ L 57/17.

European Commission (2001). 'A European Union Strategy for Sustainable Development'.

European Commission (2010). 'EUROPE 2020 A strategy for smart, sustainable and inclusive growth', COM(2010)2020.

European Commission (2011). 'Roadmap to a Resource-Efficient Europe', COM/2011/0571.

European Commission (2015). 'An EU Action Plan for the Circular Economy', COM/2015/0614 final.

European Commission (2018). 'A European Strategy for Plastics in a Circular Economy', COM/2018/028 final.

European Commission (2019). 'The European Green Deal', COM(2019)640.

European Commission (2020a). 'Communication from the Commission to the European Parliament, the Council, the European Economic and Social Committee and the Committee of the Regions. Sustainable Europe Investment Plan. European Green Deal Investment Plan', COM(2020)21 final.

European Commission (2020b). 'Proposal for a Regulation of the European Parliament and of the Council establishing the Just Transition Fund', COM(2020) 22 final.

European Commission (2020c). 'Proposal for a Regulation of the European Parliament and of the Council establishing a Recovery and Resilience Facility', COM(2020) 408 final.

European Commission (2020d). 'Stepping up Europe's 2030 climate ambition. Investing in a climate-neutral future for the benefit of our people', COM/2020/562 final.

European Commission (2021a). 'Political agreement on new Common Agricultural Policy: Fairer, greener, more flexible', IP/21/2711, https://ec.europa.eu/commission/presscorner/detail/en/IP_21_2711.

European Commission (2021b). 'EU budget: European Commission welcomes the adoption of the EU's long-term budget for 2021–2027'. European Commission press release. Europe direct.

European Council (2019). 'A New Strategic Agenda', www.consilium.europa.eu/media/39914/a-new-strategic-agenda-2019-2024.pdf.

Fleming, R. C., & Mauger, R. (2021). 'Green and just? An update on the "European green deal"'. *Journal for European Environmental and Planning Law*, 18(1), 164–180, https://doi.org/10.1163/18760104-18010010.

Fukuda-Parr, S., & Hegstad, T. S. (2019). '"Leaving no one behind" as a site of contestation and reinterpretation'. *Journal of Globalization and Development*, 9(2), 20180037, https://doi.org/10.1515/jgd-2018-0037.

Gravey, V., & Jordan, A. J. (2020). 'Policy dismantling at EU level: reaching the limits of "an ever-closer ecological union"?' *Public Administration*, 98(2), 349–362, https://doi.org/10.1111/padm.12605.

Haas, T., & Jürgens, I. (2021). 'Die europäische Landung auf dem Mond? Der European Green Deal als Projekt ökologischer Modernisierung'. *PROKLA. Zeitschrift für kritische Sozialwissenschaft*, 51(202), 133–140, https://doi.org/10.32387/prokla.v51i202.1927.

Hay, C. (1999). 'Crisis and the structural transformation of the state: interrogating the process of change'. *British Journal of Politics and International Relations*, 1(3), 317–344, https://doi.org/10.1111/1467-856X.00018.

Heinelt, H., & Münch, S. (eds) (2018). *Handbook of European Policies: Interpretive Approaches to the EU*, Edward Elgar Publishing.

Hutter, S., Grande, E., & Kriesi, H. (2016). *Politicising Europe: Integration and Mass Politics*, Cambridge University Press.

Jordan, A. J., & Liefferink, D. (eds) (2004). *Environmental Policy in Europe: The Europeanization of National Environmental Policy*, Routledge, https://doi.org/10 .4324/9780203449004.

Lehndorff, S. (2021). 'Vom New Deal der 1930er Jahre zum Grünen New Deal'. *PROKLA. Zeitschrift für kritische Sozialwissenschaft*, 51(202), 149–161, https://doi .org/10.32387/prokla.v51i202.1924.

Lightfoot, S., & Burchell, J. (2005). 'The European Union and the World Summit on Sustainable Development: Normative Power Europe in Action?' *JCMS: Journal of Common Market Studies*, 43(1), 75–95, https://doi.org/10.1111/j.0021-9886.2005 .00547.x.

Mastini, R., Kallis, G., & Hickel, J. (2021). 'A Green New Deal without growth?' *Ecological Economics*, 179, 106832, https://doi.org/10.1016/j.ecolecon.2020 .106832.

Meadowcroft, J. (2007a). 'National sustainable development strategies: features, challenges and reflexivity'. *European Environment*, 17, 152–163.

Meadowcroft, J. (2007b). Who is in charge here? Governance for sustainable development in a complex world'. *Journal of Environmental Policy & Planning*, 9(3), 299–314, https://doi.org/10.1080/15239080701631544.

Munta, M. (2020). *The European Green Deal: A Game Changer or Simply a Buzzword?* Friedrich-Ebert-Stiftung.

Oberthür, S., & Dupont, C. (2021). 'The European Union's international climate leadership: Towards a grand climate strategy?' *Journal of European Public Policy*, 28(7), 1095–1114, https://doi.org/10.1080/13501763.2021.1918218.

Pantzer, Y. (2021). 'The CAP is parting ways with the EU Green Deal'. Slow Food, www.slowfood.com/eu-farming-policy-is-parting-ways-with-the-eu-green-deal/.

Pianta, M., & Lucchese, M. (2020). 'Rethinking the European Green Deal: An industrial policy for a just transition in Europe'. *Review of Radical Political Economics*, 52(4), 633–641, https://doi.org/10.1177/0486613420938207.

President of the European Commission & President of the European Council (2020). 'A roadmap for recovery. Towards a more resilient, sustainable and fair Europe', www.consilium.europa.eu/media/43384/roadmap-for-recovery-final-21-04-2020 .pdf.

Redaktion, P. (2021). 'Editorial: Green New Deal!? Wie rot ist das neue Grün?' *PROKLA. Zeitschrift für Kritische Sozialwissenschaft*, 51(202), 4–7, https://doi.org/ 10.32387/prokla.v51i202.1933.

Rietig, K. (2021). 'Accelerating low carbon transitions via budgetary processes? EU climate governance in times of crisis'. *Journal of European Public Policy*, 28(7), 1018–1037, https://doi.org/10.1080/13501763.2021.1918217.

Rosamond, J., & Dupont, C. (2021). 'The European Council, the Council, and the European Green Deal'. *Politics and Governance*, 9(3), 348–359, https://doi.org/10 .17645/pag.v9i3.4326.

Rosenbloom, D., & Markard, J. (2020). 'A COVID-19 recovery for climate'. *Science*, 368(6490), 447, https://doi.org/10.1126/science.abc4887.

Schepelmann, P., & Fischedick, M. (2020). 'Perspektiven des "European Green Deal" in Zeiten der Corona-Pandemie'. Diskussionspapier, Wuppertal Institut, 6.

Schmidt, V. A. (2008). 'Discursive institutionalism: the explanatory power of ideas and discourse'. *Annual Review of Political Science*, 11(1), 303–326, https://doi.org/10 .1146/annurev.polisci.11.060606.135342.

Schmidt, V. A. (2018). 'The role of ideas and discourse in European integration'. In H. Heinelt & S. Münch (eds), *Handbook of European Policies: Interpretive Approaches to the EU*, Edward Elgar Publishing, 35–54.

Serricchio, F., Tsakatika, M., & Quaglia, L. (2013). 'Euroscepticism and the global financial crisis'. *JCMS: Journal of Common Market Studies*, 51(1), 51–64, https://doi.org/10.1111/j.1468-5965.2012.02299.x.

Siddi, M. (2020). 'The European Green Deal: Assessing its current state and future implementation'. Finnish Institute of International Affairs, Working Paper 114.

Simonis, U. E. (2020). 'Vom "Green New Deal" zum "European Green Deal"'. Wissenschaftszentrum Berlin für Sozialforschung (WZB) Discussion Paper, EME 2020-002.

Skjærseth, J. B. (2021). 'Towards a European Green Deal: the evolution of EU climate and energy policy mixes'. *International Environmental Agreements: Politics, Law and Economics*, 21(1), 25–41, https://doi.org/10.1007/s10784-021-09529-4.

Skovgaard, J. (2014). 'EU climate policy after the crisis'. *Environmental Politics*, 23(1), 1–17, https://doi.org/10.1080/09644016.2013.818304.

Steinebach, Y., & Knill, C. (2017). 'Still an entrepreneur? The changing role of the European Commission in EU environmental policy-making'. *Journal of European Public Policy*, 24(3), 429–446, https://doi.org/10.1080/13501763.2016.1149207.

Steurer, R. (2010). 'Sustainable development as a governance reform agenda: principles and challenges'. In R. Steurer & R. Trattnigg (eds), *Nachhaltigkeit regieren: Eine Bilanz zu Governance-Prinzipien und -Praktiken*, Oekom Verlag, 33–52.

Thieme, A., & Galariotis, I. (2020). *The European Council's Strategic Agenda: 2019–2024*. European University Institute, https://doi.org/10.2870/900570.

Vogel, D. (2003). 'The hare and the tortoise revisited: the new politics of consumer and environmental regulation in Europe'. *British Journal of Political Science*, 33(4), 557–580.

Von der Leyen, U. (2019a). 'A Union that strives for more. My agenda for Europe. Political Guidelines for the Next European Commission 2019–2024. By candidate for President of the European Commission Ursula von der Leyen', www.europarl.europa.eu/resources/library/media/20190716RES57231/20190716RES57231.pdf.

Von der Leyen, U. (2019b). 'Opening Statement in the European Parliament Plenary Session by Ursula von der Leyen, Candidate for President of the European Commission'. SPEECH/19/4230.

Von der Leyen, U. (2019c). 'Press remarks by President von der Leyen on the occasion of the adoption of the European Green Deal Communication'. SPEECH/19/6749, https://ec.europa.eu/commission/presscorner/detail/en/SPEECH_19_6749.

Weale, A. (1996). 'Environmental rules and rule-making in the European Union'. *Journal of European Public Policy*, 3(4), 594–611, https://doi.org/10.1080/13501769608407055.

Weale, A., Pridham, G., Cini, M., Konstadakopulos, D., Porter, M., & Flynn, B. (2002). *Environmental Governance in Europe: An Ever Closer Ecological Union?* Oxford University Press. https://doi.org/10.1093/acprof:oso/9780199257478.001.0001.

Wolf, S., Teitge, J., Mielke, J., Schütze, F., & Jaeger, C. (2021). The European Green Deal – more than climate neutrality. *Intereconomics*, 56(2), 99–107, https://doi.org/10.1007/s10272-021-0963-z.

Wolff, S., & Ladi, S. (2020). 'European Union responses to the covid-19 pandemic: adaptability in times of permanent emergency'. *Journal of European Integration*, 42(8), 1025–1040, https://doi.org/10.1080/07036337.2020.1853120.

Wurzel, R. K. W., Connelly, J., & Liefferink, D. (eds) (2016). *The European Union in International Climate Change Politics: Still Taking a Lead?* Routledge.

Zeller, C. (2021). 'Green New Deal als Quadratur des Kreises'. *PROKLA. Zeitschrift für kritische Sozialwissenschaft*, 51(202), 31–51, https://doi.org/10.32387/prokla .v51i202.1932.

8. The Multiannual Financial Framework for 2021–2027 and the struggle over ideas about migration and border management

Sybille Münch

INTRODUCTION

Many institutions of the European Union have been characterized by a 'consensus-building style of discourse' (Bach, 2008, p. 119), where cognitive convergence with regard to problem perceptions, policy ideas and approaches to solutions abounds (Lahusen, 2016, p. 115). Negotiations about the EU budget, on the other hand, 'are most often perceived as classical domains of fierce intergovernmental bargaining between EU member states in the (European) Council' (Selle, 2017, p. 149). This edited volume is based on the assumption that the negotiations about the EU Multiannual Financial Framework (MFF) 2021–2027 took place in a setting that was politicized as never before. This assessment is shared by scholars of European integration who have scrutinized how the EU's 'polycrisis' has increased issue salience, the polarization of views and mobilization of public opinion (Zeitlin et al., 2019).

Therefore, we argue that the 'struggle over ideas' (Stone, 2002) during the MFF negotiations should be easily identified. Rather than taking negotiations over the EU budget as reflections of given national interests, this chapter takes an interpretivist approach to the production and circulation of knowledge about migration that is embedded in narratives and argumentation for priorities in the EU budget (cf. Geddes, 2013). This moves processes of collective meaning-making (Schwartz-Shea & Yanow, 2012) as well as persuasion and justification, to the centre of inquiry (Fischer, 2007).

Asylum and migration are policy areas that had proven to be particularly polarized in the run-up to the MFF negotiations. Following the 'migration crisis' around 2015, we have seen disputes about the scope of cooperation and harmonization in this field, and struggles over the lack of solidarity among member states and vis-à-vis refugees. As Niemann and Zaun (2018) maintain, the so-called 'refugee crisis' can be more accurately characterized as a crisis of the Common European Asylum System (CEAS). The rise of right-wing populism and the Brexit referendum are also closely related to disagreements over migration. Hadj Abdou makes an even stronger point for linking EU integration and migration as twin issues: 'If we want to fully understand the underlying dynamics of the politicization of European integration, processes of de-integration and rising sovereigntist demands, we have to turn our attention to immigration' (Hadj Abdou, 2020, p. 644). To Genschel and Jachtenfuchs (2018), the novelty of the EU's crises is caused by the shift from economic integration as traditional rationale to the integration of core state powers (like controlling immigration). While labour and regular migration continue to remain in the hands of the member states, the EU has become increasingly important for issues of border control, asylum and irregular migration (cf. Münch, 2018). New regional alliances among EU member states emerged or strengthened over immigration, like the Visegrád Group, consisting of Poland, Hungary, the Czech Republic, and Slovakia (Koß & Séville, 2020), that later also featured during the MFF negotiations (see Heinelt & Münch, Chapter 1 in this volume).

Polarization and rifts are, however, not only identifiable between countries of arrival, transit and destination among the member states, but also within domestic political systems (Hutter et al., 2016; Schmidt, 2019; Zeitlin et al., 2019). Whereas anti-immigrant narratives have contributed to populism's success, at the same time we observe a strong welcoming attitude among large parts of civil society across the member states. These movements continue to volunteer for the incorporation of refugees and even provide search and rescue missions in the Mediterranean where the EU and its member states fail to ensure that no one dies at sea (Funke, 2021). To many, the neglect, securitization and externalization that are causing thousands of deaths at the external borders have cast serious doubts on the role of the EU as a promoter of human rights in the world (Niemann & Zaun, 2018).

Consequently, migration had already been high on the agenda of all relevant institutions before the beginning of the EU budget negotiations: the European Council discussed this divisive topic most often between December 2014 and January 2017. The European Commission under Jean-Claude Juncker used the issue strategically to place the Commission back on the political stage and counter rumours that its relevance was in decline (Wolff, 2020). The reinforcement of both the non-executive agencies, the European Border and Coast Guard (EBCG), formerly known as Frontex, and the European Asylum Support Office (EASO), had been announced by the Commissioner in charge, Avramopoulos, as a 'way to "ensure EU solidarity on the ground at all times, in all situations, whilst fully respecting Member states' competences"' (European

Commission, 2018b). With the Treaty of Lisbon, the European Parliament (EP) had formally gained importance, without playing the pro-immigrant role that had formerly been predicted (cf. Ripoll Servent & Trauner, 2014). Nevertheless, Stępka (2022) identifies the EP as the main promotor of a human security logic, putting human lives on the agenda. Following the 2015 migration crisis, migration and refugee policies were 'experiencing conflicting trends of liberalization, politicization, de-politicization and securitization' (Wolff, 2020). As far as the public discourse is concerned, civil society has organized and actively used the internet as a transnational, de-securitizing forum (Crepaz, 2020). Against this backdrop, and reflecting the high salience of the issue, the European Commission created a new and specific 'heading' for migration and border management in the post-2020 Multiannual Financial Framework.

This chapter focuses on the negotiations around the MFF and tries to analyse and anticipate changes in this policy area. It does so by introducing the reader to its methodology before reconstructing the policy and discursive context at the beginning of the negotiations. It goes on by briefly sketching out the main developments of the migration heading in the MFF negotiations. Finally, it zooms in on the main rationales in the debate over the MFF heading.

METHODOLOGY: IDENTIFYING STORYLINES

EU budget negotiations have been described as the 'mother' of European package deals and are associated with institutional bargaining (Selle, 2017, p. 152). This mode of communication is often distinguished from argumentation: bargaining is defined as a process 'in which pragmatic demands are made, underpinned by promises, threats and hints to exit-options' (Saretzki, 2009, p. 162). Arguing, on the other hand, is defined as a mode of communication 'in which empirical and normative assertions are made with the claim to being valid' (ibid.). In interpretive policy analysis, authors in the tradition of the argumentative turn have foregrounded how 'policy ideas are arguments that favor different ways of seeing and relating to social problems' (Fischer, 1998, p. 141) and how they serve to naturalize inherently political claims. So why does this chapter focus on the MFF *negotiations* in the field of migration as a 'struggle over ideas', a process often associated with arguing rather than bargaining? Two remarks are in order at this point, one of a theoretical, the other of a more empirical nature. First, there are significant distinctions between the subdisciplines of public policy on the one hand and European studies or international relations on the other, that we have discussed elsewhere (Heinelt & Münch, 2018), drawing from Barbehön (2015) and Diez (2016): the subdiscipline of European studies or international relations saw debates between constructivists and rationalists about whether rationalists could 'accommodate communication at all' (H. Müller, 2004, p. 398), tried to establish under what conditions bargaining gave way to arguing (ibid.) or what kind of situations fostered the dominance of either interests or ideas (Risse, 2018).[1] While proponents of constructivism in EU research have traditionally been more conciliatory towards rationalist approaches or even calling for a 'synthesis' (H. Müller, 2004),[2] interpretivism in the study of public policy has been more confrontational in linking its postpositivist epistemology with social and political theory and a methodology that focuses on meaning. 'Interpretive approaches to political studies focus on meanings that shape action and institutions, and the way in which they do so' (Bevir & Rhodes, 2016, p. 3). Policy analysis is thus taking an interpretive (Yanow, 2000) or argumentative turn (Fischer & Forester, 1993a), in which policy processes are no longer explained solely on the basis of cost–benefit calculations. Instead, they are understood as linguistically mediated and shaped processes of interpretation and struggles for interpretation. This means that 'participants in plural political processes not only bargain, given their interests, but also refine and learn about those interests' (Fischer & Forester, 1993b, p. 13). Therefore, we can scrutinize negotiations as communication rather than as a mere display of neutral facts and given interests.

The second reason why this chapter goes beyond notions of given national or institutional interests is the fact that debates about the MFF go way beyond official negotiations between member states and different EU institutions: the voices in the 'struggle over ideas' are manifold, because the proposals and discussions trigger further reactions from other stakeholders, including academics, think tanks, (human rights) NGOs and commentators, but also national parliaments of the member states (cf. Selle, 2017 on the last MFF). When developing its proposals, the European Commission already conducts stakeholder consultations regarding specific funds and draws from *ex post* evaluations of existing funds and programmes, in the case of the Asylum, Migration and Integration Fund (AMIF) in the form of a programmed interim evaluation together with member states. The European Parliament (2018) requested another evaluation of allocation, implementation and oversight of migration funds based on publicly available information, stakeholder interviews and a survey of non-governmental organizations (NGOs).

As the editorial introduction by Heinelt and Münch (Chapter 1 in this volume) and Peter Becker's chapter (Chapter 2 in this volume) have demonstrated, negotiations for the MFF involve different complex legislative procedures for the overall MFF and the sector-specific instruments. While the Treaty on the Functioning of the European Union (TFEU) requires unanimity in the Council following Parliament's consent for the adoption of the entire MFF, the EP and the Council are on an equal footing under the ordinary legislative procedure when it comes to negotiating about the funds and decentralized agencies in the areas of migration and border management (D'Alfonso, 2020). Following a proposal by the European Commission, the European Parliament, the Council and the European Council start working on their responses. While the European Council is not formally involved in the legislative processes leading to the adoption of the MFF, it had already become accepted practice to reach unanimity among member states in the context of the 2014–2020 budget (EPRS, 2018). While recent studies of the European governance of migration around 2015 are dominantly (implicitly) intergovernmentalist and therefore privilege the role of member states, an analysis of the negotiations around the MFF allows the decentralizing of what is often portrayed as coherent EU migration governance or discourse. Disentangling the different voices in the struggle over ideas around the MFF makes clear

> that an a priori understanding of 'the EU' as a unitary discourse participant is problematic because its institutions constantly interact and renegotiate perceptions of situations and problems as well as claims to define, form(ulate), represent and articulate into effect a specific EU identity through governmental activity. (Simon, 2021, pp. 52–53)

As opposed to rationalist approaches that treat ideas as causal factors, interpretivists often draw from analyses of discourse 'that is, the examination of argumentative structure in documents and other written or spoken statements as well as the practices through which these utterances are made' (Hajer, 2006, p. 66).[3] More specifically, in what follows, we identify storylines in documents issued by EU institutions, stakeholders, NGOs and think tanks that act as short cuts for a specific understanding of the challenges the budget is supposed to mitigate. The corpus was collected by drawing from a keyword search and snowballing to other sources. The focus is first and foremost on the heading 'migration', but in some instances cohesion policies are mentioned when they are dedicated to the integration of third-country nationals.[4] According to Hajer (2006), storylines are condensed statements that contain complex narratives that are often left untold but reduced to short 'cues', a notion that is also used by Hadj Abdou (2020). Narratives are ordering devices through which (political) actors make sense of reality. The analyst then tries to identify patterns of political storytelling across different sources (Gadinger et al., 2019), with sequential and causal orderings being ubiquitous. Policy coalitions, hence, are held together by 'narrative storylines that interpret events and courses of action in concrete social contexts' (Fischer, 2003, p. 102), rather than by deeply entrenched belief systems. In line with Bevir and Philipps (2019), who aim at 'decentering European governance', we highlight the significance of narratives, rationalities and resistance in European governance.[5]

In what follows we briefly introduce the reader to the discursive and budgetary context under the MFF for 2014–2020. We shall then briefly and chronologically present the main milestones and actors in the policy area of migration leading up to the final EU budget, before identifying key heuristics or rationalities ('cues') in the policy documents.

PROLOGUE: ASYLUM, MIGRATION AND BORDERS UNDER THE MULTIANNUAL FINANCIAL FRAMEWORK FOR 2014–2020

In the EU context, asylum, migration and borders are part of the broader area of freedom, security and justice. The Treaty of Lisbon (TFEU) introduced various changes to this area in 2009, establishing the competences for a common policy on asylum, immigration and external border control, 'based on solidarity between Member States and fairness to non-EU nationals' (D'Alfonso, 2020, p. 2). As mentioned above, both objectives have not materialized since then. Article 80 explicitly mentions pooling financial resources in their support in order to share the financial implications of shared responsibilities (D'Alfonso, 2020). Moreover, the policy area is one of differentiated integration. Therefore, some countries opted out, whereas others that are not member states of the EU, but of the Schengen area, participate and contribute to the overall policy objectives.

The preparations for the negotiations on the 2014–2020 budget had started under the pressure of the economic and financial crisis. During the funding period of the 2014–2020 MFF, the internal dimension of the policies for asylum, migration and external borders was under its smallest budget ('Security and citizenship'; Heading 3). The funding was dedicated to three different categories:

- EU funding programmes to co-finance measures of the member states;
- decentralized EU agencies such as Frontex and the European Asylum Support Office (EASO);
- IT systems such as the Schengen Information System.

In its proposal the European Commission had

> underlined the growing importance of these policies in recent years, their role in the creation of an area without internal borders and the changes introduced to them by the Treaty of Lisbon, concluding that the mobilization of the EU budget produced an obvious added value. The Commission pointed to the fact that pooling resources in these policy areas is meant to ensure synergies and economies of scale by facilitating cooperation and joint solutions to issues that Member States cannot tackle acting individually. (D'Alfonso, 2019, p. 11)

While the European Parliament had argued along similar lines, the European Council significantly cut Heading 3 during its negotiations, particularly the transnational dimensions. The sensitivity of the policy field close to the core of state functions and the attempts of member states to retain control have been interpreted as reasons for the slow progression of budgetary envelopes (D'Alfonso, 2019, p. 15), even though the Commission had repeatedly tried to alert member states to an increase in migration following the Arab Spring.[6]

Subsequently, the resources provided under the MFF 2014–2020 did not suffice to meet the demands in the face of the rise in arrivals around the year 2015. Hence, EU institutions made excessive use of the MFF's flexibility provisions, while the high numbers of new arrivals following political instability in the EU's neighbourhood laid bare the weaknesses of the Common European Asylum System. As a consequence, the mid-term revision of the MFF in 2017 led to reinforcements of the heading that were actually higher than the original cuts (D'Alfonso, 2020). Drawing from these past experiences, flexibility and leeway for emergency assistance were stressed in the run-up to the new round of MFF negotiations. Yet observers like Goldner Lang (2019, p. 16) maintained that the right balance should be struck between flexibility and predictability and attaining the long-term strategic objectives of funding.

The negotiations and responses that led to the new MFF cannot be isolated from ongoing and overlapping policy processes in the European multilevel governance of migration. Attempts to reform the Common European Asylum System have been ongoing since 2016 and a number of new and recast legislative proposals were already under negotiation. Sarah Wolff (2020) identifies three trends in EU migration policymaking following the 2015 'crisis' narrative: agencification, a leadership of JHA (Justice and Home Affairs) bureaucrats in favour of the status quo and strong divergences between EU member states. First, even though often framed as neutral, depoliticized 'credible actors and experts' and problem-solvers, the legitimacy of agencies like Frontex were often challenged during the period of the last EU budget. Not only by pro-migrant NGOs, but also by some member states and countries of arrival, who perceive these agencies as 'proxies' of stronger member states (Ripoll Servent, 2018, p. 83). Moreover, in the European Court of Auditors' (ECA) analysis of expenditures in the field of migration, asylum and border control, the European Asylum Support Office (EASO) was the only EU agency that did not receive a clean opinion regarding the legality and regularity of its payments. Even though it found indicators of improvements compared to earlier ECA reports, the EP refused to grant EASO discharge for the financial years 2016 and 2017 (D'Alfonso, 2020, p. 4). In terms of the legality and regularity of its budget, the close cooperation with third countries following 2015 has led to a consistent problem according to the ECA. Even though the Frontex budget was regularly discharged, the proof of equipment-related costs claimed by cooperating countries was often deemed to be insufficient (D'Alfonso, 2020).

Second, Wolff (2020) maintains that the crisis mode has perpetuated the monopoly of Justice and Home Affairs (JHA) bureaucrats in favour of border controls and restrictive policies. While the fact that European integration was famously used by restrictive-venue shoppers from the member states (Guiraudon, 2003) is well established, Wolff (2020) and others (Andersson, 2016; Münch, 2018) demonstrated how the constant crisis mode allowed for 'more of the same' in terms of definition and direction of policies. While research in some member states like Germany has found a 'meritocratic turn' that introduces notions of skills and labour market demands to the asylum process (Schammann, 2017; Bonjour & Chauvin, 2018), little of this framing has made it into the discourse at EU level.

For instance, proposals for a recast of the EU return policy had been put forward. The issue of return had become more salient after 2015, due to a perception of crisis and how borders did not sufficiently stop irregular migration. As Majcher and Strik (2021) identify, the Commission refrained from conducting an impact assessment of the old Return Directive by pointing at an 'urgent need':

> In response to criticism of this lack of evidence, the Commission often refers to confidential reports from Member States, including under the Schengen Evaluation Mechanism, and exchanges with senior officials. This reasoning ignores the importance of transparent decision-making and affects the role of the European Parliament ... as a co-legislator. (Majcher & Strik, 2021, p. 108)

Hence, it needs to be stressed that the intergovernmental and secretive modus that has been characteristic for the field of migration policymaking in earlier phases of EU integration (cf. Guiraudon, 2003) has not been entirely replaced. This means that the officially published data that forms the basis of our analysis for this chapter most likely only covers some processes and not all. The monopoly of JHA is also relevant for our later analysis of the MFF negotiations, because Hadj Abdou in her analysis of over 100 interviews with governance actors from EU institutions and agencies, as well as selected member states, demonstrates how similar interpretations of immigration emerge among similar actors. Influenced by their social context, they turn to like-minded actors to make sense of the situation in times of crisis. 'The frames that emerge are supported by specific cues that circulate within actors' networks and that provide "evidence" for a certain perspective' (Hadj Abdou, 2020, p. 646). The author finds that actors in home affairs were central in shaping dominant frames of migration as tragedy and the problematization of pull factors, that is those that re-emerged or were also referred to by actors with opposing views. This is a pattern we also detect in our data (see below).

The third trend according to Wolff (2020) is the continuing, if not growing, divergence among member states in terms of aims and goals of migration policymaking. The distrust is specifically apparent between Eastern and Western member states and featured heavily in the negotiations on the MFF as well (see below). In parallel to the negotiations on the MFF, European Commission President Ursula von der Leyen had made a new pact on migration and asylum a priority on the new Commission's agenda. Her 2020 work programme stated that she aims for a more resilient, humane and effective migration and asylum system. According to reports, some EU member states, including Germany, then drafted various reform proposals aimed at mandatory registration and/or asylum application procedures at the EU's external borders (Deutsches Institut für Menschenrechte et al., 2020, p. 3). In June 2020 the Commission's proposal on migration reform was postponed, however, because it was assumed that it could fuel tensions during the ongoing MFF negotiations. One of the expected controversies was around the redistribution of refugees from countries of arrival in Southern Europe across all member states as 'a mandatory solidarity mechanism' (Barigazzi, 2020).

In drawing a longitudinal picture, Trauner (2016) highlights how policymakers' reactions to the 'migration crisis' in 2015 are closely intertwined with previous experiences and perceptions of the financial and economic crisis following 2008. While the Dublin system, according to which the responsibility for dealing with asylum requests lies with the country of entry, operates on the assumption that all member states provide similar procedures, substantial differences became apparent; all the more so in respect of a country like Greece that had been hit badly by the economic crisis. The resistance by Eastern and Central European member states to agreeing on the relocation of 160,000 asylum-seekers from Greece and Italy had clearly demonstrated how polarized decision-making had become, even before the MFF negotiations (cf. Trauner, 2016).

THE NEGOTIATIONS ABOUT THE MULTIANNUAL FINANCIAL FRAMEWORK FOR 2021–2027: CONTENT AND PROCESSES

In the following section we will reconstruct the main steps and objectives leading up to the final MFF agreement.

Final Results

When the European Parliament and EU member states in the Council, with the support of the European Commission, reached an agreement on the new MFF on 20 November 2020, the heading Migration and Border Management saw an allocation of €22.7 billion. Migration was among the ten programmes that received top-ups compared to the European Council agreement of 21 July 2020: the Integrated Border Management Fund, formerly at €6.5 billion, received an extra €1 billion; and the European Border and Coast Guard allocation of €5.6 billion received an extra €0.5 billion (European Commission, 2020, p. 3). When the funds were adopted by the European Parliament in July 2021, the Asylum, Migration and Integration Fund (AMIF) was €9.88 billion to support asylum and migration policy and the Integrated Border Management Fund received €6.24 billion (ECRE, 2020b).

A press release by the European Parliament of 9 December 2020 identifies the following aims:

> The co-legislators agreed that the new AMIF should contribute to strengthening the common asylum policy, develop legal migration in line with the member states' economic and social needs, support third-country nationals to effectively integrate and be socially included, and contribute to the fight against irregular migration. Other objectives include ensuring that those without a right to stay in the EU are returned and readmitted in an effective, safe and dignified way. The fund will also support those people to begin reintegrating in non-EU countries to which they have been returned. (European Parliament, 2020b)

The European Commission (n.d.) website on the new AMIF states the following objectives:

- to strengthen and develop all aspects of the common European asylum system, including its external dimension
- to support legal migration to the Member States, including by contributing to the integration of third-country nationals
- to contribute to countering irregular migration and ensuring effectiveness of return and readmission in third countries
- to enhance solidarity and responsibility sharing between the Member States, in particular towards those most affected by migration and asylum challenges.

Processes and Milestones

Given the salience of migration on the EU agenda leading up to the MFF negotiations, many analysts and policymakers had argued that asylum, migration and border management should be among the policy areas where the contribution of the EU budget should be stepped up: according to the interinstitutional High-Level Group tasked with a review of the EU's financing system, 'the EU budget should increase its focus on policy areas relating to EU public goods and European added value, where joint action at Union level is deemed not only relevant but indispensable' (D'Alfonso, 2020, p. 5).[7]

Nevertheless, when the European Commission initiated the hot phase of the MFF negotiations in May 2018, it proposed a new heading for migration and border management for the new MFF. Heading 4 would be organized around 'migration' and 'border management' as two policy clusters, with the strengthening of external borders receiving potentially stronger reinforcements (European Commission, 2018a). The paradigm of 'migration management' has been promoted by the International Organization for Migration (IOM) since the 1980s and is the dominant framing of migration governance in the EU (cf. Scheel & Ustek-Spilda, 2019, p. 665). According to a briefing by the European Parliamentary Research Service (D'Alfonso, 2020, p. 1), the EC's proposal for the new heading with a value of €30.8 billion was intended to increase synergies with other EU funding instruments and capacity to react to evolving needs.

The new funding programmes should be (1) the Asylum and Migration Fund (AMF), building on the former Asylum, Migration and Integration Fund (AMIF; see above), and (2) the Integrated Border Management Fund (IBMF), the latter composed of two separate instruments for border management and visas (86% of IBMF resources) and for customs control equipment (14%). The second cluster was going to build on the Internal Security Fund (ISF) borders and visa instrument as well as filling gaps in the 2014–2020 MFF for the purchase, maintenance and upgrading of customs control equipment for goods (D'Alfonso, 2020).

According to D'Alfonso (2020, p. 6), the Commission's proposal built on various interim evaluations and an impact assessment of the existing AMIF and ISF borders and visa instrument. First, the administrative burden on beneficiaries and managing authorities of the old AMIF was considered to be too high. Many NGOs in particular had complained that the funding rules for the AMIF created significant barriers to the participation of civil society organizations (Goldner Lang, 2019, p. 22).[8] What is more, the NGOs criticized that the old AMIF generation was often managed by those national authorities in charge of migration and internal affairs, while the European Social Fund (ESF), which was tackling, among others, the integration of third-country nationals, was coordinated by ministries of social policy – often with insufficient coordination (PICUM & ECRE, 2018). Second, the EC intended to strengthen the external dimension of both funding programmes and allow for cooperation with and in third countries. Relevant measures include 'implementation of readmission agreements and secondment of joint liaison officers to third countries' (D'Alfonso, 2020, p. 6).

In a joint reaction to this proposal of the European Commission, the United Nations High Commissioner for Refugees (UNHCR) and the non-profit European Council on Refugees and Exiles (ECRE) maintained:

> The AMF's Policy Objective thus relates solely to migration management, with no overall commitment to building a European protection system. The proposed AMF would additionally be implemented 'in line with' the Union acquis, rather than with a commitment to 'strengthen and develop' it. The specific reference to the Charter of Fundamental Rights (CFEU) included in the General Objective of the AMIF has been replaced by a more general requirement for implementation 'in compliance with the Union's commitments on fundamental rights'. (UNHCR & ECRE, 2018, p. 30)

According to UNHCR and ECRE (2018), the specific objectives in the Commission's AMF proposal reflected the migration management paradigm with a broad provision for cooperation with third countries, the reframing of resettlement from a humanitarian tool to a measure for enhancing cooperation with third countries and by envisaging AMF support for capacity-building in third countries to counter irregular migration.

While it could be expected that those regional alliances like the Visegrád group (V4; see above), who were strengthened by their shared disagreement on relocations of refugees and mandatory solidarity mechanisms, would favour a strengthening of the budget for migration control, in fact a more nuanced pattern emerged. In their analysis of 50 press statements originating from 35 meetings of V4 Prime Ministers in the 2004–mid-2018 period, Koß and Séville (2020) find: 'With the exception of border controls, the V4 accordingly opposed any allocation of EU money to migration policies at the detriment of cohesion policy' (Koß & Séville, 2020, p. 103). In their joint statement of June 2018, the V4 maintain:

> In line with the repeated conclusions of the European Council, the V4 countries believe that it is time to take divisive concepts off the table and focus instead on elements which unite us and are working on the ground, like designing a border protection-based system, which aims at stemming the irregular migratory pressure by common European action in the area of the external dimension and by effective, responsible and enforceable border protection. (V4 Prime Ministers, 2018)

The emphasis on border protection is, of course, not new and border control policies have been harmonized since the creation of a free movement area by the Schengen agreement. In this widely shared logic, Schengen could only eliminate internal border controls between member states at the cost of intensified border controls on the outside. Koß and Séville (2020, p. 103) suggest that the V4's resistance towards the mandatory relocation of refugees around 2015 aimed to protect the principle of free movement at a time when Western member states had suspended this principle, with the V4 calling on 'all true friends of Schengen'.[9]

Both the Council and the EP started examining the proposals, leading to an agreement to increase the European Border and Coast Guard Agency's operational staff with the aim of raising a standing corps of 10,000 EU border guards by 2027. In June 2018, the European Council asserted that the new MFF should contain 'flexible instruments, allowing for fast disbursement, to combat illegal migration. The internal security, integrated border management, asylum and migration funds should therefore include dedicated, significant components for external migration management' (European Council, 2018, p. 3). It went on to stress the need for member states to protect external borders, and work on the effective return of irregular migrants (ibid.). In November 2018, the EP issued an interim report, asserting to endow the 'Migration and border management' heading with sufficient resources. It argued for confirmation of the increased level as suggested by the European Commission and called for further resources for decentralized agencies.

In 2018, the negotiations reached a point that triggered institutionalized reactions from advisory committees, like the European Economic and Social Committee (EESC) and the Committee of the Regions (CoR). The EESC welcomed the increase in financial resources for the two 'very different' funds under the migration heading and their increased flexibility. However, the EESC (2018) also noted

> Equal treatment and anti-discrimination policies represent the pillars of European policies, including those concerning the integration of third-country nationals. The removal of the word 'integration' from the title [of the AMF] is worrying, as this could be seen as reflecting diminishing concern for this aspect. (EESC, 2018, p. 4)

It went on to call for a strengthening of solidarity among member states, so as to not leave it an 'empty word' and 'regrets that there is no specific mention of the protection of fundamental rights at border installations' (EESC, 2018, p. 4).

The Committee of the Regions (CoR), in its 'Opinion' from October 2018, 'reiterates the need for a coordinated approach by the EU and the Member States to build a common asylum and migration policy based on the principles of solidarity and fair sharing of responsibility' and 'welcomes the increases in funding for migration in the EU budget, but is concerned by the bias in these increases which are far more significant for measures on border protection, than for the AMF'.

While it welcomed close cooperation with third countries in order to tackle the 'root causes' of migration, it stressed that external 'development funding should not, however, be instrumentalised solely to prevent migration' (Committee of the Regions, 2018, p. 1). This is a case where we can reveal the dominance of certain 'cues' feeding into external cooperation, like tackling 'root causes' (Council of the European Union, 2020, p. 47) even among opposing opinions. Supporting countries of origin and transit in their economic development and stability to get rid of push factors is one of the often-told 'stories of control' (Stone, 2002, cf. Terlizzi, 2021 on the Italian case). The CoR's suggested amendments to the Commission's proposal are also interesting in how certain wordings are shared while the CoR simultaneously tries to underline the responsibilities of the European Union towards forced migrants: long-established metaphors like 'migratory pressures' and 'inflows' are easily shared (Committee of the Regions, 2018, p. 3; European Parliament, 2018; Münch, 2018), but the CoR opinion adds 'vulnerable persons' and the need to create infrastructure to receive newcomers. It goes on to suggest the creation of channels for legal migration and amends the Commission's objective for the fund 'to contribute to countering irregular migration and ensuring effectiveness of return and readmission in third countries' by adding 'while ensuring that human rights are respected' (Committee of the Regions, 2018, p. 4).

In its attempt to summarize the main reactions from different stakeholders at this point, the European Parliamentary Research service (D'Alfonso, 2020) picks up a research brief for the European Trade Union Institute that 'depicts the significant increase in the resources for borders and migration as among the most striking elements of the proposals, but notes that, nevertheless, proposed funding remains moderate in scale, given its low starting point' (D'Alfonso, 2020, p. 9).

Further to the discussions in Council preparatory bodies, the Romanian presidency in May 2019 reinserted the word 'integration' into the title of the Fund (Council of the European Union, 2019b, p. 6). It would take until July 2020 for EU heads of state to reach a political agreement and until November 2020 for the EP and the Council to agree on the package.

As Becker (Chapter 2 in this volume) describes, the simultaneous negotiations in the Council did not reach an agreement in time for the EP elections. The new EP that was constituted after the elections in May 2019 confirmed its former negotiating mandate, but introduced a modified name (Asylum, Migration and *Integration* Fund), extended provisions for emergency assistance, and increased involvement of regional and local authorities to the proposal following a report from the Committee on Civil Liberties, Justice and Home Affairs (LIBE).

In a joint statement from November 2019, the UNHCR, the IOM and the ECRE, together with other NGOs, published a statement of shared concerns asking the co-legislators to address 'groups which are most vulnerable to violence, exploitation and abuse such as human trafficking victims, regardless of their residence status'. They demanded, among other things, avoiding the use of funds for building detention facilities and limiting the amount of spending outside the EU (ECRE, 2019a).

When in December 2019 the Finnish presidency of the Council published an updated MFF draft negotiating box, the heading for migration and border management was among those that were to be cut significantly in relative terms compared to the Commission proposals. While the proposal for the AMF was confirmed, funding for the Integrated Border Management Fund (IBMF) and the European Border and Coast Guard Agency (EBCGA)/Frontex would be significantly reduced. Both the EP's negotiating team and Commission President von der Leyen criticized the proposal for undermining key policy objectives in the field of border management (D'Alfonso, 2020, p. 9).

In July 2020, the NGO EuroMed Rights reported that the European Commission had proposed 'a 441% monetary value increase compared to its 2014 proposal for the 2014–2020 budget and a 78% increase compared to the 2015 budgetary review for the same budget' (EuroMed Rights, 2020). In its resolution following the conclusions of the extraordinary European Council meeting of 17–21 July 2020, the EP heavily criticized the agreement as it then stood, and stressed its beliefs 'that the proposed cuts to asylum, migration and border management imperil the EU's position in an increasingly volatile and uncertain world' (European Parliament, 2020a, p. 2).

In its newsletter of 11 December 2020, the European Council on Refugees and Exiles commends that

> the European Parliament has secured minimum shares of allocations to national programmes, earmarking 15% of these for strengthening the common asylum policy and 15% for the objective of promoting integration and regular migration. … Another achievement of the European Parliament regards the increase of the lump-sum payments provided per every resettled person (€10,000, up from the €7,000 intended by the Council). The same amount will be provided for every person relocated from another member state. (ECRE, 2020a)

As the chronological reconstruction should have made clear, discussions around the migration heading featured some established controversies around notions of migration management and border protection as opposed to pathways to integration, protection of human rights and the participation of regional authorities and civil society. With both the AMIF and the Integrated Border Management Fund under the same heading, very heterogeneous discourse coalitions could generally agree on sufficient resources.

STRUGGLES OVER THE INTERPRETATION OF THE CHALLENGES AND PERSPECTIVES OF ACTION LINKED TO MIGRATION AND ASYLUM

While the main milestones have been highlighted in the previous section, we shall now zoom into five storylines that were dominant in the 'struggle over ideas' on migration and asylum: inside/outside dichotomies, an emphasis on return, the need for externalization, conditionality, and solidarity. Readers familiar with the rationalities of EU migration governance will realize that most of these 'cues' have been around for some time.

Inside/Outside Dichotomies

From an interpretive perspective, it becomes clear that the financial framework not only allocates resources, but in doing so, it conveys a certain understanding of what the problem it is trying to solve 'really is'. One could argue that already the press release by the European Commission (2018a) that announced the first proposals fuelled this framing by labelling it 'a modern budget for a Union that protects, empowers and defends', introducing it as 'an honest response to today's reality in which Europe is expected to play a greater role in providing security and stability in an unstable world'. While 'protection' would certainly be needed by asylum-seekers from third countries, it seems clear that this is not what the slogan tries to insinuate. It can be assumed from the outset that it is the interior of the European Union that is perceived to be in need of protection and defence. This resonates with Simon's finding that 'since 2011, the concept of risk has consistently been relevant in the productive organisation of the relational identities of the EU Self and the migrant Other' (Simon, 2021, p. 64). This resonates with the draft conclusions of a meeting of the European Council in July 2020:

> Coordinated action at EU level offers significant EU added value as effective control of external borders is a prerequisite for ensuring more efficient migration management and a high level of internal security while safeguarding the principle of free movement of persons and goods within the Union. (Council of the European Union, 2020, p. 47)

As highlighted in a Council document, external border management is portrayed as a 'precondition for the free movement of persons within the Union and is a fundamental component of an area of freedom, security and justice'

(Council of the European Union, 2019a, p. 7). Drawing from a well-known migration–security narrative, it goes on to stress the need for a Union budget

> to support Member States in managing the crossing of the external borders effi-
> ciently and in addressing migratory challenges and potential future threats at those
> borders, thereby contributing to addressing serious crime with a cross-border
> dimension while acting in full respect of fundamental rights. (Council of the
> European Union, 2019a, p. 9)

Hence, the rise in the budget in the area of asylum and migration that the Commission suggested in July 2020 was interpreted and hence criticized by pro-immigrant human rights NGOs for its securitization and externalization motives:

> Is this good news to ensure the well-being of thousands of migrants and refugees
> currently living on the streets or stuck in overcrowded reception centres in EU
> member states? Actually, this increase is mainly directed towards strengthening the
> security approach: in the current proposal, approximately 75% of the EU's migra-
> tion and asylum budget would be allocated to returns, border management and the
> externalisation of controls. (EuroMed Rights, 2020)

The increased funding for border protection supports this interpretation. The approval of the new Frontex Regulation in November 2019, together with earlier MFF proposals by the European Commission, have provided Frontex with the opportunity to invest heavily in infrastructure and new technologies (cf. Noori, 2021 on how practices of bordering are entangled with material artefacts). In 2020, the NGO Statewatch was already reporting the acquisition of dozens of vehicles equipped with thermal and day cameras, surveillance radar and sensors, maritime analysis tools, new software to access the Schengen Information System, etc. (Statewatch, 2020). The emphasis on border control as a long-standing motive in EU migration governance materi-alizes in a border regime that has been characterized as a 'state of suspicion' (Borrelli et al., 2021). Drawing from the enactment approach in science and technology studies (STS) it is clear that these attempts at generating (quanti-fiable) knowledge about migration 'perform the realities they allegedly only study and describe' (Scheel & Ustek-Spilda, 2019, p. 665). The substantial upgrade of the Frontex mandate, personnel and budget, which can be attributed to a plethora of policy developments of which the MFF is only one piece of the jigsaw, has led to calls for accountability measures in the face of accusations for potential fundamental rights abuses and attempted push backs (Rasche, 2019). Nevertheless, the EP's rapporteur is quoted with maintaining that

> the EU's borders in future must be efficient, digital, humane and safe. These new
> instruments [the border instruments] guarantee progress towards this goal. Together

we can bring border, visa and asylum policy back in line with our human rights obligations, notably with increased funding for search and rescue to aid those drowning on Europe's borders. (European Parliament, 2021)

Digitalization, effectiveness and border management hence are storylines that are shared yet hold different meanings to those who portray migrants as vulnerable and to those who stress the vulnerability of the EU (cf. Simon, 2021).

In 2019, in assessing how the budget negotiations for the migration heading evolved, Goldner Lang maintained that the emphasis on fighting irregular migration and smuggling and enhancing border-control capacity suggested not only a significant rise in allocations to the external dimension. In addition, the

> fact that the budget for these policies is undergoing the highest increase in relative terms supports the argument that it is politically easier to negotiate a budgetary increase in this politically sensitive area than to agree on a change of EU migration and asylum legislation. (Goldner Lang, 2019, p. 16)

We have argued elsewhere that in the case of the EU, metaphors discursively construct a European identity based on binary inside/outside oppositions that serve as a substitute for the lack of myths and shared founding stories (Münch, 2016). This dichotomy is also reflected in the MFF.

Return

While border protection is the most established aspect of EU migration governance, the readmission and return are increasingly portrayed as the other side of the coin of a functioning asylum system. This is also reflected in the MFF. Already the old AMIF generation was intended to enhance 'fair and effective return strategies' (UNHCR & ECRE, 2018, p. 20). The widespread problematization of a so-called 'deportation gap' among European policymakers is a guiding principle for action (cf. Ataç & Schütze, 2020, p. 119). According to this interpretation, the number of persons who are legally obliged to leave the respective EU member state considerably exceeds the number of those who have actually been deported or have left voluntarily. After 2015, calls for effective return 'have been voiced more often and more assertively, resulting in the adopting of numerous legally non-binding instruments entitled "Statements", "Joint Way Forward", "Handbooks" or "Action Plans"' as 'soft law' (Slominski & Trauner, 2021, p. 84).

In the documentation of its meeting on 6–7 December 2018, taking place during the initial months of the MFF negotiations, the Council of the European Union (2018, p. 10) maintains that 'Member states identified migration, returns, cooperation with third countries and the fight against migrant smuggling as priorities. Some member states emphasized the need for flexibility and sufficient funding.' Already in the evaluation on the old AMIF generation, the European Parliament (2018) had noted that even though the Fund required at least 20% of funds to be allocated to each of asylum and integration, some member states only went for the minimum. 'Some countries prioritise asylum, others integration, while others prioritise returns' (European Parliament, 2018, p. 6).

In their assessment of the new MFF proposal, the UNHCR and the ECRE (2018, p. 12) criticized that indicators prioritize return. They predicted that seven member states (Greece, Bulgaria, Croatia, Hungary, Poland, Slovakia and Slovenia) would effectively be financially rewarded for asylum recognition rates far lower than the EU average. In its meeting in December 2018, the Council of the European Union (p. 6) had even suggested that a 'Debate should still take place on the possibility to return a third country national to any safe third country and not only the country of origin or transit.' The European Council on Refugees and Exiles stresses that the Asylum and Migration Fund should be preserved to play a 'considerable role in ensuring fair and effective asylum systems in Europe, dignity in returns of third-country nationals and contribute to the harmonization of standards in relation to asylum, reception conditions and integration' (ECRE, 2019b, p. 3). While the right of return is central to international law, 'voluntary return' is increasingly co-opted as a migration management strategy, with member states investing in financial incentives, professional training and reintegration measures.

Externalization

In addition to its emphasis on fighting irregular migration and smuggling, and border-control capacity-building, consecutive proposals on the MFF have suggested 'a significant increase in allocations to the external dimension of migration management and asylum and a comparably smaller raise for their internal dimension' (Goldner Lang, 2019, p. 16). The expansion of EU policies beyond the European Union's borders started in the early 2000s, with the 2005 Global Approach to Migration and Mobility (GAMM) revised in 2011 as a main policy framework. Wolff (2020) notes that, interestingly, before 2011, asylum was not an external priority.

While the 2014 budget did not include an external dimension, externalization has become an established practice since 2015 with the EU Trust Fund for Africa (€4.7 billion) and €6 billion to implement the EU–Turkey deal of March 2016. According to Goldner Lang (2019), between 2015 and 2018, 57% (€12.5 billion) of the total EU funding planned in response to the experience of 2015–16 had been allocated to measures outside the EU, whereas 43% had been allocated to the internal dimension. Both the Trust Fund and the EU–Turkey deal established a conditionality between development aid and migration control. Moreover, at least 10% of the budget foreseen for the Neighbourhood, Development and International Cooperation Instrument (NDICI) is earmarked for migration management projects in origin and transit countries. The externalization is therefore linked to attempts to prevent migration in the first place, but also to return and readmission.

During the MFF negotiations, NGOs like EuroMed Rights (2020) worried about accountability and transparency on the use of the funds and stressed how this cooperation paved the way for human rights violations: the

> more funds are allocated to the 'Libyan Coast Guard', the more pushbacks (refoulements) can be observed on the Central Mediterranean route. ... In Turkey, another long-term EU partner when it comes to outsourcing migration controls, the authorities do not hesitate to play with the lives of migrants and refugees, opening and closing borders, to negotiate the disbursement of funds, as the recent example at the Greek–Turkish border attests. (EuroMed Rights, 2020)

The ECRE worried that externalization could lead to substandard asylum systems:

> It must be ensured that actions in or in relation to a third country fully respect the rights and principles enshrined in the Charter of Fundamental Rights of the European Union and the international obligations of the Union and the Member States. The EU otherwise runs the risk of becoming complicit in human rights violations. The mid-term review of the Internal Security Fund – Borders and Visa (ISF) found that it was not supporting Member States to apply the non-refoulement principle, the most likely and significant human rights violation a fund supporting border management could contribute to. (ECRE, 2019b, p. 3)

In spite of this criticism, the delegation and externalization prevail. In the final MFF, no ceiling to the funds which can be spent in third countries was set, despite requests by both the European Parliament and civil society organizations. Instead, additional safeguards were included 'to ensure that only actions in line with the internal dimension of asylum can be funded' (ECRE, 2020b).

Conditionality

The motive of externalization feeds into that of conditionality. As Becker (Chapter 2 in this volume) shows, disputes around conditionality were characteristic of the negotiations on the MFF overall. While these arguments touch upon rule of law conditionality, conditionality is also dominant in the EU's externalization strategy towards third countries, linking aid with cooperation on migration management and readmissions (Goldner Lang, 2019, p. 24). From the point of view of international development aid, the Confederation of Relief and Development NGOs (CONCORD) called the agreement on the Neighbourhood, Development and International Cooperation Instrument (NDICI) as part of the MFF 'shameful' and 'tarnished by EU migration politics'. Not only had member states agreed on cuts to the budget in summer 2020, but they had also partially agreed that partner countries' cooperation with the EU's migration governance be a condition for funding (CONCORD, 2020). We see how in the negotiation of the cohesion funds (ESF and ERDF) a different kind of conditionality comes into play: the number of refugees taken in by each member state was supposed to play a role for the budget allocation. This suggestion had been brought forward in a German diplomats' leaked position paper in early 2018, before the official MFF negotiations had started. Even though one could argue that this is more of a distribution key than conditionality in the strict sense of the word, the proposal generated resistance among some member states, such as Hungary (Kleist, 2018).

Solidarity

Even before the beginning of the MFF negotiations, appeals to 'solidarity' had been widely documented in EU migration governance. Particularly around 2015, the storyline of solidarity condensed negotiations around cooperation, European integration and burden-sharing. Wallaschek (2020) scrutinized how solidarity was often portrayed as lacking, with actors attributing different meaning to what solidarity entails. When in September 2015 160,000 refugees from border countries like Italy and Greece were supposed to be distributed to other member states according to a certain quota, the Visegrád group opposed this mechanism and tried to repeal it in the European Court of Justice (ECJ), although unsuccessfully (Wallaschek, 2019, p. 76). During the MFF negotiations, the motive of solidarity continued to appear in public statements. In its 'last call' from November 2020 (ECRE, 2020b), a group of NGOs strongly recommended

> a dedicated objective on solidarity and fair sharing of responsibility across Member States, in line with Article 80 of the Treaty on the Functioning of the European Union (TFEU). Linking such an objective to a dedicated spending target will ensure that funds for activities contributing to solidarity, including capacity building, will not be competing with emerging priorities.

It goes on to stress that in the face of the Covid-19 pandemic and increasing resettlement needs worldwide the international community as a whole needs to 'operationalize solidarity' (ECRE, 2020b). The signatories here refer to the TFEU, stating that the common policy on asylum, immigration and external border control should be 'governed by the principle of solidarity and fair sharing of responsibility, including its financial implications, between Member States' (ibid.).

Integration

Not surprisingly, NGOs have stressed the relevance of funding dedicated to the integration of migrants. While we have introduced the notion of venue shopping (Guiraudon, 2003) of conservative policymakers using the EU's backstage to promote their policy preferences, this tactic is also employed by immigrant rights activists. According to a policy paper by PICUM and ECRE (2018), they consider EU funding of immigrant integration for local and civil society organizations as a key resource in the face of the increasing anti-refugee and anti-migration rhetoric taking hold in many EU member states. They commended that for the first time the ESF+ added a specific objective on socio-economic inclusion of third-country nationals, with the Commission promoting a mainstreaming approach that includes immigrants, asylum-seekers and refugees as eligible. Mainstreaming, they stress, should also imply a 'firewall' guarantee for users of funded services irrespective of their legal status. 'Firewall' means the separation of service providers from migration authorities. As regards the AMF proposal at that point, however, they criticized a lack of earmarking for integration measures, leaving it up to the member states to decide the amount of resources. Furthermore, the NGOs worried that this could lead to a competition between third-country nationals and other marginalized groups. In a similar vein, in a joint statement by different NGOs in November 2019, the signatories warned that the fact that the ESF+ supports integration only beyond the early stages after arrival could lead to a gap between target groups eligible under the AMF and later the ESF+ (ECRE, 2019a).

CONCLUSION

The discourse around the governance of migration as manifest in official policy documents has been characterized as surprisingly stable over the past 20 years (Norman, 2006; Carmel, 2011; Münch, 2018). The negotiations over the Multiannual Financial Framework are no exception. We detect a high continuity when it comes to notions of migration management, border protection and motives of drawing migration into the realm of security as well as certain well-established metaphors like 'migratory pressure' or problematizing 'illegal migration'. The MFF perpetuates these existing 'cues' by allowing funding for technologies such as those used for border protection or encouraging existing processes of externalization. Needless to say, there are conflicting voices, particularly among NGOs, who stress the vulnerability of migrants (rather than the risk they pose to the European Union), the need to protect human rights, solidarity and meaningful integration. Given our analysis, it seems, however, that it is not so much a 'struggle over ideas' in the sense of incompatible frames but more of a struggle over evaluating those ideas, given how vague most of the 'cues' are in the first place.

In the meantime, some of the storylines reflected in the MFF negotiations, such as the emphasis on return and calls for intra-EU solidarity, have fed into the New Pact on Migration and Asylum. Labelled as a 'fresh start' upon its presentation in September 2020 by the Commission, the pact picks up on many existing ideas, such as those reflected in the budget negotiations and tries to overcome old deadlocks at the same time. In linking the two storylines of conditionality and solidarity, it introduces the notion of *mandatory, flexible solidarity*, where member states have a degree of flexibility in how to demonstrate solidarity in the face of 'migratory pressures' (Sundberg Diez et al., 2021). 'Return sponsorship', under which a member state would carry out the return of specific third-country nationals from another member state stands out as a new concept in this respect. It could be assumed that return was a policy goal around which very different member states' interests converged.

Standards of refugee reception and integration are not off the table, however. At the time of writing in March 2022, the Russian invasion had led to an estimated 3.5 million people fleeing Ukraine in less than a month. As opposed to 2015, Central and Eastern European countries currently display an immense willingness to help – in sharp contrast to the 'migration crisis', when they strongly criticized Germany and Sweden's alleged 'open-door policy' (Szalai et al., 2017).

NOTES

1. Saretzki (2009) critically scrutinises early attempts in the field of European integration and international relations that first tried to take into account the role of argument and discourse in a field formerly dominated by power and interest.
2. It needs to be stressed, however, that the theoretical and methodological landscape has become far more diverse in IR in recent years (F. Müller, 2019; Kurowska & Bliesemann de Guevara, 2020).
3. We share Nullmeier's (2013, p. 33) sentiment that the analysis of arguments in political science rarely keeps up with argumentation analysis because it has only a limited interest in inference procedures; and not all arguments, but only those based on assertions and propositions, are presented.
4. As an evaluation issued by the European Parliament (2018) states, in the previous MFF, funds such as Horizon 2020, the Fund for European Aid to the Most Deprived (FEAD), the European Regional Development Fund (ERDF) and the European Social Fund (ESF) also allocated funds to migration, more specifically to the integration of refugees and migrants. Moreover, there are trust funds for external measures under the EU budget but outside the MFF 2014–2020.

5. As opposed to Goetz and Patz (2016) who draw from interviews, we are methodologically unable to disentangle potential cases of dissent or centralization within the European Commission.
6. The author would like to thank Julia Simon for pointing this out.
7. This interpretation reflects a consensus of the financial literature on the EU budget. Various studies have dealt with the European budget structure in recent years, applying the criteria of the economic theory of federalism. According to this reading, those policy fields are recommended for European funding in which pan-European responsibility promises economies of scale and thus cost advantages (Heinemann, 2018). In his assessment of the May 2018 Commission proposal, Heinemann (2018, p. 4) stresses, however, how the contrast between the rhetoric of added value and a defence of the status quo is unmistakable.
8. The same complaint continues to come from academic institutions across Europe who told this author of seemingly arbitrary and 'no less than bizarre' funding and reporting regulations.
9. Roos (2021), however, draws a more nuanced picture. On the one hand, freedom of movement is highly appreciated among citizens of the Central and Eastern European member states. On the other, the unbalanced emigration has led to a politicization within both the Council and the European Council. In preparing for the final round of MFF negotiations, various policymakers from Central and Eastern Europe demanded compensation for the 'brain drain' their countries encountered.

REFERENCES

Andersson, R. (2016). 'Europe's failed "fight" against irregular migration: ethnographic notes on a counterproductive industry'. *Journal of Ethnic and Migration Studies*, 42(7), 1055–1075, https://doi.org/10.1080/1369183x.2016.1139446.

Ataç, I., & Schütze, T. (2020). 'Crackdown or symbolism? An analysis of post-2015 policy responses towards rejected asylum seekers in Austria'. In S. Spencer & A. Triandafyllidou (eds), *Migrants with Irregular Status in Europe. Evolving Conceptual and Policy Challenges*, Springer International Publishing, 117–137, https://doi.org/10.1007/978-3-030-34324-8_7.

Bach, M. (2008). *Europa ohne Gesellschaft. Politische Soziologie der Europäischen Integration*, Springer.

Barbehön, M. (2015). 'Europeanisation as discursive process: urban constructions of Europe and the local implementation of EU Directives'. *Journal of European Integration*, 38(2), 163–177, https://doi.org/10.1080/07036337.2015.1110147.

Barigazzi, J. (2020). 'EU migration reform plan postponed until after budget deal'. *Politico*, 19 June, www.politico.eu/article/migration-reform-to-be-postponed-after-a-deal-on-the-eu-budget-said-commissioner-ylva-johansson/.

Bevir, M., & Philipps, R. (2019). *Decentring European Governance*, Routledge.

Bevir, M., & Rhodes, R. A. W. (2016). 'Interpretive political science. Mapping the field'. In M. Bevir & R. A. W. Rhodes (eds), *Routledge Handbook of Interpretive Political Science*, Routledge, 3–27.

Bonjour, S., & Chauvin, S. (2018). 'Social class, migration policy and migrant strategies: an introduction'. *International Migration*, 56(4), 5–18, https://doi.org/10.1111/imig.12469.

Borrelli, L. M., Lindberg, A., & Wyss, A. (2021). States of suspicion: how institution-
    alised disbelief shapes migration control regimes'. *Geopolitics*, 1–17, https://doi.org/
    10.1080/14650045.2021.2005862.
Carmel, E. (2011). 'European Union migration governance: utility, security and inte-
    gration'. In E. Carmel, A. Cerami & T. Papadopoulos (eds), *Migration and Welfare
    in the New Europe. Social Protection and the Challenges of Integration*, Policy
    Press, 49–66.
Committee of the Regions (2018). 'Opinion. Asylum and Migration Fund'.
    COR-2018-04007-00-01-AC-TRA (EN), Brussels, 8–10 October 2018.
CONCORD. European Confederation of Relief and Development NGOs (2020). 'EU
    seven year development aid instrument finally agreed – but tarnished by EU migra-
    tion politics'. Brussels, 18 December, https://concordeurope.org/resource/eu-seven
    -year-development-aid-instrument-finally-agreed-but-tarnished-by-eu-migration
    -politics/.
Council of the European Union (2018). 'Outcome of the Council Meeting. Justice and
    Home Affairs', 15252/18, Brussels, 6–7 December 2018.
Council of the European Union (2019a). Interinstitutional File, 2018/0249(COD),
    Brussels, 24 May 2019.
Council of the European Union (2019b). 'Proposal for a Regulation of the European
    Parliament and of the Council establishing the Asylum and Migration Fund – Partial
    general approach'. Interinstitutional File. 2018/0248(COD), Brussels, 29 May 2019.
Council of the European Union (2020). 'Special meeting of the European Council –
    Draft Conclusions'. Doc. 9515/20, Brussels, 10 July 2020.
Crepaz, K. (2020). 'Overcoming borders: the Europeanization of civil society activism
    in the "refugee crisis"'. *Journal of Ethnic and Migration Studies*, 1–14, https://doi
    .org/10.1080/1369183x.2020.1851471.
D'Alfonso. A. (2019). 'External border control and asylum management as EU
    common goods: a budgetary perspective'. EUI RSCAS, 2019/05, http://hdl.handle
    .net/1814/61044.
D'Alfonso, A. (2020). 'Migration and Border Management: Heading 4 of the
    2021–2027 MFF'. European Parliamentary Research Service, Briefing PE 646.135,
    January 2020, Brussels, www.europarl.europa.eu/RegData/etudes/BRIE/2020/
    646135/EPRS_BRI(2020)646135_EN.pdf.
Deutsches Institut für Menschenrechte, Greek National Commission for Human
    Rights, Ombudswoman of the Republic of Croatia, & Institution of Human
    Rights Ombudsman of Bosnia and Herzegovina (2020). 'Die Situation an den
    EU-Außengrenzen und die zukünftige Europäische Asylpolitik', https://nbn
    -resolving.org/urn:nbn:de:0168-ssoar-67338-7.
Diez, T. (2016). 'European politics'. In M. Bevir & R. A. W. Rhodes (eds), *Routledge
    Handbook of Interpretive Political Science*, Routledge, 268–281.
ECRE (2019a). 'The Future of the Asylum, Migration and Integration Fund: Our Call
    for More Humane, Transparent and Effective Resources for Asylum and Migration
    in the Union', https://ecre.org/the-future-of-the-asylum-migration-and-integration
    -fund-our-call-for-more-humane-transparent-and-effective-resources-for-asylum
    -and-migration-in-the-union/.
ECRE (2019b). 'Outspending on Migration?' Policy Note #18, https://ecre.org/wp
    -content/uploads/2019/05/Policy-Note-18.pdf.
ECRE (2020a). 'EU Budget: Agreement Reached on the Regulation for the Asylum,
    Migration and Integration Fund (AMIF)', 11 December 2020, https://ecre.org/

eu-budget-agreement-reached-on-the-regulation-for-the-asylum-migration-and -integration-fund-amif/.

ECRE (2020b). 'Last call: The future Asylum, Migration and Integration Fund. Making the case for humane, transparent and effective use of EU resources for asylum and migration in the Union', 24 November 2020, https://ecre.org/joint-statement-last -call-the-future-asylum-migration-and-integration-fund/.

EESC (2018). 'Asylum and Migration Fund (AMF) and Integrated Border Management Fund'. SOC/600-EESC-2018-03636-00-02-AC-TRA. Brussels, 17 October 2018.

EPRS – European Parliament Research Service (2018). 'The European Council and the Multiannual Financial Framework'. EPRS_BRI(2018)615644_EN, Brussels, February 2018.

EuroMed Rights (2020). 'EU migration budget: more border management, less respect for human rights'. Press Release, Brussels, 16 July 2020.

European Commission (n.d.). 'Asylum, Migration and Integration Fund (2021–2027)'. Retrieved 27 January 2022 from https://ec.europa.eu/home-affairs/funding/asylum -migration-and-integration-funds/asylum-migration-and-integration-fund-2021 -2027_en.

European Commission (2018a). 'EU budget: Commission proposes a modern budget for a Union that protects, empowers and defends'. Brussels, 2 May 2018, https://ec .europa.eu/commission/presscorner/detail/en/IP_18_3570.

European Commission (2018b). 'State of the Union 2018 – Commission proposes last elements needed for compromise on migration and border reform'. Press release, Brussels, 12 September 2018.

European Commission (2020). 'EU's Next Long-Term Budget & NextGenerationEU. Key Facts and Figures'. Brussels, 11 November 2020, https://doi.org/doi:10.2761/ 567087.

European Council (2018). 'European Council meeting (28 June 2018) – Conclusions'. EUCO 9/18, Brussels, 28 June 2018.

European Parliament (2018). 'EU funds for migration, asylum and integration policies'. Study requested by the European Parliament's Committee on Budgets. PE 603.828, Brussels, April 2018.

European Parliament (2020a). 'Conclusions of the extraordinary European Council meeting of 17–21 July 2020.' P9_TA(2020)0206.

European Parliament (2020b). 'Deal on EU funds for common asylum, migration and integration policies up to 2027'. Brussels, 9 December 2020, www.europarl.europa .eu/news/de/press-room/20201207IPR93209/deal-on-eu-funds-for-common-asylum -migration-and-integration-policies-up-to-2027.

European Parliament (2021). 'EU Parliament adopts two funds for asylum and border policies'. Brussels, 7 July 2021, www.europarl.europa.eu/news/en/press -room/20210701IPR07514/eu-parliament-adopts-two-funds-for-asylum-and-border -policies.

Fischer, F. (1998). 'Beyond empiricism: policy inquiry in postpositivist perspective'. *Policy Studies Journal*, 26(1), 129–146, https://doi.org/10.1111/j.1541-0072.1998 .tb01929.x.

Fischer, F. (2003). *Reframing Public Policy. Discursive Politics and Deliberative Practices*, Oxford University Press.

Fischer, F. (2007). 'Deliberative policy analysis as practical reason: integrating empirical and normative arguments'. In F. Fischer, G. J. Miller & M. S. Sidney (eds), *Handbook of Public Policy Analysis. Theory, Politics and Methods*, Taylor & Francis, 223–236.

Fischer, F., & Forester, J. (eds) (1993a). *The Argumentative Turn in Policy Analysis and Planning*, Duke University Press.

Fischer, F., & Forester, J. (1993b). 'Editors' Introduction'. In F. Fischer & J. Forrester (eds), *The Argumentative Turn in Policy Analysis and Planning*, Duke University Press, 1–20.

Funke, B. (2021). 'Voices from liminality: civil society search and rescue organisations as agents of migration de-securitisation'. In N. Fromm, A. Jünemann & H. Safouane (eds), *Power in Vulnerability: A Multi-Dimensional Review of Migrants' Vulnerabilities*, Springer Fachmedien Wiesbaden, 71–91, https://doi.org/10.1007/978-3-658-34052-0_4.

Gadinger, F., Ochoa, C. S., & Yildiz, T. (2019). 'Resistance or thuggery? Political narratives of urban riots'. *Narrative Culture*, 6(1), 88–111, https://doi.org/10.13110/narrcult.6.1.0088.

Geddes, A. (2013). 'The Transformation of European Migration Governance'. KFG/FU Berlin Working Paper No. 56.

Genschel, P., & Jachtenfuchs, M. (2018). 'From market integration to core state powers: the Eurozone crisis, the refugee crisis and integration theory'. *JCMS: Journal of Common Market Studies*, 56(1), 178–196, https://doi.org/10.1111/jcms.12654.

Goetz, K. H., & Patz, R. (2016). 'Pressured budgets and the European Commission: towards a more centralized EU budget administration?' *Journal of European Public Policy*, 23(7), 1038–1056, https://doi.org/10.1080/13501763.2016.1162835.

Goldner Lang, I. (2019). 'Financial framework'. In P. De Bruycker, M. De Somer, & J.-L. De Brouwer (eds), *From Tampere 20 to Tampere 2.0: Towards a New European Consensus on Migration*, European Policy Centre (EPC), 15–26.

Guiraudon, V. (2003). 'The constitution of a European immigration policy domain: a political sociology approach'. *Journal of European Public Policy*, 10(2), 263–282, https://doi.org/10.1080/1350176032000059035.

Hadj Abdou, L. (2020). '"Push or pull"? Framing immigration in times of crisis in the European Union and the United States'. *Journal of European Integration*, 42(5), 643–658, https://doi.org/10.1080/07036337.2020.1792468.

Hajer, M. A. (2006). 'Doing discourse analysis: coalitions, practices, meaning'. *Netherlands Geographical Studies*, 344, 65–74.

Heinelt, H., & Münch, S. (2018). 'Introduction'. In H. Heinelt & S. Münch (eds), *Handbook of European Policies. Interpretive Approaches to the EU*, Edward Elgar Publishing, 1–16, https://doi.org/https://doi.org/10.4337/9781784719364.00006.

Heinemann, F. (2018). 'Mehrjähriger EU-Finanzrahmen: Die schwierige Transformation in Richtung europäischer Mehrwert'. *ifo Schnelldienst*, 71(12), 3–7.

Hutter, S., Grande, E., & Kriesi, H. (2016). *Politicising Europe*, Cambridge University Press.

Kleist, O. (2018). 'Will Finance Policies Solve the EU "Refugee Crisis"?', VerfBlog, 2018/2/28, https://verfassungsblog.de/will-finance-policies-solve-the-eu-refugee-crisis.

Koß, M., & Séville, A. (2020). 'Politicized transnationalism: the Visegrád countries in the refugee crisis'. *Politics and Governance*, 8(1), 95–106, https://doi.org/10.17645/pag.v8i1.2419.

Kurowska, X., & Bliesemann de Guevara, B. (2020). 'Interpretive approaches in political science and international relations'. In L. Curini & R. Franzese (eds), *The SAGE Handbook of Research Methods in Political Science & IR*, Vol. 2, SAGE, 1221–1240.

Lahusen, C. (2016). 'Auf dem Weg zu einem europäischen Verwaltungsfeld? Zur Soziologie der Bürokratisierung Europas am Beispiel des Gemeinsamen Europäischen Asylsystems'. *Berliner Journal für Soziologie*, 26(1), 109–133, https://doi.org/10.1007/s11609-016-0304-4.

Majcher, I., & Strik, T. (2021). 'Legislating without evidence: the recast of the EU Return Directive'. *European Journal of Migration and Law*, 23(2), 103–126, https://doi.org/10.1163/15718166-12340096.

Müller, F. (2019). 'Der kürzeste Weg zwischen zwei Lagerfeuern. Ein Dialog zwischen interpretativen und postkolonialen Perspektiven der Internationalen Beziehungen'. *Zeitschrift für Politikwissenschaft*, 29(2), 227–244, https://doi.org/10.1007/s41358 -019-00181-8.

Müller, H. (2004). 'Arguing, bargaining and all that: communicative action, rationalist theory and the logic of appropriateness in international relations'. *European Journal of International Relations*, 10(3), 395–435, https://doi.org/10.1177/ 1354066104045542.

Münch, S. (2016). 'Beyond national policymaking: conceptions of myth in interpretive policy analysis and their value for IR'. In B. Bliesemann de Guevara (ed.), *Myth and Narrative in International Politics*, Palgrave Macmillan, 47–66.

Münch, S. (2018). 'EU migration and asylum policies'. In H. Heinelt & S. Münch (eds), *Handbook of European Policies*, Edward Elgar Publishing, 306–330, https://doi.org/ https://doi.org/10.4337/9781784719364.00025.

Niemann, A., & Zaun, N. (2018). 'EU refugee policies and politics in times of crisis: theoretical and empirical perspectives'. *JCMS: Journal of Common Market Studies*, 56(1), 3–22, https://doi.org/10.1111/jcms.12650.

Noori, S. (2021). 'Suspicious infrastructures: automating border control and the multiplication of mistrust through biometric e-gates'. *Geopolitics*, 1–23, https://doi.org/10 .1080/14650045.2021.1952183.

Norman, L. (2006). 'Asylum and Immigration in an Area of Freedom, Security and Justice: EU policy and the logic of securitization'. Master's Thesis.

Nullmeier, F. (2013). 'Wissenspolitologie und interpretative Politikanalyse'. In S. Kropp & S. Kuhlmann (eds), *Wissen und Expertise in Politik und Verwaltung. Der Moderne Staat Sonderheft*, Verlag Barbara Budrich, 21–44.

PICUM & ECRE (2018). 'Promoting socio-economic inclusion of migrants and refugees in the next EU budget (2021 – 2027)'. Policy Paper.

Rasche, L. (2019). 'Frontex: Great power warrants great responsibility. Four proposals to strengthen Frontex' accountability'. Jacques Delors Institut.

Ripoll Servent, A. (2018). 'A new form of delegation in EU asylum: agencies as proxies of strong regulators'. *JCMS: Journal of Common Market Studies*, 56(1), 83–100, https://doi.org/10.1111/jcms.12652.

Ripoll Servent, A., & Trauner, F. (2014). 'Do supranational EU institutions make a difference? EU asylum law before and after "communitarization"'. *Journal of European Public Policy*, 21(8), 1142–1162, https://doi.org/10.1080/13501763.2014 .906905.

Risse, T. (2018). 'Social constructivism and European integration'. In Antje Wiener, Tanja A. Börzel, and Thomas Risse (eds), *European Integration Theory* (3rd edn), Oxford University Press, 128–147, https://doi.org/10.1093/hepl/9780198737315 .003.0007.

Roos, C. (2021). 'Compensating for the effects of emigration. Eastern Europe and policy response to EU freedom of movement'. *Journal of European Public Policy*, 1–19, https://doi.org/10.1080/13501763.2021.1984547.

Saretzki, T. (2009). 'From bargaining to arguing, from strategic to communicative action? Theoretical distinctions and methodological problems in empirical studies of deliberative policy processes'. *Critical Policy Studies*, 3(2), 153–183, https://doi.org/10.1080/19460170903385650.

Schammann, H. (2017). 'Eine meritokratische Wende? Arbeit und Leistung als neue Strukturprinzipien der deutschen Flüchtlingspolitik'. *Sozialer Fortschritt*, 66(11), 741–757.

Scheel, S., & Ustek-Spilda, F. (2019). 'The politics of expertise and ignorance in the field of migration management'. *Environment and Planning D: Society and Space*, 37(4), 663–681, https://doi.org/10.1177/0263775819843677.

Schmidt, V. A. (2019). 'Politicization in the EU: between national politics and EU political dynamics'. *Journal of European Public Policy*, 26(7), 1018–1036, https://doi.org/10.1080/13501763.2019.1619189.

Schwartz-Shea, P., & Yanow, D. (2012). *Interpretive Research Design: Concepts and Processes*, Routledge.

Selle, L. (2017). 'What multi-level parliamentary system? Parliamentary discourses in EU budgetary negotiations (MFF 2014–2020)'. In S. Becker, M. W. Bauer & A. De Feo (eds), *The New Politics of the European Union Budget* (1st edn), Nomos Verlagsgesellschaft mbH & Co. KG, 149–172, https://doi.org/10.5771/9783845278032-149.

Simon, J. (2021). 'Whose vulnerability? EU identity formation processes and the risks of migration'. In N. Fromm, A. Jünemann & H. Safouane (eds), *Power in Vulnerability: A Multi-Dimensional Review of Migrants' Vulnerabilities*, Springer Fachmedien Wiesbaden, 49–69, https://doi.org/10.1007/978-3-658-34052-0_3.

Slominski, P., & Trauner, F. (2021). 'Reforming me softly – how soft law has changed EU return policy since the migration crisis'. *West European Politics*, 44(1), 93–113, https://doi.org/10.1080/01402382.2020.1745500.

Statewatch (2020). 'EU: Frontex splashes out: millions of euros for new technology and equipment', www.statewatch.org/news/2020/june/eu-frontex-splashes-out-millions-of-euros-for-new-technology-and-equipment/.

Stępka, M. (2022). *Identifying Security Logics in the EU Policy Discourse : The "Migration Crisis" and the EU*, Springer International Publishing, https://doi.org/10.1007/978-3-030-93035-6_6.

Stone, D. A. (2002). *Policy Paradox: The Art of Political Decision Making* (rev. edn), Norton.

Sundberg Diez, O., Trauner, F., & De Somer, M. (2021). 'Return sponsorships in the EU's new pact on migration and asylum: high stakes, low gains'. *European Journal of Migration and Law*, 23(3), 219–244, https://doi.org/10.1163/15718166-12340101.

Szalai, M., Csornai, Z., & Garai, N. (2017). 'V4 migration policy: conflicting narratives and interpretative frameworks'. In P. Morillas (ed.), *Illiberal Democracies in the EU: The Visegrad Group and the Risk of Disintegration*, CIDOB edicions, 19–30.

Terlizzi, A. (2021). 'Narratives in power and policy design: the case of border management and external migration controls in Italy'. *Policy Sciences*, 54(4), 749–781, https://doi.org/10.1007/s11077-021-09440-4.

Trauner, F. (2016). 'Asylum policy: the EU's "crises" and the looming policy regime failure'. *Journal of European Integration*, 38(3), 311–325, https://doi.org/10.1080/07036337.2016.1140756.

UNHCR & ECRE (2018). *The Way Forward. A Comprehensive Study of the New Proposals for EU Funds on Asylum, Migration and Integration*, UNHCR & ECRE.

V4 Prime Ministers (2018). 'Stronger together: V4 joint statement'. Press release, www .visegradgroup.eu/documents/official-statements/final-stronger-together.

Wallaschek, S. (2019). 'Mapping Solidarity in Europe: Discourse Networks in the Euro Crisis and Europe's Migration Crisis'. Dissertation, http://nbn-resolving.de/urn:nbn: de:gbv:46-00107787-17.

Wallaschek, S. (2020). 'Contested solidarity in the euro crisis and Europe's migration crisis: a discourse network analysis'. *Journal of European Public Policy*, 27(7), 1034–1053, https://doi.org/10.1080/13501763.2019.1659844.

Wolff, S. (2020). 'Managing the refugee crisis: a divided and restrictive Europe?' In R. Coman, A. Crespy & V. A. Schmidt (eds), *Governance and Politics in the Post-Crisis European Union*, Cambridge University Press, 238–257, https://doi.org/ https://doi.org/10.1017/9781108612609.015.

Yanow, D. (2000). *Conducting Interpretive Policy Analysis*, SAGE.

Zeitlin, J., Nicoli, F., & Laffan, B. (2019). 'Introduction: the European Union beyond the polycrisis? Integration and politicization in an age of shifting cleavages'. *Journal of European Public Policy*, 26(7), 963–976, https://doi.org/10.1080/13501763.2019 .1619803.

9. EU research, technological development and innovation policy

Matthias Weber, Peter Biegelbauer, Michael Dinges and Katja Lamprecht

INTRODUCTION

The framework programmes are the main instrument of the EU's research and innovation (R&I) policy, combining elements of innovation, industry, regional development, research and education policy.[1] Since the establishment of the EU framework programmes for research and innovation (FPs) in the mid 1980s, they have been characterised by regular, if infrequent, change in terms of underlying narratives and instruments used (Biegelbauer and Weber, 2018).

Decision-making about the framework programme follows the ordinary legislative procedure, a formalised co-decision procedure involving the European Commission, the European Parliament and the European Council (Kluger Dionigi and Rasmussen, 2019; Brandsma et al., 2021). Yet the process leading to the formulation of the proposal for a framework programme is less clearly structured. It may benefit from political leadership, such as in the case of the Horizon 2020 programme (2014–2021), which drew a lot of inspiration from the Lund declaration of the Swedish European summit.[2] It also usually involves several elements of formal and informal consultations with Member States, stakeholders and experts (Pernicka et al., 2002).

Overall, however, it is largely developed within the European Commission services. As formulated by one of the high-level expert groups looking into this issue, there is a great deal of strategic intelligence available to feed into the development of the framework programme, but the actual sense-making involved in the preparation of the specific proposal is opaque (EFFLA, 2012).[3]

Given the importance of the FP for R&I in Europe, both in financial and in symbolic terms, the governance question of how the FPs are actually 'shaped' and by whom is of major importance for the legitimacy of the entire endeavour. This leads to the research questions of this chapter: how has the process of preparing the initial proposal of a framework programme worked in the case of Horizon Europe (2021–2027)? What was the role of policy discourses and frames and who deployed them, or, put differently: how was the battle of ideas (Heinelt and Münch, Chapter 1 in this volume) waged over Horizon Europe?

Inspired by work on this matter, but also through involvement in the most recent process of this kind, we argue that the influence of external stakeholders, including the Member States, on the shaping of the framework programme proposal is rather limited, and that the processes, dynamics and debates within the European Commission are the key levers of change. In order to strengthen the legitimacy of the framework programmes, it might be sensible to provide more transparency to the internal processes and open them up even in the preparatory phase.

In order to illustrate our argument, we will look at the three main novelties that have been introduced to the EU framework programmes by Horizon Europe: EU missions, the redesigned European partnerships and the European Innovation Council. We will then reconstruct the process of how these new elements came into being. The final section will draw some conclusions based on these findings.

CONCEPTUAL AND METHODOLOGICAL FRAMEWORK

In conceptual terms, the chapter draws from several approaches. First, a network perspective on governance provides a perception of how the internal governance networks within the European Commission interact with external stakeholders and networks in the course of the shaping of the framework programme (Torfing and Sørensen, 2014). These interactions exhibit features of advocacy and interest representation. Member States are part of this game and use formal as well as informal channels to bring in their views on the future shape of the framework programme (Pernicka et al., 2002). However, the actors are not driven by political interests alone and the whole process also features elements of policy learning (Biegelbauer, 2016) in the sense of learning from past experience with previous framework programmes.

Yet importantly, these interactions are all taking place in a context of discourses that shape the policy field, and which rest on policy frames and narratives produced since the early days of the European unification process (Biegelbauer and Weber, 2018). In the past such frames have recurrently stressed arguments of Europe being a 'laggard in S&T' or the so-called 'European Paradox'.[4] We want to follow Finlayson (2004) in arguing that this emphasis on discourses, narratives and frames is of special significance for the study of informal processes and governance – as we will show, this is exactly what our study is about.

Policy frames create a widely used narrative environment in which political measures can be situated. They provide a context for collective sense-making activities, which are an important part of policymaking (Hoppe, 1999). Policy frames entail options for political actors, allowing them to distinguish between important and less important elements of a policy (Laws and Rein, 2003). Framing may have specific functions, such as selecting, highlighting and utilising elements of a narrative to construct an argument about problems, causation, evaluation and solution (Entman, 1993, p. 53). Policy frames, therefore, are important in policy contests to strengthen the credibility and legitimacy of political proposals.

Indeed, policy frames may be strategically utilised in confrontations. The political opponents may try to 'immunise' their argument against other arguments. For instance, they may want to 'blackbox' their narrative and establish it as a truism, an axiom that cannot be contested (Callon, 1986).

Policy frames are not static; on the contrary, they are continuously produced, contested, reproduced, changed and/or replaced during political discourses by various actors featuring specific interests under specific framework conditions (Benford and Snow, 2000, p. 628).

Frames also offer an understanding of how a certain policy problem arises, through which instruments it may be tackled and how these instruments may impact upon the problem. By changing the framing to a specific policy problem, not only does the perception of the problem change, but the problem itself changes (Fischer, 2003, p. 145).

To provide a concrete example for this from the policy field under discussion, R&I may be framed as a problem of enterprises, whose main goal is to create profits through new products, processes and services, which they often build on new research results. However, it also may be understood as a public concern, since firms often underinvest in R&I in respect of the development of products that are not likely to create profits quickly and/or of sufficient volume. Indeed, enterprises often do not invest in basic science, where new findings are still a long way from profitable market innovations (Arrow, 1971; Vignola-Gagné and Biegelbauer, 2013). These two frames are reflected in the actual R&I policies of different countries. While, for instance, Switzerland and Denmark decided not to directly fund R&I of firms, because of the governments' position that this should be part of corporate activities, Austria and Germany have a long tradition of programmes in which they directly fund firms' R&I.

A helpful analysis of the role of frames in R&I has been written by Godin, who describes conceptual frameworks (i.e. frames) as central element of R&I policies. He states that a 'narrative gives meaning to [R&I], and to policy actions. It helps to put [R&I] on the political agenda' (Godin, 2009, p. 14). We fully subscribe to the argument that frames and narratives are of key importance to understand policies. However, we would like to distinguish between these, with frames as emblematic narrative elements providing perspectives and meaning to activities and policies around which narratives are built. Frames do not have to have full storylines with beginning, plot and end, yet narratives do. Frames provide perspectives, narratives illustrate and embed these (Shanahan et al., 2018; Kuhlmann and Blum, 2021).

Frames are also important for the analysis of policies. Rein and Schön (1994) contend that it is important to identify meanings of policies, relevant actors, their roles and interests. The identification of conflicts is essential, reflecting the varying interpretations of policies, including policy problems, theories of instrument usage and impact. It is also important to understand how different frames are set up, how they change over time and what their assumptions are. For a thorough understanding of policies, conflicting policy frames have to be determined and their qualities should become visible. This way it becomes possible to understand the dimensions of political disputes and devise measures to overcome these conflicts (Fischer, 2003, p. 146).

Following this logic, we will concentrate on the analysis of our three examples (EU missions, European partnerships and European Innovation Council) through the following aspects: as well as tracing their patterns of emergence, we look into the rationales, narratives and policy frames underlying these, and also at the role of internal and external networks for shaping them.

As we will show, the key actor in the construction of the three analysed elements characterising Horizon Europe has been the European Commission, which has virtuously utilised and recombined existing narratives and policy frames. We will analyse the frames, narratives and discourses, such as the fear of falling behind economic competitors like the US and Asia (Servan-Schreiber, 1968) and show how the discourses became more powerful and pre-structured the options of the further development of EU R&I policy.

In methodological terms, this chapter draws on a combination of document analysis and participation in some of the preparatory processes leading to the formulation of the Horizon Europe proposal, and a series of interviews with individuals involved in that process.

THE PATTERNS OF EMERGENCE OF FP9

As a foundation for the deeper analysis of the three examples of 'EU missions', 'European partnerships' and 'European Innovation Council', it is instructive to briefly reconstruct the main phases of the shaping of Horizon Europe as a whole. The predecessor framework programme, Horizon 2020, started off with high ambitions regarding the role and contribution of European research and innovation funding, by addressing societal challenges that are at the core of the largest pillar of Horizon 2020. However, it soon became clear that the envisaged impacts on societal challenges could at best arise in the long term and that the linkages between specific R&I projects and higher-order policy goals like addressing societal challenges were at best vague (see, e.g. European Council, 2015) as governance practices did not really change compared to previous framework programmes. In addition, the overall research and innovation performance of Europe did not meet the ambitions initially formulated – a fact acknowledged even by the European Commission, which speaks of the slowing down of progress towards its original goals (European Commission, 2020f, p. 1). A growing pressure on EU (R&I) policy to demonstrate its value added to Member States and citizens raised the need to formulate convincing narratives in order to justify rising, or at least stable, budgetary provisions in the multi-annual financial framework (MFF). These observations may serve as backdrop for the four main phases of preparing the new framework programme.

Phase 1: Early Thoughts about a New Framework Programme

First ideas about what a new framework programme should look like were launched back in 2015/16 at the level of the research commissioner's cabinet. The RISE high-level expert group identified important issues to be considered for future R&I policy, such as (i) Europe's difficulties in retaining fast-growing firms (partly due to a shortage of second-phase venture capital, partly as a result of an incomplete single market; see Soete et al., 2015); (ii) the need for a more transformative and at the same time more open R&I policy (Andree et al., 2015); (iii) the 'double deficit' as compared to the US in terms of lagging behind not only in innovation, but also in key areas of science (Sachwald, 2015), and (iv) the growing divide between Member States in terms of innovation performance (Tsipouri, 2017). At the national level, first initiatives were also taken to think ahead in terms of what the next framework programme should be about (see, e.g. the Austrian FP9 Think Tank, 2017). The 'Lund revisited' conference (European Council, 2015) and the Madelin Report further fuelled the early debates about 'Europe's mission to innovate' (Madelin and Ringrose, 2016).

Phase 2: Learning from the Past, and Identifying Challenges for the Future

The culmination point of this second phase must be seen in the publication of the Lamy Report in mid 2017 (Lamy et al., 2017). Based on the interim evaluation of Horizon 2020, the modelling of possible impacts of European research, and a major foresight project, the expert group chaired by Pascal Lamy put together 11 guiding principles for the next framework programme. Amongst these were mentioned the adoption of a mission-oriented approach,

the promotion of a European Innovation Council (EIC) and also a closer alignment of national and EU R&I investments through better targeted partnerships.

Phase 3: Elaborating Key Elements

Subsequent debates led to a further refinement of the ideas on the new framework programme, in particular regarding EU missions and the European
Innovation Council. Various expert groups of the European Commission,
in particular RISE (Research, Innovation and Science Policy Experts High
Level Group), ESIR (Expert Group on the Economic and Societal Impact
of Research and Innovation) and the High-Level Group of Innovators, were
involved in this process. A policy paper by Mariana Mazzucato (2018) as
well as support studies on past experiences with missions (JIIP, 2018) and on
future candidate themes for missions (Weber et al., 2018b) also fed into this
phase of debates. As regards the European Innovation Council, a high-level
advisory board was established in 2019 to strategically position and define its
guiding principles and supervise the first EIC pilot activities under Horizon
2020. Taking up the findings of the Lamy Report, the Council Conclusions of
1 December 2017 asked the European Commission and Member States to consider ways to rationalise the EU R&I partnership landscape, and ensure closer
links between partnership initiatives, EU and national policies. The European
Commission and Member States should jointly establish a long-term strategic
coordinating process for R&I partnerships by establishing suitable governance
structures (European Council, 2017).

Phase 4: Feedback and Refinement

In the second half of 2018, Member States, the European Parliament and
other stakeholders gave feedback and made suggestions for changes to the
Commission proposal. Under the scrutiny of its advisory board, an enhanced
pilot of EIC was launched in 2019, in order to test some of the elements proposed for the European Innovation Council and pave the way for its implementation under Horizon Europe. The identification and selection of missions was
achieved during 2019, with the five mission boards presenting their proposals
and agendas in mid 2020. The operational governance of missions in between
the different pillars and clusters of Horizon Europe, but also in alignment with
national mission initiatives, will be developed in the initial phase of Horizon
Europe, with dedicated coordination and support actions. For the European
partnerships, in 2018 an Ad Hoc Working Group of the European Research
and Innovation Area Committee (ERAC) proposed criteria for selecting,
implementing, monitoring and phasing out the R&I partnerships. In May 2019
a list of close to 50 candidate European partnerships was established following

a consultation of EU Member States. In May 2020 the Commission started to publish detailed Draft Partnership Proposals.

THE SHAPING OF 'MISSIONS'

Patterns of Emergence: How the 'Missions' Came About

The 'Grand Challenges' policy frame became programmatically incorporated into the framework programmes with Horizon 2020 (2014–2020), but the high programmatic ambitions could not be met. The actual revisions to the governance and instrumentation of Horizon 2020 were not changed in line with the new ambitions, but largely relied on well-established instruments, structures and procedures. As a consequence, the cross-cutting, inter- and transdisciplinary nature of research in support of societal challenges could not be adequately addressed. The recognition of this deficit stood at the beginning of the debate about missions in the preparation of Horizon Europe.

The notion of missions was not used explicitly by the Commission in the debate about the next framework programme until the publication of the Lamy Report in 2017. However, similar ideas had already been raised. Drawing on earlier work on demand-side innovation policy in the European Commission (Aho et al., 2007), Andree et al. (2015), in a report of the RISE group advising the research commissioner, called for a more demand-centric mission-oriented approach in future R&I policy in order to move beyond the technology-centric approach of Horizon 2020:

> While the move towards a challenge-driven approach in Horizon 2020 has been a good step forward, addressing now broader societal challenges, to have a real impact, such a programme would have to be truly 'mission-oriented', fitting in as an integral part of larger policy objectives. To achieve this, R&I will have to be linked closer to the other EU policies, defining concrete missions in the realm of a broader EU energy policy, transport policy, environment policy, etc. In other words, what is lacking is coordination and synergies between supply and demand of R&I. (Andree et al., 2015, p. 5)

The term 'mission' was explicitly used for the first time in a Commission report by Robert Madelin and David Ringrose (2016). Here the notion of 'mission' was used in a comprehensive sense, in order to promote a positive commitment to innovation in order 'to make society attentive to its future and resilient in face of crisis' (Madelin and Ringrose, 2016, p. 49).

After this first phase, the idea that a mission-oriented approach should be adopted in the EU framework programmes was discussed in several circles, as reflected, for instance, in the first thesis paper of the Austrian FP9 Think Tank (2017), which argues that 'Contributing to the grand societal challenges of our times and bringing science closer to the people should be a main objective of FP9. With respect to the societal challenge element of the programme, a redesign is required to give full justice to the specificities of new mission-oriented programmes' (p. 6). Other national papers outlining initial ideas about the future framework programme came up with similar suggestions.

In the follow-up to the Lamy Report, policy papers by different expert groups (ESIR, 2017; RISE, 2018a) further contributed to the elaboration of a mission-oriented approach in the new framework programme. Two further expert reports, published in early 2018 and 2019, elaborated on how the concept of missions could be operationalised in the context of the next framework programme, and it contributed to consolidating the political legitimacy of the concept of missions (Mazzucato, 2018, 2019). This was necessary because missions reassign a stronger role to the state in matters not only of research, but also of innovation and diffusion. The subsequent consultation on the mission-oriented approach lent a lot of support to the concept, but also raised quite some scepticism as to the governance capabilities and capacities of the European Commission to deliver on the ambitious promises. This scepticism was underpinned by experiences from past mission-oriented initiatives, showing that missions require a highly developed governance and management system, with strong leadership, to succeed. Furthermore, a range of other critical success factors have to be taken into account, in particular when addressing 'transformative' and 'systemic' rather than just technological challenges such as the moonshot mission of the 1960s (JIIP, 2018). Moreover, the approach presented by Mazzucato (and adopted in large parts by the EC) draws strongly on the rather technocratic experience of 'old' missions, which may well be suitable for technology-centric missions but is less adapted to 'new' missions geared towards addressing societal challenges, which are more complex in nature (Wanzenböck et al., 2020).

When the European Commission presented its proposal for Horizon Europe in 2018 (European Commission, 2018a), the contours of its new mission-oriented approach were still rather vague, but it soon turned out that the Commission took the challenging requirements of transformative missions seriously, by proposing five areas to Member States in which dedicated missions should be piloted and implemented: (i) climate-neutral and smart cities; (ii) cancer; (iii) adaptation to climate change including societal transformation; (iv) soil health and food; and (v) healthy oceans, seas and inland water. The debates about the identification and selection of priority themes for future missions to be addressed in Horizon Europe gave evidence of the difficulties faced by the European Commission in putting the missions concept into practice, and which were also anticipated in a memorandum by the ESIR expert group (ESIR, 2018).

In line with the multiple interests and contributions needed to realise these missions, and the novel governance requirements they brought with them, mission boards (and supporting mission assemblies) were set up following a call for expressions of interest. These high-level boards, chaired by a politically high-ranking chairperson, were highly autonomous in defining the scope of the specific mission(s) to be implemented in their respective areas, as well as the envisaged mode of implementation. They were not only informed by dedicated foresight and other support actions,[5] but also accompanied by a range of Directorates-General with responsibilities for policies of major relevance to the achievement of the missions.[6] In September 2020, the mission boards presented their proposals to the European Commission at the European Research and Innovation Days, with concrete proposals and roadmaps of how the missions shall be achieved by a combination of R&I policy and domain-specific policy measures. The proposals by the mission boards were also presented and discussed at stakeholder events in Member States, involving a broad range of stakeholders from science and industry to citizens. Due to the COVID-19 crisis, only the first of these national events could be held, while most others had to be cancelled or postponed.

The attention paid to Member States' voices was important, because the five missions cannot be achieved by means of European-level measures and policies alone, but their success will ultimately depend on local and national actions. Therefore, one of the incentives provided by the European Commission is support measures to establish national governance structures for missions, in order to complement the mission-oriented funding provided as part of the framework programme. In the framework programme, the missions operate as cross-cutting 'virtual' programmes, with specific topics earmarked for their relevance to one of the five missions but funded from within the different programme lines of Horizon Europe. In order to achieve the necessary coordination of activities associated with the five missions, mission managers, high-ranking European Commission officials, were appointed in February 2021.

Rationale: Turning a Vision into Practice

Although the strengthening of an orientation of European R&I towards societal challenges received a lot of support when Horizon 2020 was launched, it soon turned out that the gap between highly abstract challenges and the reality of specific projects was very wide. Even if explicit reference was made in project proposals to the relevance of the envisaged work for addressing societal challenges, the challenges often served only as an overarching frame to which lip service had to be paid. Neither was it possible to seriously assess or evaluate impacts of specific projects on the ability to address societal challenges, due to attribution problems resulting from the many other intervening factors and the lengthy time horizon. What was missing was often an intermediate layer that would allow the targeting of ambitious but achievable goals with the help of a bundle or cluster of projects. Moreover, research and innovation activities at best promise a potential for impact, but whether an actual impact will be achieved depends on demand-side conditions and sectoral policies determining the uptake and diffusion of new solutions.

Overall, the governance mode of implementing Horizon 2020 had not changed significantly as compared to earlier framework programmes. Guiding ideas or visions were translated into a systematic process of strategic programming, and work programme development was translated into individual topics in respect of which consortia could apply, but limited room was given to non-conventional ideas.

In this light, missions represent an opportunity to introduce an intermediate level of orientation and guidance, in between the highly abstract societal challenges and the reality of specific projects, which should help overcome the fragmentation into a myriad of individual projects. Functionally, they describe a credible claim to make the change happen that is needed on the pathway towards successfully addressing societal challenges. A very important promise tied to this claim was the promise of impact. A clear goal, a clear timeline and a clear plan of how to bundle complementary projects into a package should contribute to achieving an impact beyond the level of individual projects.

This technocratic vision of enhanced planning and implementation of research and innovation activities for impact was meant to help overcome growing scepticism about the ability to achieve the ambitious goals tied to societal challenges under Horizon 2020. Such a convincing narrative was also important to ensure support for an increase of the research budget within the multi-annual financial framework of the EU.

However, the appealing idea of missions also raised very serious challenges. If taken seriously, a mission-oriented approach, in particular when applied to systemic and wicked problems (e.g. urban transformation, adaptation to climate change, etc.) opens up many interfaces with policy areas and policy levels that would need to revisit the demand-side instruments and framework conditions that are key for the uptake of novel solutions; in short: no uptake, no impact. This issue of who ultimately 'owns' the missions has not yet been resolved. Seen from an impact perspective, sectoral policies often 'own' the issues to be addressed (e.g. health policy for cancer, agricultural policy for soil) and should therefore lead the definition of missions. However, by restricting the EU missions first and foremost to R&I agendas, the lead could be claimed to remain within R&I policy.

Missions and External Stakeholders: Support for an Ambitious and Vague Governance Approach

The simple narrative behind missions was well received by the majority of external stakeholders. Several Member States had already adopted similar ideas in their national policies and adapted them to their specific conditions. The Challenge-Driven Innovation programme in Sweden may serve as an example. The German government presented 12 missions as part of its revised High-Tech Strategy 2025 (BMBF, 2018). In the meantime, the OECD has also shown much interest in mission-oriented innovation policy by launching a first project on this matter (OECD, 2021). In the Netherlands, the idea of missions has been combined with the established Top-Sector programme. So, the idea of 'missions' has taken on momentum, even if interpretations may vary across Member States.

This is also reflected in the generally rather positive reactions to the mission-oriented approach in national position papers to the Horizon Europe proposal. The main points of criticism refer to the governance of the missions, and in particular the question of respective influence of Member States and the Commission on the definition, selection and subsequent implementation of missions. Other critical issues, such as the coordination and alignment of R&I policy with sectoral policies, received less attention, at least initially.

Some other stakeholders, in particular in industry, remain more reserved about the mission-oriented approach. Not only do they fear the complexity of implementation, but also declining support for traditional key enabling technologies. Others, such as many research and technology organisations, perceive missions as an opportunity to bring their interdisciplinary competencies and their ability to manage large-scale programmes involving different stakeholders to bear in the implementation of missions.

Missions and Internal Networks: Trickling Down of a Political Idea

Within the European Commission, the mission-oriented approach gained support through a range of mechanisms. First, the societal challenges were widely accepted as overarching frames, and further strengthened by the launch of the sustainable development goals as an external source of legitimacy. As regards implementation, two different perspectives can be distinguished. On the one hand, the 'traditionalist stance' was in favour of preserving the well-established approach to implementing framework programmes through thematic work programmes. On the other hand, the 'modernist stance' sought a revision of the implementation approach in order to truly deliver on the ambitions formulated with the societal challenges. In practice, the actual approach to mission implementation was developed in real time with the various stages of decision-making, leading to a combination of traditionalist and modernist elements.

A second important concern was the autonomy of the Directorate-General for Research and Innovation (DG RTD) in defining its policy agenda, a move supported by the creation of the Research Executive Agency in 2007, which outsourced programme implementation from DG RTD. Recent years have seen a transformation of DG RTD from a programme-implementing DG into a policy DG with a strong political agenda of its own. This political agenda was focused on matters like the European Research Area, but also the strengthening of the political and economic significance of R&I policy in general. In this light, missions were a means to enhance the political visibility of DG RTD, but it implied tying missions to political goals that were largely defined in other policy areas. This tension was overcome by stressing the R&I-centric nature of the missions to be pursued, as an argument that the control over missions remains largely within DG RTD.

At the same time, the engagement with other Directorates-General was intensified in the preparatory debates about possible themes for future missions. The foresight correspondents' network, for instance, bringing together key strategic thinkers from the majority of DGs, was closely involved in the implementation of the EC's foresight project BOHEMIA, which helped prepare the thematic orientation of Horizon Europe, and thus also of possible missions. In other words, the network already served as a soft coordination and harmonisation mechanism between R&I policy and various other EU policy fields prior to the presentation of the Horizon Europe proposal.

Assessment

The introduction of the mission-oriented approach in Horizon Europe is based on the widely shared recognition that the implementation model of Horizon 2020 was not sufficient to achieve the expected impacts on societal challenges that were promised at the outset of Horizon 2020. This view was also backed by many Member States. The commitment to missions is thus a confirmation of the commitment to the policy frame that regards R&I policy as a major contributing force to resolving major societal challenges, and at the same time a novel framework and approach for implementing R&I policy in a more impactful way.

While it is difficult to reconstruct precisely how and when the notion of 'missions' found its way into the Lamy Report, it was a concept under discussion in many different circles and tested in several Member States. In other words, the time was ripe for a new approach to implementing the framework programme; a necessity that was not strongly contested in its general line of reasoning.

The situation is more complicated when it comes to the governance details of the mission-oriented approach. The overall appeal of the mission concept has led to an under-estimation of the governance challenges that a mission-oriented approach involves, from the selection of missions and the establishment of carrier organisations to the need for coordination with demand-side sectoral policy and with coherent implementation of supply- and demand-side policy instruments. It is of little surprise that this also led to conflicts and tensions within the European Commission because missions tend to put into question existing boundaries between Directorates-General, with their respective organisational interests. These intra-EC actor constellations continue to have an influence on the shaping of the more detailed specifications of responsibilities in relation to missions.

Finally, it is also interesting to observe the verve with which the proponents of missions in the European Commission pursued this new concept and designed both its content and its governance structure in a process of co-creation with stakeholders in the mission boards, and subsequently in the Commission's internal development of work programmes. In view of the potential influence of missions on policy fields other than R&I policy, as well as on Member States policies, missions could well evolve into a strong lever of more coherent national and European policies in the European Research Area.

EUROPEAN PARTNERSHIPS

In Horizon Europe, 'European partnership' means an initiative where the Union, together with private and/or public partners (such as industry, research organisations, bodies with a public service mission or civil society organisations), commit to jointly support the development and implementation of a programme of R&I activities (European Council, 2019).

Patterns of Emergence

From a historical perspective, European partnerships are strongly linked to the concept of a European Research Area (ERA), which was defined at the EU level in the early 2000s. The initial ERA concept put a focus on the fragmentation of R&I policy at the level of the EU Member States and linked challenges of European policy coordination. The European Commission's Communication 'Towards a European Research Area' (European Commission, 2000) presented a diagnosis of (1) a principal national reference framework for research activities in Europe, (2) limited European cooperation efforts (not exceeding 17% of total public R&D expenditures) and (3) limited financial power of Europe's main funding mechanism for collaborative research, that is, the FP, accounting for only about 5.4% of total public expenditure on R&D.

In the words of former Commissioner Philippe Busquin: 'The problem is not money but the fragmentation of the efforts carried out at European level ... So it is imperative that we mobilise resources and create a movement towards coherence of research policies in Europe. This is why I have launched the idea of a European Research Area' (European Commission, 2020e).

The Fragmentation Rationale

As a medication against the ill of fragmentation, a more coordinated implementation of national and European research programmes, and the application of the principle of the mutual opening of national programmes, as well as means to better share information on the objectives and content of programmes and R&I activities, were agreed upon.

In turn, the first types of European R&I partnerships emerged in the form of so-called ERA-NETs in FP6. They were originally designed to support networking, coordination and cooperation between national R&I programmes of different EU Member States, including their mutual opening and the development and implementation of joint activities to overcome the fragmented nature of the ERA. As a core principle of these partnerships, public authorities from several EU Member States (typically ministries or agencies) designed specific research programmes which they wished to coordinate as programme 'owners', while management of joint calls for R&D actions was mostly provided by national programme 'managers' (i.e. research councils or other research funding agencies). Notably, while coordination on the scope of joint R&D activities across Member States took place, funding for national R&I actors was still provided individually by each Member State on the terms and conditions of their respective programmes.

Since FP6, the evolution of these public–public partnerships (P2Ps) has undergone continuous development. In FP7, the ERA-NET scheme was complemented by a means to provide EU top-up funding for single joint calls (ERA-NET Plus) and in Horizon 2020, both schemes were merged into a single instrument (ERA-NET Co-Funds). The scope of European funding shifted towards the top-up funding of joint calls in selected areas with high European added value and relevance for Horizon 2020. In addition, a proliferation of partnership instruments happened, reinforcing the rationale to reduce fragmentation and enhance ERA, but also adding new frames to the partnership instruments.

Since FP7, Article 185 of the Treaty on the Functioning of the European Union (TFEU) provided the basis for long-term collaboration between the EU Member States and the European Commission on a voluntary basis. The ambition of Article 185 partnerships is to achieve scientific, managerial and financial integration amongst national research programmes in a given field. The currently existing Article 185 partnerships feature a high degree of diversity in terms of thematic and regional scope, participation, management and funding modes but they all seek to demonstrate their relevance to the objectives of the European Framework Programme for R&I and to contribute to broader EU policy objectives by creating a 'critical mass' of investment and more coherent planning across the EU Member States.

The Competitiveness Rationale

Going beyond the ERA frame with its narrative of existing fragmentation and necessary coherence, the rationale of strengthening the competitiveness of European industry also played a key role in the emergence of new European partnership instruments. Innovation and technological leadership at a European scale was aimed to be achieved by the creation of public–private partnerships (PPPs), which were first launched in FP7. Joint technology initiatives (JTIs) based on Article 187 TFEU (ex-Article 171 TEC) are long-term PPPs that are managed within dedicated governance structures (joint undertakings), whose members include (1) the European Commission, (2) a not-for-profit industry-led association, and (3) EU Member States and Associated States. The core ambition of these partnerships is to boost industrial innovation by providing a clear framework for joint research investment by industry, the Member States and the European Commission. JTIs are based upon a jointly defined, industry-driven common Strategic Research Agenda that deals with general aspects such as research infrastructure, education, support for small and medium-sized enterprises (SMEs) and international collaboration.

The Societal Challenges Rationale

Finally, transgressing the thematically narrow research topics and joint funding of calls in the ERA-NET scheme, the creation of joint programming initiatives (JPIs) constituted a turning point in the orientation of European partnerships. JPIs were a response to the Lund Declaration in 2009 that called upon the Member States and European institutions to focus research on the grand challenges of our times by moving beyond rigid thematic approaches and aligning European and national strategies and instruments. JPIs should build partnerships based on common visions and strategic research and innovation agendas (SRIAs) to address major societal challenges. Thereafter JPIs should be implemented through a variety of measures including joint calls, fast-track activities, knowledge hubs, task forces, etc. The practical implementation of joint programming relies on the 'alignment' of existing or planned national (and regional) research and innovation strategies, programmes, activities, and funding. It was defined as a strategic approach to modify national programmes, priorities or activities as a consequence of the adoption of joint research priorities in the context of joint programming, with a view to implement changes and thereby improve the efficiency of investment in research at the level of Member States and the European Research Area (Meyer et al., 2017). Alignment thus aims to structure both research and innovation efforts of EU Member States to help establish a single ERA and tackle global societal challenges more effectively.

The Partnership Reform in Horizon Europe

With the adoption of the proposal for Horizon Europe, the development of the partnership approach has gone through a major reform. Twenty years after the first ERA Communication, the New ERA Communication (European Commission, 2020f) set out to achieve four key strategic objectives: prioritise investments in R&I to successfully accomplish the green and digital transformation, improve access to excellence, transfer R&I results into the economy and deepen policies that promote the free circulation of knowledge. Therein, European partnerships in key policy areas[7] are seen to be essential for prioritising investment and reform in research and innovation towards the green and digital transition, for supporting Europe's economic recovery after the COVID-19 pandemic, and for meeting a target of spending of 5% of national public funding on joint research and development programmes and European partnerships by 2030.

To speed up the transfer of research results into the economy, the communication also specifies that the European Commission will guide the development of common technology roadmaps, which shall be part of the strategic innovation agendas agreed with Member States and industry, under the Horizon Europe R&I Partnerships. To achieve greater societal impact and increased trust in science, emphasis shall also be put on the engagement of citizens, local communities and civil society in respect of the new ERA.

From a more practical perspective, the major aim of the partnership reform is to streamline the number and types of partnerships while achieving greater alignment with the research topics of Horizon Europe. Horizon Europe now distinguishes between three types of European partnerships: (1) co-funded partnerships with a (more or less centralised) blending of EU and national public and/or other R&I funding sources (in particular former ERA-NETs and JPIs); (2) co-programmed partnerships between the EU, Member States/ Associated States, and/or other stakeholders, based on memoranda of understanding or contractual arrangements with partners; and (3) institutionalised partnerships (based on Arts 185 or 187 TFEU, and the regulation on the European Institute of Innovation and Technology).

Assessment

The partnerships have been introduced to the European R&I programming scene with the aim of increasing joint funding from EU Member States and industry in areas of specific concern. As a result, institutionalised public–private partnerships focusing on industrial competitiveness and a diverse set of public–public partnerships (Art. 185) with European interest under the patronage of the European Commission have been built. In addition, a large number of co-funded public–public partnerships emerged, in which EU Member States participated on a voluntary basis in areas of their specific concern and the societal challenge-oriented JPIs were created. By the end of 2020 about 100 public–public partnership networks were active and some 747 joint calls had been implemented by these networks, with cumulative investment of some €9 billion in more than 9,300 transnational projects (ERA-LEARN 2021). Despite the considerable size of this investment, the ambition to better align national and European R&I funding, and to create the critical mass necessary to tackle global challenges more effectively, were only partly fulfilled. For the joint programming process, the independent expert group evaluation showed that the overall level of ambition to really support the societal challenges to be addressed was disappointing. Furthermore, the central executive resources needed to effectively implement the strategic agendas were not provided (Hernani et al., 2016). However, the joint programming process also demonstrated that a collaborative creation of strategic research and innovation agendas allows better tailoring of R&I agendas towards societal challenges and elaborating of pathways to impact. Against this background, the present partnership reform in Horizon Europe can be seen not only as another attempt to bundle efforts across Europe in a more coherent manner, but the ambition to better contribute to solving societal challenges is also reflected in the partnership proposal process with its focus on delineating strategic research and innovation agendas (as introduced in the context of joint programming) and their specific pathways to impact.

THE SHAPING OF THE EUROPEAN INNOVATION COUNCIL

Patterns of Emergence

The idea of establishing a European Innovation Council (EIC) was announced for the first time by Carlos Moedas, Commissioner for Research, Science and Innovation,[8] following the perception of an ongoing deficit of the European innovation system to commercialise high-quality European research and to scale up innovative business, in particular in comparison with the US (the 'European paradox').

Against this backdrop, the European Commission ran an open call for ideas in spring 2016 to further develop discussion, accompanied by publication of numerous stakeholder position papers (European Commission, 2016a, 2016b). In that period, the spectrum of ideas varied from bundling innovation-supporting instruments to reduce complexity (the 'one-stop shop'), to allocating financial support for upscaling, or to concentrating on providing strategic intelligence and helping to reduce regulatory barriers in cooperation with other sectoral DGs.

Subsequently, the 'High Level Group on Maximising the Impact of EU Research and Innovation Programmes' (Lamy et al., 2017) and particularly the 'High Level Group of Innovators' (HLG Innovators, 2018) stressed the need to support and invest in European high-risk, market-creating breakthrough innovations, particularly in 'deep tech' innovation, and to overcome hindering factors in Europe (a lack of large-scale investments over a significant period, national and local initiatives too small to compete on global level, an incomplete single market and regulatory barriers). The EIC was recommended to take a bottom-up approach to funding (grant-based at an early stage and a combination of grants and financial instruments when larger investments are needed). It should also encourage collaboration between European innovators, firms and investors in order to stimulate scaling-up at EU level, and to help innovators overcome regulatory barriers.

With the initial phase of an EIC pilot (launched in October 2017) as part of the Horizon 2020 Work Programme 2018–2020, the European Commission bundled together existing funding instruments: the SME Instrument, the Fast Track to Innovation programme, the Future and Emerging Technologies (FET) Open programme, and the EIC Horizon Prizes, accompanied by opportunities for networking, mentoring and coaching (European Commission, 2018a).

The design of the third pillar of the proposed Horizon Europe programme (European Commission, 2018b) basically followed this approach, with the idea of providing financial support throughout the innovation cycle and of overcoming the growing lack of equity funding for risky companies. In addition, the InvestEU Programme was meant to mobilise further public and private investment by a factor of about 14 times the anticipated total guarantees (European Commission, 2018d). Concerning the EU added value, it was argued that the only possibility of providing large-scale venture capital is to act on the EU level, with more effectiveness and comprehensiveness (e.g. common regulation, synergies with other EU programmes) and with increasing coherence of the overall innovation ecosystem.

The Rediscovery of a Frame

As noted, the main rationale used to underpin the call for a European Innovation Council is rooted in the 'rediscovery' of the European paradox, a notion that was first coined in the mid 1990s, when the European Commission in its Green Paper on Innovation argued that 'one of Europe's major weaknesses lies in its inferiority in terms of transforming the results of technological research and skills into innovations and competitive advantages' (European Commission, 1995). The paradox, then, was suggesting that Europe was performing comparatively well in research but was not successful in exploiting that potential economically.

A decade later, the existence of this paradox was increasingly questioned. Dosi et al. (2006), for instance, argued that this paradox does not exist because Europe is also behind the US in scientific terms, for instance when looking at publication output per capita of population or at research personnel. Sachwald (2015) confirms this scepticism and speaks of a 'double deficit', because although Europe produces more scientific publications, these are less cited and less relevant to innovation. Also, sectoral differences matter, because the US have their strongest scientific base in ICT, health and medicine, that is, in areas where the mode of science-based innovation is particularly prevalent. Other reasons are seen in a less-developed entrepreneurship and start-up culture in Europe (Henrekson and Sanandaji, 2017), and in the limited capacities of many European firms to absorb new scientific knowledge (Czarnitzki et al., 2012). Still, the remaining barriers to a truly single market in Europe hamper the incentives for firms to innovate.

However, in spite of these insights, the European paradox was adopted as the guiding narrative underpinning the call for the creation of a European Innovation Council. The European Commission postulated that the upcoming wave of breakthrough innovation will be science-based and emphasised the need for swift action (European Commission, 2018c).[9]

External and Internal Networks: Handling Scepticism

A round of consultation launched in 2016 raised support for the intention for, but also criticism of, the proposed concept of the EIC. The position papers of Member States, as well as the joint position of ERAC (ERAC, 2016) and the reflection papers of the RISE group are interesting in this regard (RISE, 2017).

Member States came up with a diverse range of proposals regarding the focus of the EIC. The statements as synthesised by Weber et al. (2018a) ranged from (i) the EIC as supporting instrument for start-ups with high potential to scale up on European and global levels with entrepreneurs as the main beneficiaries; (ii) the EIC as supporting instrument for an 'excellence in innovation' model (partly described in BMBF, 2016) for a wider target group; (iii) the EIC as driver for the integration of existing instruments enabling synergies; to (iv) the EIC as key to an integrated research and innovation policy. The latest EIC model should be achieved through coordinating and thus enhancing policy coherence between research policy, innovation policy and sectoral policy fields which define terms for innovation from a demand-side perspective, taking into account the national policy level as well (Austrian FP9 Think Tank, 2017; IPM, 2017).

Furthermore, the RISE expert group emphasised that a new narrative 'From Innovation to Innovators' will be one of the guiding principles of the EIC, aiming to align innovation policy in Europe with the characteristics of emerging models of innovation. Moreover, the EIC was meant to become a one-stop shop for various types of innovators, be they driven by technology, new business modes, new design, customer experience, or organisational development (RISE, 2017).

Criticism first addressed aspects concerning potential duplication of national funding initiatives for SMEs and therefore an unclear division of labour between national and regional policies. Other points of critique referred to the limited European added value because the EIC addresses individuals or individual firms rather than collaborative innovation activities across borders. Finally, there were questions as to the ability of a public institution like the European Commission to identify excellent innovations/innovators with a market-creating potential and to manage risk capital and entrepreneurship-centric initiatives (RISE, 2018b).

In the phase of elaborating Horizon Europe, national position papers mainly followed the HLG of Innovators. Some items still remained unclear at that stage and were the subject of heated debate:

– *Narrowing down of scope of the EIC mission* to 'deep-tech' innovation and supporting individual entrepreneurs: the RISE Group recommended carefully distinguishing between 'deep-tech' and 'architectural' disruptive innovation and further suggested the concept of 'Innovator Readiness Levels' instead of 'Technology Readiness Levels' (RISE, 2018b).
– *Complementarity with other segments of Horizon Europe:* the positioning of the EIC with regard to EU missions and the European Institute of Technology (EIT) was unclear.
– *Missing details in the proposed governance concept:* the suggested EIC portfolio management approach, which was meant to follow the DARPA and ARPA-E model[10] of the USA (European Commission, 2018c), was not yet well specified and its implementation was unclear.
– *Complementarity with innovation initiatives of Member States:* several EU Member States already had support initiatives for start-ups, scale-ups and

other types of innovation entrepreneurship in place. This raised concerns about duplication of funding opportunities.

– *Appropriateness of budget allocation within the third pillar of Horizon Europe (including the EIC):* budget allocation to the EIC was criticised for neglecting equally, if not more important, measures to overcome barriers to the scaling-up of deep-tech start-ups and to boost the effectiveness of the European innovation ecosystem, in particular the need to strengthen the single market and overcome European fragmentation (European Commission, 2018b; RISE, 2018b).

The first EIC pilot was followed by a 'reinforced EIC pilot' in March 2019, already introducing some of the key elements of the EIC concept foreseen for Horizon Europe. Subsequently, recommendations of expert groups focused mainly on the differentiation between these core elements and their implementation, and fundamental debates on the EIC mission and concepts have been concluded.

The recruiting process for the EIC 'programme managers' (a key element following the DARPA/ARPA-E approach) started in June 2019. The EIC Advisory Board – appointed by the European Commission – published its vision statement and roadmap one year later (European Commission, 2020a) with key indicators that have already been taken up in the 'EIC pilot impact report 2020' (European Commission, 2020b). The feedback from the European Commission consultation process provided some additional comments related to issues of connectedness, competence and access to and deployment of capital (European Commission, 2020c).

An Independent Expert Group, invited by the European Commission to reflect on lessons from the US's DARPA/ARPA-E model and other international practices, stated that to support breakthrough innovations, the EIC must itself be an organisational breakthrough (European Commission, 2020d) and also give the programme manager a very central role for both portfolio management and ecosystem coordination. Shortly after, in March 2021, the EIC was officially launched.

Assessment

EU Member States have raised concerns regarding the European Innovation Council, and as a result, the initial approach was considerably narrowed down to address a much more specific group of innovators than initially envisaged. Many other points of criticism have not been addressed, such as the extension of the single-beneficiary approach of the EIC – the announced budget allocation for the EIC accelerator (70% of total EIC budget) underlies this tendency (European Commission, 2021). Also unchanged from the original plans is the extensive role that the European Commission assumes in handling a variety of financial instruments which are well beyond the scope of funding instruments that the European Commission has been used to handling so far.

Possibly the most fundamental argument questioning the EIC concept as a whole concerns the main barriers to realising market-creating breakthrough innovations in Europe, which some experts and Member States see in the remaining shortcomings of the European single market and the regulatory rigidities residing in sectoral policies, rather than in funding and advice to innovators. In other words, the wider ecosystem may hamper the success of market-creating breakthrough innovations more than lack of funding. Interestingly, the ecosystem-oriented element of the EIC pillar of Horizon Europe is by far the smallest component in financial terms.

However, the strong support to the EIC concept from the Commissioner and his cabinet, backed largely by the high-level group installed in its development phase, demonstrates that the EIC is a good example of the rather limited influence of external voices – including those of the Member States – on the shaping of a key element of Horizon Europe.

DISCUSSION AND CONCLUSIONS

The three elements of Horizon Europe described here, missions, European partnerships and EIC, can be attributed to specific policy frames, which have been described in more detail elsewhere (Biegelbauer and Weber, 2018). Interestingly, all four frames played a role in the construction of Horizon Europe.

'Europe as laggard' in R&I serves as the 'basso continuo', the very background not only for the history of EU R&I policy, but also for Horizon Europe. We understand it as a 'master frame' and the argument goes back a long time, to Jean-Jacques Servan-Schreiber's 1968 book, *Le Defi americain*, and has been taken up frequently by the European Commission to justify Europeanised policy initiatives in R&I.

The 'European paradox', with the idea of the EU excelling in science and technology, but lagging behind in industrial innovation, came to the fore with the Green Paper on Innovation (European Commission, 1995). It was framing the attempt to strengthen EU R&I policymaking and was much more recently utilised for building the EIC as well as public–private cooperation in the framework of the European partnerships.

The European Research Area was a frame created to extend the reach of EU R&I policymaking in the 2000s (European Commission, 2000). It was the basis for the creation of the European partnerships and remains a point of reference for EU policy debates (European Parliament, 2016).

Table 9.1   Policy frames of the EU R&I policy

Frame	Identified problem	Proposed solution	Intended goal	Key outcome
'Europe as laggard' in R&I	EEC/EU technologically and thus also industrially lags behind in international competition	Common European industrial/ technological programmes	EEC/EU catches up with other countries and regions	Industrial and technological excellence
'European paradox', 'Europe as a laggard' in innovation	EU excels in science and technology, but lags behind in industrial innovation	More emphasis on EU innovation programmes and ecosystems	EU catches up with other countries and regions and forges ahead	Industrial and technological excellence
European Research Area	EU's international competitiveness is hindered by missing common market/area for R&I	More emphasis on cooperation and networking in EU R&I programmes	EU excels in international competition	Industrial, scientific and technological excellence
'Grand Challenges'	EU faces societal challenges asking for trans-/inter-disciplinary R&I solutions providing opportunities for international competition	Emphasis on trans- or interdisciplinary problem-centred and application-oriented R&I	Societal problems are diminishing and EU excels in international competition	Societal resilience and industrial, scientific and technological excellence

Source: Based on Biegelbauer and Weber, 2018, p. 255.

Finally, the 'Grand Challenges' frame, with a particular focus on societal challenges serving as a basis for EU R&I policymaking, was of central importance for creating the framework programme, Horizon 2020. The missions of Horizon Europe have been argued on the basis of this policy frame, against the backdrop of the realisation that Horizon 2020 did not contribute enough to solving the societal challenges. This frame was also important for the public–public cooperation in the framework of the European partnerships.

In Table 9.1 the four policy frames are depicted in terms of the identified problem, proposed solution, intended goal and the key outcome that they feature.

Our conclusion is that EU R&I policy continues to be dominated by the four policy frames, which have been created from the 1960s to the 2010s. Over time they have undergone accentuations but have not been changed markedly. They have been used by certain political actors and during specific times, but they have never been unimportant at any point in time since their creation.

Furthermore, they have been utilised, especially by the European Commission, to establish and stabilise EU R&I policy, to defend it against other policy fields and actors and to enlarge its budgets and relative importance vis-à-vis other areas.

The four frames have also been found not to be mutually exclusive. In fact, they frequently build upon and complement each other. They can therefore be understood as creating a discourse stretching over several decades of European R&I policy debates (Biegelbauer and Weber, 2018), thus creating a stable frame of reference for an expanding EU policy field, which was charged with an increasing number of tasks. These were, since the 1960s, to serve the economy; from the 1990s onwards and especially since the creation of the European Research Council (ERC) in 2007 (König, 2017), to finance basic research;[11] and since 2013, with the advent of Horizon 2020, to solve key societal problems.

These are not trivial observations, since over the last decades a number of framework conditions have changed in R&I policy on the European, and especially on the national level. Perhaps most importantly, the idea of the role of the state in governance has changed over time. Interestingly, the concomitant argument in R&I policymaking has made almost a 360 degree turn. In the 1960s and 1970s technology policy, as one of the precursors of innovation policy, was dominated in many countries by industry policy, that is, by policies attempting to 'pick the national winners' in the sense of leading corporate actors against the backdrop of international economic competition (Ergas, 1987). From the 1980s to the 2000s innovation policymakers in most countries abhorred such policies and concentrated on providing an enticing environment for corporations and research institutions to engage in R&I (see, e.g., Biegelbauer, 2000).

In the wake of the economic crisis starting in 2008 and the questioning of globalisation, discussions arose about the role of the state in economic and innovation policymaking. In the late 2010s this led to a resurgence of debates on industrial policy, which also reached the EU and helped to create, amongst others, the Important Projects of Common European Interest (IPCEI). IPCEI projects enable EU consortia with partners bringing knowledge, expertise, financial resources and economic actors into large structures, which finance large industrial endeavours in key technologies. An example is the attempt to create a major pan-European battery ecosystem costing several billion euros, which started in 2019; other initiatives focus on microelectronics, hydrogen and life sciences.

The missions of Horizon Europe are another example of the state again taking a stronger role in devising and coordinating R&I policy. Both European Commission and Member State governments openly take on a much more active role than in the decades before regarding agenda setting, political negotiation, decision-making and potentially also the implementation of R&I missions. It remains to be seen whether the state can fulfil all the high expectations in orchestrating a multitude of actors with very different backgrounds, rationales and objectives over several years and across several policy fields.

NOTES

1. We would like to thank the editors and two anonymous reviewers for valuable feedback.
2. The Lund declaration was at the origin of the emphasis put in Horizon 2020 on addressing grand or societal challenges (see European Council, 2009).
3. EFFLA was tasked to revisit the role of foresight in EU policymaking, and it stressed the importance of foresight for opening up the second phase of 'sense-making', in particular in order to make it more transparent and hence strengthen the legitimacy of policy actions proposed by the European Commission. The subsequent phases of decision-making and implementation are much more formalised.
4. The 'laggard' argument has been used since the first framework programmes that stressed the scientific backwardness of Europe in key technology areas, whereas the 'European paradox' was first used in 1995 in the European Commission's Green Paper on Innovation (European Commission, 1995), which fed into the preparation of the fourth framework programme (Biegelbauer and Weber, 2018).
5. See the studies by JIIP (2018) and Weber et al. (2018b), but also five 'Foresight on Demand' projects in support of each mission board, as well as several expert groups on European missions and their governance in general.
6. In the case of the mission board 'Climate Neutral and Smart Cities', no less than 11 DGs were observers to the debates of the mission board.
7. The communication mentions health, accessibility, digital, industrial competitiveness, climate, energy, mobility, natural resources and food systems.
8. Carlos Moedas, Commissioner for Research, Science and Innovation (2015):
    Europe does not yet have a world class scheme to support the very best innovations in the way that the European Research Council is the global reference for supporting excellent science. So I would like us to take stock of the various schemes to support innovation and SMEs under Horizon 2020, to look at best practice internationally, and to design a new European Innovation Council.
9. The European Commission (2018c):
    The EU innovation ecosystem generates as many start-ups as the US in number but only a few of them grow-up rapidly. This is even truer for start-ups carrying out breakthrough innovation and for the science-based ones ('deep tech'). The fact that the next wave of breakthrough innovation will be science-based calls for immediate action.
10. The Advanced Research Projects Agency (ARPA), as a model for research funding, has its origin in the defence domain. DARPA was launched by the US Department for Defence in 1958 with the idea of realising radically new technologies. Later it was adapted as ARPA-E by the US Department of Energy, featuring key elements such as organisational flexibility, high autonomy for programme design and project selection and active project management. Recently, the model and its applicability for approaching challenges in other domains have been under discussion.

11.   One of the reviewers has pointed out that the ERC is based on a narrative of 'basic/ frontier research', which might be interpreted as a fifth frame. Acknowledging this finding, we have decided not to include this frame, since we would argue that it provides structure for only a comparatively small and specialised part of the EU R&I policy, while the other frames are more generally applicable.

REFERENCES

Aho, E., Cornu, E., Georghiou, L., and Subira, A. (2007). 'Creating an Innovative Europe'. Report of the Independent Expert Group on R&D and Innovation appointed following the Hampton Court Summit, European Commission, Brussels.

Andree, D., Weber, M., and Llerena, P. (2015). 'A new role for EU Research and Innovation in the benefit of citizens: towards an open and transformative R&I policy', Policy Paper by the Research, Innovation, and Science Policy Experts (RISE), European Commission, Brussels.

Arrow, K. J. (1971, 1st edn 1962), 'Economic welfare and the allocation of resources for invention', in N. Rosenberg (ed.), *The Economics of Technological Change – Selected Readings*, Harmondsworth: Penguin Books, 609–626.

Austrian FP9 Think Tank (2017). 'Fostering Impact and Sustainable Collaboration in FP9 within a new Common Research, Technology and Innovation Policy', Technical Report, ZSI – Centre for Social Innovation.

Benford, R., and Snow, D. (2000), 'Framing processes and social movements: an overview and assessment'. *Annual Review of Sociology*, 26, 611–39.

Biegelbauer, P. (2000). *130 Years of Catching Up with the West: A Comparative Perspective on Hungarian Industry, Science and Technology Policy-Making since Industrialization*, Aldershot: Ashgate Publishing.

Biegelbauer, P. (2016). 'How different forms of policy learning influence each other: case studies from Austrian innovation policy-making'. *Policy Studies* 37(2), 129–146.

Biegelbauer, P., and Weber, M. (2018). 'EU research, technological development and innovation policy', in Hubert Heinelt and Sybille Münch (eds), *Handbook of European Policies: Interpretive Approaches to the EU*, Cheltenham, UK and Northampton, MA, USA: Edward Elgar Publishing, 241–259.

BMBF (2016). European Innovation Council (EIC) – Position paper of the Federal Ministry of Education and Research (BMBF), Berlin. www.bmbf.de/bmbf/shareddocs/downloads/files/eic_position_paper_eng.pdf?__blob=publicationFile&v=1. Retrieved 10 January 2022.

BMBF (2018). 'Forschung und Innovation für die Menschen. Die Hightech-Strategie 2025'. Bundesministerium für Bildung und Forschung, Berlin.

Brandsma, G. J., Greenwood, J., Ripoll Servent, A., and Roederer-Rynning, C. (2021). 'Inside the black box of trilogues: introduction to the special issue'. *Journal of European Public Policy* 28(1), 1–9.

Callon, M. (1986), 'The sociology of an actor-network: the case of the electric vehicle', in M. Callon, J. Law and A. Rip (eds), *Mapping the Dynamics of Science and Technology: Sociology of Science in the Real World*, Basingstoke: Palgrave Macmillan, 19–34.

Czarnitzki, D., Hussinger, K., and Schneider, C. (2012). 'The nexus between science and industry: evidence from faculty inventions'. *The Journal of Technology Transfer*

37, 755–776, https://doi.org/10.1007/s10961-011-9214-y (last accessed 11 July 2022).

Dosi, G., Llerena, P., and Labini, M. S. (2006). 'The relationships between science, technologies and their industrial exploitation: an illustration through the myths and realities of the so-called "European Paradox"'. *Research Policy* 35(10), 1450–1464.

EFFLA (2012). 'How to design a European foresight process that contributes to a European challenge driven R&I strategy process', Policy Brief No. 2, European Forum on Forward-Looking Activities, European Commission, Brussels.

Entman, R. (1993), 'Framing: towards clarification of a fractured paradigm'. *Journal of Communication*, 43(4), 51–58.

ERA-LEARN (2021). 'Annual Report on Public–Public Partnerships 2020', Brussels.

ERAC (2016). 'ERAC Opinion on the idea of a European Innovation Council'. ERAC 1209/16. Brussels, 14 July 2016.

Ergas, H. (1987), 'Does technology policy matter?', in P. Dasgupta and P. Stoneman (eds), *Economic Policy and Technological Performance*, Cambridge, UK: Cambridge University Press, 51–96.

ESIR (2017). 'Towards a mission-oriented research and innovation policy in the European Union. An ESIR memorandum', Report of the ESIR expert group, European Commission, Brussels, December 2017.

ESIR (2018). 'ESIR memorandum II. Implementing EU missions', Report of the ESIR expert group, European Commission, Brussels, October 2018.

European Commission (1995). 'Green Paper on Innovation', European Commission, Brussels.

European Commission (2000). 'Towards a European Research Area, Communication from the Commission to the Council, the European Parliament, the Economic and Social Committee and the Committee of the Regions', COM(2000) 0006 final, Brussels.

European Commission (2016a). 'Ideas for a European Innovation Council – Overview of Responses to the Call for Ideas', European Commission, Brussels.

European Commission (2016b). 'Ideas for a European Innovation Council – Summary of a Validation Workshop with Stakeholders held on 13 July 2016'. Brussels, https:// careersdocbox.com/Financial_Aid/79105624-Ideas-for-a-european-innovation -council.html (last accessed 11 July 2022).

European Commission (2018a). 'H2020 Work-Programme 2018–2020, Towards the next Framework Programme for Research and Innovation: European Innovation Council (EIC) pilot (revised version)', European Commission, Brussels, https://ec .europa.eu/research/participants/data/ref/h2020/wp/2018-2020/main/h2020-wp1820 -eic_en.pdf (last accessed 2 October 2018).

European Commission (2018b). 'Proposal for a Regulation of the European Parliament and of the Council establishing Horizon Europe – the Framework Programme for Research and Innovation', COM(2018) 435 final, European Commission, Brussels, https://eur-lex.europa.eu/resource.html?uri=cellar:b8518ec6-6a2f-11e8-9483 -01aa75ed71a1.0001.03/DOC_1&format=PDF (last accessed 2 October 2018).

European Commission (2018c). 'Impact Assessment Accompanying the document establishing Horizon Europe', SWD(2018)307 final, European Commission, Brussels, https://ec.europa.eu/transparency/documents-register/detail?ref= SWD(2018)307&lang=en (last accessed 2 October 2018).

European Commission (2018d). 'Factsheets on InvestEU', European Commission, Brussels, https://ec.europa.eu/info/publications/investeu-programme_en (last accessed 2 October 2018).

European Commission (2020a). 'Vision and Roadmap for Impact, to pave the way for the fully-fledged EIC in Horizon Europe (2021–2027)', EIC Advisory Board Brussels, 30 June 2020, https://eic.ec.europa.eu/system/files/2021-03/ec_rtd_eic -vision-roadmap-impact.pdf (last accessed 2 May 2021).

European Commission (2020b). 'A robust innovation ecosystem for the future of Europe, Report on the results of the stakeholder consultation: October 2019– February 2020', Brussels, 14 September 2020, https://data.europa.eu/doi/10.2777/ 524268 (last accessed 2 May 2021).

European Commission (2020c). 'Deep Tech Europe, European Innovation Council Pilot Impact Report', Brussels, 22 September 2020, https://data.europa.eu/doi/10 .2826/770124 (last accessed 2 May 2021).

European Commission (2020d). 'Implementing the pro-active management of the EIC pathfinder for breakthrough technologies & innovations, Lessons from the ARPA model & other international practices – Independent expert report'. Brussels, 10 November 2020, https://data.europa.eu/doi/10.2777/698838 (last accessed 2 May 2021).

European Commission (2020e). 'History of the European Research Area', Factsheet, Brussels.

European Commission (2020f). 'A new ERA for Research and Innovation', Communication from the Commission to the Council, the European Parliament, the Economic and Social Committee and the Committee of the Regions, COM/2020/628 final, Brussels.

European Commission (2021). 'EIC Work Programme 2021', European Innovation Council (EIC) established by the European Commission, under the Horizon Europe programme (2021–27), Brussels, 17 March 2021, https://ec.europa.eu/info/funding -tenders/opportunities/docs/2021-2027/horizon/wp-call/2021/wp_horizon-eic -2021_en.pdf (last accessed 2 May 2021).

European Council (2009). 'The Lund Declaration. Europe must focus on the Grand Challenges of our time', European Council, Brussels.

European Council (2015). 'Background paper to the Lund declaration 2015', European Council, Brussels.

European Council (2017). 'From the Interim Evaluation of Horizon 2020 towards the ninth Framework Programme – Council conclusions' (adopted on 1/12/2017), 15320/17, RECH 404, COMPET 851, Council of the European Union, Brussels.

European Council (2019). 'Proposal for a Regulation of the European Parliament and of the Council establishing Horizon Europe – the Framework Programme for Research and Innovation, laying down its rules for participation and dissemination – Common understanding, Art. 8', 2018/0224(COD), Council of the European Union, Brussels.

European Parliament (2016). 'The European Research Area: Evolving concept, implementation challenges', European Parliamentary Research Service, Brussels.

Finlayson, A. (2004). 'Political science, political ideas and rhetoric'. *Economy and Society* 33(4), 528–549.

Fischer, F. (2003), *Reframing Public Policy: Discursive Politics and Deliberative Practices*, Oxford: Oxford University Press.

Godin, B. (2009). *The Making of Science, Technology and Innovation Policy: Conceptual Frameworks as Narratives, 1945–2005*, Montréal: Centre Urbanisation Culture Société de l'INRS.

Henrekson, M., and Sanandaji, T. (2017). 'Schumpeterian entrepreneurship in Europe compared to other industrialized regions', IFN Working Paper No. 1170, Stockholm.

Hernani, J. T., Giry, C., Antoniou, L., Danielsen, K., and Hunter, A. (2016). 'Evaluation of joint programming to address grand societal challenges – Final report of the expert group', Brussels.

HLG Innovators (2018). Funding – Awareness – Scale – Talent (FAST) – Europe is back: accelerating breakthrough innovation – Full set of recommendations from the Independent High-Level Group of Innovators on establishing a European Innovation Council', https://data.europa.eu/doi/10.2777/96701 (last accessed 2 October 2018).

Hoppe, R. (1999). 'Policy analysis, science, and politics: from "speaking truth to power" to "making sense together". *Science and Public Policy*, 26(3), 201–210.

IPM (2017). 'Draft Recommendations on the European Innovation Council, High Level Group on Innovation Policy Management', June 2017, Brussels.

JIIP (2018). 'Mission-Oriented Research and Innovation: Inventory and characterisation of initiatives', Final report, Joint Institute for Innovation Research, European Commission, Brussels.

Kluger Dionigi, M., and Rasmussen, A. (2019). 'The Ordinary Legislative Procedure', in F. Laursen (ed.), *Oxford Research Encyclopedia of Politics*, Oxford: Oxford University Press.

König, T. (2017). *The European Research Council*, Cambridge: Polity Press.

Kuhlmann, J., & Blum, S. (2021). 'Narrative plots for regulatory, distributive, and redistributive policies'. *European Policy Analysis* 7(S2), 276–302.

Lamy, P., et al. (2017). 'LAB – FAB – APP Investing in the European future we want', Report of the independent High Level Group on maximising the impact of EU Research & Innovation Programmes, https://op.europa.eu/en/publication-detail/-/publication/1b101eff-a7e5-11e7-837e-01aa75ed71a1/language-en/format-PDF/source-253594411 (last accessed 2 October 2018).

Laws, D., and Rein, M. (2003). 'Reframing practice deliberative policy analysis', in M. Hajer and H. Wagenaar (eds), *Understanding Governance in the Network Society*, Cambridge: Cambridge University Press, 172–208.

Madelin, R., & Ringrose, D. (eds) (2016). 'Opportunity now: Europe's mission to innovate', European Commission, Brussels.

Mazzucato, M. (2018). 'Mission-oriented research & innovation in the European Union: a problem-solving approach to fuel innovation-led growth', European Commission, Brussels.

Mazzucato, M. (2019). 'Governing missions in the European Union', European Commission, Brussels.

Meyer, S., Dinges, M., and Wang, A. (2017). 'Toolbox of Current and Novel Alignment Modalities', ERA-LEARN 2020 Technical Report, Vienna.

Moedas, C. (2015). 'Open Innovation, Open Science, Open to the World'. Speech at 'A new start for Europe: Opening up to an ERA of Innovation' Conference, 22 June 2015, Brussels.

OECD (2021). 'The Design and Implementation of Mission-Oriented Innovation Policies. A new systemic policy approach to address societal challenges', OECD Science, Technology and Industry Policy Papers, Organisation for Economic Co-operation and Development, Paris.

Pernicka, S., Feigl-Heihs, M., Gerstl, A., and Biegelbauer, P. (2002). *Wie demokratisch ist die europäische Forschungs- und Technologiepolitik? Der politische Entscheidungsprozess zum fünften Forschungsrahmenprogramm aus österreichischer Perspektive*, Baden-Baden: Nomos.

Rein, M., and Schön, D. A. (1994). *Frame Reflection. Toward the Solution of Intractable Policy Controversies*, New York: Basic Books.

RISE (2017). 'Europe's Future: Open Innovation, Open Science, Open to the World. Reflections of the Research, Innovation and Science Policy Experts High Level Group', European Commission, Brussels.

RISE (2018a). 'Mission-Oriented Research and Innovation Policy. A RISE Perspective', European Commission, Brussels.

RISE (2018b). 'The academic underpinnings of the European Innovation Council. Summary and recommendations of the RISE subgroup on EIC', European Commission, Brussels.

Sachwald, F. (2015). 'Europe's twin deficits: excellence and innovation in new sectors', Policy Paper by the Research, Innovation, and Science Policy Experts (RISE), European Commission, Brussels.

Servan-Schreiber, J.-J. (1968). *Le Défi américain*, Paris: Éditions Denoël.

Shanahan, E., Raile, E., French, K., and McEvoy, J. (2018). 'Bounded stories'. *Policy Studies Journal* 46(4), 922–948.

Soete, L., Veugeleurs, R., Sundgren, J.-E., and Glover, A. (2015). 'R&I in times of crisis: dynamic interactions between R&I, public finances and economic growth', RISE presentation, January 2015.

Torfing, J., and Sørensen, E. (2014). 'The European debate on governance networks: towards a new and viable paradigm?' *Policy and Society* 33(4), 329–344.

Tsipouri, L. (2017). 'Pockets of excellence as drivers of regional growth', Policy Paper of the RISE high-level workshop on 'The impact of smart specialisation strategies on pockets of excellence and regional growth' (Crete, 6–8 October 2015), European Commission, Brussels.

Vignola-Gagné, E., and Biegelbauer, P. (2013), 'Translational research', in E. G. Carayannis and D. F. J. Campbell (eds), *Encyclopedia of Creativity, Invention, Innovation, and Entrepreneurship*, New York: Springer, 1834–1843.

Wanzenböck, I., Wesseling, J. H., Frenken, K., Hekkert, M. P., and Weber, K. M. (2020). 'A framework for mission-oriented innovation policy: alternative pathways through the problem–solution space'. *Science and Public Policy*, 47(4), 474–489.

Weber, M., Rammer, C., Dinges, M., Dachs, B., Hud, M., and Steindl, C. (2018a). 'Erkenntnis- und Wissenstransfer im Kontext europäischer F&I-Politik'. Studien zum deutschen Innovationssystem Nr. 12-2018.

Weber, M., Andreescu, L., Cuhls, K., Dragomir, B., Gheorghiu, R., Giesecke, S., Ricci, A., Rosa, A., Schaper-Rinkel, P., Sessa, C., Baiocco, S., Curaj, A., Giuffrè, G., and Zern, R. (2018b). 'Transitions on the Horizon: Perspectives for the European Union's future research and innovation policies', Final Report of Project BOHEMIA (Beyond the Horizon. Foresight in Support of the EU's Future Policies on Research and Innovation), European Commission, Brussels.

PART III

Do we have to reconsider theories of European integration?

10. Consensus politics and EU disequilibrium: the German Council Presidency 2021 and the rule of law mechanism

Uwe Puetter

INTRODUCTION

With the German presidency of the Council of the European Union (EU) coming to an end in December 2020, the EU had once more avoided crucial challenges to its own existence, it seemed. Not only had EU institutions sealed decisions on the EU's new seven-year Multiannual Financial Framework (MFF), a traditionally difficult negotiation exercise, they also had reached agreement on the €750 billion Covid-19 recovery fund 'NextGenerationEU'. For students of European integration these events are noteworthy for several reasons.[1]

With the baseline decision of the European Council on the MFF and the recovery fund, the EU seemed to have fended off once more a substantial threat to the integrity of the Eurozone and, thus, to the Union more generally (van Middelaar & Puetter, 2021). Especially Italy, the EU country the hardest hit after the initial outbreak of the Covid-19 pandemic in Europe in the first half of 2020, had been threatened with the prospect of extremely constrained public finances in view of economic slowdown and rising public expenditure in response to the crisis. Unlike in the case of the long-delayed response to Greece's problems at the beginning of the euro crisis, the EU acted far more swiftly and resolutely (Hodson & Puetter, 2022). The fact that the recovery fund NextGenerationEU provides true subsidies to national budgets as opposed to loans, as in the case of the euro crisis, can even be seen as sign of once more intensifying EU integration. This is all the more so as the fund involves a solidarity mechanism which allocates considerably higher contributions to countries which have been more heavily affected by the pandemic and which have been facing comparatively greater restraints on their public finances. For example, Italy and Spain are each to receive allocations which are approximately 2.7 times higher than those of the EU's largest economy, Germany.

With Germany holding the rotating presidency of the Council in the second semester of 2020 and Chancellor Angela Merkel personally playing a crucial role in the negotiations on the MFF and the recovery fund in the European Council, the country's most senior decision-makers can claim some credit for what is seen by them as effective crisis management. The paths towards reaching agreement on the MFF and the recovery fund were by no means trivial. The negotiations revealed big divisions within the Union at the centre of which were not only disputes over burden-sharing and finances but the question of whether and how the EU continues to tolerate governments with autocratic leanings inside its own ranks (Kelemen, 2020). The so-called rule of law mechanism, a legislative instrument, which allows for EU institutions to make the release of funds to individual member states dependent on the existence of an independent judiciary, sparked controversy between different member state coalitions (Heinelt & Münch, Chapter 1 in this volume). Finally, a majority within the European Parliament (EP) found itself opposed to the negotiation positions of the European Council and the Council on the matter. As the issue of the rule of law mechanism became closely entangled with the negotiation of the MFF and the recovery fund, this question was at the centre of efforts by the German Council presidency and Chancellor Merkel, as a member of the European Council, to bring about a consensus position in these intergovernmental forums.

This chapter discusses Germany's role in negotiating the MFF, the recovery fund and the rule of law mechanism in the second semester of 2020 from a new intergovernmentalist perspective. Two hypotheses of new intergovernmentalist analysis are central to the discussion: first, that member states in contemporary EU politics see consensus as an end in itself and as a guiding norm in intergovernmental relations (Bickerton et al., 2015a). Second, that member state governments seek to circumvent resistance to integration, or, for that matter, to core EU principles, rather than resolving political conflicts. Even though this behaviour may resolve decision-making impasses it does little to ease tensions within contemporary EU politics, which may even lead to disintegration, a state which new intergovernmentalism refers to as disequilibrium (Hodson & Puetter, 2019). This chapter thus seeks to document the commitment of the German government to consensus politics in the European Council and the Council.

It will explain why Germany, and notably Chancellor Merkel and the governing party duo of the Christian Democratic Union (CDU) and the Christian Social Union (CSU) can both be seen to have been associated with a coalition of member states favouring the introduction of the rule of law mechanism (Heinelt & Münch, Chapter 1 in this volume) while at the same time seeking to actively accommodate challenger governments in Budapest and Warsaw. With this double strategy, it is argued, Germany may have successfully helped to overcome obstacles to EU unity and consensus within the European Council but at the same time has amplified rather than reduced problems threatening the normative foundations of the EU's post-Maastricht political and legal order. Rather than having been transformed into a political community in equilibrium the EU remains in a state of disequilibrium, as new intergovernmentalist theory expects. Moreover, the analysis shows that Germany's EU policy during the chancellorship of Angela Merkel and partisan politics within the CDU/CSU and European People's Party (EPP) have been a crucial pillar of this policymaking approach. Having missed the opportunity to design a more hard-hitting rule of law mechanism, the EU continues to remain devoid of any credible sanctioning mechanisms in relation to member states that opt for challenging the EU's political and legal order.

In terms of its meta-theoretical and methodological foundations the chapter shares some common ground with other interpretive or discursive perspectives, which are represented in this volume. Even though new intergovernmentalism as a theory of contemporary European integration is not committed to a single meta-theoretical perspective, such as rationalism or constructivism, it operationalises consensus politics as an institutional practice within the European Council, the Council and EU expert committees, based on routinisation, informal norms, deliberation and socialisation processes (Puetter, 2012, 2015). More specifically, the chapter seeks to identify discursive interventions by leading political actors which document adherence to consensus politics.

THE EUROPEAN UNION IN DISEQUILIBRIUM AFTER THE NEGOTIATION OF THE MFF

As a theory of post-Maastricht EU politics and institutional change, new intergovernmentalism (Bickerton et al., 2015a; Puetter, 2014) can provide key insights into the process of decision-making on the MFF and the Covid-19 recovery fund NextGenerationEU. One of the core hypotheses of the new intergovernmentalism is that consensus has become the guiding norm in post-Maastricht European Council and Council decision-making. This is because member states rely on mutual commitment to implement common decisions domestically in the absence of strong sanctioning powers on part of supranational institutions, such as the Commission and the Court of Justice (in the following: the Court), in a range of new areas of EU activity which have become central to the Union's political and economic stability. These domains include economic governance under the EMU, foreign and security policy, and crucial aspects of justice and home affairs.

Moreover, new intergovernmentalism sees post-Maastricht EU integration progressing, even though in non-conventional ways, by shifting new executive powers towards the European Council and the Council as opposed to delegating them to the Commission. While emphasising the centrality of consensus politics, new intergovernmentalism at the same time has also given attention to key challenges to the EU's legitimacy, as well as its political and legal order. Here the theory shares common ground with postfunctionalism (Hooghe & Marks, 2009, 2018). However, while highlighting that EU politics are impacted by a constraining dissensus, postfunctionalism remains unclear about how and why the EU's multiple crises in the 2010s and early 2020s have continued to lead to a further intensification of EU integration rather than its abandonment. The new intergovernmentalist concept of the post-Maastricht disequilibrium in EU politics offers an explanation of this puzzle (Hodson & Puetter, 2019).

Hodson and Puetter (2019, pp. 1155–1157) highlight the importance of the concept of equilibrium to the study of politics, including classic theories of European integration. They cite David Easton's (1965, pp. 103–135) flow model of the equilibrating forces in politics. Easton argues that authorities must generate outputs that respond to demands and support for the political system while triggering further demands and support for future policy action instead of undermining further demand and support. This idea is detected to reappear in the classic neofunctionalist scholarship of Lindberg and Scheingold (1970) who saw the European Community as either evolving towards an equilibrium or as facing spillback. Their concept of the permissive consensus is central to explaining the existence of systemic support for community institutions and policies. Neofunctionalists have sought to integrate the question of popular legitimacy, which could either advance or impede integration, into their models. However, they remain optimistic overall with regard to the underlying progress of integration. In contrast, Andrew Moravcsik's liberal intergovernmentalist theory of EU integration is most explicit about the EU's status quo as a state of systemic stability. He attests the Union to be in a state of 'a stable constitutional equilibrium' (Moravcsik, 2005, p. 349). Central to this stability are the compromises reached in intergovernmental bargaining at the EU level, which ensure that member state governments back 'the European constitutional compromise' (Moravcsik, 2005).

New intergovernmentalism does not share this confidence in systemic stability. Even though new intergovernmentalists deliberately do 'not seek to put forward an optimistic or a pessimistic account' (Bickerton et al., 2015a, p. 716). They insist that contemporary integration theory needs to consider disruption and sources of instability more systematically. Hodson and Puetter (2019) consider 'the EU's tendency to produce policy outputs that polarise politics in ways that cast doubt on the future of the Union' (ibid., p. 1157) as a key feature of post-Maastricht EU decision-making. The key point is that disequilibrium is seen here as 'a concept that suggests continuity and rupture' (ibid., p. 1158). If the disequilibrium were to unwind, the EU's political system would face 'a large and potentially disorderly adjustment' (ibid.). Examples of this are scenarios to which the EU came extremely close during the crises of the 2010s, including a so-called Grexit spilling over into an unwinding of the Eurozone. The rise of challenger parties, which reject the foundations of EU integration as we know it, to become governing parties in multiple member states, including some of the largest EU countries, is another scenario which has not been impossible to contemplate in the 2010s. The stand-off between the pro-European candidate Emmanuel Macron and the Eurosceptic challenger Marine Le Pen in the second round of France's 2017 presidential election constituted such a moment.

The new intergovernmentalist argument on disequilibrium seeks to prevent treating evidence of a near miss of disorderly adjustment as proof of the EU's consolidated systemic stability. Hodson and Puetter (2019) identify a number of key patterns of post-Maastricht EU decision-making, which, while either avoiding the unravelling of the disequilibrium and/or enabling further integration, result in policy outputs which increase rather than decrease tensions surrounding the foundations of the EU's post-Maastricht political order as it has been known so far. The central question for them in this regard is 'to understand how EU elites have responded to – and accommodated – challengers without interrupting integration' (ibid., p. 1159).

In the 2000s the rise of studies on significant popular Eurosceptic sentiments, as well as on the importance of populism, as a political current which can be linked to fundamental shifts in Europe's partisan politics, signals the relevance of these developments for studying the systemic stability of the EU. While scholars of Euroscepticism have highlighted the centrality of so-called challenger parties as actors who channel and advocate political demands to disrupt and unravel integration (Szczerbiak & Taggart, 2008), they have also found evidence which suggests that for a long time such parties could, at best, hope to join coalitions or make minority governments dependent on them (Taggart & Szczerbiak, 2013). Quoting these findings, Hodson and Puetter (2019) shift the focus onto a more recent but already persistent phenomenon: challenger parties which rise to power, so that they are able to fully control or dominate government. These governments, as far as they openly contest the EU's post-Maastricht political order, are referred to as challenger governments. Challenger governments have persisted in Hungary and Poland for long periods, while Italy had a challenger government from June 2018 until September 2019.

Because of the centrality of intergovernmental decision-making in the European Council and the Council for the EU's political processes, challenger governments are by default directly involved in shaping EU policy. Moreover, by avoiding compliance with EU principles and laws as well as by publicly denouncing EU institutions and representatives, they particularly take on the Commission and the Court as the EU's central supranational actors. This in turn allows challenger governments to remain more muted in relation to the EU's leading intergovernmental institutions, the Council and the European Council. The potential of challenger governments to disrupt the EU's foundations can be explained by reference to the new intergovernmentalist hypothesis that consensus has become the guiding norm in EU intergovernmental decision-making (Bickerton et al., 2015a, p. 711). Pro-EU mainstream governments rely on support from challenger governments in crucial areas of EU activity, such as economic governance, foreign policy and migration and asylum. They also depend on them in important budgetary decisions, notably the MFF and the recovery fund. Hodson and Puetter (2019) identify a set of sample interactions between pro-EU mainstream governments and challengers in which both sides challenge each other yet find ways of interaction which allow them to still adhere to consensus politics. Most importantly, despite the individual actions taken by the EP and the Commission against challenger governments, the Council and the European Council have avoided any pronounced criticism of challenger governments in the 2010s and early 2020s. The invocation of Article 7 of the Treaty on European Union (TEU) by these institutions has been unrealistic.

Here the new intergovernmentalist argument on disequilibrium meets Kelemen's (2020) concept of an 'authoritarian equilibrium' within the EU. Kelemen highlights that a number of socio-economic factors help autocrats to survive not despite EU integration but because of it. Yet, the other key factor explaining their survival is the 'politics of authoritarian protection' (Kelemen, 2020, p. 487). Kelemen agrees with the new intergovernmentalist emphasis on the centrality of member state governments and, thus, the European Council and the Council in EU decision-making, as well as with the importance of 'norms of mutual trust and deference to national sovereignty' (ibid., p. 489) within these institutions. Moreover, he emphasises how deeply institutionalised the protection of autocrats, notably of Viktor Orbán's Fidesz party, has become in the context of EU partisan politics within the 2010s and 2020s. The centre-right European People's Party (EPP) is seen to have played the most important role in this regard, as it has protected its own member party, Fidesz, from the adoption of sanctioning measures within the EP and the European Council (ibid., pp. 487–489). Moreover, the EPP relied on the votes of Fidesz MEPs within the European Parliament's EPP group when Jean-Claude Juncker was elected president of the Commission in 2014.

To conclude, the discussion of the new intergovernmentalist argument on the disequilibrium in post-Maastricht policymaking is of key relevance when studying the negotiations relating to the MFF, the EU's Covid-19 recovery fund NextGenerationEU and the related rule of law mechanism in 2020. Moreover, new intergovernmentalist explanations of European Council and Council decision-making coupled with Kelemen's argument on the centrality of partisan politics, notably the role of the EPP, in protecting EU member state governments with autocratic leanings, provides a particularly suitable conceptual framework for reviewing the role of the German Council presidency as well as Chancellor Merkel's agency in the negotiations. In particular, the new intergovernmentalist argument about disequilibrium can help to unravel the puzzle of why Germany has played a double role as a supporter of the rule of law mechanism and as a facilitator of agreement with Hungary and Poland at the cost of weakening the very same mechanism. The guiding question for the following review of the German Council presidency's role in negotiating the MFF, the recovery fund and the rule of law mechanism is whether the achieved policy output increases rather than decreases tensions surrounding the foundations of the EU's post-Maastricht political order as it has been known so far.

To understand the above theoretical argument in relation to alternative explanations of contemporary EU decision-making it is helpful to revisit the five discourse coalitions and two unlinked camps that are identified by Heinelt and Münch (Chapter 1 in this volume) as signifying the central controversies surrounding the negotiation of the MFF, the recovery fund and the rule of law mechanism in 2020. Within this framework Germany is associated with the coalition of the 'promoters of the rule of law' while Hungary and Poland are included within the 'Visegrad 4' coalition, which acted as an adversary on the issue of the rule of law mechanism. Conventional approaches to integration theory, notably a liberal intergovernmentalist account, could simply assess the actions of the German Council presidency in terms of Germany's potential to bridge the boundaries between the different coalitions and camps. Seen in this way, Germany's approach to accommodating the interests of Hungary and Poland in the negotiations would be interpreted as an expression of Germany's role as an honest broker and compromise seeker. Moreover, it could be concluded that the EU's intergovernmental negotiation regime provides evidence of a 'constitutional equilibrium' (Moravcsik, 2005), as it safely prevents the EU from breaking up at times of heightened crisis.

An alternative, new intergovernmentalist, way of interpreting the policy stance of the German 2020 Council presidency emerges from considering the central role of the German government under Chancellor Merkel in EU consensus politics and its track record in dealing with challenger governments in Budapest and Warsaw in the 2010s and early 2020s. Moreover, partisan politics within the EPP, of which Germany's governing centre-right parties CDU and CSU are key members, are considered too. While the negotiation outcome is considered to have been aimed at enabling consensus within the European

Council, it has avoided addressing a major tension surrounding the EU's political and legal foundations: the abandoning of the rule of law, democracy and
pluralism by some of the Union's member states.

The following empirical sections seek to provide evidence for this interpretation. More specifically, they document actions and discursive interventions
of the German government and Chancellor Merkel, which reveal commitment
to consensus generation. Moreover, these actions and interventions are interpreted with a view to their longer-term consequences, which means whether
and how they might prepare the ground for further tensions regarding persistence of the EU's post-Maastricht political and legal order.

GERMANY'S RECORD AS A CHAMPION OF CONSENSUS AND THE ROLE OF PARTISAN POLITICS

Before reviewing the German Council presidency of 2020 in greater detail, it is
important to recall some of the core elements of the track record of the German
government in EU consensus politics and in the context of partisan politics
within the EPP. While a more encompassing analysis of these aspects is clearly
beyond the scope of this chapter, it is important to identify sample patterns
of interaction between the German government and challenger governments,
as well as these governments' attitudes to major EU-level negotiations.
Considering the limitations of scope of this chapter, emphasis is placed on
Chancellor Merkel and interactions with the challenger government of Viktor
Orbán in Hungary.

A central actor in this context is Chancellor Merkel herself. Having been in
office as head of government since November 2005, the chancellor by 2020
was the longest-serving member of the European Council. At home she had led
two grand coalitions of her centre-right CDU and its Bavarian sister party, the
CSU, with the centre-left Social Democratic Party (SPD) from 2005–2009 and
from 2013 onwards. In between Merkel had led a coalition government with
the liberals. The chancellor had also acted as CDU party leader until 2018.
Representing the largest EU economy and the EU's most populated member
state, Merkel, throughout her term, remained committed to finding agreement
within the European Council. She sought to pursue decision-making which
would facilitate rather than roll back integration. A major programmatic
statement which documents this approach is her 2010 speech at the College
of Europe in Bruges (Merkel, 2010) in which she hailed the centrality of the
European Council in EU decision-making, highlighting that agreement among
the heads is the most crucial condition for the EU to function at all.[2]

Moreover, the chancellor identified herself as a 'firm believer in Europe'
(ibid.) and placed special emphasis on the experience of European support for
German reunification and the importance of the legacy of Chancellor Helmut

Kohl, a Christian democrat too, for informing Germany's policy stance on European integration. Finally, Merkel used her Bruges speech to make a key reference to the then ongoing euro crisis. This statement can be read as a fundamental commitment to act whenever collective EU action is required 'to bring Europe back from disaster' (ibid.). Moreover, Merkel quoted herself as stating in front of the German parliament, the Bundestag: 'if the euro fails, Europe fails' (ibid.). She also flagged that she had been ready to propose to her own parliament 'unusual and previously unimagined routes in order to help Greece and thus to ensure the stability of the eurozone as a whole' (ibid.) despite facing 'severe criticism' for this (ibid.).

In 2010 Viktor Orbán, leader of Hungary's Fidesz party, emerged as the first EU prime minister who wasted no time in transforming his own party, a member of the EPP centre-right alliance, into a challenger party, and, thus, his own government into the EU's first challenger government. Orbán systematically took aim at core EU principles domestically by attacking the independence of the Hungarian Constitutional Court, by reducing pluralism and media freedom and by preventing civil society from accessing foreign funding sources. By 2020 he had secured re-election twice. He continued to ensure, through changes to the electoral law, attacks on the independence of the judiciary at all levels, and through the curtailing of academic freedom, the endurance of Hungary's authoritarian turn (Csehi, 2019, 2022). In 2014 he touted that he believed in the possibility of building 'an illiberal nation state within the EU' (Orbán, 2014).

Following the so-called EU refugee crisis of 2015, Orbán positioned himself directly against Germany's Chancellor Merkel within the EPP, as he identified her as an enabler of migration, citing her decision to open Germany's borders to refugees in that year. With this move Orbán also deliberately opened a flank in EPP partisan politics as he sought to emerge as a right-wing alternative to more moderate conservatives like Merkel. In an appearance at an EPP conference in Malta in March 2017 he stated that 'migration turned out to be the Trojan horse of terrorism' (Brunsden, 2017). Merkel made no secret of her antipathy to Orbán's attempts to challenge both the EU and her personally. When the EU's Court finally ruled against Hungary's policy to ignore a Council majority decision from 2015 on sharing refugees to lessen the burden for Greece and Italy, Budapest reaffirmed its determination to ignore the decision of the Court too. Merkel denounced this move with the words, 'That one government says it isn't interested in a verdict by the European Court of Justice cannot be accepted' (Byrne & Buckley, 2017). Yet Merkel refrained from more radical steps towards taking action against Hungary, notably in the European Council and the Council, over the coming years.

How much Merkel and Orbán have sought to deal with each other in ways which would not allow their antagonism to ultimately break consensus politics in the European Council can also be illustrated by the fact that by 2020 Orbán was, after Merkel, second in line as longest-serving member of the European Council. Another major factor in explaining German EU policy in the 2010s and early 2020s is the role of German CDU/CSU MEPs as members of the EPP group within the EP. Clashes with EU institutions, notably the Commission, became inevitable as Orbán continued domestic pushbacks against judicial independence, civil society, media and academic freedoms in the second half of the 2010s. Yet, the EPP group neither moved to sanction Fidesz or even to expel it. The EPP also successfully prevented the EP as an EU institution from adopting a tougher stance on Orbán's authoritarian moves. A central actor in this context was CSU politician Manfred Weber, who acted as EPP group chair from the beginning of the 2014 EP electoral period. In 2017 when Orbán moved to close down the Central European University in Budapest, voices within the EPP demanding a tougher stance towards Fidesz became louder. Yet, while publicly emphasising his unequivocal support for EU values, Weber sought to keep the EPP group together and avoided demands to sanction Fidesz, a party which provided crucial votes in the EP to the group (King, 2017). Weber was thanked by Orbán for supporting Fidesz' Hungarian campaign for domestic re-election in the same year at the EPP Congress in Helsinki in November 2018 (Fortuna, 2018). But when the EP eventually voted in favour of launching Article 7 TEU proceedings against Hungary in September 2018, Weber voted with the EP majority, even though CSU MEPs and many other EPP group members voted against the decision. Attempts to continue accommodating Fidesz even continued when divisions within the EPP became bigger. Most importantly, Fidesz supported Weber's candidacy as lead candidate of the EPP in the 2019 EP elections. At the same time Weber sought to publicly keep a distance from Orbán ahead of the elections by stating: 'Enough is enough' (Amann & Müller, 2019).

To conclude, this section has documented Chancellor Merkel's fundamental commitment to consensus seeking and EU integration. Most importantly, Merkel viewed agreement in the European Council as key to preserving EU integration. The positioning of Hungary's Prime Minister Orbán and his Fidesz party as a challenger to the EU's normative foundations did not lead Merkel and her CDU/CSU party family to abandon consensus politics in the 2010s. Equally did Orbán not miss the opportunity to pay tribute to consensus politics in some way, even though he had positioned himself as a challenger towards Merkel.

THE GERMAN COUNCIL PRESIDENCY 2021: THE EU'S FINANCES AND THE RULE OF LAW MECHANISM

In her speech at the EP at the beginning of Germany's presidency of the Council in July 2020, Merkel identified fundamental rights as well as cohesion and solidarity as the key priorities of the presidency, stating that 'fundamental rights are the issue, which I feel most strongly about in relation to this Council presidency' (Merkel, 2020; translation by the author). Interestingly, in this context Merkel mentioned the Commission, the Court and the EP as the EU's 'strong institutions' which safeguard fundamental rights. However, she left out the Council and the European Council. Moreover, the statement came only days after a joint video press conference with Commission President Ursula von der Leyen about the priorities of the German presidency in which Merkel had put the emphasis differently and stressed that: 'time is of the essence' (Chazan & Fleming, 2020). The chancellor said that 'The issue of rule of law is not just about money. It's an overarching issue which will go on for years' (Khan et al., 2020). With regard to the upcoming July European Council meeting, Merkel stressed: 'That's why the first task of the 17–18 July … must of course be to ensure that we aren't left with nothing on Jan[uary] 1, 2021. We need an agreement. And that's why the central task is to make progress on the recovery fund and the MFF, so we have a basis for being able to work' (ibid.).

When the European Council met later in July for a record four-day-long meeting, leaders indeed reached agreement in principle on the MFF and the recovery fund. Observers wrote that the negotiation outcome was 'orchestrated' (Fleming et al., 2020b) by Chancellor Merkel and European Council President Charles Michel. Moreover, Merkel, working together with Latvia's Prime Minister Krisjanis Karnis, was seen to have been instrumental in enabling agreement on a compromise regarding the rule of law mechanism (ibid.). The issue had emerged as a central point of contention among European Council leaders during the preceding days (Fleming et al., 2020a). The eventual compromise included the softening of conditions in view of the threat to veto the recovery plan on the part of Hungary's Prime Minister Orbán. At the same time, it was agreed that any potential decisions on withholding eventual payments would be subject to qualified majority voting (Fleming et al., 2020b).

While the agreement in principle on the MFF and the recovery fund, which was reached at the July 2020 European Council meeting, largely proved to be solid with regard to the financial and redistributional side of the negotiations, disputes about the rule of law mechanism were reopened shortly afterwards. This issue became the central obstacle to the eventual implementation of the July European Council compromise by the Commission, the EP and the Council and, thus, the main challenge for the German Council presidency. At the beginning of August, France's European Affairs Minister Clément Beaun told the *Financial Times* that 'If any government breaches the rule of law there should be elements of sanctions – financial and legal' (Khan, 2020). The German Council presidency made a first attempt at proposing a basis for agreement within the Council and with the EP by the end of September. The proposal was met with immediate criticism from MEPs and flanked by rebuttals from members of the Commission and the Hungarian government about the country's adherence to democracy and the rule of law (Fleming & Peel, 2020).

In the second week of October 2020, the German Permanent Representative to the EU, Michael Clauss, sought to win over MEPs by suggesting to them in a letter that they agree on a 'package deal' (Fleming & Khan, 2020d). Clauss indicated that the Council could be ready to accept an unspecified increase in EU spending while he sought to lower expectations regarding the rule of law mechanism. Most importantly, the Permanent Representative emphasised that the mechanism should be restricted to rule of law violations, which impact on the management of the EU budget, and stressed that Article 7 TEU would be the appropriate instrument to deal with instances of 'general disrespect' (ibid.).

An actual agreement between negotiators from the EP and the Council, led by the German presidency, was reached in early November. The EP's lead negotiator, Petri Sarvamaa, even praised the agreement, as he saw room for broader applications of the mechanism: 'The EU will not only be able to stop EU funding once the rule-of-law principles have already been breached, but also in cases where it is evident that recent governmental decisions represent a future risk for EU finances' (Khan & Peel, 2020). Only days later, Michael Clauss also announced agreement with EP negotiators on the MFF while Orbán instantly signalled disagreement (Fleming & Khan, 2020a).

Even though the EP had moved towards the Council position, as represented by the German presidency, with the two agreements, on 16 November 2020 Hungary and Poland formally declared in COREPER that they would veto agreement on the MFF and the recovery fund because of the latest decisions on the rule of law mechanism (Fleming & Khan, 2020c). Differences had hardened. In response to the veto threat the possibility was floated that 25 EU member states could sign off on an agreement outside the EU treaties to unlock money from the recovery fund. Yet there also were signs from Budapest and Warsaw that both governments were eager to seek compromise (Fleming & Khan, 2020b). This context set the scene for another European Council meeting to take the ultimate decision.

Merkel and the German government were attributed with a key role in bringing about the final agreement on the MFF and the recovery which was reached at the 10–11 December 2020 European Council (*Süddeutsche Zeitung*, 2020). European Council President Charles Michel praised the chancellor in a press conference for having 'rolled up her sleeves' to bring about agreement

(Kolb, 2020). A key element of the compromise was that the German Council presidency could claim that it had not asked the EP and the Council to alter the text on the rule of law mechanism, which had been agreed on in early November. Instead, the European Council adopted as part of its conclusions a set of qualifications regarding the actual application of the mechanism and also granted Hungary and Poland reassurances that a declaration would be prepared by the Commission for submission to the Council when the latter institution was supposed to hold the final vote on the EU regulation containing the rule of law mechanism. Formally, European Council conclusions are not legally binding but politically, or de facto, bind EU institutions and member state governments (Puetter, 2014, pp. 133–140). Regarding the disputed issue of how broad the scope of the use of the rule of law mechanism could be, the conclusions contain a set of limiting guidelines (European Council, 2020, Section 1). More specifically, the conclusions refer to Article 7 TEU as the legal instrument to deal with violations of the EU's values (ibid., para. 1). The Commission was asked to develop guidelines on the application of the mechanism. Yet, the European Council also asked the Commission to delay the finalisation of these guidelines until after the Court had itself pronounced on the legality of the rule of law mechanism. This implied a postponement of the application of the mechanism altogether (ibid., para. 2). The conclusions state that 'The measures under the mechanism will have to be proportionate to the impact of the breaches of the rule of law on the sound financial management of the Union budget' and that 'the causal link between such breaches and the negative consequences on the Union's financial interests will have to be sufficiently direct and be duly established'. Most significantly, the European Council reaffirms that 'The mere finding that a breach of the rule of law has taken place does not suffice to trigger the mechanism' (ibid.).

In his own way of paying lip service to Merkel's consensus politics, Orbán, in a newspaper interview with *Die Welt* later in December 2020, stated that

> the rule of law has been already defined by the European treaties. The [European] Parliament wanted to unlawfully bypass this. Angela Merkel's proposal for an agreement [in the European Council], thus, was ingenious: She did clarify that a [rule of law] mechanism only can be regarded as being subordinated to the EU Treaty. (Aust & Volkmann-Schluck, 2020; translation by the author)

Merkel herself had stressed immediately prior to the beginning of the European Council on 10 December 2020 that a negotiation success would amount to a 'very important sign for the European Union's ability to act' (Peel et al., 2020).

CONCLUSION

The final stages of the negotiations on the MFF and on the historical recovery fund NextGenerationEU coincided with Germany holding the rotating Council presidency in the second half of 2020. While there were many obstacles to agreement, as addressed by several chapters in this volume, a central point of contention which nearly led to derailing an agreement among all 27 member states was the rule of law mechanism. The review of events leading up to the December 2020 European Council in the previous section showed that the German government, and notably Chancellor Merkel personally, played a key role in bringing about agreement. The findings show that a central motive for Merkel was to preserve the European Council's ability to reach consensus agreements among all 27 member states, including in this case the challenger governments of Hungary and Poland, which sought to prevent the EU from adopting a conditionality mechanism with the potential to sanction their rule of law violations. For Merkel, the emergence of consensus within the European Council has been synonymous with the EU's ability to act. In this sense her approach to crisis management in 2020 is consistent with her earlier approach to euro crisis decision-making. This confirms intergovernmentalist integration theory: for Merkel, consensus has become an end in itself (Bickerton et al., 2015b, p. 29).

Merkel undoubtedly succeeded in her ambition to bring about agreement between July and December 2020, yet she made key decisions in this context which may impact on the further course of EU development and, most importantly, may be suited to further increasing rather than decreasing tensions surrounding the normative foundations of the EU's post-Maastricht political and legal order, as suggested by the new intergovernmentalist hypothesis of the EU being in disequilibrium (Hodson & Puetter, 2019). In their model of discourse coalitions mobilising around the negotiation of the MFF and the recovery fund, Heinelt and Münch, in Chapter 1, as the editors in this volume, attributed to Germany the role of a member of the so-called rule of law coalition. The evidence provided in the previous section, indeed, suggests that the German government and Merkel were signed up to demand a conditionality mechanism in relation to rule of law violations as a precondition for agreeing on the Union's medium-term and emergency financing. Alongside Merkel, even EPP group leader and lead candidate in the 2019 EP elections, Manfred Weber, had expressed his support for protecting the EU's normative foundations. Moreover, there is little doubt that Merkel personally had misgivings about the policy course pursued by Viktor Orbán as the leader of the EU's most persistent challenger government.

Yet, the notion of a close affiliation of both the German government and Merkel, personally, with the rule of law coalition requires qualification when it comes to tracing the unfolding of negotiations during the German Council presidency in 2020. The findings in the previous section clearly suggest that Merkel prioritised consensus in the European Council over the ambition to devise a novel mechanism to sanction challenger governments in the EU more effectively than through the defunct Article 7 procedure. This line of action is not only consistent with her crisis management approach during the euro crisis but also with an established pattern of interaction between the different governments that Merkel was leading in Germany and the challenger governments of Viktor Orbán in the 2010s and early 2020s. While the two politicians have challenged each other routinely, they equally paid attention to not completely abandoning consensus politics within the European Council. Moreover, partisan politics within Merkel's own transnational centre-right party alliance, the EPP, ensured that Orbán and his Fidesz party were kept on board within the European Council, the Council and the EP in areas which were dependent on consensus decision-making.

The German Council presidency and Merkel were decisive in engineering a consensus agreement, which implies substantial qualifications regarding the future application of the rule of law mechanism. Not only were they successful in leading member states of the so-called rule of law coalition and, notably, the EP majority away from more far-reaching conceptions of the mechanism, but they also succeeded in at least temporarily breaking the veto by Hungary and Poland by diluting the eventual application of the mechanism. In view of the enormous economic and financial consequences of the Covid-19 pandemic, the dispute about the rule of law mechanism may seem a minor issue. Indeed, the decision to enable the release of fresh EU finances can be viewed as part of a series of key crisis management decisions of the European Council and EU institutions to prevent an immediate threat to the Union, notably the financial collapse of one of the EU's biggest economies, Italy. Yet, the negotiation of the seven-year MFF and the recovery fund was a rare opportunity for the Union to counter the creeping process of the erosion of rule of law principles and the EU's overall political and legal order, which is heavily based on mutual trust and functioning member states' democracies. Viewed in this way, the negotiation output did little to interrupt the endurance of Hungary's authoritarian turn (Csehi, 2019), nor to prevent further challenges to the rule of law, to basic freedom and democracy in Poland and other EU member states. Given that the EU's Article 7 procedure remains seriously defunct, the EU remains in disequilibrium. The 10 December 2020 European Council decision prevented the disequilibrium from unravelling but increases rather than decreases tensions surrounding the EU's political and legal foundations.

NOTES

1.   I would like to thank the editors, Robert Csehi, Chiara Terranova and two anonymous reviewers for their comments on drafts of this chapter.
2.   Merkel directly quoted the then European Council President Herman Van Rompuy with the words: 'Often the choice is not between the community method and the intergovernmental method, but between a coordinate European position and nothing at all' (Merkel, 2010).

REFERENCES

Amann, M., & Müller, P. (2019). 'Viktor Orbán Is Following the Wrong Political Path. Interview with EPP Lead Candidate Manfred Weber'. *Der Spiegel*, 1 March (online edition). www.spiegel.de/international/germany/manfred-weber-viktor-orban-is-following-the-wrong-political-path-a-1255779.html (accessed on 5 May 2021).
Aust, S., & Volkmann-Schluck, P. (2020). 'Manfred Weber hat unser ganzes Volk beleidigt'. *Die Welt*, 21 December.
Bickerton, C. J., Hodson, D., & Puetter, U. (2015a). 'The new intergovernmentalism: European integration in the post-Maastricht era'. *Journal of Common Market Studies*, 53(4), 703–722.
Bickerton, C. J., Hodson, D., & Puetter, U. (2015b). 'The new intergovernmentalism and the study of European integration'. In C. Bickerton, D. Hodson, & U. Puetter (eds), *The New Intergovernmentalism. States, Supranational Actors, and European Politics in the Post-Maastricht Era*, Oxford University Press, 1–48.
Brunsden, J. (2017). 'Europe refugee policy is "Trojan horse of terrorism", says Orban'. *Financial Times*, 30 March. www.ft.com/content/538b2a0a-154e-11e7-80f4-13e067d5072c (accessed on 5 May 2021).
Byrne, A., & Buckley, N. (2017). 'Hungary defies German call to accept EU refugee ruling'. *Financial Times*, 13 September.
Chazan, G., & Fleming, S. (2020). 'Merkel urges swift agreement on EU coronavirus recovery plan'. *Financial Times*, 2 July. www.ft.com/content/20930fb0-4322-4e78-a942-272ee3dc98f8 (accessed on 5 May 2021).
Csehi, R. (2019). 'Neither episodic, nor destined to failure? The endurance of Hungarian populism after 2010'. *Democratization*, 26(6), 1011–1027.
Csehi, R. (2022). *The Politics of Populism in Hungary*, Routledge.
Easton, D. (1965). *A Systems Analysis of Political Life*, John Wiley & Sons Ltd.
European Council (2020). 'Conclusions'. www.consilium.europa.eu/media/47296/1011-12-20-euco-conclusions-en.pdf (accessed on 5 May 2021).
Fleming, S., & Khan, M. (2020a). 'EU negotiators strike deal over seven-year budget'. *Financial Times*, 10 November. www.ft.com/content/b33d6c52-7930-4c11-b1e7-13df852b42c7 (accessed on 5 May 2021).
Fleming, S., & Khan, M. (2020b). 'EU scrambles to resolve rule of law stand-off as economy suffers'. *Financial Times*, 20 November. www.ft.com/content/ab29fcd8-26de-4b34-85da-e7790beef1b5 (accessed on 5 May 2021).
Fleming, S., & Khan, M. (2020c). 'EU's budget and recovery package stalls over rule of law spat'. *Financial Times*, 16 November. www.ft.com/content/328ea149-e849-47eb-b53c-61344cfd4bb0 (accessed on 5 May 2021).

Fleming, S., & Khan, M. (2020d). 'Germany tables EU budget offer to break impasse with parliament'. *Financial Times*, 7 October. www.ft.com/content/c8db5629-9d11 -484c-b9dc-ad6673306dc2 (accessed on 5 May 2021).

Fleming, S., & Peel, M. (2020). 'Hungary's Orban demands resignation of EU's rule-of-law chief'. *Financial Times*, 29 September. www.ft.com/content/7f1d03fb -75b9-49d2-8aea-72678b7b1309 (accessed on 5 May 2021).

Fleming, S., Khan, M., & Brunsden, J. (2020a). 'EU leaders remain deadlocked on recovery fund in protracted summit'. *Financial Times*, 19 July. www.ft.com/content/ 4553ea05-189c-44d1-8e9d-08ea4dd6efba (accessed on 5 May 2021).

Fleming, S., Khan, M., & Brunsden, J. (2020b). 'EU leaders strike deal on €750bn recovery fund after marathon summit'. *Financial Times*, 21 July. www.ft.com/ content/713be467-ed19-4663-95ff-66f775af55cc (accessed on 5 May 2021).

Fortuna, G. (2018). 'EPP warns Orbán, but Fidesz still influences the line'. Euractiv. www.euractiv.com/section/eu-elections-2019/news/epp-warned-orban-publicly-but -fidesz-still-influences-the-line/ (accessed on 5 May 2021).

Hodson, D., & Puetter, U. (2019). 'The European Union in disequilibrium. New inter-governmentalism, postfunctionalism and integration theory in the post-Maastricht period'. *Journal of European Public Policy*, 26(8), 1153–1171.

Hodson, D., & Puetter, U. (2022). 'The euro crisis and European integration'. In M. Cini & N. Pérez-Solórzano Borragán (eds), *European Union Politics* (7th edn), Oxford University Press, 373–388.

Hooghe, L., & Marks, G. (2009). 'A postfunctionalist theory of European integration: from permissive consensus to constraining dissensus'. *British Journal of Political Science*, 39(1), 1–23.

Hooghe, L., & Marks, G. (2018). 'Cleavage theory meets Europe's crises: Lipset, Rokkan, and the transnational cleavage'. *Journal of European Public Policy*, 25(1), 109–135.

Kelemen, R. D. (2020). 'The European Union's authoritarian equilibrium'. *Journal of European Public Policy*, 27(3), 481–499.

Khan, M. (2020). 'France to push for rule-of-law sanctions as part of EU recovery plan'. *Financial Times*, 2 August. www.ft.com/content/5e065f7a-0895-402f-881b -067a49336b3b (accessed on 5 May 2021).

Khan, M., & Peel, M. (2020). 'EU reaches deal to suspend funds to member states that breach rule of law'. *Financial Times*, 5 November. www.ft.com/content/523adf3c -0c4a-41a7-9527-20b36b039a99 (accessed on 5 May 2021).

Khan, M., Fleming, S., & Chazan, G. (2020). 'Bitter divisions over the rule of law haunt EU recovery fund talks'. *Financial Times*, 3 July. www.ft.com/content/79843ffa -5ab8-445c-a590-e150f6bbb3dc (accessed on 5 May 2021).

King, T. (2017). 'Ties that bind Hungary's Fidesz and European Parliament'. Politico, 7 April. www.politico.eu/article/ties-that-bind-hungarys-fidesz-and-european -parliament/ (accessed on 5 May 2021).

Kolb, M. (2020). 'Stein vom Herzen'. *Süddeutsche Zeitung*, 12 December.

Lindberg, L. N., & Scheingold, S. A. (1970). *Europe's Would-Be Polity: Patterns of Change in the European Community*, Prentice Hall.

Merkel, A. (2010). *Rede anlässlich der Eröffnung des 61. akademischen Jahres des Europakollegs Brügge*. www.coleurope.eu/file/content/news/Speeches/Rede %20Merkel%20Europakolleg%20Bruegge.pdf (accessed on 5 May 2021).

Merkel, A. (2020). 'Rede von Bundeskanzlerin Merkel zur deutschen EU-Ratspräsidentschaft 2020 vor dem Europäischen Parlament in Brüssel'. www.bundesregierung.de/breg-de/suche/rede-von-bundeskanzlerin-merkel-zur

-deutschen-eu-ratspraesidentschaft-2020-vor-dem-europaeischen-parlament-am-8
-juli-2020-in-bruessel-1767368 (accessed on 5 May 2021).

Moravcsik, A. (2005). 'The European Constitutional Compromise and the neofunction-alist legacy'. *Journal of European Public Policy*, 12(2), 349–386.

Orbán, V. (2014). 'Prime Minister Viktor Orbán's Speech at the 25th Bálványos Summer Free University and Student Camp'. www.kormany.hu/en/the-prime -minister/the-prime-minister-s-speeches/prime-minister-viktor-orban-s-speech-at -the-25th-balvanyos-summer-free-university-and-student-camp (accessed on 5 May 2021).

Peel, M., Khan, M., & Fleming, S. (2020). 'EU countries agree historic €1.8tn budget and recovery package'. *Financial Times*, 11 December. www.ft.com/content/ 03d72613-1745-4520-9ba3-5a94c8a3963f (accessed on 5 May 2021).

Puetter, U. (2012). 'Europe's deliberative intergovernmentalism – the role of the Council and European Council in EU economic governance'. *Journal of European Public Policy*, 19(2), 161–178.

Puetter, U. (2014). *The European Council and the Council. New Intergovernmentalism and Institutional Change*, Oxford University Press.

Puetter, U. (2015). 'Deliberativer Intergouvernementalismus und institutioneller Wandel: die Europäische Union nach der Eurokrise'. *PVS Politische Vierteljahreszeitschrift*, 56(3), 406–531.

Süddeutsche Zeitung (2020). 'EU-Mitgliedstaaten einigen sich auf Finanzpaket'. *Süddeutsche Zeitung*, 10 December. www.sueddeutsche.de/politik/eu-haushalt -rechtsstaatsmechanismus-ungarn-polen-einigung-1.5143429 (accessed on 5 May 2021).

Szczerbiak, A., & Taggart, P. (2008). *Opposing Europe?: The Comparative Party Politics of Euroscepticism, Volume 2: Comparative and Theoretical Perspectives*, Oxford University Press.

Taggart, P., & Szczerbiak, A. (2013). 'Coming in from the cold? Euroscepticism, gov-ernment participation and party positions on Europe'. *JCMS: Journal of Common Market Studies*, 51(1), 17–37.

van Middelaar, L., & Puetter, U. (2021). 'The European Council: the Union's supreme decision-maker'. In D. Hodson, U. Puetter, & S. Saurugger (eds), *The Institutions of the European Union*, Oxford University Press.

11. What do the negotiations about the Multiannual Financial Framework 2021–2027 mean for theories of European integration? Reflections from an actor-centred constructivist perspective

Sabine Saurugger

INTRODUCTION

Among the variety of public policy instruments, budget negotiations are probably considered the most rational and interest-based processes. Hence the question of what negotiations of the Multiannual Financial Framework (MFF) 2021–2027 mean for theories of European integration seems to call for a short and simple answer: rational choice approaches, be they institutionalist or liberal intergovernmentalist should best explain the processes and the outcomes of budget negotiations. Rational choice approaches start from the assumption that actors make their decisions based on an economic cost–benefit analysis, hardly influenced by ideas or cognitive frames.

However, under closer scrutiny, the MFF negotiations for the EU's 2021–2027 budget show signs of both dependency (Ackrill & Adrian, 2006) and innovation (Becker, Chapter 2 in this volume) as well as the influence of cognitive frames, which question a purely cost–benefit reading of the process. On the one hand, we find path dependency in the preferences of member states, which seem relatively fixed. While coherent with their domestic economic situation, these preferences are also influenced by well-established economic ideas independent of the economic conjuncture of the country. Path dependency can also be found in the Commission's suggestion of a set of own resources to improve the EU's financial resources. On the other hand, innovation can be found in the introduction of the 'NextGenerationEU' proposal by the Commission, comprising a temporary €750 billion recovery fund of which

€500 billion should be disbursed as grants and €250 billion as loans. This is a novelty, which some scholars and commentators did not fear to compare to a Madisonian moment in European integration history. Borrowing in order to finance the budget is indeed an entirely novel fiscal instrument in European integration. Once created, it establishes a precedent.

This chapter argues that these elements question a theoretical understanding of MFF negotiations as processes purely based on cost–benefit calculations. While these calculations definitely exist – and hence rational choice approaches offer useful starting points in our understanding of the process (Benedetto, 2013, 2017; Crombez & Høyland, 2015) – taking into account the influence of specific cognitive frames is fundamental in the explanation of both the process and the outcomes of European MFF negotiations.

In order to discuss this issue, the chapter is structured as follows. A second section will present the main issues of the 2021–2027 MFF negotiations, before the third section interprets these elements through two classic rational choice integration theories – liberal intergovernmentalism (LI) and rational choice institutionalism. The fourth section will then present an actor-centred constructivist analysis of the MFF, linking strategic elements with ideational underpinnings in which actors react. This section will argue for the importance of measuring both the influence of path dependency and cognitive frames in the processes and outcomes of the 2021–2027 MFF, which will help us to understand the innovations we find in the new European budget.

THE MULTIANNUAL FINANCIAL FRAMEWORK NEGOTIATIONS IN BRIEF

Described as 'budgetary dramaturgy' (Laffan, 2000, see also Laffan, 1997), the EU's budget negotiations, or officially 'negotiations for the Multiannual Financial Framework (MFF)' are constituted of a series of institutional and political elements that are intrinsically linked. The MFF is the frame for the EU's annual budget negotiations. The process of the MFF negotiation is described as a three-step model, starting with a Commission proposal, followed by Council discussions, and finally, the bargaining stage between the Council of Ministers and the Parliament. Second, as a classic EU bargaining process, the MFF is characterised by coalition building amongst member states as well as between member states and European institutions. Finally, the context in which the MFF takes place is a powerful variable, opening or closing windows of opportunity for policy entrepreneurs, either individual or collective ones.[1] The three-step model of budget negotiations for the 2021–2027 MFF started in 2016 when the European Commission published its mid-term review for the MFF 2014–2020, in which it developed its ideas for better-equipped flexibility instruments (Becker, 2016). In June 2017, the Commission (European

Commission, 2017) discussed key budgetary challenges for the coming years in developing five scenarios, ranging from a drastic reduction of the budget to the continuation of the current system. This scenarios approach is not without similarity to the five presidents' report on the Future of the European Union published in 2017, which sketched out five possibilities for the economic development of the European integration project, and more specifically, its Economic and Monetary Union (EMU). In January 2018, the High-Level Conference on the Future of the European budget, presented 'a new modern long-term budget', adding the idea of a €26 billion fund, outside the financial framework that might be foreseen, for flexibility instruments, specific facilities and reserves – a European Solidarity Fund, a Globalisation Fund and a European Peace facility. At the same time, the proposal foresaw cuts in the budget of the Common Agricultural Policy (CAP) and a rise in the financial instruments of the European border agency, Frontex. On the revenue side, the Commission proposed a basket of own resources to improve the EU's financial resources, such as revenues stemming from the emissions trading system, a new levy on recyclable waste and a consolidated corporate tax (European Commission, 2018a, 2018b).

The Commission proposal was discussed by successive EU presidencies: Bulgaria, Austria (which put a procedural 'negotiating box' in place), Romania and Finland. In 2019, the Finnish presidency handed the negotiations over to the European Council. Charles Michel, the Council president, presented a new negotiation box in February 2020, of both a procedural and substantive nature, including an increase to 1.074 per cent of the 27 gross national incomes (GNI), an additional €7.5 billion for the new Just Transition Fund proposed by the European Commission (European Commission, 2020a), and digressive rebates for several member states. The third stage, negotiations between the Council of Ministers and the European Parliament took place in two stages – from February to May 2020, ending with a new Commission proposal which foresaw, under the name 'NextGenerationEU', a new framework for the 2021–2027 MFF (European Commission, 2020b, 2020c); this took up an idea initially developed by the Italian government, supported by the French, and transformed it into a Franco-German proposal (Howarth & Schild, 2021). The Commission foresaw in its proposal an increase of the budget to €1.1 trillion, complemented by an additional €750 billion recovery fund, of which €500 billion should be disbursed as grants and €250 billion as loans.

A discussion between the President of the European Commission, the President of the European Parliament and the chair of the rotating Council Presidency on 29 July 2020 aimed at preparing the next steps in the adoption of the Recovery Plan for Europe. More precisely, it elaborated the terms of the interinstitutional negotiations based on the political agreement reached by the European Council and the Resolution subsequently adopted by the Parliament.

The first trilogue talks were held on 27 August 2020, followed by a second meeting on 7 September and a third on 11 September. It was during these meetings that the conditionality attached to respecting the rule of law, focusing on the Hungarian and Polish governments' breaches of the rule of law, became one of the main issues of the negotiations.

Negotiations continued into October and November, with co-legislators stuck on the rule of law matter. By the end of October, the Parliament put forward a so-called breakthrough proposal, which aimed at bridging the gap between the two sides. Only on 5 November, however, was a political agreement reached on a proposed rule of law mechanism aimed at safeguarding the EU budget. An informal agreement between the co-legislators was reached on the financial package comprising the MFF and the Recovery Plan for Europe on 10 November. Six days later, Hungarian and Polish representatives refused to endorse the informal agreement reached the previous week due to the rule of law mechanism; they were later joined by Slovenia in that opposition. Heated negotiations took place between, on one side, Hungary, Poland and Slovenia, and on the other, the other 24 member states, the former calling for changes to the rule of law mechanism. On 17 December 2020, the Council of the European Union adopted the final version of the 2021–2027 MFF.

The negotiations of the MFF were structured, typically, through member state positions as well as Commission proposals. More specifically, five factions were particularly salient: the European Commission's positions including most prominently its own resources proposals and the NextGenerationEU, the two member state coalitions – 'Friends of Cohesion' opposed to any cuts in the CAP and cohesion fund, and the 'Frugal Four' (Sweden, Denmark, the Netherlands and Austria) asking for rebates and calling for spending control[2] – the Franco-German coalition (with the European Commission's support) and the European Parliament.

Finally, however, the element of context in which the negotiations took place reveals a crucial aspect of MFF negotiations. The COVID-19 pandemic becoming salient in March 2020 took everyone by surprise. Initially, the Italian government's call for 'corona bonds' (which aim to finance the debt that states are accumulating in the COVID-19 health crisis by resorting to a large loan) was rejected, despite the fact that it received support from the French government. The Franco-German coalition split over this issue before launching a new intense coordination phase (Crespy & Schramm, 2021; Howarth & Schild, 2021; Krotz & Schramm, 2022). This led to one of the most surprising proposals in the past history of European integration, not only supported but promoted by the German government: a large-scale post-COVID-19 recovery fund, an idea taken up by the Commission. The NextGenerationEU and its key component, the Recovery and Resilience Facility, were adopted in July 2020 by an EU-wide agreement. The experience of the economic crisis and its management, characterised by the establishment of new European institutions, in particular in the field of banking supervision, in which an important degree of supranationalisation took place (Busuioc, 2013), represents another contextual frame illustrating the path dependency necessary to analyse the process of MFF negotiations. Parallel to the institutional developments, the issue of environmental policies became ever more salient. The global 'Fridays for Future' movements, coupled with the alarming annual reports by the Intergovernmental Panel on Climate Change (IPCC), Conference of the Parties (COP) meetings and the significant success of Green parties during the EP elections in 2019 made it difficult, if not impossible, for European decision-makers to ignore the demands for the creation of more efficient policy instruments in favour of environmental protection. This was particularly visible in the programme presented by the new Commission President Ursula von der Leyen, in which environmental protection plays a crucial role (see Bornemann, Chapter 7 in this volume; Ferrera et al., 2021). This element is important also in the context of the compromises found with the European Parliament. In addition to environmental protection, rule of law issues, in particular with regard to laws that question judicial and media independence (in Poland or Hungary) or do not protect the political system in question from bribery and corruption (such as in Romania and Bulgaria) intervened in the MFF negotiations. Last but not least, the outbreak of the COVID-19 pandemic in February 2020 influenced the MFF negotiations considerably, with the pandemic's potential repercussions not only for the health of European citizens but also for the economic system due to lockdown situations and financial means made available by member state governments to support temporary unemployment and lockdown measures (Armingeon et al., 2021; Bongardt & Torres, 2021).

CLASSIC INTEGRATION THEORIES AND BUDGET NEGOTIATIONS

Conventional wisdom has it that budget negotiations are rational preference-based processes. Agreeing on how much money will be spent on which issues is a question of bargaining, based on carefully prepared positions. These positions might be based on on-the-spot cost–benefit calculations, influenced by domestic groups or the wish to reduce transaction costs. Theoretically speaking, these arguments can be found in liberal intergovernmental or rational choice institutionalist explanations.

Liberal Intergovernmentalism

Liberal intergovernmentalism explains the politics of budget negotiations as the interaction of national preferences, governmental bargaining power and institutional choices designed to commit EU member states to a six-year budget cycle, in line with its general three-step model (Moravcsik, 1998; Schimmelfennig, 2015). According to liberal intergovernmentalism, domestic preference formation more specifically leads to interstate bargaining and, finally, to supranational institution building according to the principal–agent model.

Liberal intergovernmentalism convincingly explains, on the one hand, the role of interstate bargaining as the main decision-making mode in producing a new budget, and on the other hand, why member states prefer to agree on a budget based on multiple compromises, instead of accepting negotiation failure and ultimately the obligation to continue future budget cycles based on past budgetary agreements. A common budget is the most effective means to reduce transaction costs.

The first step in liberal intergovernmentalism is to explain how national preferences are established on a specific issue. Hence liberal intergovernmentalism, in acknowledging the influence of domestic politics, argues that the preferences of governments on European integration result from a domestic process of preference formation. These preferences are based on national economic interests. Liberal intergovernmentalism distinguishes between organised interests (economic interest groups) and diffuse interests (public opinion), arguing that the more institutionally represented and organised they are, the more influence they have. Diffuse interests, on the contrary, are more likely to lead to the prevalence of ideological preferences (Moravcsik & Nicolaïdis, 1998; Schimmelfennig, 2015). Once defined, preferences are supposed to remain stable throughout negotiations (Moravscik & Schimmelfennig, 2009). As a consequence, liberal intergovernmentalism does not take into account feedback loops, such as the influence of EU-level debates on national preferences during the negotiation. We observe, however, empirically, that domestic preferences in intergovernmental bargaining processes are indeed influenced by negotiations at the EU level. Since European integration has become an issue for domestic politics, since the end of the so-called permissive consensus, there is an adaptation of negotiations from the domestic level to the EU level. This, on the one hand, does not allow for considering preferences as fixed or stable, and on the other, blurs the distinction between economic and identity-based preferences. Utilitarian concerns about the EU's institutional effectiveness and benefits of integration, including financial issues as well as economic solidarity, have increased amongst the general public, as Hobolt and Tilley (2014), Hobolt and Wratil (2015), and Kriesi and Grande (2015), have shown (see also Saurugger, 2016).

This challenges, however, one of the main assumptions of liberal intergovernmentalists, which argues that preferences remain stable. We observe indeed a relative stability in most member states' preferences during the MFF negotiations (the preferences of the Frugal Four as well as those of the 'Friends of Cohesion' are indeed stable and long-standing constructions), as well as those of institutions such as the Commission (the increase in the Commission's own resources is a long-standing demand). Germany's position, particularly in the context of the Franco-German coalition, however, is more difficult to explain through the idea of stable preferences. Indeed, the German government had rejected the idea of the creation of a common debt issuance with joint liability during the economic and financial crisis that started in 2008 (Eurobonds), and it did the same when the Italian government suggested the creation of 'corona bonds'. The ultimate German agreement to the creation of a common debt issuance, despite the fact that it was elaborately defended by the German Chancellor Angela Merkel as a transitory agreement, or one-of-a-kind that will not be repeated, potentially questions this stable preference. The explanation for this preference change seems to come less from the pressure stemming from the domestic level, but in the renewed cooperation of the Franco-German coalition. Hence, through the interaction with its French counterpart, the German government, and more precisely Angela Merkel, surprised the EU partners by openly defending the idea of European financial solidarity. While during the euro crisis, the national mood composed of public opinion and economic voting, inter- and intra-party competition and the parliamentary arena (Târlea et al., 2019) remained true to the ordoliberal understanding of economic answers based on spending control guaranteed by the state, this understanding changed in 2020, and hence seemed to lead to a change in preferences. Through intense cooperation, which the Franco-German coalition is wont to launch very rapidly through a long-standing institutional structure, as well as through the debates that took place inside the Council and the Council of Ministers (Kassim et al., 2020; Puetter, 2021), the German government position had changed. Howarth and Schild (2021, pp. 218–219) argue indeed that during the negotiations for the 2021–2027 MFF, the German government broke

> two taboos. First it advocated grants in addition to loans in favour of member states most hit by the economic impact of the crisis. Second, it proposed that these grants should be financed by allowing the Commission to borrow massively on financial markets on behalf of the EU, creating thus a joint liability for debts.

The reasons for this can be found, for some authors, in the 'unwavering German commitment' to European integration (Howarth & Schild 2021, p. 222) as well as domestic events such as the German Federal Constitutional Court (FCC) Public Sector Purchase Programme (PSPP) judgment of 5 May 2020. The FCC declared the Court of Justice of the EU's ruling legitimising the ECB's PSPP ultra vires. In other words, the FCC argued that this CJEU judgment went beyond the European Court's competences (see Saurugger and Terpan, 2020). Simon Bulmer (2022, p. 178) argues that the judgment reinforced the view amongst German politicians that politics should not be left to unelected bodies but that elected representatives should get involved in macroeconomic policies through budget decisions. The central German preference for European integration is so significant that the government accepted extraordinary fiscal capacity building of a temporary nature.

The second incident of the MFF negotiations, concerning the rule of law conditionality, was another challenge for liberal intergovernmentalism, albeit a lesser one. The Hungarian and Polish agreement to the MFF was only secured after these governments had been assured that the conditionality regime to protect the EU budget through a direct linkage to the rule of law had been significantly watered down. Instead of an automatic application of financial sanctions in the case of a breach of the rule of law in a member state, the Commission was authorised to start the procedure that could lead to sanctions such as the suspension of payments or a non-disbursement of loans. Here, liberal intergovernmentalism is clearly useful to illustrate that member state vetoes in case of non-attainment of national preferences remain a powerful tool in negotiations based on unanimity and only consensus seeking will allow the reaching of a conclusion that opens up possibilities for a decrease in transaction costs; in this case, the conclusion of the MFF and the Recovery Fund.

Rational Choice Institutionalism

Rational choice institutionalism explains the process and the outcome of the MFF negotiations based on the idea that cooperation, and the subsequent establishment of institutions, decrease transaction costs. The framework originated in analyses of decision-making processes in the USA's Congress, where political choices were unstable and wavered according to different majorities (McKelvey, 1976; Riker, 1980). However, in certain circumstances, Congress was capable of forming stable majorities around certain public policies (Shepsle, 1979). The main variable explaining the emergence of these equilibria was a system of committees producing a structure-induced equilibrium by authorising or, conversely, blocking, certain political options (Moe, 1984; Shepsle & Weingast, 1984).

On the basis of this research, two influential models emerged: the principal–agent model showing that, under certain circumstances, Congress delegates powers to independent bureaucratic authorities (Moe, 1984), and the transaction-cost model showing that institutions reduce costs that emerge in any typical transaction between actors (Epstein & O'Halloran, 1999).

Scholars in European studies seek primarily to understand why national governments consent to abandon or at least share their sovereignty at supranational level by creating supranational institutions. While this question is also prominent in liberal intergovernmentalism, rational choice approaches are less interested in the other two steps leading to European integration: neither in the reasons for domestic preference formation – these are taken as given – nor in the details of the bargaining process amongst actors. In the context of our research on the MFF, rational choice approaches seek to understand why member states as a unified collective principal decide on a budget and delegates its implementation to an agent, putting in place a series of control mechanisms (Dijkstra, 2017). The central assumption here is that state actors rationally pursue their own interests while transferring competencies to institutions. States understand perfectly well that the *ex post* control of these institutions can be problematic. They nevertheless transfer competencies to the European level. Why? Because institutions help to decrease the uncertainty linked to the imperfect division of power between competing European actors. Furthermore, delegating powers to supranational institutions helps to reduce transaction costs involved in the decision-making process. States agree to act according to international agreements they have signed and benefit to this end from the expertise of supranational actors.

In exchange for delegating competencies, these supranational bodies provide the states with control instruments to implement policies decided at European level. However, if the rules of implementation are not respected, the European Commission refers cases to the European Court of Justice. Thus, *principals*, meaning the states, accept being controlled by *agents* – the Commission and the European Court of Justice – to ensure that implementation is equally applied to all member states.

When adopting this theoretical understanding in the analysis of MFF negotiations and outcomes, we would argue that member state preferences for fiscal capacity building, that is, the creation of both an MFF and the more specific tool of the NextGenerationEU, will only last as long as state elites perceive the costs of fiscal capacity building to be lower than the costs of non-action. In more general terms, when the costs become higher than the benefits, member state governments will not further pursue the establishment of institutions such as the budgetary instruments, like NextGenerationEU.

Formulated as such, we would believe that MFFs are solely dependent on the preference of member states and the costs of capacity building. MFF negotiations are, on the contrary, embedded in a very strict institutional setting. Budget negotiations do indeed leave room for manoeuvre but are designed in such a strict manner that a no-deal brings European integration to a standstill. The question of why member states, and particularly the German government, agreed to a large-scale recovery plan in the first place is not answered by this analysis. It can be explained by a path dependency frame combined with a cognitive framework approach, which will be developed later in the chapter. This conceptual combination allows us to understand the institutional constructions as a consequence of the economic and financial crisis from 2008 to 2012, which opened up a possibility to frame institutional answers to crisis situations, such as the economic crisis triggered anew by the COVID-19 pandemic.

Rational choice institutionalism focusing on institution building in order to decrease transaction costs is a particularly useful tool in structuring the analysis of the compromise found with Hungary and Poland. In putting forward the idea to go forward with 25 member states, thus without Poland and Hungary, the French and German governments signalled their willingness to move ahead and to establish the recovery fund on a supranational basis (Krotz & Schramm, 2022). This strategy made it ultimately possible to transfer the management of potential breaches of rule of law to the Commission, the EU's supranational institution, in order to ensure that all member states comply with the rule that has been decided and hence reduce the transactions costs that would have arisen if the agreement had remained intergovernmental.

The two rational choice approaches to European integration thus explain large parts of MFF negotiations and particularly the outcome of those negotiations. Scholars share overall the conviction that despite the agreement leading to a common budget and the Recovery Fund, deep divisions remain among member states on the future of fiscal politics. France and Germany, despite having been pivotal to the agreements, remain divided regarding their economic preferences (Krotz & Schramm, 2022, p. 14). While the French government wished for the creation of a permanent recovery fund, thus creating the possibility of EU indebtedness, the German government rejected the idea of common debts and the establishment of a permanent direct financial transfer instrument at the EU level.

In these circumstances, what can the constructivist approaches that are at the heart of this edited volume add to our understanding of budgetary decision-making processes in the EU?

OVERCOMING BLIND SPOTS BY COMBINING CONSTRUCTIVISM AND STRATEGIC THINKING

Constructivist approaches have shed new light onto policymaking in the EU in insisting on the embeddedness of actors in construction of problems and solutions, socialisation of agents through interaction and the influence of specific cognitive frames of actors in policymaking processes more generally. As we have seen, however, budgetary negotiations are strongly preference-based and seem to leave little space for constructivist or critical theories to explain negotiation outcomes. At the same time, an understanding based purely on rational choices does not include the underlying reasons for these preferences. Policy actors are constantly embedded in cognitive frames, which guide their actions and define their preferences. Ideational factors frame the understanding of material factors, or in other words allow an 'intellectual topography of ideational explanations' (Gofas & Hay, 2010, p. 3). These ideational factors shed light on the influence of 'worldviews', mechanisms of identity formation, and principles of action in public policy analysis (Hall, 1993; McNamara, 1998; Surel, 2000; Blyth, 2002; Parsons 2002; Jabko, 2006).

Concentrating on embeddedness, socialisation and cognitive frames, however, leads to a situation where individuals are sometimes implicitly perceived as passive, and not as active beings who, through strategic action, coalition building and power politics can change outcomes. While constructivism, according to which the understanding of situations is always mediated by ideas and worldviews, is shedding light on one aspect of individual action, it is the way these ideas, worldviews or more generally cognitive frames are used that will allow us to understand the entire policy and political process. In other words, 'political actors use narrative story lines and symbolic devices to manipulate so-called issue characteristics, all the while making it seem as though they are simply describing facts' (Stone, 1989, p. 282).

Hence, actor-centred or strategic constructivism helps us to understand actors' usages of ideas and worldviews in budget negotiations. They emphasise the importance of taking into account how and why specific actors use these ideas (see Saurugger, 2013). The central question to which the so-called actor-centred constructivism seeks to find an answer is to understand how precisely ideas and cognitive frames count in policy outcomes and why they count at specific times and not at others. Mark Blyth argues in this respect that constructivist perspectives have for too long opposed interests, preferences and ideas and considered them to be radically different and unrelated concepts (Blyth, 2002; see also McNamara, 2006).

Ideas, Belief Systems and Cognitive Frames

How do ideas frame preferences, then, and how can one understand the practices of actors and, more generally, the policymaking process as a whole? When and why, for example, does the German government agree to a recovery fund included in the MFF being based on loans, hence creating a de facto financial solidarity, which was so forcefully resisted during the previous negotiations to solve the economic and financial crisis? Why, on the other hand, did the Hungarian and Polish governments agree to the compromise in which the rule of law was included in the MFF? These questions lead to identifying the agents who pay attention to certain ideas and not to others, as well as the reasons why certain decisions are made at a specific point in time and not at another (Zahariadis, 2008).

Actor-centred constructivism considers ideas, worldviews and cognitive frames as malleable objects – they can be used for strategic purposes. The purely rhetorical use of these notions underestimates the forms of mobilisation and instrumentalisation to which these frames have been subject (Surel, 2000). While strategies are indeed socially constructed, in order to have an impact, actors must create broad coalitions around common strategies to carry out major reforms.

Actor-centred constructivist perspectives are particularly prominent in the field of European political economy approaches (Saurugger, 2013) and might therefore be of particular use in the analysis of budget negotiations. The main question in this context refers to the reasons explaining why and how a convergence of beliefs or ideas around economic and political solutions to specific European problems has emerged (Hall, 1993; Berman, 1998; McNamara, 1998, 2006; Blyth, 2002; Parsons, 2002; Jabko, 2006, 2010; Woll, 2008; Abdelal et al., 2010; Meyer & Strickman, 2011; Clift & Woll, 2012).

These scholars agree that the actors' understanding of economic, political and social challenges, their interpretation and their analysis, is filtered by cultural and ideational structures in which political actors operate. In order to be visible, ideas can both serve the interest of the dominant actors by strengthening their position in the game (Hall, 1993; McNamara, 1998; Parsons, 2002; Béland, 2009), or be used quite independently from the position of the actors themselves, and hence could refer to a truth-seeking endeavour (Blyth, 2002; Jabko, 2006).

Cognitive Frames and Coalitions in MFF Negotiations

What we observed during the MFF negotiations was precisely that: the creation of six different factions, based on individual actors with specific preferences but reunited around specific common ideas.

First, the European Commission, on the one hand, was arguing according to a long-standing Commission cognitive frame existing in its midst, its 'own resources' proposal. On the other hand, the new Commission presidency was defending, from 2019 onwards, as a reaction to the success of the Green parties at the European Parliamentary elections, the NextGenerationEU proposal, proposing green investment and economic recovery linked to the institutional answer to the COVID-19 crisis. Second, the member states regrouped in the 'Friends of Cohesion' coalition, opposed to cuts to the funding of the Common Agricultural Policy and the Cohesion Fund. A third group brought together four member states known as the 'Frugal Four', opposed to spending increases and defending strict budget control, composed of Sweden, Denmark, the Netherlands and Austria. Fourth, the Franco-German coalition, supported by the Commission, formed a coalition late during the negotiations; and fifth, the

European Parliament. A final, sixth group, was formed when the rule of law conditions were introduced into the MFF negotiations – the Hungarian, Polish and, for a short time, Slovenian governments.

These different factions opposed each other during the negotiations. The successful action of the Franco-German coalition, supported by the Commission, which was the result of leaving opposing preferences behind and agreeing to create a common financial transfer instrument – the Recovery Fund – created a strong pull factor that could be adopted by all 27 member states, even those whose preferences were initially opposed to this idea.

However, the difficulty of showing the empirical influence of ideas remains. Sometimes the beliefs of actors guide their actions and sometimes perceived beliefs only rationalise strategies that can be chosen for other reasons. Empirically distinguishing between the two situations remains difficult (Parsons, 2002).

To solve this problem, actor-centred constructivism argues that, in order to observe the influence of ideas, it is crucial to consider the agenda setting power of the actor in question (Parsons, 2002; Jabko, 2006). The issue, however, is not only one of power relations. In order to have influence, an idea must be shared by a coalition of actors.

This approach helps us to understand through which mechanism two phenomena occurred: on the one hand, the establishment of the Recovery Fund, based on loans, to address the challenges of the pandemic and on the other, the environmental framing of the Recovery Fund and the MFF in general.

Coalition Building through Agenda Setting Powers: The Recovery Fund and the Environment

The Recovery Fund is based on a Franco-German plan to create a fund financed through common debts and allocated in grants to the regions worst hit by the coronavirus. While the German government consistently rejected the creation of a common debt instrument during the economic and financial crisis starting in 2008 (the so-called Eurobonds idea), it approved this idea in May 2020 (Crespy & Schramm, 2021; Howarth & Schild, 2021; Krotz & Schramm, 2022). Initial assessments of the situation created deep divisions amongst member states. The German government, consistent with its earlier positions, initially rejected the idea of a collective debt issuance. This preference for caution was shared throughout the political spectrum, as Howarth and Schild (2021) show in their analysis of Bundestag debates, where party members of all major parties presented in the Bundestag rejected the idea of common debt bonds. In 2020, though, this preference changed. Crespy and Schramm (2021, p. 17) show how the perception and framing by political elites served to construct the very nature of the crisis as one requiring a common European response based on solidarity. The Recovery Fund became an instrument of action. The crisis became a public health issue, not involving any responsibility of or wrongdoing by other European actors. Following this preference change, a Franco-German coalition became possible. The fact that the French and German governments did agree on the common plan made it possible for the other coalitions – the 'Frugal Four' as well as the 'Friends of Cohesion' – to agree to the Recovery Fund, despite deep divisions in their initial preferences. The German government also agreed to empower the Commission with the management of the disbursement of grants and loans, departing from its long-standing position in favour of strict intergovernmental control of the disbursement of funds and conditionality (ibid.). The reasons for the agreement are a combination of ideational factors, national public mood and EU-level political bargains (see also Kleine & Pollack, 2018).

To what extent did ordoliberal ideas influence these preferences? Howarth and Schild (2021) argue that while ordoliberalism remained an important ideational source of German preference formation during the Eurozone crisis (see Matthijs, 2016; Schäfer, 2016), this influence seemed to have been less predominant in the case of the Recovery Fund, which made the coalition with the French government and the European Commission possible. Hence, according to Howarth and Schild (2021), none of the three assumptions linked to the ordoliberal argument can be entirely observed in the Recovery Fund decision: first, while a strong preference remains for a rules-based system and hence an emphasis on regulating national fiscal policies, the support for pandemic-impacted regions trumps strict spending control. Second, while policymakers influenced by ordoliberal ideas should stress moral hazard concerns, Angela Merkel did not. Third, ordoliberal ideas should shape material cost–benefit calculations, and most importantly, their time horizon. In this understanding, the German government's response to the creation of a recovery fund can be seen as an exceptional policy position contrary to German economic traditions.

The second innovation of the MFF negotiations is the prominent inclusion of the fight against climate change and in favour of an energy transition in the MFF. The new European Commission under Commission President Ursula von der Leyen turned the fight against climate change into one of the core policies for the European Commission, partly in response to the high score the Green party group achieved in the 2019 European Parliamentary elections. Policies focusing on energy transition and the fight against climate change were at the heart of the Green Deal the European Commission presented in December 2020. During the European Council of 17–21 July 2021, Council President Charles Michel and Ursula von der Leyen insisted on the link between the Green Deal, the EU's long-term economic strategy and the Recovery Plan. The resulting Recovery Plan foresees that 30 per cent of the NextGenerationEU's financial support must focus on ecological transition policies and projects, an amount of €550 billion over the 2021–2027 period. Amongst those policies, digitalisation and green transition are central elements to be implemented. The idea of fighting climate change is shared by an extremely large number of member states and was reinforced through the EP election results and also those of national parliaments. This made it even more possible to include it centrally not only in the MFF, where the fight against climate change has been included under the heading of environmental mainstreaming since the 1980s, but also in the Recovery Plan, which is establishing the rules for spending the budget for the next generation of Europeans.

This analysis shows the capacities of an actor-centred constructivist approach, not as a conceptual framework replacing the rational approaches to the study of budgetary negotiations, but as a necessary enlargement of those. It allows for focusing, on the one hand, on who the carriers of ideas and norms are and, on the other, how their power relations shape the policy outcomes under scrutiny. Economically rationalist thinking is brought back into the analysis and linked to the use actors make of these ideas. Agents are purposeful actors, embedded in ideational structures, which they use according to their interests. Hence policies are not simply a translation of beliefs or cognitive frames. The translation requires the exercise of power, and we therefore need to understand how power is distributed amongst policy actors.

Complexity and Legitimation

As I have argued elsewhere (Saurugger, 2013), actor-centred constructivism allows us to deal particularly well with two structural issues of EU policymaking that we can find in EU budgetary policymaking too: on the one hand, the complexity of policymaking processes and, on the other, legitimation issues.

The combination of a constructivist and rationalist research design makes actor-centred or 'strategic' constructivist perspectives particularly interesting in public policy studies aimed at explaining a multilevel system such as the EU. As in public policy generally, actors often lack a clear and well-articulated set of preferences in policy processes, and have contradictory preferences, which are embedded in specific values and belief systems.

While these characteristics are central elements in the analysis of the *complexity* of contemporary societies in general, the notion of complexity seen by actor-centred constructivists goes beyond the difference in positions or interests. While these differences undoubtedly exist, these scholars question the origin of these differences and find them in different belief systems of actors. Agents evolve in different subsystems at the same time and their interests are therefore influenced by a multitude of values and ideas. All constructivist perspectives seem at first sight particularly apt to address the problems of issue complexity that arise in contemporary systems of governance, and more particularly in the EU, because they aim at uncovering rather than assuming material rationality of policy agents in their research. Actor-centred constructivists, however, have allowed for reintroducing tools that address the question of why, under certain circumstances, some policy solutions win, whereas others lose. These scholars argue that higher institutional complexity, which we observe in budgetary negotiations, gives rise to potential conflict, in which a high number of actors with overlapping and often conflicting competencies increase the possibility of power struggles for control of agendas and resources. Actor-centred constructivists insist on the fact that ideas, belief systems and norms do not exist independently from the users of these ideas and the institutional conditions in which they are embedded. Interests defended in budgetary negotiation, whilst economically rational, are equally informed by the worldviews in which they are embedded.

Beyond the treatment of the complexity of social systems, actor-centred constructivist approaches are equally useful to explain *legitimation* strategies that actors pursue in policymaking processes, as they foreground power struggles amongst actors in their analysis (Blyth, 1997). This very clearly is an issue in budget negotiations where questions of power struggles between different national governments, institutions and belief systems, including solidarity questions, structure the debates. Constructivist public policy approaches have addressed this issue, as we have seen above, but they have often done so implicitly. This is important for public policy studies in the EU, as in both political and academic debates the question of legitimate and accountable governance in the European Union remains a central feature.

This conceptualisation does in no way exclude behaviour based on cost–benefit analysis. However, this attitude only occurs when actors have chosen the instruments available to them in order to pursue a specific objective. Again, and this seems somewhat circular, these objectives, however, are influenced through the cognitive and normative frames available to them. More precisely, negotiating a budget is about priorities on which the money should be spent, and these priorities depend, on the one hand, on factual necessities but, on the other hand, on decisions about which of these multiple necessities take priority and why. These norms or cognitive frames are not homogeneous amongst actors, either within a particular member state or amongst member states. Conflict amongst actors negotiating within these frames occurs constantly. The regulation of these conflicts allows us to explain why positions change.

Seen under this light, legitimacy thus is no longer an absolute value but must be understood in the light of a permanent framing process in which different ideas about legitimacy confront each other, as this chapter has pointed out earlier.

Finally, budget negotiations are not a one-time game, but a repetitive one. Patz and Goetz (2019) underline that, through budgeting, delegation contracts are routinely and regularly re-negotiated. In this understanding, MFF negotiations are not a single event, but an organisational routine that is indeed based on preferences and positions influenced by cognitive frames as much as it is on the application of a sense of a standard operating procedure. This is crucial when applying a rational choice model in the analysis of budget negotiations, as it must include an element of repetition amongst actors' interactions.

CONCLUSION

We have seen that the Multiannual Financial Framework negotiations are particularly prominently studied through rational choice approaches such as liberal intergovernmentalism or rational choice institutionalism. In the European Union, the financial bargaining amongst member state governments leading to a multiannual budget is well understood in the analysis of member states' economic and financial preferences. However, several puzzles remained: the greening of the MFF; the agreement of the German government to a financial solidarity principle; and the retreat of the Polish and Hungarian veto against the rule of law conditionality. These outcomes can be explained through a combination of rational choice approaches and an actor-centred constructivist approach. Financial negotiations are about financial and economic preferences. But these preferences and positions change through interaction, coalition building and cognitive framing, all of which can be used strategically.

The Franco-German coalition's defence of a recovery fund based on loans and grants was made possible because the German government broke with its former opposition to fiscal solidarity in the European Union, through a framing process amongst the elite, and based on the public mood, arguing that a response to the crisis needed a European solidarity instrument. Whether this is a permanent or temporary preference change remains to be seen.

Finally, the fight against climate change becoming the central element of the MFF and subsequently the Recovery Fund is strongly influenced by a common reading of climate change as a major challenge for future generations. Hence while all member state and institutional positions during the MFF negotiations were based on cost–benefit calculations, the origin of these preferences and the change in these positions can be explained by an actor-centred constructivist approach.

The 2020–2027 MFF negotiations did not fundamentally challenge cost–benefit analysis, or at least, no more than previous negotiations. But a number of puzzling features made it necessary to reach out to an approach that not only includes strategic thinking but also the embeddedness of ideals.

NOTES

1. For details of the three-step model of budget negotiations for the 2021-2027 MFF, see Becker, Chapter 2, and Heinelt & Münch, Chapter 1, both in this volume.
2. For a more detailed analysis of different discourse coalitions among member states' governments formed during the MMF negotiations, see Heinelt & Münch, Chapter 1 in this volume.

REFERENCES

Abdelal R., Blyth, M., & Parsons, C. (2010). *Constructing the International Economy*, Ithaca, NY: Cornell University Press.

Ackrill, R., & Adrian, K. (2006). 'Historical-institutionalist perspectives on the development of the EU budget system'. *Journal of European Public Policy*, 13(1), 113–133.

Armingeon, K., de la Porte, C., Heins, E., & Sacchi, S. (2021). 'Voices from the past: economic and political vulnerabilities in the making of NextGenerationEU'. *Comparative European Politics*, 20, 144–165.

Becker, P. (2016). 'The EU budget's mid-term review. With its promising reform proposals, the Commission lays the groundwork for the next, post-2020 budget'. SWP Comments, 2016/C 48, November.

Béland, D. (2009). 'Ideas, institutions, and policy change'. *Journal of European Public Policy*, 16(5), 701–718.

Benedetto, G. (2013). 'The EU budget after Lisbon: rigidity and reduced spending?' *Journal of Public Policy*, 33(3), 345–369.

Benedetto, G. (2017). 'Institutions and the route to reform of the European Union's budget revenue, 1970–2017'. *Empirica*, 44(4), 615–633.

Berman, S. (1998). *The Primacy of Politics: Social Democracy and the Making of Europe's Twentieth Century*, Cambridge: Cambridge University Press.

Blyth, M. (1997). '"Any more bright ideas?" The ideational turn in comparative political economy'. *Comparative Politics*, 29(2), 229–250.

Blyth, M. (2002). *The Great Transformation: Economic Ideas and Institutional Change in the 20th Century*, Cambridge: Cambridge University Press.

Bongardt, A., & Torres, F. (2021). 'The European Green Deal: More than an exit strategy to the pandemic crisis, a building block of a sustainable European economic model'. *JCMS: Journal of Common Market Studies*, 60(1), 170–185.

Bulmer, S. (2022). 'Germany, the Eurozone crisis and the Covid-19 pandemic: Failing forward or moving on?' *Comparative European Politics*, 20, 166–183, https://doi.org/10.1057/s41295-022-00278-5.

Busuioc, M. (2013). *European Agencies: Law and Practices of Accountability*, Oxford University Press.

Clift, B., & Woll, C. (2012). 'Economic patriotism: reinventing control over open markets'. *Journal of European Public Policy*, 19(3), 307–323.

Crespy, A., & Schramm, L. (2021). 'Breaking the budgetary taboo: German preference formation in the EU's response to the Covid-19 crisis'. *German Politics*, https://doi.org/10.1080/09644008.2021.2020253.

Crombez C., & Høyland, B. (2015). 'The budgetary procedure in the European Union and the implications of the Treaty of Lisbon'. *European Union Politics*, 16(1), 67–89.

Dijkstra, H. (2017). 'Collusion in international organizations: how states benefit from the authority of secretariats'. *Global Governance*, 23, 601.

Epstein, D., & O'Halloran, S. (1999). *A Transaction Cost Politics Approach to Policy Making Under Separate Powers*, Cambridge: Cambridge University Press.

European Commission (2017). 'Reflection Paper on the Future of EU Finances', COM(2017)358, 28, Brussels, 7 June 2017.

European Commission (2018a). 'A new, modern Multiannual Financial Framework for a European Union that delivers efficiently on its priorities post-2020. The European Commission's contribution to the Informal Leaders' meeting on 23 February 2018', COM(2018) 98 final, Brussels, 14 February 2018.

European Commission (2018b). 'A modern budget for a Union that protects, strengthens and defends. Multiannual Financial Framework 2021–2027', COM(2018)321 final, Brussels, 2 May 2018.

European Commission (2020a). 'Proposal for a Regulation of the European Parliament and of the Council establishing the Just Transition Fund', COM (2020) 22 final, Brussels, 14 January 2020.

European Commission (2020b). 'The EU budget powering the Recovery Plan for Europe', COM(2020) 442 final, Brussels, 27 May 2020.

European Commission (2020c). 'Europe's moment: Repair and Prepare for the Next Generation', COM(2020) 456 final, Brussels, 27 May 2020.

Ferrera, M., Miró, J., & Ronchi, S. (2021). 'Walking the road together? EU polity maintenance during the COVID-19 crisis'. *West European Politics*, 44(5–6), 1329–1352.

Gofas, A., & Hay, C. (2010). 'The ideational turn and the persistence of perennial dualisms'. In A. Gofas & C. Hay (eds), *The Role of Ideas in Political Analysis: A Portrait of Contemporary Debates*, London: Routledge, 3–10.

Hall, P. A. (1993). 'Policy paradigms, social learning, and the state: the case of economic policymaking in Britain'. *Comparative Politics*, 25(3), 275–296.

Hobolt, S. B., & Tilley, J. (2014). *Blaming Europe? Responsibility without Accountability in the European Union*, Oxford: Oxford University Press.

Hobolt, S. B., & Wratil, C. (2015). 'Public opinion and the crisis: the dynamics of support for the euro'. *Journal of European Public Policy*, 22(2), 238–256.

Howarth, D., & Schild, J. (2021). 'Nein to "Transfer Union": the German brake on the construction of a European Union fiscal capacity'. *Journal of European Integration*, 43(2), 209–226.

Jabko, N. (2006). *Playing the Market*, Ithaca, NY: Cornell University Press.

Jabko, N. (2010). 'The hidden face of the euro'. *Journal of European Public Policy*, 17(3), 318–334.

Kassim, H., Saurugger, S., & Puetter, U. (2020). 'The study of national preference formation in times of the euro crisis and beyond'. *Political Studies Review*, 18(4), 463–474.

Kleine, M., & Pollack, M. (2018). 'Liberal intergovernmentalism and its critics'. *JCMS: Journal of Common Market Studies*, 56(7), 1493–1509.

Kriesi, H. & Grande, E. (2015). 'The Europeanization of the national political debate'. In O. Cramme & S. B. Hoboldt (eds), *Democratic Politics in a European Union Under Stress*, Oxford: Oxford University Press, 67–86.

Krotz, U. & L. Schramm (2022). 'Embedded bilateralism, integration theory, and European crisis politics: France, Germany, and the birth of the EU Corona Recovery

Fund'. *Journal of Common Market Studies*, 60(3), 526–544, https://doi.org/10.1111/jcms.13251.

Laffan, B. (1997). *The Finances of the European Union*, Basingstoke: Palgrave Macmillan.

Laffan, B. (2000). 'The big budgetary bargains: from negotiation to authority'. *Journal of European Public Policy*, 7(5), 725–743.

Matthijs, M. (2016). 'Powerful rules governing the euro: the perverse logic of German ideas'. *Journal of European Public Policy*, 23(3), 375–391.

McKelvey, R. D. (1976). 'Intransitivities in multidimensional voting models and some implications for agenda control'. *Journal of Economic Theory*, 12(3), 472–482.

McNamara, K. (1998). *The Currency of Ideas: Monetary Politics in the European Union*, Ithaca, NY: Cornell University Press.

McNamara, K. (2006). 'Economic governance, ideas and EMU: what currency does policy consensus have today?' *Journal of Common Market Studies*, 44(4), 803–821.

Meyer, C. O., & Strickman, E. (2011). 'Solidifying constructivism: how material and ideational factors interact in European defence'. *Journal of Common Market Studies*, 49(1), 61–81.

Moe, T. M. (1984). 'The new economics of organization'. *American Journal of Political Science*, 28, 739–777.

Moravcsik, A. (1998). *The Choice for Europe*, Ithaca, NY: Cornell University Press.

Moravcsik, A., & Nicolaïdis, K. (1998). Keynote article: 'Federal ideals and constitutional realities in the treaty of Amsterdam'. *Journal of Common Market Studies: Annual Review*, 36, 13–38.

Moravcsik, A., & Schimmelfennig, F. (2009). 'Liberal intergovernmentalism'. In A. Wiener & T. Diez (eds), *Theories of European Integration*, Oxford: Oxford University Press, 67–87.

Parsons, C. (2002). 'Showing ideas as causes: the origins of the European Union'. *International Organization*, 55(1), 47–84.

Patz, R., & Goetz, K. H. (2019). *Managing Money and Discord in the UN: Budgeting and Bureaucracy*, Oxford: Oxford University Press.

Puetter, U. (2021). 'The Council of the European Union: co-legislator, coordinator, and executive power'. In D. Hodson, U. Puetter, S. Saurugger & J. Peterson (eds), *The Institutions of the European Union*, Oxford: Oxford University Press, 78–105.

Riker, W. H. (1980). 'Implications from the disequilibrium of majority rule for the study of institutions'. *American Political Science Review*, 74(2), 432–446.

Saurugger, S. (2013). 'Constructivism and public policy approaches in the EU. From ideas to power games'. *Journal of European Public Policy*, 20(6), 888–906.

Saurugger, S. (2016). 'Constructivism and agenda setting'. In N. Zahariadis (ed.), *Handbook of Public Policy Agenda Setting*, Cheltenham, UK, and Northampton, MA, USA: Edward Elgar Publishing, 132–154.

Saurugger, S., & Terpan, F. (2020). 'Integration through (case) law in the context of the Euro area and Covid-19 crises: courts and monetary answers to crises'. *Journal of European Integration*, 42(8), 1161–1176, DOI: 10.1080/07036337.2020.1852233.

Schäfer, D. (2016). 'Banking union of ideas? The impact of ordoliberalism and the vicious circle on the EU Banking Union'. *Journal of Common Market Studies*, 54(4), 961–980.

Schimmelfennig, F. (2015). 'Liberal intergovernmentalism and the euro area crisis'. *Journal of European Public Policy*, 22(2), 177–195.

Shepsle, K. A. (1979). 'Institutional arrangements and equilibrium in multidimensional voting models'. *American Journal of Political Science*, 23(1), 27–59.

Shepsle, K. A., & Weingast, B. R. (1984). 'Uncovered sets and sophisticated voting outcomes with implications for agenda institutions'. *American Journal of Political Science*, 28(1), 49–74.

Stone, D. (1989). 'Causal stories and the formation of policy agendas'. *Political Science Quarterly*, 104(2), 281–300.

Surel, Y. (2000). 'The role of cognitive and normative frames in policy making'. *Journal of European Public Policy*, 7(4), 495–512.

Târlea, S., Bailer, S., Degner, H., Dellmuth, L., Leuffen, D., Lundgren, M., Tallberg, J., & Wasserfallen, F. (2019). 'Explaining governmental preferences on economic and monetary union reform'. *European Union Politics*, 20(1), 24–44.

Woll, C. (2008). *Firm Interests: How Governments Shape Business Lobbying on Global Trade*, Ithaca, NY: Cornell University Press.

Zahariadis, N. (2008). 'Ambiguity and choice in European public policy'. *Journal of European Public Policy*, 15(4), 514–530.

Index